THE FLAGS CHANGED
AT MIDNIGHT

Gogo warrior

Lushoto market

The author, Chief Majebele and the Governor, His Excellency, Sir Edward Twining, with a crowd of Sukuma tribesmen in Lake Province.

The Governor's Train bearing the Governor's Flag.

THE FLAGS CHANGED AT MIDNIGHT

Tanganyika's Progress to Independence

Michael Longford

GRACEWING

First published in 2001

Gracewing
2 Southern Avenue, Leominster
Herefordshire HR6 0QF

ISBN 0 85244 551 2

Typeset by
Action Publishing Technology Ltd, Gloucester GL1 5SR

Printed in England by
MPG Books Ltd,
Bodmin PL31 1EG

Contents

Author's Preface and Acknowledgements

I would like to thank very sincerely all those who have helped me in many different ways to complete this book.

In particular, I want to express my warmest thanks to Dorothy Kingdon and Patricia Prentice for permission to reproduce their paintings; to Don Barton, Geoff Bullock, David Suckling, and the late John Mitchell-Hedges for providing many of the photographs; to Don Barton, Geoff Bullock, Chris Christodoulou, Michael Dorey, Reg Clarke, Robin Denniston, John Grigg, Tony Kirk-Greene, Denis Loretto, Randal Sadleir, John Smith, and David Suckling for helpful comments and advice; to Stephen Goddard for preparing the sketch map and the ink drawings included in the text; to Sir John Margetson for writing the foreword, and to the last British Governor of Hong Kong, Chris Patten, whose book *East–West* gave me the idea for the title of this book. I am grateful to Mirror Syndication International for their permission to reproduce the photograph of H.R.H. Princess Margaret's visit to Tabora School.

Above all, I want to thank my beloved wife Jennifer, who read every word of the text, and whose comments and suggestions were invaluable. The letters from Tanganyika which she wrote to her mother, and which her mother wisely kept, were a useful source of contemporary material, much of which I have included in the book, using Jennifer's own words.

When I started to write this book, I had many different aims. I wanted to tell my children, Ruth, Catherine, and Philip, all of whom were born in Tanganyika but do not remember it well, how their parents came to work, get married, and have a family so far from Britain.

Tanganyika achieved its Independence in December 1961. Sadly, the number of people who were involved in this transition gets smaller year by year, and people of every race should be given the opportunity, now and in the future, to read a personal account given by an eyewitness of what were very eventful years in the history of Africa.

There are many people who believe that colonialism is inherently evil and oppressive. Others say that any poor and underdeveloped country should be given guidance to enable it to assume its rightful place in world affairs. I hope readers will find this book gives a balanced account of the successes and failures of the last ten years of British colonial rule in Tanganyika, and that those who object to some of the views I express will find others with which they can agree.

After my family and I came back to Britain, I worked first for a large pharmaceutical company for two years, then for a children's charity for nearly three years, and finally as a Whitehall civil servant for over twenty. I sincerely believe that the work I did in Tanganyika was of more value to those I was seeking to help, and infinitely more satisfying for me, than any of the jobs I did later.

January 2001

Foreword

by Sir John Margetson K.C.M.G.
formerly British Ambassador to the Netherlands

In August 1951 the *Llanstephan Castle*, oldest and most decrepit of the Union Castle liners, set sail from Tilbury. On it were some 20 cadets of the Colonial Administrative Service, bound for various colonial territories in East and Central Africa. Michael Longford and I were amongst them; our destination Tanganyika.

The process of African decolonisation was by then well under way. That very year Nkrumah's party had triumphed in the Gold Coast election and Nkrumah had become effectively prime minister. But that was West Africa; and the colonies there were far ahead of those in East Africa in political, economic and educational progress. Indeed Tanganyika at that point did not have a single African with a university degree in government service. None of us, as we sailed slowly but very enjoyably to Africa in 1951, could have foreseen the extraordinary pace of decolonisation during the rest of that decade. Rather, we looked forward to several decades of hard endeavour before the East African colonies would be ready for independence.

In fact Tanganyika reached independence in 1961 and the careers of the vast majority of British colonial servants there came to an end soon after. Michael Longford was one of the majority of district officers who chose to leave rather than continue in the very different circumstances of independence. As the book relates, he saw from his position as District Commissioner in Lindi which way the wind was likely to blow. *The Flags Changed at Midnight* is therefore a record of just ten years' service in Tanganyika. It is an extraordinarily accurate and detailed account of the life of a district officer, reflecting the honesty and complete integrity of the author. It will certainly take its place alongside other memoirs of members of the Colonial Service as an invaluable record and source of material for historians of the closing years of the British Empire.

Just as the work of a district officer was remarkable for its variety, so too it differed considerably from district to district. Michael Longford never served in the Lake Province, Dar es Salaam (except in the special position of private secretary to the Governor), nor in North East Tanganyika. These were the major areas of African political unrest. He therefore never experienced directly the protest rallies, the refusal to pay taxes and the difficulties of working in an atmosphere of political tension. He was lucky. But the reader should not assume that the political progress of Tanganyika was quite as smooth as the experience of the author in the districts of Tabora and Ulanga might suggest.

Michael Longford's admiration for the Governor, Sir Edward Twining, whom he served as private secretary, is something which I share wholeheartedly. Twining admitted to me in 1956 that eventually Tanganyika would have to become an African country. He saw his policy of multi-racial political development as a necessary stage to give time for the economic development of the country and the training of Africans to take over the machinery of government. This deliberate pace of development, linking all three races, was overwhelmed by the effects of the 1954 UN Visiting Mission and by the 1958 election in which TANU swept to victory. The new governor, Sir Richard Turnbull, grasped the situation and with the co-operation of Julius Nyerere brought the country peacefully to independence. Perhaps some may think that Michael Longford is a little less than generous in his assessment of Sir Richard's motives, but he recognises his achievement.

Anthony Kirk-Greene in his history of the Colonial Service quotes the pan-colonial lament: 'Yes, you gave us law and order, you gave us schools, hospitals and roads ... But how often did you give us your hearts?' This book answers that question, at least for two people. Michael and Jennifer Longford had, and still have, a profound love of Tanganyika and its people. This emerges quite naturally from the book. And although Michael Longford went on after Tanganyika to play a major role in such important things as the framing of the UN Convention on the Rights of the Child, it is, I suspect, his service in Tanganyika of which he is proudest – and justly so. Those of us who shared those years in Tanganyika must be very grateful that he has written so fully and interestingly about them.

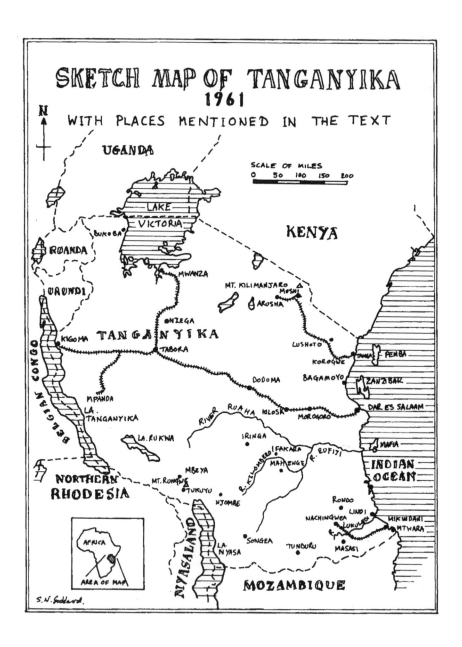

SKETCH MAP OF TANGANYIKA
1961
WITH PLACES MENTIONED IN THE TEXT

N

SCALE OF MILES
0   50   100   150   200

UGANDA

LAKE
VICTORIA

KENYA

BUKOBA

RUANDA

URUNDI

MWANZA

MT. KILIMANJARO
MOSHI
ARUSHA

NZEGA

TANGANYIKA

KIGOMA

TABORA

LUSHOTO

KOROGWE

TANGA   PEMBA

BELGIAN CONGO

DODOMA

BAGAMOYO

ZANZIBAR

MPANDA

LA. TANGANYIKA

RIVER RUAHA KILOSA

MOROGORO

DAR ES SALAAM

LA. RUKWA

IRINGA

KILOMBERO FAKARA
MAHENGE

R. RUFIJI

MAFIA

INDIAN
OCEAN

MBEYA
MT. RUNGWE

NORTHERN
RHODESIA

TUKUYU

NJOMBE

RONDO

LINDI

NACHINGWEA

NIKWDANI

MTWARA

LUKULEDI

NYASALAND

SONGEA

LA. NYASA

TUNDURU

MASASI

MOZAMBIQUE

AFRICA

AREA OF MAP

S.N. Goddard.

Chapter 1

Journey to Tanganyika

(August–October 1951)

Slowly Round the Cape of Good Hope

On the afternoon of 2nd August 1951, the oldest liner in the Union Castle fleet, S.S. *Llanstephan Castle*, set sail from Tilbury on its last journey before being broken up. Passengers joining the ship had travelled in a special boat-train from London to Tilbury, together with friends and relatives who were coming to see them off. Most of the passengers looked excited, while most of the relatives looked tearful. I was one of the passengers, and was travelling to Africa to take up my appointment as a cadet in the Colonial Administrative Service. I was twenty-three years old, and I expected to be away from England for the next thirty months.

My mother travelled in the boat-train with me. My father's cousin, Desmond Longford, a doctor who practised in Kent, came too. I was very fond of Desmond, but I think he was really more concerned about keeping my mother company on the journey back to London after the ship had sailed than he was about seeing me off. My father had died at the beginning of 1951, and Desmond did not want my mother to spend the evening completely alone on the day her son left England.

The ship was divided into first- and tourist-class, and the first-class passengers included over twenty cadets on first appointment. Ten had completed a preliminary course at London University, and were on their way to Uganda. They were to disembark in Mombasa. The others were heading for Dar es Salaam or Tanga. Three members of the Tanganyika group had done their course at Oxford, but I was one of ten cadets who had spent a year together on the Colonial Service Course at Cambridge, and we already knew each other quite well.

Travelling first class at someone else's expense seemed splendid, but I later travelled 'cabin class' in single-class ships, and I think the first-class cabins in the *Llanstephan Castle* were no better than even the cheapest cabins in the more modern single-class liners.

A few of the cadets were already married. The Colonial Office tried to discourage the wives of cadets from going to Africa until their husbands had passed the appropriate law and language examinations, but this policy was not strictly enforced in 1951. However, a berth in a cabin for three costs less than a berth in a cabin for two, and the authorities who booked our passages refused to pay the full cost of a two-berth cabin for married couples going out on first appointment, so they booked us all in three-berth cabins. I shared a cabin with a bachelor, John Margetson, and a married man, Mike Sadler. Mike's wife Cynthia had to share an all-female three-berth cabin with the wives of two other cadets. One couple did reserve a two-berth cabin, but they had to pay the extra cost out of their own pocket. I felt it was hard for newly-married couples to have no place where they could spend time alone in privacy, and the policy certainly had a detrimental effect on the way in which some of the wives settled to their new way of life.

I did not much like the colour of the Union Castle liner, which reminded me of a raspberry milk-shake, but there were many features about the ship which I liked. The first-class public rooms were old-fashioned but attractively furnished, and I admired the oak panelling in the bar. There was a well-stocked library, The food served in the first-class dining saloon in the bowels of the ship was excellent.

As we passed through the English Channel, the sea was calm, but a storm arose in the Bay of Biscay. The young steward called Hunter, who served at the table which I shared with three other bachelor colleagues, had only just left school. Like us, he was on his first voyage, and he became extremely seasick and was unable to carry on working in the dining saloon. His place was taken temporarily by a competent but very effeminate table steward. After he had finished serving our dinner for the first time, he minced back to our table and asked, 'Is there anything really special which I could do to give pleasure to any of you nice-looking young men?'. Homosexual acts between consenting adult males were still a criminal offence at that time, and I was amazed that a crew member should make such an offer simultaneously to four passengers. I was told later that the crews of many ocean liners included stewards who were openly gay, and were willing to make themselves available to any passengers who might be interested.

The cabin stewardess who looked after our cabin was very different. Miss White was seventy-four years old, and spoke with a refined accent. She had spent most of her life working as a nanny, but she loved her work as a cabin stewardess, and was still energetic and competent, albeit rather eccentric. She hoped to be transferred to another ship in the Union Castle fleet when the *Llanstephan Castle* finished its last voyage. One day she asked me how tall I was, and when I told her I was 6 foot 6 inches tall, she commented that there had recently been another passenger on the ship who was just as tall as me. He was, she added, 'only a knighted person, sir, but very gentlemanly!'

The route which we were taking to East Africa was not via the Suez Canal but round the west coast and the Cape of Good Hope. Our first port of call was Las Palmas, in the Canary Islands. We were encouraged to see the view from the top of the Cathedral tower, and a group of us took a lift – free of charge – to get us to the top. The view was quite impressive, but when we wanted to come down again, our guide demanded an exorbitant payment for use of the lift, and we could find no alternative way to get down to the bottom.

After visiting the Cathedral, four of us took a taxi to the top of a mountain where a new five-star hotel had just been opened. It was already receiving guests, but the water supply was not yet functioning properly. The wash-basins and toilets were absolutely disgusting. The sun was shining, and the sea was sapphire blue, but I have never felt any wish to return for a holiday to the Canary Islands.

A few days later, the ship called at Ascension Island, but passengers were not permitted to land there, and the next place where we were allowed to disembark was Saint Helena.

I generally find small islands fascinating, and I was enchanted by Saint Helena. It is a volcanic island with an area of less than 50 square miles. The capital, Jamestown, was in festive mood to welcome the ship and its passengers, and smiling women sat in front of pretty little cottages offering to sell us beautiful lace goods which they had made.

I joined a group of friends to walk up to the highest point on the island, which is over 2,700 feet high. We climbed up the side of a cliff overlooking Jamestown, using a stairway called Jacob's Ladder. The view from the top was spectacular. We visited the garden of the Governor's house where we saw the biggest tortoises I had ever seen. We then walked on to a house called Longwood, a few miles east of the capital, where Napoleon had died in 1821. It was not in good repair, and I found it somewhat depressing. I nevertheless had the childish idea that it might be pleasant to end my colonial service career as Governor of Saint Helena. In fact, life there must be rather dull in the weeks between the departure of one ship and the arrival of the next, and there are very few employment opportunities for the island's residents. There is not even any scope to develop the tourist industry, as the island is too small and mountainous to build an airstrip, and the time it takes to reach Saint Helena by ship rules it out as a holiday destination.

Soon after the ship left Saint Helena on its way towards Capetown, there was a mechanical breakdown, and we remained for a few days on a calm sea without making any progress at all. I did not mind about the delay. If the journey lasted a few days longer, so much the better.

The main reason for my cheerful acceptance of this delay was that there were two extremely pretty girls, Hazel Walford and Susan Leach, travelling out to Africa together on the *Llanstephan Castle*, and I had made friends with both of them. Their plan was to travel by sea as far as Port Elizabeth, and then to travel overland to Nairobi, staying with friends on the way. I found Susan particularly attractive. She was the daughter of a university lecturer in tropical agriculture who had spent some years in what used to be called Nyasaland.

Shipboard romances are notorious, but I found myself thinking of Susan at all hours, and I suspected that I was falling in love with her. I had not yet actually told her that my intentions were serious and honourable, however, when she told me that she was travelling out to Kenya to announce her engagement to someone else. She told me she had met the man she planned to marry while he was an undergraduate at Cambridge, and that she was now going out to visit him and his family at their home a few miles outside Nairobi.

The fact that Susan was already in love with someone else was bad enough, but my emotions became still more confused when she told me his name and asked me if I had ever met him. The man she was planning to marry was called George Knaggs. I replied that I had indeed met him: he had been to Trinity, the same college as me, and we had even rowed together in the college First May Boat in 1948. He had rowed at bow when I rowed at 5, and I regarded him as a very close friend. I was genuinely pleased that two such delightful people were planning to get married, and I resolved that I would never give Susan the slightest hint of how I felt about her. I told myself in the severest possible terms that Trinity oarsmen never stole each other's girl-friends. However, I think the real reason for my reticence was probably my fear that she would reject any overtures which I might make to her.

When we at last reached Capetown, the berth in the harbour which had been reserved for the *Llanstephan Castle* had been taken by another ship, and we had to wait outside the harbour until another berth became available. This went on happening in all the other ports in South Africa where we were scheduled to land.

Capetown provided my first glimpse of Africa. It is an extremely beautiful city, with splendid parks and an esplanade running along the seashore, planted with flowering shrubs and palm-trees. The architecture of some of the old buildings in the Dutch colonial style is superb. I was thrilled by some of the plants which I saw for the first time in the Botanical Gardens, and by Table Mountain, which rises 3,000 feet above the city.

Capetown was said to be more racially tolerant than the Afrikaans-speaking areas of South Africa, but even so I was revolted by the manifestations of legalised apartheid which I met there for the first time. Segregated beaches, with all the best ones reserved for whites only, segregated park benches, and segre-gated public transport all seemed morally repugnant. I did not see much of the areas where black people lived, but I saw enough of them to feel shocked by the way in which Africans, Asians, and people of mixed race were treated, and by the contrast between the slums where black people were compelled to live and the prosperous white areas.

Table Mountain, Capetown

We arrived in Capetown on a Saturday evening, and a colleague and I decided to attend a service in Capetown Cathedral the following day. We were not sure how to get to the Cathedral, and walked into a police station to ask. Three white constables were sitting behind the counter in the part of the police station designated as being for blacks only, and they pointedly ignored the two British visitors who were waiting in the section reserved for whites at the other end of the counter. At last one of them spoke rather discourteously to us, and we asked him how to find the Anglican Cathedral. He and both his companions said they did not know, and that they did not have a map of the city that we could look at for ourselves. The constables were either telling the truth, in which case they were extremely inefficient, or else they were lying. Whatever the reason for their unhelpfulness, we formed an unfavourable first impression of the South African police.

One of the manifestations of the apartheid regime was that marriage or any form of sexual relation between people of differ- ent races was prohibited, but while we were walking back to the ship, a black prostitute accosted us. We declined her offer, but I felt sure that, whatever the legal prohibitions might be, she had often done business before with white as well as black customers.

At every port in South Africa where the *Llanstephan Castle* was due to land, the procedure was the same as it had been in Capetown. As soon as the ship reached the approaches to the harbour at Port Elizabeth, East London, or Durban, the passen- gers who were ending their journeys at those ports were allowed to disembark with their baggage, and transfer into a small motor boat which took them to the shore. The ship itself then lay for some days at anchor a short distance from land, waiting for a berth in the harbour to become available. Passengers who were continuing their journeys were given the option of going ashore with the disembarking passengers if they wanted to go sight- seeing at their own expense. Most of us decided to stay on board the ship, however, as our food and accommodation were still being provided for us.

Port Elizabeth was not so beautiful as Capetown. I formed my first impression of the town from a distance, when I was standing on the deck of the *Llanstephan Castle* waving to Susan and Hazel as they were taken ashore in a small motor boat to start their overland journey to Nairobi. A few days later, the remaining passengers were permitted to go ashore. I joined a few friends to explore the town and we found it rather dull. We went into the main post office to post some letters, and, as expected, had to stand at a counter for whites only.

One of the cadets who was going to Uganda was the son of a very senior army officer, and had been to an elitist public school. I already knew how strongly he disapproved of apartheid, and I was therefore surprised to hear him ask the clerk behind the counter where white men were expected to post their letters. The clerk pointed to a letter box which was being used by black as well as white customers. My companion then raised his voice and said, adopting an extremely pompous accent for the purpose, that it was absolutely outrageous that white men like himself should be expected to post their letters in the same box as kaffirs. I then realised that his remarks were intended to ridicule the system, but the post office clerk, who was himself white, took them completely seriously. He offered to take the letters himself and to arrange for them to be posted from a room at the back of the building.

The ship left Port Elizabeth and arrived in East London after yet another wait until a berth became available there. East London was no more exciting than Port Elizabeth, and made no lasting impression on me at all.

Durban, on the other hand, was quite different. When the ship berthed there I felt envious of one of my closest friends, who was later my best man when I got married. Geoff Thirtle had been the stroke of the Jesus College First Boat at Cambridge which was Head of the River when I was rowing in the Trinity crew. The stroke of the Jesus College Second Boat was a South African called Mike Butcher, whose family lived in Durban. Mike was spending the summer vacation in Britain, but he urged Geoff to meet his family when the ship was in Durban, and Geoff had already received a letter from Mike's parents inviting him to stay in their house for as long as the ship remained in Durban. Not long after the *Llanstephan Castle* moored, Mike's sister Pam arrived in a smart little Hillman Minx car to collect Geoff and take him to their home.

About an hour later, Geoff and Pam returned to the ship. There was room in the Butchers' house to accommodate three guests, and Geoff was invited to bring two of his friends to join him. He chose me and another close friend, John Cooke, and Pam drove us all to meet her parents.

The Butcher family were extremely hospitable. They also seemed to be very wealthy. I had no reason to doubt it when I heard someone mention that Pam's father owned a sugar estate of 30,000 acres. Their house was situated at the top of a hill over-looking Durban, and its views were breath-taking. It was beauti-fully furnished, and several indoor domestic servants kept it all immaculately polished, while an army of gardeners tended the lawns and the colourful tropical trees and shrubs which surrounded the house.

Pam herself drove us on several sightseeing expeditions round the town and into the surrounding countryside. When she was busy, she allowed me to drive her car around Natal with Geoff and John, who did not have driving licences.

The routes which we were recommended to follow in Pam's car took us through many small isolated villages, where we saw Zulu women adorned with brightly coloured bead necklaces and bracelets, sitting outside their huts playing with their children. The scene gave the impression of peace and tranquillity, and if I had had a camera I would have loved to take a lot of photo-graphs. It did not occur to me until later that we hardly ever saw a Zulu man. I think the reason for the absence of men was that they were probably working on the sugar estates, or in the mines near Johannesburg. Coming from Britain at a time when the welfare state was narrowing the gap between the very rich and the very poor, I found the extremes of living standards in South Africa disturbing, but I enjoyed my luxurious stay with the Butchers, and found it a memorable visit.

Our stay in Lourenço Marques (now called Maputo) was memorable for quite a different reason. Soon after we arrived there, eight or nine of us went for an evening walk in the town looking for a place to have a glass of beer. We found a quiet beer-garden, and sat down under a large mango tree which had coloured lights in its branches. The proprietor was friendly and the prices reasonable, and the bar seemed to be a delightful place to spend the evening. At midnight we had no wish to go back to the ship, but the proprietor, who was Portuguese, said he was closing his bar. He recommended us to try the Café Imperium, where drinks went on being served after midnight.

The name Café Imperium sounded innocuous, but it did not take us very long to find out that it was not a respectable bar at all. We had misguidedly ordered our beers and sat down at a large table in the basement when half a dozen raddled old whores advanced towards us. The first whore ogled John Cooke, and asked him, 'You like your beer or me?' John, whose judgement was always sound, replied, 'My beer thank you, madam,' but the whore was not in the least discouraged, and sat down at our table.

A second whore, who was wearing an emerald green satin creation, then joined us. She said her name was Clementine and that she came from Elsinore in Denmark. She acted as if she had taken a fancy to me. She danced what looked like an extremely energetic flamenco. She then grabbed my hand and clamped it firmly onto her left breast, saying – in English – 'Just feel how my heart is beating!' I noticed that even in a country where Portuguese is the main language, all the whores spoke to us and to each other in English, albeit with some pretty terrible accents. A few were of mixed race, but most would have passed for white in South Africa. None was black.

Within a few minutes of our arrival, we had about six women sitting at our table. Margie was the ugliest of the lot, and offered to give a nice time to anyone who would have her. This offer was treated by the other women with unmitigated scorn. Clementine shrieked with laughter as she announced that the only customers willing to pay for Margie's services were those who gave money to watch her perform with a donkey. Margie took offence at this and began to shout threats at Clementine.

I was beginning to feel extremely uncomfortable in every way. I did not want to become involved in a brawl, and my beer had by this time reached my bladder. Any relief I might have felt on getting to the urinal was offset by discovering a new cause for anxiety. Four or five villainous looking pimps were standing near the door of the toilet, and each had what looked like a sheath-knife in his belt. I returned to our table with only one desire – to get back to the *Llanstephan Castle* in one piece as quickly as possible.

Some of my colleagues who had not noticed the pimps and their knives wanted a bit more time to finish their beers, and while they were drinking up I became more and more uneasy. I was sure that if we tried to go back to the ship without paying any money to the whores or their pimps, we were likely to be attacked.

Rescue came unexpectedly, if rather noisily. A party of American seamen in uniform staggered down the steps into the basement, singing discordantly. The prostitutes all left us very abruptly to go and join the Americans, and my colleagues and I all made our way back to the ship without being molested.

The rest of the journey was comparatively uneventful. After calling briefly at Beira and the Island of Mozambique, the

Dar es Salaam Harbour with S.S. Kenya Castle

Llanstephan Castle reached Dar es Salaam on 24th September, seven weeks and four days after setting sail from Tilbury. A new chapter in my life was about to begin.

By Train and Bus to the Southern Highlands

The name Dar es Salaam means 'Haven of Peace', and the harbour is perfectly sheltered and extremely beautiful. The *Llanstephan Castle* entered the harbour by passing through a narrow opening between two sandy beaches that were lined with coconut palms swaying gently in the breeze. By 1951, the port already had a wharf where ships could berth, but the facilities were very limited, and most ocean-going liners had to anchor in the lagoon while their cargo was off-loaded in lighters, and passengers waited on deck for small motor boats to take them ashore.

The old part of the town was a fascinating mixture of different styles of architecture. I had not been to any Arab countries, but there were signs of Arab influence in many of the buildings. There were some large buildings which looked out over the sea. These included a Roman Catholic Cathedral, a Lutheran Church, Government House – the official residence of the Governor – and a large government hospital known as the Ocean Road Hospital. There were some old and some new offices. Most of the buildings that I found particularly attractive dated from before the First World War, when Tanganyika had been administered by the Germans. It was often alleged that the Germans saved on building costs by underpaying their African construction labourers, or even by not paying them at all. They certainly put up many very attractive public buildings and imposing houses for their senior government officials. The Germans also laid out a network of attractive avenues in Dar. By 1951, most of these were lined with a variety of glorious flowering trees and shrubs. I had often been told that I would like Dar, but I was overwhelmed by my first glimpse of the capital of the country where I was planning to spend the rest of my working life.

All the new cadets spent a few days completing various formalities before travelling overland to the provinces where they were to be stationed. These formalities included swearing a judicial oath in front of the Chief Justice, and swearing an oath of allegiance before the Chief Secretary, Sir Rex Surridge, deputising for the Governor, Sir Edward Twining, who was on leave.

As soon as I had taken the oath, Sir Rex invited me to come with my colleagues to have a drink at his house that very evening to meet a few of the people with whom we might sooner or later be working. When I left his office, an official car took a small group of us to sign the visitors' books of certain senior officials. Signing visitors' books was a common form of courtesy which was later to play an indirect but extremely important part in my life. Sir Rex's visitors' book was on a table in the front hall of his house, and visitors were requested to go straight in and sign, without ringing the doorbell. As we were signing, a door leading off the hall was ajar, and we heard the cultivated voice of an English lady whom we could not see, but who sounded extremely annoyed. 'Darling,' she said, 'who the *hell* will want to meet *them*? How on earth can I get hold of enough suitable people to come at such ridiculously short notice? For heaven's sake don't ever do it again!' It was clear that, however hospitable Sir Rex himself might be, Lady Surridge was not very enthusiastic about being asked by her husband to prepare a sundowner party at a few hours' notice.

That evening, Sir Rex and Lady Surridge both received us with a warmth and cordiality which seemed completely genuine, and we all thoroughly enjoyed the party. Any criticism I might have secretly felt for Lady Surridge's insincerity was outweighed by my admiration for the way in which she and her husband both appeared to be genuinely interested in all their guests, and managed to make us feel welcome.

While we were still in Dar, I was also invited to spend an evening with an old Cambridge friend, Bob King, and his wife Margaret. Bob was several years older than me. He had served in the forces during the war and returned to Trinity to complete the Colonial Service Course while I was still an undergraduate straight up from school. Bob was small but he was very muscular. He had been the scrum-half of our college rugger fifteen. He was also exceptionally able, and was one of the few colonial administrators in Tanganyika to have got a first-class degree. I liked and respected him enormously. Bob and his family lived in a modern suburban bungalow built by the Public Works Department for government officials, and half-way through the evening I suddenly spotted the reason for something about his living room that had been puzzling me. It had no fireplace. There was, of course, no need for one in Dar, or indeed in any other coastal stations in Tanganyika. One of the things which I came to like about working in a hill station was that after sunset the evenings often became chilly, and it was then very pleasant to sit in front of a log fire. Even when the fire was not alight, the fireplace still provided a sitting room with a focal point which was lacking in houses on the coast.

Towards the end of our course at Cambridge, every cadet had been told which Province he was to be posted to on his arrival in Tanganyika, and I already knew that I was going to Southern Highlands Province, which sounded delightful. In one of my conversations with officials in the Secretariat, I was told that I would initially be posted to Mbeya, the Provincial Headquarters. Most of my colleagues appeared to agree with my opinion that this sounded a very attractive posting, and I looked forward to another journey, this time by rail and bus, to reach my eventual destination.

The first part of the journey from Dar to Mbeya was by train, and punctually at 10 o'clock on the Saturday morning after the *Llanstephan Castle* had docked, our train left Dar es Salaam Station, heading inland. The Central Railway Line had been built by the Germans, and by 1951 many stretches of the track were in such poor condition that trains were limited there to a speed of twenty miles an hour. The distance from Dar to the terminus at Kigoma on Lake Tanganyika was nearly 800 miles. Even without stopping on the way, the journey would have taken a couple of

Central Railway Line passenger train

days. At every station, however, some passengers got on and others got off the train with their baggage, the residents of the villages wanted to come and greet their friends, farmers wanted to sell their fruit and vegetables to the passengers, and the train had to take on more water and firewood for the engine. This added considerably to the total time the journey took. I did not mind about the length of the journey, as the first-class compartments in the train were clean and comfortable, the food served in the restaurant car was simple but quite good, and I found the changes of scenery exciting.

There were three cadets travelling to Southern Highlands Province. Peter Hollis was a graduate of Edinburgh University who had done the Colonial Service Course with me at Cambridge, and I liked him very much. He was travelling with his Scottish wife, Morag, who seemed a bit apprehensive about how she would be able to manage without the kind of electrical gadgets she had used in Britain. John Lewis-Barned had done his course at Oxford, and I did not know him so well. I was the third cadet in our group.

After our train left Dar, it climbed slowly towards Morogoro, the Provincial Headquarters of Eastern Province, and then on to Dodoma, the Provincial Headquarters of Central Province, where the countryside seemed arid and infertile. The train was due to divide at Tabora, the Headquarters of Western Province, one half continuing westwards as far as Lake Tanganyika, the other half turning northwards to reach Lake Victoria and the terminus at Mwanza, the Headquarters of Lake Province.

My colleagues and I left the train before it got to Tabora. We changed on to a bus at a tiny village called Itigi, where a road going from north to south crossed the railway line going from east to west. Itigi consisted of a few peasant huts, a couple of shops, the basic necessities of a halt on the railway line, a parking space for buses that were operated by East African Railways and Harbours, and a rest-house for first-class passengers. The rest-house was spotlessly clean, and the caretaker/cook had a reputation for serving delicious food. It was, de facto, a rest-house for Europeans, as they were then just about the only category of passengers who travelled first class, but any African or Asian who could have afforded it would have been allowed to use the rest-house facilities, in contrast to the legalised segregation on grounds of race which I had seen in South Africa.

The bus for Chunya and Mbeya left towards sunset, and travelled through the night. Soon after we left Itigi, when it was not yet quite dark, the front wheel of the bus ran over the tail of a long, thin snake which was crossing the road. I thought it was a black mamba, and the driver assured us that anyone bitten by that kind of snake would not reach hospital alive. Certain other types of snake were quite common in parts of Tanganyika, but I do not think I ever saw another one that I suspected of being a black mamba.

We reached Chunya soon after dawn. Chunya District was said to be the Cinderella of Southern Highlands Province. There had been a gold rush on the Lupa Goldfields in Chunya District during the inter-war years, but the gold had run out, and the town had become very shabby and depressing. The District Commissioner and his wife, Harry and Mary Braddell, welcomed Peter and Morag, who were going to live there, and they also invited John and me to have breakfast with them.

Over breakfast, Harry Braddell mentioned to me that I would not be going to Mbeya, as I expected, but to a place called Tukuyu, about fifty miles beyond Mbeya, on the road leading to Lake Nyasa (now called Lake Malawi). John would be remaining in Mbeya, but I would stay one night in a hotel in Mbeya before completing my journey to Tukuyu.

I reached Tukuyu on 2nd October, exactly two months after I

had left London. I had been rather disappointed at being told by Harry Braddell that I would not be going to Mbeya, but the beauty of the scenery as we approached Tukuyu completely reconciled me to my change of posting.

Chapter 2

Rungwe District

(October 1951–November 1952)

Tukuyu Boma

First Impressions of Tukuyu

Tukuyu was the Headquarters of Rungwe District, named after
Mount Rungwe, an extinct volcano a few miles north-east of
Tukuyu township. Usually the first comment one heard about
Rungwe District was that it was the wettest district in the whole
of Tanganyika. The rainfall in Tukuyu averaged about 120 inches
per year, in contrast, for example, to Chunya, which was less than
100 miles away, but where the average annual rainfall was only
about 30 inches. There was a quite simple geographical reason to
explain the freak climate of Tukuyu. The district was surrounded
to the west, north, and east by a range of mountains shaped like a
horseshoe. To the south lay Lake Nyasa. When water from the

lake evaporated, the clouds were usually blown towards the mountains, but were seldom high enough to pass over the top of the mountains, so the water condensed and fell as rain over a comparatively small area. Unlike most of Tanganyika, which was only green during the rainy season, Rungwe District remained green the whole year round. The soil was fertile, and on the high ground the peasant farmers grew abundant crops of coffee and bananas. On the low-lying plains near the lake they grew rice.

The countryside along the Mbeya–Tukuyu road was lovely, and the final approach into the town itself was even more beautiful. Flowering tropical trees lined the road on both sides. I had seen jacaranda trees and flame trees in other towns, but never before in such profusion. The houses were all neat and in good repair, and many of them had pretty gardens, a luxury which was rare in other districts.

When the bus arrived at the bus station, there were two men waiting there to welcome me. The older and taller of the two was the District Commissioner, Teddy Kingdon. The District Officer, Robert Paterson, was with him. Both men seemed very friendly, and Teddy invited me to stay in his house for a few days, until I could engage a cook and a houseboy, unpack my boxes, and move into the new Government quarter which had already been allocated to me. Expatriate officials were provided with houses, for which they paid a rent of ten per cent of their salary. Each house was equipped with very simple basic furnishings, but the officer himself was expected to provide the personal items needed to make a home.

Teddy Kingdon and his wife Dorothy were extremely kind and generous hosts, who immediately made me feel welcome in their exceptionally attractive home. They lived with Dorothy's charming old mother, who was then eighty-seven years old and was always known within the expatriate community as 'Gran'. I did not meet their children, Jonathan and Jane, until later, as they were both away at boarding school when I arrived. The Kingdons' garden was one of the most beautiful in the whole of Tanganyika, and Dorothy was one of the many very gifted artists, most of them women, who found the time to paint landscapes of Tanganyika or portraits of its citizens. One of the wedding presents which my wife and I particularly treasure is a portrait by Dorothy of a Gogo warrior in traditional tribal dress. Jonathan Kingdon inherited his mother's ability as an artist, and his work on an atlas of evolution, *East African Mammals*, which he started when he was a lecturer in Fine Art at Makerere University, earned him an international reputation, both as an artist and as an ecologist.

The District Office, referred to as the Boma, was one of several which had been built when the country was still being administered by the Germans before they were forced to surrender their colonies at the end of the 1914–18 war. It was a rectangular fort standing on the top of a hill. The DC's office was in the south-east corner of the fort, with the offices of the two District Officers, a correspondence office and a cash office with a strong-room also on the east side of the building. A police station, a magistrate's court, and a very small room with a thunder-box latrine were on the south side of the Boma. The north side was occupied mainly by the Native Treasury and the African District Council offices. Other offices, such as the Agricultural Office or the Labour Office, were housed on the west side of the fort or in small buildings outside the walls of the main Boma compound.

I could not have started my career under a better boss than Teddy Kingdon. He had been promoted to the rank of 'Senior District Officer', and already had over twenty years' experience of Tanganyika. Prior to that, he had graduated at Oxford and got a job as a schoolmaster at a famous public school in Britain, but he had become disillusioned when he learned that housemasters at that school were not given an adequate allowance to run their houses, but were expected to make a profit for themselves by giving the pupils in their care too little to eat. Teddy had all the patience and lucidity of a dedicated teacher, and whenever I asked him any question he not only advised me on me what I ought to do, but also explained the advantages and disadvantages of the various options. He also loved and was loved by the African people among whom he worked.

Robert Paterson also had many fine qualities. He was very intelligent and energetic, and had won a medal for bravery in the Second World War. There was one great difference between Teddy's personality and his. Robert seemed to think that paper was more important than people. He did not appear to have much patience with Africans, or indeed with anyone who was less able than himself. I quickly discovered that most of the local Nyakyusa tribesmen cordially disliked him. Robert later served in the Secretariat, which I regarded as a far more suitable posting for a man of his temperament than an up-country District Office.

During my first few days in Tukuyu, Teddy introduced me to all the colleagues with whom I would be working. Rungwe District was small in area, but it was densely populated. The complement of expatriate officials totalled about fifteen, most of whom were married with young children. We had a Medical

Officer, a Health Inspector, an Assistant Superintendent of Police, two Health Visitors, a Nursing Sister, and a Sister Tutor who ran a training school for African nurses. The Agricultural Department and the Veterinary Department each had its own Field Officer. A Co-operative Officer had responsibilities connected with the marketing of the cash crops produced by African farmers, mainly coffee and rice. There was an official with the title 'District Assistant', whose work involved simple engineering tasks which, in a bigger district, would normally have been carried out by an officer of the Public Works Department. We also had a qualified engineer of the Water Development Department posted temporarily to Tukuyu in order to instal a piped water supply in the township, but he was expected to move on as soon as that assignment was completed.

When I arrived in Tukuyu, water was still delivered every day to the houses of Government officials by a gang of convicts who each carried a couple of four-gallon cans filled with water drawn from one of the many local streams. The convicts then poured the water into a pair of forty-four-gallon drums that had formerly been used for oil or petrol, but were now fixed onto an elevated wooden plat-form, from which the water could flow down into the domestic water supply of the house. All the houses occupied by expatriate officials in Tukuyu had water-borne sanitation, but in many up-country districts bucket latrines were still in use. There was no electricity supply in Tukuyu at that time. Cooking was done on wood-burning stoves, and lighting was provided by pressure lamps or hurricane lamps fuelled by paraffin. The heat given off by pressure lamps was tolerable in highland districts like Tukuyu, where we often sat by log fires in the evenings, but it could be very oppressive in a humid coastal station which did not have electricity.

There were, of course, far more Africans than Europeans working in the Boma, and for several weeks I found it hard to distinguish one smiling black face from another. I was quick to recognise Katoto Musyani, the Head Messenger, who was tiny and had two stripes on his khaki drill uniform. I also recognised Abel Seme, my own personal messenger, who was plump and exceptionally dark-skinned, but for some weeks I hesitated to address by name an African of average size in case I mixed him up with someone else. I got over this problem in due course, and never had any more difficulty in recognising individual black faces, but I still have a problem sometimes when I visit an unfamiliar country for the first time, and meet a group of people whose faces and clothes all look alike to an untrained eye. There were surprisingly few Asian officials in Tukuyu, though we had an outstanding Indian Sub-Assistant Surgeon, and most of the shopkeepers in the town were Asian.

Teddy Kingdon let it be known that I wanted to employ a number of servants including a cook and a houseboy-dhobi*, and I was astonished at the huge number of people who turned up at the Boma to be interviewed at the appointed hour. My Swahili was still not good enough to do the interviewing myself, so Teddy asked all the questions and interpreted the answers to me. At the end of an afternoon which I found great fun, I had taken on a cook called Bernard Mwakilima, who was to be paid 55 shillings a month, a houseboy-dhobi, Timothy Mwakapombe, an ex-askari[†] in the King's African Rifles, who would receive 45 shillings a month, and a woodcutter called Atupele, whose sole task was to keep my household supplied with firewood for cooking and heating. He would receive 15 shillings a month. I also engaged a 'kitchen toto', *toto* being the Swahili word for child. This was the cook's son Isaac, who would scrub the pots and pans and be taught by his father the rudiments of European style cooking. He was delighted to be offered 12 shillings a month.

I felt slightly ashamed at the very low rates of pay that were eagerly accepted by the people who were looking for work, but my own starting salary was only £550 per annum. While it seemed excessive for a bachelor to have four domestic servants, they had no labour-saving gadgets like washing machines or vacuum cleaners to help them, and the derisory wages which I paid helped my staff and their families to pay their poll tax and to have a marginally higher standard of living than they would have got either from casual labour or from the sale of their cash crops. The cook and the houseboy were also provided with free living quarters for themselves and their families behind the bungalow where I lived.

Most of the Government officials in Tukuyu lived in a group of houses on the south side of the Boma, but my bungalow stood by itself on the side of a hill to the east of the township. It had two bedrooms, a large living room which also served as a dining room, a verandah, and a bathroom. The kitchen was separate, but connected to the main house by a covered passageway. The footpath from my house up to the Boma was extremely steep, and occasionally, when the ground was very wet, I slipped on the way down to my house and landed painfully on my backside.

*dhobi: Indian word for laundry boy, washerman, washerwoman.
[†]*askari*: any uniformed official in the public sector.

There were two things I did not like about the house. It had been painted with paint which would have been fine in the arid climate which was typical in other parts of Tanganyika. In Tukuyu, however, the inside walls got spots of mildew only a few weeks after I moved in. The other thing I didn't like was the way my clothes, and in particular my shoes, became mouldy if left in a cupboard for just a couple of days. This involved a lot of extra work for Timothy Mwakapombe drying my clothes with a charcoal iron and brushing the mould off my shoes. On balance, however, the advantages outweighed the disadvantages, and I got constant pleasure from the superb view of Mount Rungwe from my living room. Sometimes the mountain looked bright and sunny; by the light of a full moon it was even more beautiful; but when the storm clouds gathered it could look very threatening indeed. It never looked dull.

Apprenticeship in the Boma

In every District Office in which I served, there was always a list of the distribution of duties of the District Commissioner and the District Officers. One aim of this list was to inform the officers themselves of who was responsible for what, and to ensure that the workload was fairly shared between them. The list also advised members of the public who were uncertain about whom to approach regarding a particular type of problem. The list had to be applied flexibly, however, as officers were often on safari, and when they were not in the Boma someone else had to deputise for them.

The duties that an officer was expected to perform varied greatly from district to district. There were two main reasons for this. Environmental factors meant that problems which were important in a coastal district, for example, might not even exist in a highland area six or seven hundred miles away. The complement of officers of specialist departments in a station also had an effect on the tasks that a District Officer had to do. There was no point in a District Officer becoming involved in tasks for which specialist officers from technical departments were already responsible. When there was no such specialist officer available in the district, however, the responsibility for such functions fell to one of the District Officers. There was no Forestry Officer or Labour Officer stationed in Tukuyu, so the list of my duties included matters connected with forestry and labour, although these did not take up very much of my time.

I spent much more time in the District Court. All District Officers were magistrates and coroners, but there were three classes of magistrate. District Commissioners were first-class magistrates, with power to impose sentences of up to two years' imprisonment. District Officers who had been confirmed in their appointments were second-class magistrates, with less extensive powers. Cadets were third-class magistrates with very limited powers. For the first six months of his service, every case tried by a cadet had to be submitted for inspection to a Judge of the High Court, and sentences of more than one month's imprisonment had to be confirmed by a first-class magistrate. The standard practice was that each case was heard by the most junior magistrate with the power to deal with it. This meant that a cadet usually dealt either with comparatively trivial cases like petty shoplifting, minor traffic offences, wilful neglect to pay poll tax, or preliminary enquiries into very serious cases. Every magistrate of whatever class had the power to commit an accused person for trial by the High Court.

In my very first preliminary enquiry, the name of the accused was Mugilege d/o Mkakilwa. The symbol 'd/o' was an abbreviation for 'daughter of', which implied that she was a peasant woman. (A peasant man would be referred to in court records as X s/o Y, which meant X son of Y.) There was a form of class distinction which crept into the way we referred on paper to individual Africans. An educated town-dwelling African man was usually referred to by his family name, usually with the prefix Mister. No one would have dreamed of referring, for example, to Julius Nyerere as Julius s/o Nyerere. Most Christian names like John or Mary, or Islamic names like Abdullah or Fatima, were clearly male or female, but with an unfamiliar tribal name like Mugilege it was not always apparent to expatriates whether the person who bore that name was a man or a woman.

Mugilege was quite definitely a woman. I thought that her case was a very sad one. She was not married, but had become pregnant. All the rest of the people who lived in her village had gone to join in the wailing at an important funeral a few miles away when Mugilege started to give birth as night was falling. She was completely alone in her hut, and I believed her story that her confinement was distressing and took the whole night. She gave birth just before dawn, and she immediately went outside and threw her baby down her neighbour's pit latrine.

Later that morning, when the mourners had returned from the funeral, her neighbour went to his latrine for the usual reason, and was surprised to hear from the pit the sound of a baby

crying. He ran to tell the Village Elder, who told the Chief of
Busokelo. The Chief then ordered a drum to be beaten to
summon all the pregnant women immediately. I never discovered how such messages could be transmitted by drum, but all
the pregnant ladies arrived within a short space of time. They
were then ordered to stand in a straight line and to undress
completely while the Chief and his Headmen scanned their
profiles. When the Chief reached Mugilege, she at first denied
that the baby was hers and said that she was still pregnant. This
did not fool the Chief, who ordered her to go down into the pit
and retrieve her baby. Mugilege then washed the baby and put
it to her breast.

The Chief said, quite correctly, that he did not have the power
to hear a case involving an attempt to kill a baby, and that the
case would have to be reported to the police in Tukuyu. Mugilege
was placed under escort and ordered to walk to the Police
Station, which was 26 miles away. By the time she got there, she
was so ill that she was immediately admitted to Tukuyu Hospital
rather than being locked up on remand. In his medical evidence,
Dr Mehta, the Sub-Assistant Surgeon, said that when she was
admitted to hospital Mugilege was suffering from the effects of
severe haemorrhage, and that her condition was critical. He
described the baby as being 'extremely healthy'.

After receiving treatment for a couple of weeks, Mugilege was
allowed to go back to her village with her baby. All the witnesses
confirmed that while she was in hospital she cared for her baby in
an exemplary way, but on the walk back to Busokelo there was a
typical Rungwe District rainstorm. The baby got completely
soaked and died of pneumonia two days later.

I had no choice but to commit Mugilege for trial on a charge of
attempted infanticide, and the High Court in due course
convicted her and imposed a deterrent prison sentence on her. I
felt that the circumstances of the case were exceptional, and that
a more merciful sentence might have been appropriate.

Only a small proportion of judicial work was dealt with by the
District Court itself. Local Native Courts, presided over by chiefs or
headmen, dealt with very large numbers of criminal and civil cases
at village level. These courts had no power to hear very serious
cases or cases involving non-natives, and litigants could not engage
advocates to represent them, but the maintenance of law and order
within a tribe depended to a great extent on the competence and
integrity of its Native Courts. The court records were written in
Swahili, and they were submitted regularly to the Boma for inspec-

tion by a District Officer. While on safari, District Officers also gave
high priority to inspecting the records of any court they were visiting, and would query any long delays in dealing with pending cases
or in collecting fines imposed for criminal offences. They would
also investigate the reasons for imposing sentences which seemed
either unduly severe or unduly lenient.

I came to learn that Africans did not always share the views of
Europeans about the gravity of particular types of offence, and that
a verbal insult was often regarded more seriously in a Native Court
than an assault causing actual bodily harm. Even childish remarks
like 'You've got an ugly face' were regarded as deeply hurtful. The
Nyakyusa were not as sensitive as the tribesmen in some other
districts where I later served, but in some tribes it was regarded as
quite commonplace for a person who had been insulted to feel so
humiliated that he or she decided to commit suicide.

One of my main tasks in Tukuyu involved the close supervision of the day-to-day running of the Government Cash Office,
and a daily audit of the accounts kept by a very experienced
cashier, Mr Malik Burra Selemani Madenge. He had been in
Government service for over twenty-five years, and he taught me
everything that I needed to know about financial procedures in a
District Office. Every morning I checked the counterfoils of each
revenue receipt and payment voucher issued the previous day,
and satisfied myself that they had been entered correctly in the
main cash book. I then checked that the cash on hand in the
strong-room tallied with the figure in the cash book, and signed a
certificate to the effect that the accounts were in order.

Within my first few weeks at Tukuyu, I received through the
Provincial Commissioner's Office at Mbeya a directive, endorsed
by the Provincial Commissioner himself, calling on me to reply
without delay to a Treasury query and a series of reminders
which had remained unanswered for much too long. I looked up
the papers, and found that there had been a slip of the pen by a
junior clerk who had entered in the cash book a figure which did
not tally exactly with the amount stated on the counterfoil of the
revenue receipt. The Sub-Accountant was required either to
explain the error or refund the cash deficiency. The amount
involved was one cent, or the equivalent in sterling of one twentieth of a new penny, and I happily refunded the shortfall from
my own pocket, but I wondered how any audit clerk could think
that such a trivial sum could justify the amount of work he had
created in the Treasury in Dar, the Provincial Office in Mbeya,
and in the Cash Office in Tukuyu.

Unfortunately, the amount of real theft of public money which went on was a serious problem. During the thirteen months that I was stationed in Tukuyu, five out of the six cash clerks working in the offices of Rural Councils went to prison for the theft of cash entrusted to them. What saddened me even more was that, nearly a year after I had been transferred to Iringa, a station about 250 miles north-east of Tukuyu, I was told that Mr Madenge had been convicted of stealing nearly £1,000.

It had been Mr Madenge himself who had told me of the need to check regularly on the stocks of all accountable documents held in the strong-room. However, after my departure, he had managed to remove a book of revenue receipts from the strong-room, and to use it to collect money from members of the public without entering the transactions in the cash book. While he and I were working together, I had had complete confidence in his honesty, and I was shattered to learn that he had been sentenced to several years in prison and had lost his pension entitlement after serving honestly for twenty-six years. I knew he was a strict Muslim, and believed that he never touched alcohol, but I was told that he had suddenly acquired a taste for brandy, which he could not afford on his salary, and that this was what had caused his downfall.

Dishonesty exists in every country across the world, but there were certain local factors in Tanganyika, and probably in other colonies as well, which seemed to make it especially hard for people in positions of trust to resist temptation. A sentence of imprisonment imposed by a colonial legal system appeared to carry very little stigma. Africans often jokingly referred to prison as 'The Queen's Hotel', and did not seem to regard a spell inside as a great hardship. When cash was stolen, any efforts made to recover the money were rarely, if ever, successful. Any colleagues of the thief who might have an idea about where the money had been hidden were likely to get a bigger share of the loot if they kept quiet than if they informed the police.

Perhaps the biggest incentive to steal lay in the low salaries of junior clerks and messengers. The economy of the country could not afford substantial pay increases, but a messenger carrying a cash box into the Boma during the harvest season, when most peasant farmers paid their poll tax, would be aware that the amount of money in the cash box could easily exceed his own total salary for twenty or thirty years. If he stole the money and successfully hid it, he would then probably serve a few years in prison, but on his release he would be able to retrieve the money from the place where he had hidden it, and enjoy a much higher material standard of living than he could ever have hoped to achieve if he had remained honest.

It was easy for expatriates to deplore the numbers of African employees who were convicted of theft. Too few of us were prepared to give proper credit to those Africans who resisted temptation, and worked honestly till they reached old age. There were certainly too many people employed in the public sector who yielded to temptation, but I think that in the 1950s those people were outnumbered by the others who remained honest.

A District Officer could usually guess fairly accurately how much time he would be likely to spend on each of his most important tasks. However, there was one aspect of our work which could either take no time at all or be extremely time-consuming. Many illiterate Africans used to come into the Boma with personal problems, and the District Commissioner or the District Officer was often the agony aunt whom they asked to help them. If an African had a relative who had gone, for example, on a labour contract to work on the copper belt in Northern Rhodesia, or in the gold mines of South Africa, and then failed to write home or remit any money to maintain his wife and children, his dependants often came in to the Boma to seek help. It was surprising how often a short letter signed by a District Officer would achieve the desired objective. Complaints by villagers about the refusal of a chief or a court clerk to accept a case for hearing in a Native Court often proved to be the first symptom of laziness or even of serious corruption. A few officers thought it paternalistic and a waste of time to listen carefully to everyone who came with a problem, and they were sometimes very impatient with petitioners. This meant that the flow of customers for them dried up, and they were then able to handle their paperwork without so many interruptions.

Teddy Kingdon set a very different example, which I tried to follow. There seemed always to be a long queue of people waiting to be admitted to his office. As soon as my Swahili became fluent enough to deal with them I also started to get a steady increase in the number of people bringing their problems to me.

A young woman came into my office one day and complained that her husband had not come to visit her for more than two months. I guessed what she implied by her husband's failure to visit, and I asked her to tell me his name. She told me that she was married in accordance with tribal law and custom to Chief Mwakatumbula of Mpuguzo Chiefdom. This put a new light on the case. There was no limit to the number of women a Nyakyusa man could marry, as long as the bride's father agreed to accept the bride-price and the bridegroom paid up. The views of the bride herself were comparatively unimportant. Mwakatumbula was very rich, and had already got about 120 wives. The young ones lived in an immaculate village which he called London. The middle-aged ones lived in another village to which he gave the name of Dar es Salaam. The old and ugly wives lived in a village he called Bagamoyo, after the port where David Livingstone had started his journeys inland in the nineteenth century.

There were some tribes which regarded adultery as a criminal offence, but the Nyakyusa treated it as a civil matter, and any cuckolded Nyakyusa husband could claim compensation from his erring wife and her lover in the appropriate Native Court. Mwakatumbula could not himself preside over a case in which he was personally involved, so his cases were dealt with at the next level. Mwakatumbula was a shrewd capitalist, and he employed a number of plain-clothes private detectives to patrol the banana groves in order to catch 'in flagrante delicto' any neglected wives who might be seeking consolation with partners who were younger than he was. He later told me that when he was awarded damages for the adultery of one of his wives he generally used the money towards paying the bride-price for a new wife. I doubt whether the young woman in my office was very happy when I told her that, if my calculations were right, she would probably have to wait another couple of months before her husband got round to visiting her again.

Mwakatumbula was a likeable old rascal with an engaging sense of humour. In spite of all the other calls on his energy, he still managed to rule his Chiefdom well. Unfortunately, he suffered from syphilis, and this meant that most of his wives and their boyfriends had it too. The records of the dispensary in Mpuguzo, where they usually went to be treated, showed a higher incidence of sexually transmitted diseases than I ever came across anywhere else in Tanganyika, and propaganda based on the message 'clean living is the only safeguard' was not very effective. There has not been much change in attitudes since the 1950s, but the main disease is now not syphilis but AIDS, which is killing off thousands of young adults every year all over East Africa.

Government Offices in Tanganyika were normally open from Monday to Friday and also on Saturday mornings. The Boma in Tukuyu was always busy, and at the end of a working day, either Teddy or Robert would often spontaneously invite me to come home with them for a cup of tea, or occasionally something stronger.

Robert and his wife had three delightful young sons, and

whenever I visited them the boys would always ask me to read bits of *Thomas the Tank Engine* to them. The Patersons also had a sealyham bitch, Ginger, which had recently given birth to puppies following an unplanned encounter with a dachshund. Male dachshunds had an unrivalled reputation for their determination and resourcefulness in all sexual matters, and often managed to mate successfully with bitches more than twice their size. The results often looked very odd.

I wanted a dog to keep me company, but I was initially rather embarrassed at the idea of owning a small dog with very short legs when I myself was very large and had extremely long legs. The more I saw of Ginger's puppies, however, the more enchanting I found them, and before long I had agreed to Robert's suggestion that I should give one a home. I never regretted my decision. I called her Susan, after the girl I had met on the sea journey from England. She was the most intelligent and affectionate dog I have ever known, and remained with me throughout my whole service in Tanganyika. She had a lovely sense of humour, and grinned whenever I played with her. While I was a bachelor, she normally accompanied me to my office and lay silently under my office chair while I was working. After I got married she usually stayed at home protecting my wife and children. She was a brave little watch-dog who barked at intruders, but she never attacked anyone.

One afternoon when I was having tea with the Patersons and the atmosphere seemed cheerful, Robert's wife suddenly noticed a cobweb in the corner of the ceiling of her living room. She called for her houseboy and started to rebuke him in my presence in a way that I thought was objectionable. The houseboy thought so too, and when the tirade came to an end he replied softly, 'I am leaving work, Memsahib,' and walked out.

The houseboy had been working on a monthly contract of service. If he had been sacked before the completion of the contract period, Robert would have had to pay him his full month's wages. As the houseboy had left work voluntarily before completing his contract, however, he was not legally entitled to be paid for those days that he had worked. It was very close to the end of the month, and Robert was exultant about unexpectedly saving a few pounds. He then asked me, as the officer responsible for the Labour Office, to find him another houseboy.

The Labour Office had a list of people looking for various types of employment, but it had no system to indicate the competence of potential applicants. My own houseboy Timothy Mwakapombe was a good judge of the merits of other houseboys, however, and when I got home that evening I asked him to invite three possible applicants whom he knew to come to the Boma as soon as possible to be interviewed for a job. Timothy then asked me the name of the employer who was looking for a houseboy, and when I told him he replied, 'I am sorry, but I do not think any of those good houseboys would agree to work for Mr Paterson. We do not like him at all.'

Expatriate wives used often to chatter in club bars about the shortcomings of their domestic servants, but I found that European employers who treated their domestic staff well got excellent service from them, whereas those who were rude or unjust seldom kept a servant for more than a month or two.

I had brought out a second-hand 'His Master's Voice' portable gramophone with me from England, and when I was alone I used to spend most evenings sitting in front of a log fire listening to records, mainly of classical music. To a background of scratchy performances by artists most of whom are now forgotten, and getting up from my chair every four or five minutes to change the gramophone needle and the record, I read books in Swahili and memorised my own list of useful Swahili words. I had a strong motive to learn the language as quickly as possible, as Teddy Kingdon had told me that he would arrange for me to go on safari as soon as I became fluent enough in Swahili to cope on my own.

Swahili is not a particularly difficult language. Unlike English, where it is a nightmare for a foreigner to pronounce correctly words like cough, enough, plough, though, thorough and through, in Swahili every word is spelt as it is pronounced and pronounced as it is spelt. A voiced sound, as in the English word 'that' is spelt 'dh', but 'thing' would be spelt using the letters 'th'. The letter 's' is always pronounced as in the word 'this'. For a voiced sound like 'these', the letter 'z' is used in Swahili.

However, there is one aspect of the language which beginners usually find causes big problems. English sentences are formed by joining nouns, adjectives, verbs, and pronouns together in the correct word order. Where there are grammatical changes in English, for example changing a singular noun into the plural or a present tense into the past, the changes are usually made at the end of the word – 'one book/two books', for example, or 'I play/I played'. A beginner learning English has no problem in looking up 'book' or 'play' in the dictionary.

Swahili follows clearly-defined grammatical rules, but they are not the same as the rules of English, or indeed of most other

European languages. The English sentence 'I will follow you' consists of four words. 'I will not follow you' consists of five words. 'I have not yet followed you' consists of six words. In each of these examples, one single Swahili word is enough to convey the exact meaning of four, five, or even six English words. Unfortunately, the single Swahili word is often very complicated, consisting of a 'subject prefix', a 'tense prefix', an 'object prefix' and the root of a verb. The root of the verb in the above examples is *fuata* – to follow, but a beginner is likely to spend many frustrating minutes or even hours trying to look up complete words as they appear in printed or written documents.

I found learning Swahili as entertaining as a cryptic crossword puzzle, and made rapid progress. I was the first cadet to pass the Government Higher Standard Written and Oral Swahili examinations within a year of landing in Tanganyika.

I did not spend every evening at home by myself studying Swahili. My colleagues were very hospitable, and I was often invited to dinner in their houses. The meals in Tukuyu usually consisted of produce which had been grown locally, although in infertile areas in other parts of Tanganyika one depended much more on imported tinned food. At first I felt diffident about returning hospitality in a bachelor quarter which I had not yet equipped with curtains, floor coverings, or cushions, but if my guests thought my hospitality was spartan they were much too polite to say so.

Social Life in Rungwe District

Rungwe District is very small but very densely populated. When I was stationed there a population of 237,099, or nearly a quarter of a million people of different races, lived in an area of 1,874 square miles. The next district in which I served, Iringa, was much more typical of Tanganyika as a whole. It had an area of about 14,000 square miles, about the same size as the Netherlands and more than seven times the size of Rungwe, but its population was significantly smaller, with only 184,368 inhabitants. I later served in Tabora District, the largest district in Tanganyika, which had an area of about 25,000 square miles, nearly as big as Belgium and the Netherlands combined, but only had a population of 158,000.

My social life for the first months I spent in Tanganyika depended very much on the hospitality of colleagues, especially Teddy and Dorothy Kingdon. I had no car of my own, but during the week they frequently asked me to have a 'pot-luck' evening

Fish-eagle over Lake Masoko

meal with them, and on Sundays they often went for a family picnic beside a crater lake called Masoko, about ten miles south of Tukuyu. Whenever they went there, they invited me to come too.

Lake Masoko was a perfect place for swimming and for bird-watching. Swimming in the sea could be dangerous if waters were shark-infested, and many rivers contained the little snails which carry an unpleasant disease called bilharzia. The water in Masoko Lake did not contain anything nasty, and the temperature always seemed just right. Enjoying the company of friends, and watching the birds, in particular the fish-eagles, circling overhead, provided a magnificent way to relax after a busy week.

Not everybody had the good fortune to have Teddy Kingdon as a boss or Lake Masoko within a few miles of their home. For many people, social life depended mainly on programmes of entertainment organised by the leaders of one's own ethnic community.

According to a census of the non-African population carried out in 1952, there were at that time 549 non-Africans living in Rungwe District. These included 369 Indians, 47 Somalis, 8 Goans, 1 Arab, 10 Coloured (mixed race), 1 'other', and 113 Europeans. The population consisted of more than 400 Africans to each non-African.

In common with minority groups all over the world, the members of the racial minorities in Rungwe tended to associate for social and recreational purposes with other people with similar backgrounds and interests and who shared a common mother tongue. Even though I disapproved strongly of what I had seen of apartheid in South Africa, I accepted that freedom of association is a basic human right, and did not question the right of any group to form a recreational club and to restrict the membership to a particular category of people.

The Rungwe Club had already existed for many years by the time I arrived in Tukuyu, and its constitution stated that membership was exclusively for Europeans. It was taken for granted that any European official posted to the District would apply for membership of the Club and be elected by the Committee, and that any member and his family would then be able to make use of all the facilities which the Club provided. Reciprocal arrangements existed between the Rungwe Club and other similar clubs, so that an official from another district could use the Rungwe Club when he was visiting Tukuyu, either officially or on holiday, and vice versa.

Membership was not confined to Government officials. It also included European employees of the various tea estates in the District. Estate managers and engineers did not normally make very much use of the Club in the middle of the week, but at weekends they would drive in to Tukuyu to take part in any activities organised by the Committee, and to meet friends and have a drink or two with them. European missionaries seldom if ever applied for membership. Some missionary societies paid such low salaries that their employees probably could not have afforded to join, and I think that many evangelical missionaries did not approve of alcohol.

The Rungwe Club was quite comfortably furnished and well equipped. It had a 9-hole golf course, which I never used, a hard tennis court, which I used whenever I could, a library, a battery-operated record player, and a well-stocked bar. Although all the quarters occupied by expatriate officials had water-borne sanitation, the Club itself only had two unattractive little bucket latrines, one for Ladies and one for Gentlemen, behind the main building. After sundown, most of the male members preferred to go outside and retire behind a tree rather than patronise the Gents' loo. 'Seeing Africa' was the colloquial equivalent of 'spending a penny' in Britain.

The day-to-day management of the Club was by an elected

Committee, and not long after I arrived I was invited to become the Treasurer. This involved me in regular dealings with the Head Bar Boy, Samweli, who spoke excellent English and had been employed by the Club for many years. Whenever I checked the stocks of bottles locked in the drink cupboard, the amounts were always correct. What I found distasteful about being Club Treasurer was having to pester certain members to pay arrears of their subscriptions and bar bills.

Every Tuesday the Club had its 'music evening'. Up to a dozen members and their wives would come to listen to records played on the battery-operated record player. Unfortunately, the choice of records was very small, and the car battery used to power the player was on its last legs. Towards the end of the evening, the turntable would start to revolve more and more slowly, and a record played slowly probably sounds even worse than a record played at the correct speed on a scratchy clockwork gramophone. This meant that after a month or two I was asked to bring a choice of my own records and to play them on my own machine to those members who enjoyed an evening of music.

The problem with the record player did not arise on Saturday evenings, when the Club was always very full. Many members brought spare car batteries with them in case the Club's battery ceased to function while people were still wanting to dance.

I usually found the Club friendly and relaxing. It was pleasant to chat over a glass of beer with colleagues with whom I worked in the Boma, and the Club provided the opportunity to get to know their families as well. It also gave me the chance to meet the managers of the tea estates with whom I seldom came into contact except at the Club.

Most of the senior employees working on the tea estates were likeable and intelligent people who worked very hard and made a big contribution to the economy. The less senior expatriate staff of the tea estates included a few people who may have been skilled artisans, but got drunk most Saturday evenings, and then had noisy quarrels with their partners. My heart sank whenever I heard a shrill female voice shouting, 'You're drunk!' and the even louder reply of the woman's husband, 'Shut up!'

Matrimonial discord was not the only cause for arguments in the Club. Some Colonial Service officials were more progressive in their attitudes to social development and welfare than others, but in broad general terms the political views of non-officials were far more right-wing than those of people in Government service. At times the atmosphere in the Club became heated when tea estate workers expressed strong disapproval of progressive policies in general, and of certain actions taken by officials in particular cases. The worst example of this sort of clash between officials and non-officials involved a European crocodile hunter called Ray, who lived near Lake Nyasa.

He had been educated at one of Britain's most famous public schools, but his career had not been successful and he lived in squalid conditions with an English woman who was not his wife, though she was generally known as Mrs Ray. At that time such liaisons were not regarded with such tolerance as they are now. Anne Hartley, the Nursing Sister, had been extremely upset to discover, after they had spent a night together as guests in her house, that they were not married. She thought that this mistake on her part would cause others to think of her as not much better than a brothel-keeper.

I had become slightly involved with Ray, as he had ceased to be a member of the Rungwe Club, but still owed the Club some money, and I had been making fruitless attempts as Club Treasurer to get him to pay his debts. I thought he was destitute, and was not aware that he still owned a dilapidated old car.

By chance, my wrist-watch had broken, and I went into the shop of Makanji B Patel one evening to try to buy a replacement. While I was in the shop, Ray staggered in and ordered a large bottle of beer. I was still looking at the shop's stock of wrist-watches when he ordered a second bottle, and then a third. He was still drinking when I left the shop. Before I left, Dr Mehta, the Sub-Assistant Surgeon, came into the shop, and he also noticed Ray's condition.

I had invited the Assistant Superintendent of Police, Gordon Beal, and his wife Daphne to have dinner with me that evening, and they arrived extremely late, with many apologies. Gordon explained that he had been delayed while investigating a traffic accident on the road which went down from Tukuyu towards Lake Nyasa.

When he told me that Ray had driven his car into the back of a stationary Public Works Department lorry parked on the side of the road and had then hidden in the bush, I told Gordon that Ray had been very drunk, and that Dr Mehta would be able to corroborate my evidence.

In due course, the case was tried by Teddy Kingdon, who found Ray guilty. He had a previous conviction for drunk driving, and the relevant law in Tanganyika provided that a second or subsequent conviction for drunk driving always carried a mandatory gaol sentence. He was sentenced by Teddy Kingdon to six weeks' imprisonment. He was not given hard labour, because he was in poor health. When he came out of prison, he went off to Nairobi to celebrate his release, got very drunk and had a fatal heart attack there.

I felt a certain amount of sympathy for his former mistress, who had been with him when he died and went on bombarding Teddy with a series of hate-mail letters, but I found the remarks made in the Rungwe Club by certain people employed on the tea estates were quite intolerable. One said, fortissimo, that it was the right of any white man to drive home, even if he had drunk a bit too much. Another added that knocking down a few black children on the road was not important, as Africans bred like rabbits anyhow.

I found such comments incredibly offensive in themselves, but I was particularly shocked that they should have been expressed so shamelessly in the presence of Samweli, the Head Bar Boy, who certainly understood all that was being said.

There were three times as many Indians as Europeans in Rungwe District. Nearly all of them were traders or shopkeepers, and most adults were married with large families. They arranged their social lives with other members of their own communities, Hindus with Hindus and Muslims with Muslims. There was only one Indian working for the Government, Dr Mehta, whom I liked and respected greatly. He was later deservedly promoted to the rank of Medical Officer, but while he was still only a Sub-Assistant Surgeon he did not mix socially with Europeans. I think this was due as much to his not wanting to feel under an obligation to reciprocate hospitality on a small salary as it was to the reluctance of Europeans to befriend him, but his private life must have been very lonely.

There were ten people described in the 1952 Census as 'coloured', and I got to know three of them well. I felt particular sympathy for the plight of the first generation of children born to parents of different races. They were seldom completely accepted either by the communities of their fathers or their mothers. At that time, racial discrimination was not practised just by bigoted members of the white community. Many Africans were as prejudiced against coloured people as the most racist Europeans.

Kyela was the second largest settlement in the district after Tukuyu. It was situated in the low-lying plains not far from Lake Nyasa, and it had a thriving market, a well-attended school, and a very busy local dispensary which was mainly for out-patients but had a few in-patient beds as well. The Medical Assistant in charge of the dispensary was called William Manning. William Manning's mother was an African. His father had previously been the Governor of Nyasaland, and in the early 1950s the town in Malawi that is now called Mchinji was still called Fort Manning, in his memory.

Children of mixed race born in Tanganyika did not have access to the privileged education available to white children, and William did not have any formal qualifications as a doctor, but his medical skill and his dedication to the patients he served were very highly respected indeed, and his outstanding work was later recognised with the award of an MBE. He had married a woman who was also of mixed parentage, and they had several very intelligent children. I met two of their daughters and one of their sons. Their son Tom had blue eyes and fair hair but his features and the texture of his hair looked African. One daughter, Christine, was dark-skinned and exceptionally pretty. The other daughter, Julie, was not so pretty as her sister, but was academically brilliant. She graduated in law and became a successful lawyer. After the country achieved its independence, she became Tanzania's Attorney-General. William Manning seemed reasonably happy, because he was devoted to his family and he had a satisfying job, even though the salary of a Medical Assistant was far less than he deserved.

One of the other medical establishments in Rungwe District was also run by a person of mixed race. Cyril Wallace was a fully qualified doctor who was also an ordained Anglican priest. He was in charge of a large and well-managed leprosarium at Makete. Cyril and his assistants gave loving care to a few hundred lepers, many of whom were disfigured and evil-smelling. Cyril's father had been a doctor working in the Caribbean, and had there married a black woman. Cyril had graduated at a British university and qualified as a doctor. His wife Linda was Egyptian by birth, and a coptic Christian. They had no children. Cyril had the rank of Medical Officer and was on a much higher salary scale than William Manning, but he was not eligible for membership of the Rungwe Club. Like William Manning, Cyril Wallace was also awarded the MBE for his exceptional work, but he died of cancer soon after the award was made.

The Wallaces were on home leave in Britain when I first arrived in Tukuyu, but I met them both soon after they returned. They were very hospitable people, and we often visited each other's houses. One Sunday, I was having lunch with them at Makete when Linda started to talk about the suffering that the colour of their skin had caused them. She gave as an example the air journey that they had recently made from Britain to Dar es Salaam. The plane had developed a fault in Nairobi, and the aircrew had told all the passengers that they would not be able to continue the journey until the next day, but that accommodation had been booked at the airline's expense for all of them by name in one of the best hotels in Nairobi. When Cyril and Linda reached the hotel, however, the white girl at the reception desk absolutely refused to admit them. Linda and Cyril had called the girl's attention to a blackboard behind the reception desk, where the names of guests were entered beside the appropriate bedroom numbers. The notice-board indicated that room 23 had been reserved in the name 'Dr and Mrs Wallace', but that made no difference to the hotel's policy. After trying unsuccessfully at a number of other hotels, the Wallaces had eventually spent the night in the airport waiting-room.

I expressed my horror at the way they had been treated, and Cyril then said that they were both devoted to children, but had decided before they got married that they would never have a family of their own, as they did not want to bring children into the world to suffer in the way that they themselves had both suffered. I should have expressed myself more diplomatically, but I told them that I thought it would be a privilege for any child to have parents like them, and that I felt their decision had been understandable but misguided. Linda then began to cry gently, and Cyril put his arms round her and kissed her. I too found this visit a very painful one, but it did not harm our friendship.

The main cash crop grown in the south of the district was rice, and there was a rice mill at a village called Ipinda. The name of the manager was John Marsh. I had heard his name mentioned, and knew that he was the illegitimate son of a British gold-miner who had worked in the Lupa gold-fields and a Nyakyusa peasant woman. People said that John was very intelligent, and had been the head clerk of a tea estate before he was appointed to take charge of the mill at Ipinda. After I had been in Rungwe for nearly a year, I happened to visit Ipinda on safari, and was warmly welcomed by John Marsh, who showed me round the mill and told me everything I ever learned about the technicalities of milling rice. After we had looked round the mill, I accepted with pleasure John's invitation to have tea and biscuits with him. His quarters in the mill compound were poorly furnished and rather bleak, and the tea was served by a sulky-looking servant.

There may have been a woman somewhere on the premises, but I did not see her. After I had finished my tea and was preparing to continue on my safari, John said that his lorry had to make a journey in the same direction that I was going. If I would find it useful, I was welcome to travel on the lorry myself with my tent and camp kit and the people who were accompanying me. I left, having formed a very favourable first impression of John Marsh, though I thought he seemed sad and lonely.

A few weeks later, Police Inspector Hesron Mwakalumbwa knocked on my office door in the Boma at Tukuyu and asked if I could remand a prisoner in custody for two weeks while a case was prepared for preliminary inquiry. I agreed, and was astonished to see John Marsh in handcuffs, charged with murder. I was the magistrate who later committed him for trial by the High Court, and the facts of the case were not in dispute.

John Marsh had been one of the customers at a native beer-club. When an African had asked for his glass to be re-filled, John had been quite sober, but had said so loudly that all the other customers heard him, 'You can't have any more. There's not much left, and all there is is for me because I'm a European.' Another African had then said, 'Don't talk rubbish! You're not a European. You're a black man just like us. If you weren't black, you wouldn't be drinking beer with us now!' John said nothing, but walked out of the beer-club.

Forty minutes later he returned, carrying his shotgun which he had collected from his home. He pushed the door open and shouted, 'Who says now that I'm not a European?' The same African repeated his insulting remark, and it was the last thing he ever said. There were about twenty eyewitnesses to the killing.

There was no question about the identity of the killer, and I committed John for trial on a charge of murder. The High Court convicted him, and he was sentenced to death.

While he was awaiting execution, John asked to have an interview with me. He told me that he had a small savings account, and asked me if I would be willing to be named as the administrator of his estate. He explained that, if his illiterate old mother received his total savings as a single lump sum, the money would all be spent on one lavish funeral drinks party, and she would then be left completely destitute. John wanted me to give her a small amount of money every month to support her after he was no longer there to do so himself. I said that it would be unwise to appoint any individual officer by name to carry out his wishes, as officials were all liable to be transferred to other districts. I advised him to nominate

'District Commissioner Tukuyu' to administer his estate, and I promised to record his wishes on the appropriate file, and to do my best to ensure that they were respected.

Before any sentence of death was carried out, every case was the subject of a full report by the District Commissioner, or an officer acting on his behalf. This report was then examined by the country's Executive Council, who were required to advise the Governor on whether or not to commute the death sentence to one of life imprisonment, having regard to all the facts of the case and the previous character of the convicted murderer. In this case, the Governor exercised his prerogative of mercy, and John Marsh began a long sentence of imprisonment.

I never saw John again, but I was told that while in gaol he studied privately and that he eventually qualified as a civil engineer. After completing his sentence, he practised successfully in Dar es Salaam. Nothing could ever bring back to life the man John had killed, but the case strengthened my view that not all murderers are entirely evil.

Segregated clubs were not the only aspect of social life where racial discrimination existed during the period of British rule. Some expatriates in both the public and private sector wanted to preserve their privileged way of life for as long as possible, and regarded any moves to promote equality of opportunity for Africans as a threat to themselves. However, the reasons for what often looked like racism were not always selfish. Economic and cultural factors also played a part.

Football was popular everywhere, and teams often included non-Africans as well as Africans. Athletics was organised on multi-racial lines, and I myself later competed on several occasions alongside Africans and Asians in the territorial athletics championships. Cricket, golf, and tennis, however, were hardly ever played by Africans. The cost of the equipment needed for those sports was higher than most Africans could then afford.

Education was provided in racially segregated schools. This seems wrong to people who oppose discrimination. However, those who made the policy believed that children learn better in their own mother tongue. Putting an English-speaking or a Gujarati-speaking child into a class which is being taught in Swahili would not have been in the best interests of any of the children. Schools for non-native children were funded in part from school fees and Non-Native Education Tax, but a casual observer would notice only that they had better premises and facilities than schools for African children.

The academic standards in the best secondary schools for African children were generally regarded as being at least as good as those in non-native schools, but the competition for places in those schools was intense. At the end of their fourth year of primary schooling, African pupils took an examination, and only a very small minority were successful enough to be offered places in middle schools. At the end of their eighth and tenth years of schooling, African pupils took further competitive examinations, and a similar selection process took place at each stage. Only the most hard-working and intelligent African children had the chance to complete primary, middle and secondary schooling.

It caused much bitterness among ambitious young Africans that they were not given the opportunity to continue with their education for as long as they wanted, while non-native children did not have the same problem. However, the numbers of African children were so much larger than the numbers of non-African children that the economy could not possibly have afforded the cost of providing for every African child the quality of schooling that was available only to the brightest.

The argument of expediency was also sometimes put forward as a justification for the existence of two separate education systems. Expatriates had skills which were essential to the economic development of Tanganyika, but were still rare in the indigenous population. It was sometimes asserted that expatriates with such skills would be unwilling to work in Tanganyika at all unless their children had access to schools that compared with the standard of schools in their parents' countries of origin. I never heard any firm evidence to prove or disprove this claim.

There were several other aspects of social policy which appeared at first glance to involve legalised racial discrimination. Several such laws had nevertheless been enacted from praiseworthy motives. The 'Credit to Natives (Restriction) Ordinance', for example, had been enacted in 1923. This law provided, subject to a few minor exceptions, that a non-native was not able to sue an African for debt in a civil court. It was designed to prevent the kind of situation which still exists now in some Asian countries, that peasant farmers who become indebted to rich merchants are then exploited, either by having to pay interest at exorbitant rates, or, even worse, by being forced to pay off their debt by selling their young children into bonded labour.

The effect of this law was that indebtedness was not a serious problem in Tanganyika. However, as the people whom it sought to protect became better able to look after their own affairs, the law was increasingly criticised for being paternalistic and discriminatory.

Safari by Car

One of the features which attracted me and many of my colleagues to a career in the Colonial Service was that we would spend only part of our working lives at desks in an office. We could expect that a significant part of each year would be spent on tour in our Districts.

In my early months in Rungwe District, I sometimes accompanied experienced officers on short visits to Native Courts, primary and middle schools, rural dispensaries, markets, and trading centres. After heavy rain had fallen, there was always a risk that some earth roads would no longer be passable to cars and lorries. Very few of the roads had been bituminised, but the Public Works Department had responsibility for the maintenance of territorial main roads. The maintenance of minor local roads was a matter for the District Commissioner and his assistants. If the rain had washed away bridges or caused deep gullies in a minor road, we would arrange, as long as funds were still available in the appropriate vote, for urgent repairs to be completed as quickly as possible.

I sometimes travelled in cars owned by my colleagues, but more often I went in a Government Transport vehicle. Most 'GT' cars were short wheel-base Landrovers, which can cope with bad road conditions but are extremely uncomfortable for someone as tall as me. In Tukuyu, however, the District Office GT vehicle was an ancient box-body Ford V8 pick-up. Its driver was called Saidi. He was not a Nyakyusa, but came from a predominantly Muslim tribe which lived near the coast. Many Africans employed as drivers were excellent at their jobs and were also very competent vehicle mechanics, but Saidi inspired in me as little confidence in his skill as his vehicle did in its road-worthiness.

Any visit by a District Officer, even an inexperienced one, to a chief's headquarters normally involved certain routine tasks. He would examine the state of the buildings owned by Government or the Native Treasury. He would check the Native Court records and cash books, and satisfy himself that the amount of cash in hand was correct. He would consider applications from the elderly or frail to be exempted from payment of flat rate poll tax.

This was not just a matter of assessing the applicant's physical ability to earn money. The law provided that a District Officer could exempt from poll tax a person who was both frail and destitute. Many of the frail old men who applied for exemption were genuinely unable to pay, but a minority owned large herds of cattle, and therefore did not qualify for exemption. The District Officer needed to investigate, with the help of the chief, headman, or village elder, the circumstances of each applicant before reaching a decision.

After completing his business in the chief's court, a District Officer would also visit the primary school, and the middle school if there was one, listening to the way the teachers taught their classes and comparing the numbers of pupils in the classrooms with those on the register. If classroom attendance was poor, he would sometimes preach a little sermon about the value of education and regular attendance at school in a developing country, but I thought that such homilies ought to be addressed to the absent children and their parents rather than to those children present in the classroom. The District Officer would also visit the rural dispensary to check on the numbers of patients being treated, the illnesses from which they were suffering, the adequacy of the stocks of drugs, and any measures aimed at promoting public health. Some chiefs were diligent about mosquito control and encouraging householders to use latrines, for example, while others were not.

Rungwe differed from other districts where I served later in my career, in that enough people lived within walking distance of schools and dispensaries to mean that the staff employed there were busy all day. In more sparsely populated areas, there might be too few children living within walking distance of a primary school to fill the classrooms, and a dresser in a rural dispensary might have seen all his patients by mid-morning and spend the rest of the day with little or nothing to do.

Occasionally a District Officer would pay an unannounced visit to a chiefdom, but this was usually an indication that he suspected that something was going wrong. More often, when a safari was arranged with a particular objective in mind, a letter would be sent in advance to the chief and his headmen to notify them that a District Officer would be arriving on such and such a date, and asking the chief to arrange for anyone to be present who had business with the District Officer.

The first safari that I did with a specific task in view was to Busokelo, the chiefdom from which Mugilege, the woman who had thrown her baby down a pit latrine, had come. Soil erosion was already a serious problem in many parts of Tanganyika, but a combination of very heavy rainfall, very steep gradients, very high population density, and traditional agricultural methods meant that the stage was being reached in Busokelo where the land would soon be unable to support the population who lived there.

My assignment was to try to convince the local peasant farmers that their top-soil was being washed year by year into the sea, hundreds of miles away. If they were to prevent this from getting any worse, they needed to adopt at once new methods of cultivation to conserve their soil.

On every safari, I was accompanied by my messenger and my cook. I had recently taken on another experienced cook, Lameck Mbira, to replace Bernard Mwakilima. Bernard had not told me when I engaged him that he was still being paid a retaining fee by his previous employer, who wanted him to return to his service at the end of his UK leave.

On this safari, I was also accompanied by an Assistant Agricultural Officer called Mr Rugarabamu. He was a Mhaya by tribe, and came from Bukoba District, near Lake Victoria. He had graduated at Makerere University, and it was obvious to me from the moment we met that he was a man of exceptional ability. He was still quite young then, but I heard later that his career had been very successful, and that he had become the Permanent Secretary of one of the most important Ministries in Dar es Salaam.

Public meetings in Rungwe District were usually very well attended. People did not have to walk very far to get to their Chief's court. When the GT car arrived at Busokelo in the middle of the morning with my colleagues and me, the court was already packed with men and women, and the crowds had overflowed into the area surrounding the court building. At first the people were reasonably polite, but they did not seem very pleased to see us. I think they already suspected that we were bringing an unwelcome message.

Some expatriates praised the Nyakyusa for their intelligence and for working harder than other tribes, but many more criticised them for being argumentative and insolent. As Mr Rugarabamu and I attempted to explain the problem of soil erosion and outlined the solution which we hoped they would implement, the veneer of politeness became thinner and thinner. Over and over again, the peasant farmers we were trying to convince rejected our advice, and refused categorically to accept that there was anything wrong with the traditional methods of agriculture practised by their parents and grandparents. They disputed the suggestion that Mr Rugarabamu might perhaps know more about agriculture than they did. As far as the District Officer was concerned, I was a European, and, without saying it in so many words, they made their opinion clear that no one ought ever completely to trust the word of a European. The colonial government was probably trying to trick the tribe which owned the land into making changes which would involve a lot of unnecessary effort, but as soon as the Nyakyusa had done all the hard work on terracing and contour ridging which we had recommended, the land would then be alienated from them. Non-natives would be given rights of occupancy and permitted to cultivate land which had belonged to the Nyakyusa for generations. Hostile comments became quite commonplace in the years leading up to independence ten years later, but at that time it was unusual to hear outspoken views of that kind expressed to officials in such an uninhibited way.

Mr Rugarabamu and I listened to variations on these arguments, and to the same arguments expressed in slightly different words by many different people. Mr Rugarabamu dealt with the comments about agriculture, while I attempted to answer remarks about the untrustworthinesss of European officials. My offer to sign a document promising that the Government would never in any circumstances agree to the land being alienated to non-Africans was summarily rejected. It made no difference at all when I suggested that the Chief and all the elders could witness my signature on two copies of such a document, one of which would be kept in the Chief's court while the other would be retained in the Boma.

Towards sundown, I felt that Mr Rugarabamu and I were getting absolutely nowhere. I had very nearly despaired when one of the village elders who had not spoken all day suddenly stood up. He took me totally by surprise by saying, 'I agree with the words of the District Officer.' I did not reply directly to his remark. Instead I immediately called the meeting to a close by saying that we had all had a very busy day and were now very tired. Many of those present would want to get home before nightfall, but we would all meet again in the morning. Anyone who wanted to come to have a chat by my camp fire that evening after we had all had something to eat would be very welcome. Several people came, and the atmosphere around the camp fire was completely different from the sullen mood which had prevailed earlier in the day.

Next morning we all returned to the court, and the Chief expressed his thanks to Mr Rugarabamu and me. He announced that he and all his people had now agreed to implement the measures which the Government recommended. He promised to provide enough workers to complete the project quickly. He proved as good as his word, and the scheme which had at first seemed certain to fail eventually proved a great success.

When Mr Rugarabamu and I returned to the Boma, Teddy Kingdon congratulated us both. He then told me that, as soon as the rainy season was over, he would arrange for me to go on a long safari in the hilly Bulambia and Bundali areas in the western part of the District. There were no motor roads in Bundali or Bulambia, so I would have to go on foot with my messenger, my cook, and as many porters as I needed.

I spent much more time on safari dealing with the affairs of Africans than I did with non-Africans, but I always tried to pay courtesy calls on missions and to establish friendly relationships with European and African priests and mission workers. I never thought of them as being secret agents for the colonial regime, but they knew better than officials in the Boma what was going on in their immediate localities, and they sometimes called my attention to problems that I had not known about, for example autocratic or corrupt activities by someone in authority, or an escalating dispute between neighbouring headmen when a river which was traditionally regarded as the boundary between their lands changed its course. Most missionaries, both Protestant and Roman Catholic, were sincere men and women with a vocation to be teachers, healers or evangelists. They treated other people, whatever their religion, with equal love and respect. I admired them greatly.

Unfortunately, there were others who set a quite different example. A few missionaries were bigots who believed that all their views had been directly inspired by God, and that anyone who disagreed with them must therefore be in error. They regarded pagans as being merely ignorant, but members of other denominations were, by definition, guilty of heresy and were treated as rivals or as enemies.

I was once shown an illustrated poster which symbolised this attitude. It had been printed in Kenya. The wording was in Swahili, and the caption in large letters was 'The Ladder of Salvation'. At the top of the ladder, above the clouds, sat a repre-

sentation of God the Father on a throne, surrounded by angels, all
of whom were white and male. The angels were helping happy-
looking people, some black, some white, but all labelled as
Roman Catholics, to get to the top of the ladder and enter the
Kingdom of Heaven. Below the Roman Catholics were the
pagans, who were being beckoned upwards by the Catholics.
Then came the Muslims, who were not making much progress up
or down. At the bottom of the ladder were the Protestants, all
with faces that put me in mind of a particularly gruesome
medieval painting of the Day of Judgement. The Protestants were
all being dragged down into hell by cohorts of devils with horns
and forked tails. I am thankful to say that I only saw this repulsive poster once, but it must have represented the views of
someone with enough money and influence to get it printed.

There were also in every denomination a few missionaries who
seemed to measure their success or failure in terms of the
numbers of converts they baptised. The quickest way to draw in
new recruits was to make the mission's welfare services available
only to baptised members of their own denomination. Insisting
on giving a thorough course of instruction to anyone who wanted
to learn about Christianity might, in the long run, produce better
Christians, but what mattered most to that type of missionary
was not the quality of converts, which was hard to measure, but
the quantity, which could be recorded in annual statistics, copies
of which could be sent back to mission headquarters in Europe.

I sometimes heard it argued that donors in developed countries
gave money to help people of the same denomination as themselves, and no one else. Donors would therefore be disappointed,
and might cease to contribute funds, if they heard that the
mission's resources were being made available to anyone, of any
religion or none, who asked for help. I came across some missionaries with that sort of attitude, but they were a minority.

My first contact with a missionary who gave me a very
unfavourable impression involved the Father Superior of the
White Fathers' Mission at Kisa, about ten miles south of Tukuyu.
He seemed to me to exemplify attitudes which I found uncharitable, to say the least.

The episode which caused me to think poorly of him concerned
his treatment of my houseboy, Timothy Mwakapombe, and his
wife Tamika. A few months after he started working for me,
Timothy told me that Tamika was pregnant. Timothy was a
Roman Catholic, but Tamika was a Protestant who regularly
attended the Moravian Church in Tukuyu Township. Timothy

and Tamika had not had a Christian wedding, but Timothy had paid the bride-price to Tamika's father, and by Nyakyusa law and custom they were man and wife and their baby was legitimate.

Soon after Tamika had given birth to a delightful little girl, Timothy asked for a day off work so that he could get the baby christened at Kisa Mission. When Timothy returned home that evening with Tamika, I expected them to be proud and happy, but they both looked absolutely miserable. Timothy asked me to read a note scribbled untidily in English by the Father Superior. It said 'Bearer Dominico Kapanya may make his confession and receive communion when he has returned his concubine to her father'.

I asked who Dominico Kapanya was, and Timothy told me that that was his own religious name. I never discovered why the name Dominico was more religious than the name Timothy. Timothy told me that, as soon as the baby had been baptised, the Father Superior had told him to get rid of Tamika at once. They were both young and in love, and for a wife to be rejected and sent back to her father in such circumstances was likely to be the first step towards a life of poverty, and quite possibly of prostitution as well. For Timothy, the solution to the problem was for Tamika to become a Roman Catholic, and for them then to have a wedding in Kisa Mission, but when I asked Tamika what she thought about this suggestion, she just said two words – 'Catholic bad!'.

For the next two or three weeks I heard the sounds of constant sobbing coming from the room where Timothy and Tamika slept, but I seldom saw Tamika or the baby. Then one day Timothy came to me and asked for another day off. Tamika had at last agreed to save her marriage by becoming an extremely reluctant Roman Catholic, and to get married at Kisa Mission. She had already been baptised as a Moravian, but I believe that Tamika was given a second baptism certificate when she became nominally a Roman Catholic. It did not mean very much to her, however. On the first Sunday after her Catholic wedding, I saw Tamika sitting with her baby in the congregation of the Moravian Church.

There was no Anglican Church in Tukuyu, and services in English were very infrequent. I sometimes attended services in the Moravian Church, which were not normally conducted in Swahili but in Kinyakyusa. On Whit-Sunday there was a special festival, and the African pastor, the Reverend Robert

Mwakarukwa, asked me to give a short address in Swahili, which he interpreted into Kinyakyusa. He also asked a newly-appointed Danish missionary to speak in English, as he was not yet fluent in Swahili. The Dane's sermon must have confused the congregation. He talked about the Christian life being like a journey through a railway tunnel. Inside the tunnel everything was dark, but when the train emerged from the tunnel everything seemed brighter than one had ever realised before. The trouble with that image was that, in the year 1952, the nearest railway to Tukuyu was almost 300 miles away, and there was not a single tunnel on the whole railway system in Tanganyika.

After the service, which lasted over four hours, all the other guests and I were invited to join the church elders for a curry lunch at the Pastor's house, and I complimented the choir (spelt 'kwaya' on the Church Notice Board) on their really magnificent singing. I asked John Mwakangale, the choirmaster, who later became a prominent political leader, how often he rehearsed them. He replied, 'I'm afraid I can only take them for four evenings a week, but Absalom takes them for the other two.'

Foot Safari with Porters

Before the rainy season came to an end, I started planning my trip to Bulambia and Bundali at the western end of Rungwe District, near to the boundary with Mbeya District. I was to visit two small tribes, the Ndali and the Lambia. They spoke dialects which were very similar to Kinyakyusa.

Although the area was fertile and well-watered, it was very hilly and there were no motor roads over the hills. Anyone visiting them had to go on foot. There were one or two tiny African-owned shops which usually stocked sugar, salt, tea, cheap cigarettes, paraffin, and perhaps a blanket or two, but very little else. There were none of the Indian-owned shops that catered for the needs of town-dwellers.

Before setting out on a foot safari to a remote area, one had to plan carefully. My two most helpful advisers were the Boma Head Messenger, Katoto Musyani, and my own personal Messenger, Abel Seme. The three of us discussed together all the details of my itinerary. We first agreed on all the places where I would need to hold a public meeting, known to Swahili and English speakers alike as a 'Baraza'. We then had to work out distances, and estimate how long it would take to get by foot from A to B, with a gang of porters carrying our loads and needing to rest from time to time. This was not always easy to predict, as the weather and the condition of the footpaths and the rivers we would have to cross could affect the time spent on each stage of the journey.

We also needed to prepare a list of the equipment and rations we would need to take with us. This would include a large Government-owned tent, which was extremely heavy, a canvas ground-sheet, a 7-foot long camp bed which I had had made for me in England and used with a horse-hair mattress on every safari, my camp chair, my mosquito-net and poles, a canvas folding bath and wash-basin, and all the bedding and spare clothing I would need. I also brought a box containing copies of various official printed forms, some books for me to read if I had any spare time, some simple first aid equipment, and a supply of blank notebooks. I needed these in order to write down every evening my impressions of how well or badly each place on my itinerary was being administered by the chief or headman, and details of any matters on which I would have to take follow-up action after I returned to the Boma. The loads also included all the pots, pans, cutlery and crockery, bottled drink, and imported foods which Lameck, my cook, would use. He took great pride in producing delicious breakfasts and evening meals day after day for me and my dog Susan, even in the most difficult conditions, but in order to do so he insisted on bringing almost enough implements to equip the kitchen of a good restaurant.

We also worked out the amount of rations, mainly maize-meal, which we would need in order to feed all the people accompanying me on the safari. In all the well-watered villages where we were to spend the night, there was enough food for the resident population, but it would be difficult for the villagers to provide enough food locally to feed so many visitors. We did not yet know exactly how many porters we would employ, but we estimated that there would probably not be fewer than twenty, all of whom would need to eat.

Even though Abel had not done the journey as often as Katoto, his prodigious memory retained every bit of background information which Katoto gave us. He was also better educated than Katoto, having completed Standard VI at middle school. He had been a sergeant in the King's African Rifles before becoming a Boma Messenger, and could use a map. I had complete confidence in him, and he did not disappoint me.

Lameck, my new cook, was not young. He even remembered

the time of the German occupation before 1918, and I wondered how he would manage a long journey by foot and cooking for me as well. I need not have worried. He had stamina and skill, even though he did not have quite so ebullient a sense of humour as Abel and the porters, who laughed hilariously at things which Lameck appeared to regard as slightly beneath his dignity.

Saidi, the indolent driver, needed only to know when and where to drive the Government Transport car, and that was as far as his interest went. He showed no interest whatsoever in what we planned to do in Bundali or Bulambia. On the first day of the safari, he came with us to the end of the motor road where we had arranged to pick up the porters and start walking, and on the last day he complied with written instructions about the rendezvous point where he was to pick us up at the end of our long walk, and drive us back to Tukuyu.

It was not just Saidi who needed to have written instructions about where to be at a particular time on a particular date. The chiefs and headmen of all the villages that we were intending to visit needed to know of our plans well before the safari was due to start. This was mainly in order to let everyone who wanted to attend a Baraza in the Native Court know when it would take place. It was also to give the chief of the area where our walk would begin time to engage enough porters to carry our loads, and for the other chiefs along our route to have replacement porters standing by in case they were needed.

On the first morning of our safari, Saidi's ramshackle old GT Ford clattered up to my house, and Abel, Lameck and Timothy all helped to load up. When all the loads were safely in the car, Saidi emerged from under the tree where he had been resting from his labours – he had already driven at least a mile that morning – and we set off northwards on the Mbeya Road. My dog Susan joined us in the car, and we left Timothy in charge of my house. Saidi's laziness irritated me, but I did not rebuke him. I was sure that it would just make matters worse if I told him to perform menial tasks that he thought were beneath him. Fortunately, I never worked with such a lazy driver again.

We drove northwards for a few miles along the Tukuyu–Mbeya road until we came to a road junction, and we left what was euphemistically described as a main road, and took a much narrower and bumpier road to the west, towards the point where we were to meet our porters. This little road was just about passable in dry weather, but it came to an abrupt end a few hundred yards short of a spectacular natural bridge, known locally as *Daraja ya*

The Bridge of God

Mungu – 'The Bridge of God'. This consisted of a huge boulder spanning a ravine on the River Kiwira. I never understood why God decided to put it there.

When we reached the end of the road, we found two groups of Africans waiting for us. The first group looked dignified and were more smartly dressed than average peasant farmers. A few were even wearing shoes.

The second group were very shabbily dressed, and all had bare feet. These were the people who were to be our porters for the whole or part of a safari lasting nearly three weeks. When I saw them for the first time, I had misgivings about whether they were strong enough to carry heavy loads, and wondered whether they were volunteers or conscripts.

Politicians sometimes alleged that porters working for the Government were so poorly paid that they were little better than slaves. I do not accept that accusation. Gangs of porters usually included a high proportion of people who had not yet paid their poll tax, and work as a porter was one way to earn the money they needed in order to pay it. Most people thought that working as a porter was a lesser evil than being charged with wilful neglect to pay poll tax. There were sometimes one or two people in a group of possible porters who asked for permission to stay at home on compassionate grounds, for example to look after a sick relative, and when I had confirmed that their reason was genuine I always granted their request and took on someone else instead.

As soon as we arrived, Abel told the porters to start unloading the car while he introduced the chief and all his dignitaries to me. These included the headmen, the village elders, the court clerk, and the court messengers.

One of the characteristics of Africans which I found particularly endearing was their natural courtesy. The business of greeting old or new friends was a matter of enormous importance, and was never to be done hastily. If one knew a person's name, one used it. If one didn't, one addressed the person one was talking to by a respectful title, – 'Bwana' for a man, often with a reference to the person's occupation, 'Bibi' or 'Mama' for a woman, 'Father' or 'Grandfather' for an elderly man, and 'Mother' or 'Grandmother' for an elderly woman. In Britain to call someone 'old man' or 'old woman' or 'Granny' is not generally thought of as flattering, but in Swahili to be called *mzee* (old person) was a great compliment. Children would be addressed affectionately as 'my son' or 'my daughter', and would reply with the deference always due from children to adults. One of the respectful greetings in very common use to a person of higher status than oneself was *Shikamoo* – 'I grasp your feet'.

The ritual of shaking hands often seemed interminable, clasping the palm and then the thumb of one's companion over and over again. Convention also required people meeting one another, even after a very short period of separation, to ask for all the news – of home, of family, of health, of work, of wherever one had come from, and any other subject which might happen to be appropriate. The polite answer to such questions was always that the news was good, but this might then be qualified by adding a phrase to indicate that the news wasn't really good at all – 'Good, but this or that calamity has occurred'. To launch directly into an account of the calamity without saying beforehand that the news was good would not have been polite at all. Politeness was an essential ingredient of village life in Tanganyika, and those expatriates who failed to understand this soon acquired a reputation for being abrupt and ill-mannered.

After we had got out of the car, it took a long time for the Chief and his retinue to get through the routine of exchanging greetings with all their guests. At last, when Abel thought it suitable for him to do so, he turned his attention once again to the porters, who had been standing quietly a few yards away while those in authority were talking. He wrote down a list of all their names, and supervised the task of dividing all the baggage into loads of roughly the same weight. He then allocated one load to each porter. He reminded the porters about where we were going, the daily rate of pay authorised by the Government, and he explained that, in addition to a cash payment when they completed their task, they would be given daily rations for the journey, and that those who came with us all the way to the end would receive a supplementary payment and rations for their journey home, even though they would not then be carrying loads.

The Chief had supplied a few more porters than we needed, and Abel asked if anyone did not want to come with us. One or two asked to be excused, and Abel allowed them to go home immediately.

As soon as he had completed the briefing of the porters, Abel said loudly, 'Lift your loads,' and the porters all took from their pockets or loin-cloths circular pads of dried grass that looked rather like birds' nests, and placed them on top of their heads. The porters then balanced their loads very carefully on to the pads, and as soon as they were all ready Abel gave the order, 'Let's go.'

I was pleased to see that the Chief and his retinue were coming with us. Abel explained quietly to me in Swahili that they all intended to *sindikiza* us as far as the boundary of the Chief's area. There is, as far as I know, no exact English one-word equivalent of the word *sindikiza*. The Standard Swahili–English Dictionary uses no fewer than fifteen words to translate it. According to that dictionary, it means 'accompany a parting guest a little way on his road as a gesture of respect, &c'. The word was very commonly used in Swahili to describe an action which Africans in Tanganyika regarded as a matter of routine courtesy. Every chief or headman whose area we visited on my safari to Bundali and Bulambia made a point not only of seeing us off when we left his area but also of coming to the boundary of his land to wait for us to arrive from our previous stopping place. We were always welcomed at the boundary between two chiefdoms. This involved quite long delays that I had not expected while Chief A and his retinue said goodbye to us, and went through all the appropriate greetings when handing us over to Chief B.

We started our walk at a steady pace, and soon reached God's Bridge. This looked splendid, but the rock which spanned the river was high, the edges of the ravine were steep, and the river Kiwira was deep and still flowing fast after the heavy rains. I have always had a bad head for heights, and did not greatly enjoy clambering across the rock bridge. I wondered how the porters would cope when they had loads on their heads and were not wearing shoes. They showed no sign of unsteadiness, and there were no accidents. Those who were the first to cross the bridge waited patiently on the far side of the river until all the porters had crossed safely. We then continued on our journey, pausing for a few minutes every hour or so to rest.

The timing of these pauses for rest was not precise. None of the porters had watches, and we all preferred to rest in places which were agreeably shady, and where there was clean water, rather than stopping in a less pleasant spot simply because my watch showed that we had been walking for a specific number of minutes since the previous pause.

The schedule for each day depended on the distance between one camp site and the next. Some chiefs' headquarters were less than ten miles from the headquarters of the neighbouring chief, but others were much further apart. Our route also involved many changes of direction, as the courts we planned to visit were not situated along a straight line. The total distance we covered was much greater than it would have been if we had walked in a straight line the whole way from the start to the finish of the safari.

When Abel and Katoto had been advising me on planning the safari, they suggested that we should always set off as early in the morning as possible, before the sun got uncomfortably hot, and that if we expected to arrive at our destination by midday we should arrange to hold a Baraza in the afternoon. If the journey was likely to take from dawn until dusk, as it sometimes did, they reckoned that it would be preferable to reach the night stop, pitch our camp, and hold the Baraza the following day. This sometimes involved spending two consecutive nights in the same village.

Our departure from Tukuyu had been timed to coincide with the end of the very heavy rains, and though we still had the occasional light shower the sun shone brightly for most of the journey. It was warm at midday, but the evenings were pleasantly cool, and I enjoyed relaxing in front of a log fire.

Abel's skill as an organiser and Lameck's skill as a cook amazed me. Within minutes of reaching our camp, my tent, camp bed, camp table, and camp chair were always ready for me, assembled by the porters under Abel's guidance. I never had long to wait before Lameck served up two very appetising cooked meals, one on plates on the camp table for me, and the other in an enamel bowl placed on the grass for Susan. Susan was given meat and rice, sometimes boiled in milk. My evening meal usually consisted of a diminutive chicken and locally grown vegetables, bought from local villagers, and imported potatoes which had been carried in the car from Tukuyu, but each night the meal was cooked in a different way or with a different sauce. The main

course was usually followed by fresh or stewed fruit or fritters. In the morning, Lameck would prepare for me a hearty breakfast of eggs and toast before we left the camp. I did not have lunch on safari, as I did not think it fair to delay the journey while I ate lunch when all the people accompanying me would not get a meal until the evening. However, we all enjoyed eating the fruit which villagers offered us during our short pauses for rest.

Lameck cooked all my meals over a wood fire, using a flat sheet of iron which he placed over three very large stones. He also used the same log fire to heat a four-gallon tin can filled with water for my evening bath. This type of can was to be seen everywhere. Both English and Swahili speakers used to refer to it as a *debe* (pronounced Debbie). Debes were originally supplied for the sale and storage of paraffin, which was widely used for lighting and as fuel for refrigerators by those rich enough to possess them, but when the paraffin was finished the debe was nearly always rinsed out and used for carrying water. African women used debes every day to fetch water from the nearest river, as there were no piped water supplies to their houses.

Another facility which was provided for me but for no one else was a brand new pit latrine, built for my exclusive use. I had not mentioned in my letter to the chiefs and headmen that I wanted a loo built for me at every stopping place, but there was always one waiting for me. The design of such latrines was always similar. They consisted of a grass wall about five feet high to protect the user's privacy. The structure was shaped rather like an incomplete figure '9'. Right in the centre was a hole in the ground about a foot to eighteen inches deep, with stems of bamboo to reinforce the edges of the hole. In most latrines, the thoughtful builder left a pile of dry earth to sprinkle into the hole after it had been used.

The tasks which I performed on walking safari were generally the same as those I carried out on safaris to places that were accessible by car, but there were a few differences. Places that were only rarely visited by Government officials usually had a larger accumulation of people with personal problems than less remote chiefdoms, and there were invariably large numbers of old men applying to be exempted from payment of poll tax. There were two reasons for this. It was probably a long time since the previous visit of a District Officer, and the journey was too far for a frail old man to walk into the Boma himself to seek tax exemption there, as many who lived near the Boma were willing to do.

Some primary schools, dispensaries, markets, and courts were much better administered than others, but that is a fact of life in any country. The main difference between Bundali and Bulambia and the parts of Rungwe district that were close to Tukuyu was that the standard of administration in remote areas depended much more on the competence of the chief and his retinue than in the villages that were regularly visited by Government officials.

My task on any safari was not confined to seeing how the chief was doing his job. I also tried to teach villagers as much as I could about ways to improve the social and economic conditions in which they lived. The rudiments of democratically-elected rural councils already existed in Rungwe, but many people had very little idea of what these were likely to involve. As in other countries, tax was very unpopular, and I attempted to explain that social services such as schools and dispensaries had to be paid for by somebody. There were illnesses which caused suffering and premature death, and many of these could be prevented by improving hygiene. Productivity could be improved by adopting new methods of agriculture.

All these lessons had to be explained in the simplest possible way to an audience of peasant farmers, many of whom were illiterate. In a country with few schools, being illiterate does not mean that people are unintelligent, but it does mean that their development has to depend more on word of mouth than on the study of text-books. I would have preferred to tackle one topic at a time, but in Bundali and Bulambia I felt I had no choice but to try to cover as many themes as possible in each Baraza that I attended. I formed the impression that the people were listening to me attentively, and there was none of the hostility that I had encountered when I talked about soil erosion at Busokelo.

There was one Baraza where, even if I did not arouse active hostility, I did not respond to a unanimous request in the way the people had hoped I would.

We had set off soon after dawn, and had been welcomed by the Chief at his boundary. We had then climbed steadily all morning until we reached our destination at about midday in radiant sunshine. The distance we had travelled was quite short, but I was sweating and breathless when we reached the court and went through the usual courtesies with the people who were waiting for us. The court had only recently been built, and the view over the surrounding hills was quite magnificent.

I looked round the village, and then began to listen to the requests of the people. Almost immediately I was asked to give approval to a scheme to demolish the existing court building and reconstruct the court down in the valley a few miles away, where it was warmer. The people all volunteered to give their labour free of charge for this purpose.

I was not impressed by the idea at all, and said that, even if the labour was free, the Native Treasury had no allocation in its budget for moving the court, and there would be expenditure on new cement and building materials. The existing building was a very attractive one, and much more impressive than many other courthouses I had recently visited. The faces of my audience got gloomier and gloomier, and I decided that it would be wise to change the subject, and get on to dealing as quickly as possible with pleasanter topics like applications for tax exemption.

When I got into bed that night I began to understand why the people wanted to move their court down into the valley. My teeth started to chatter, and I felt so cold that I put on a pair of socks and a pullover over my pyjamas. That was no good at all, so I put on my long trousers, a sports jacket, a dressing-gown, and a second pair of socks. I snuggled down as far as possible under my blankets, but I still felt as if I was getting hypothermia.

Next morning, when I stepped out of my tent looking like a scarecrow, there was thick white frost everywhere. It was like a Christmas card scene. The frost on the spider webs surrounding the camp looked unbelievably beautiful, and the view would have delighted anyone who likes the Alps in winter. However, I felt concerned about how Abel, Lameck, and the porters had endured such an arctic night with far fewer clothes than I had. I also felt guilty about having been so unsympathetic in refusing the request to move the court off the crest of the hill. I could never have agreed to such a request, but at least I would have shown more compassion in turning it down if I had appreciated just how bitterly cold the place could be.

The following night we again camped on a hill, but it was not so high or so cold. However, Lameck's misfortunes were not yet over. As usual, as soon as we reached camp he had put on a cook's apron and a pair of canvas plimsolls that had seen better days. When the meals he had prepared for Susan and me were ready, he walked down a rather steep and slippery path from the hut he was using as a kitchen towards my tent, skidded on the mud and landed hard on his bottom. Susan's enamel bowl flew up into the air and landed upside down on Lameck's head. Milky rice pudding trickling gently down a black face is not a sight one sees every day, and Abel and the porters all laughed uproariously. I at first restrained myself, as I thought Lameck's feelings would be hurt if I laughed at him too, but Lameck himself then forgot all about his dignity and laughed just as hilariously as Abel and the porters. I stopped pretending it wasn't funny, and joined in the merriment too.

Ever since I had taken him on, I had regarded Lameck as an exceptionally hard-working, reliable and capable cook, but without much sense of humour. The episode of the rice pudding greatly increased my affection for him as a companion.

At the start of the safari, I had let the porters know that if they were injured or felt ill on the journey, they should tell Abel or me. I had brought with me an old tin box which had previously contained assorted chocolates, and I had put into it a few very simple household remedies such as aspirins, medicines for coughs or diarrhoea, disinfectant, ointment for sprains, bandages, and sticking plaster. When the safari began, everyone seemed to be in good health, but I was not surprised that the number of porters who came to me in the evenings for treatment for minor ailments and cuts and bruises gradually got larger as the safari progressed. What did surprise me was the way those porters who were feverish or had injuries to their bare feet continued day after day to walk long distances with loads on their heads without making any complaint. They simply expressed very warm thanks for the medicines which I offered them when we reached camp in the evening.

It was not until the safari was nearly over that I noticed that my chocolate tin was not a very suitable receptacle for use as a first aid chest. It was clearly marked on the tin that the brand of chocolates it had contained was 'Black Magic'. Fortunately none of the porters could read English, so no one suspected me of sorcery, but on subsequent safaris I always took the precaution of carrying medicines in an old chocolate tin with a different brand name on it.

On the last day of the safari, we covered a greater distance than on any previous day. We had arranged for Saidi to pick us up at sunset on a Friday evening at a point which could be easily identified on the border between Rungwe and Mbeya Districts, and we knew that we would need to go fast if we were to reach the rendezvous before dark. We all set off as early as possible in the morning, and walked steadily for about twelve hours with only very short pauses for rest for the porters.

After a foot safari lasting about three weeks, I felt very fit, but even so I was extremely tired when we at last joined up with Saidi. Never before or since have I walked so far in a day. According to a not very accurate map, I think we covered about thirty-two miles that day, but Susan must have covered more than that. As usual, she started the day dashing to and fro to explore anything which interested her, but towards the evening she walked close at my heels, looking a rather dejected little dog. Walking thirty miles in a day is quite a task for a human, especially a porter carrying loads, but for a dog with legs only eight or nine inches long it must have been really exhausting.

I enjoyed the safari immensely. Whenever we reached a village, we were welcomed with dancing, singing, and ululation, and were often invited to rest either in front of the huts of important villagers or even to step into their smoke-filled homes and sit down for a few minutes chatting there. The warmth of the welcome had nothing to do with me personally, as none of the people who gave us such a welcome had ever seen me before.

Very young children did not always join in the welcome their parents extended to me. When I arrived, many toddlers fled screaming in terror to their mothers. The adults were quick to apologise, explaining that the children had never seen a white man before, but would soon overcome their fear of me. In spite of the consternation which the colour of my skin caused to children, I got the very strong impression that the adult tribesmen trusted and were genuinely fond of British administrators like Teddy Kingdon, who had been the last official to visit Bundali and

Bulambia before me, and that they were prepared to treat me as a new friend rather than as the representative of an oppressive imperialist regime.

The steady growth of trust which the Ndali and Lambia tribesmen showed to me was reciprocated. The chiefs, headmen, and village elders were not sophisticated people. Many of them could not read or write, but I saw no sign of the corruption and tyranny of certain tribal rulers which I came across later in other parts of Tanganyika. My first impression of my porters had not been too favourable, but by the time I had got to know all of them as individuals, I found I enjoyed their company, their cheerfulness, their sense of fun, their stamina, and their eagerness to help to make the safari a success. I was very sorry to say goodbye to them when Saidi drove Abel, Lameck, and me back to Tukuyu.

Although nearly everything about walking safari gave me pleasure, there were two things about it which I did not like at all. I had met ticks in the grasslands around Tukuyu, but in the Bundali hills there were more of them than I had ever come across before, and I found them utterly repulsive. Ticks, like spiders, have eight legs. They manage, without being detected, to adhere to a host animal. They then pierce the animal's skin and suck its blood and gorge until they become grossly distended. In addition to looking obscene, ticks carry a variety of very unpleasant diseases which affect humans, dogs, and cattle. Every evening when we reached camp I would take Susan on to my lap and remove all the ticks which had got into her fur during the day. I would then examine my own anatomy to see if there were any on me which I needed to remove. It was not a task I enjoyed.

The other feature of foot safari in the hills of Bundali and Bulambia which I did not like was crossing rivers where footbridges either did not exist at all or were very primitive. In many parts of Tanganyika, river beds dried up after the rains were over, and were quite easy to cross by foot. However, rivers in Rungwe district usually flowed throughout the year. The bridges on motor roads were sometimes a bit intimidating, but they were far less terrifying than the river crossings on the footpaths that went from village to village in remote hilly areas like Bundali and Bulambia.

A few rivers had shallow points where it was possible to wade across by foot. Some fords even had stepping stones across them, but these were not always to be trusted. I had started the safari carrying an umbrella as a dual-purpose accessory, to serve as a walking stick and also to protect me in a shower of rain.

Unfortunately, while I was negotiating some particularly slimy stepping stones, my foot slipped, and I put my weight on the umbrella to prevent me overbalancing. The umbrella snapped with a noise like a rifle shot, and I landed sprawling in the river with my hand still firmly clasped round the umbrella handle and the rest of the umbrella floating downstream at some speed. All the Africans who were with me rushed to my rescue, but I was not hurt, and my clothes dried out quite quickly as we continued on our way.

I disliked rural footbridges across gorges even more than slippery stepping stones. The level of water in rivers always rose enormously during a heavy downpour, so the people who chose the sites for bridges usually opted for places where the water would not carry the bridge away in a moderate shower. Most bridges were connected to large tree-trunks on opposite banks of a gorge, and involved climbing the lower part of the tree in order to reach the bridge. The higher the bridge, the less likely it was to get washed away. One factor apparently overlooked by most of the local bridge-builders was that the higher the bridge, the more unpleasant the consequences would be if one fell off it.

One or two bridges seemed to be reasonably solid, with transverse branches to step on, connected to ropes made of liana creepers from the trees in the tropical forests, and with handrails on both sides also made of liana creepers. There were other bridges, however, which looked as if nobody had crossed them for decades, and where the liana fibres might just be strong enough to carry a person weighing eight or nine stone, as most peasant farmers did, but which looked far too fragile to carry someone who weighed nearly twice as much. One particularly horrifying bridge consisted of just one rope to walk across and one to serve as a handrail. It was nearly twenty feet above the water, and falling off it would have been painful. What made it even worse for me was that, even though she was a highly intelligent little dog, Susan was not a tight-rope walker, and the only way to get her from one side of the river to the other was to carry her. I doubted my ability to keep my balance with a dog in my arms, and I did not think Susan would take kindly to being carried in the arms of a comparative stranger. We solved the problem by putting her in a fruit basket and getting a porter who was more agile than me to volunteer to go ahead of me, dragging the basket while I followed, holding the handles to reassure Susan. We prevented the basket from falling into the water by tying the handles together and looping the rope over the handrail. I made

encouraging noises, and Susan appeared to regard the whole
episode as an exciting new adventure. I had seldom been so petri-
fied, but when she reached the far bank of the river and was set
free, she scampered round, barking triumphantly.

After we linked up with Saidi on the last day of the safari, it
was too late to attempt to drive back to Tukuyu that evening, and
we all camped overnight. Lameck and Abel lit the paraffin lamps
and set about erecting my tent, making my bed, and preparing an
evening meal for me. The porters all helped, in spite of the
distance they had walked that day, and even idle Saidi lent a
hand. I was extremely grateful for their loyalty and dedication.
The following morning, I paid off the porters and we all returned
to our respective homes.

I never had any doubts about the enormous importance for
District Officers of getting to know and be known by the people
they administered. Unless an officer saw for himself the problems
of his area and heard the views of the people affected by them, his
proposed solutions could be quite inappropriate, and, unless the
people trusted his judgement and integrity, they were not likely
to listen to his advice anyhow. My safari in Bundali and Bulambia
convinced me that such relationships of trust are cemented much
more effectively when travelling on foot than by car. The disadvantage of a foot safari, however, was that it took so long. While
I was spending weeks in a very remote area which was not accessible by car, all my other tasks had either to be carried out by
someone else or to await my return.

As roads in Tanganyika gradually improved, it became possible, at least during the dry season, to visit by car in a day or
two places that would have taken weeks to reach by foot. This
meant that foot safaris became less and less common, being
confined to those parts of the country which could not be
reached by car. I regard it as one of the greatest benefits of being
posted to Rungwe District that it contained such an area, and
that Teddy Kingdon entrusted to me the extremely rewarding
task of visiting it.

Comings and Goings

European Government officials in Tanganyika normally
completed a tour of about thirty months before returning to the
United Kingdom with their families for five or six months' leave.
Some officials, particularly those with specialist jobs, returned to

their previous station at the end of their leave, but in the Provincial Administration it was unusual to serve more than one tour in the same station. Cadets were always expected to serve in at least two different stations during their two-year period of probation, so that they could be observed at work in two different environments and reported on by two different District Commissioners. Employees working in the private sector tended to remain longer in the same place, and those who ran their own farms or businesses rarely left the country, but in most up-country stations there was a flow of people reaching the end of their tours and of newcomers arriving. The flow was uneven. Some months in Rungwe District there were no departures at all, but in others there were as many as four or five officials and their families going on leave, or being transferred for other reasons.

There were many possible reasons for being transferred in the middle of a tour of service. Some officers were transferred on promotion, others to undertake a special assignment, others because of a clash of personalities, or an affair with a colleague's wife, though I do not think this happened quite as often as is sometimes alleged. A few officers were moved because of misconduct which was not thought quite serious enough to justify prosecution or the termination of their appointment.

Teddy and Dorothy Kingdon were coming to the end of their tour of service in Rungwe District, and there was to be an inter-regnum before the arrival of the new District Commissioner, Peter Johnston. For a few weeks, Robert Paterson was to assume charge of the District. I was to be given enhanced magisterial powers for as long as I remained in Rungwe District, and a brand new cadet called Tony Moore was to be posted temporarily to the District to help out until Peter Johnston arrived. Tony had just completed the Colonial Service Course at Oxford, and he shared my house for a few weeks. I found him congenial and hard-working.

Before the Kingdons went on leave, there were innumerable farewell parties for them at which the love and respect in which Teddy, Dorothy, and Gran were held by all races were quite obvious. I knew I was going to miss them greatly, but I did not yet know quite what a difference their departure would make to me.

I did not at that time own a car of my own, and Teddy asked me if I would like to use his Standard Vanguard estate car while he was in England. The arrangement would be that I would pay the cost of the petrol I used on recreational journeys, and would claim mileage allowance at the rates approved by the Government whenever I used the car on official business. The cost of any repairs would be met from the amount I received as mileage allowance, and I would arrange for the car to be returned with any cash balance when Teddy came back from leave.

The arrangement seemed ideal, but there was one unforeseen problem. There were not many car dealers in Tanganyika at the time, and any car which proved reliable became very popular. Robert Paterson had a car the same as Teddy's and one morning when he was going off on safari he told me he wanted to take Teddy Kingdon's spare wheel with him, as the tyre on his own spare wheel was very worn. I said the wheel was not mine to lend, and that I would have to ask Teddy's permission before lending it to anyone else. Robert was furious, and said that if I did not do as he wanted he would report adversely on me when he completed my annual confidential report at the end of my first year's service.

I was appalled, and I wrote at once to ask Teddy's advice. He replied by return of post saying that my letter had distressed him but had not surprised him much. He told me that I was definitely not to lend his car or any part of it to anyone else while I was looking after it. He added that he would make himself responsible for seeing that my annual report was a fair one.

I never mentioned the matter to Alan Oldaker, the Provincial Commissioner, but after I completed my first year's service he told me quite casually when he was on a visit to Tukuyu that my report had been drafted by Teddy, not by Robert, and that it was complimentary. This was a relief, but I found working under Robert a great strain, and was not sorry when the time came for me to move to Iringa.

Shortly before I was transferred, I was chatting in the Rungwe Club with a few friends, and expressed regret that I would be leaving the District without ever having climbed Mount Rungwe. I am not a mountaineer, and I would not have attempted to climb the mountain by myself, but three colleagues, Bill Ashton, Bill Clegg, and Tony Moore, reacted by suggesting that if the weather was good we should all climb the mountain together the following Sunday. We had been told that the path up to the top of the mountain was completely safe, and that it was quite possible to reach the summit and return to Tukuyu in a day, so we arranged to set off by car very early on Sunday morning to get as close as possible to the footpath up the mountain. On the day itself, the weather was perfect, and we set off as planned, bringing with us our own food and drink, warm clothes, and very solid walking shoes. We looked forward to a good day.

Mount Rungwe is an extinct volcano, 9,717 feet high. None of the party was an expert botanist, but we were all interested to see the changes of vegetation as we got higher up the mountain. We passed through what we believed was lowland rain forest, then bamboo forest, then upland rain forest, and eventually emerged from the forest into open grassland, with flora that none of us had ever seen before. Looking down into the crater, we were amazed to see specimens of plants which normally grow to a height of just a few inches, but in the crater were several feet tall. The sun was shining, and we had a magnificent view in every direction. We all felt exhilarated.

We started the descent in the early afternoon, and had no worries about getting back to the car in good time. Suddenly Bill Clegg, the Co-operative Officer, gave a cry, and we saw him lying beside the path in agony. He had tripped and injured his ankle very badly. Within minutes the swelling had become spectacular, and it was quite clear that he was in no position to walk down the mountainside unaided.

Mount Rungwe – giant groundsel and lobelia plants

We decided that the three of us who were uninjured would take turns to help him in different ways. One would lead, and try to clear a path for the other three. Bill Clegg would put his arms round the shoulders of the other two, who would support him as he hopped down the mountainside on one leg.

Our progress was painfully slow, particularly in those places where the path was too narrow for three people to walk side by side, and we soon acknowledged to each other that we were unlikely to reach our car before dark.

Bamboo forest

Helping an injured man to walk down a steep path is quite hard work by daylight. When one can no longer see the path but knows that it is full of potholes and tree roots, it can be very unpleasant indeed. I had the additional handicap that I was much taller than my companions, and branches which they could walk under often hit my face.

At last we reached the car and drove back to Tukuyu in a chastened mood. As soon as we arrived, we called at the Club in the hope of finding the doctor there. He was not there, but some of the members who were had already begun to get worried about us. We did not waste any time talking to them about our adventures. Our first priority was to get Bill to the doctor, who, we were told, was having dinner at someone else's house. As soon as we found him, we left Bill in his care and drove on to Bill's house to let his wife know what had happened, and that Bill was not in danger but would be returning to his home with the doctor in a few minutes.

Bill had not broken any bones, but had sprained his ankle severely. In due course he made a complete recovery, but I think we all learned a salutary lesson from our foolhardiness in attempting to climb a mountain, even one which was not regarded as dangerous, without a guide and without adequate equipment. When we set off we were all so over-confident that we hadn't even thought of bringing a torch with us.

I do not climb mountains any more, but whenever I see young people trying to learn a new activity like rowing, climbing, diving, or cycling, I think that the first duty of any instructor is to teach a novice the basic essentials of safety.

I moved to Iringa a few days later, but I look back on my thirteen months in Rungwe District with real affection. It was a lovely place, and, more important than that, I was working mainly with a tribe who were progressive in an economically thriving district. I saw the beginnings of rural councils, which, even if they were not yet completely democratic, were nevertheless much more democratic than the traditional systems of local government common at that time. I enjoyed a degree of responsibility which I would never have been given in Britain at the age of twenty-four, and for almost a year I worked under the guidance of a man who was an example of the very best type of District Commissioner: hard-working, honest, intelligent, and filled with love for people of every race and creed. I saw the contrast during the couple of months that I spent working under someone who was also able and energetic, but who was not such an admirable man.

Chapter 3

Iringa District

(November 1952–April 1954)

District Officer's house in Iringa

Transfer to Iringa

On the day of my transfer I drove from Tukuyu to Iringa in Teddy Kingdon's car, accompanied by my houseboy Timothy and my dog Susan. I chose Timothy rather than Lameck to come with me, because he had served for a few years in the King's African Rifles and been trained as a driver before returning to Tukuyu and becoming a houseboy, and I thought he would be more use if the car broke down than Lameck, who had no such experience.

Vanguard cars had the reputation of being reliable, but they were also notorious for sucking in dust on dry earth roads. When we left Tukuyu my skin had clearly been white and Timothy's black, but by the time we arrrived in Iringa we were both roughly the same reddish-brown colour. I reported my arrival to the District Commissioner, Geoffrey Hucks, and his wife Aline, and the first thing they did was to invite me to stay with them for a

few nights, and offer me an immediate bath. Geoffrey's houseboy
did the same for Timothy.

My personal effects came separately in a lorry hired from the
Rungwe Native Treasury. The lorry also carried Timothy's wife
and baby, Lameck, Lameck's wife and son, and a young garden
boy called Daimon, whom I had taken on after I had been in
Tukuyu a few months, and who had shown himself to be cheerful, intelligent, honest, hard-working, and successful at growing
flowers.

Iringa District and Rungwe District had certain features in
common. The Nyakyusa were the ninth largest tribe in
Tanganyika. The Hehe, who lived in Iringa District, were the
eighth largest. The Boma in Tukuyu was 5,300 feet above sea
level. The Boma in Iringa was 5,380 feet above sea level. Both
Districts were very hilly, but the contrasts between the two
districts were much more obvious than the similarities.

The area of Rungwe District was only 1,874 square miles. Iringa
District was more than seven times as large, covering an area of
about 14,000 square miles. The total population of Rungwe
District in 1952 was more than 237,000, but in Iringa District it
was less than 185,000. However, there were nearly four times as
many non-Africans in Iringa District (2,073, including 800
Europeans) as in Rungwe (549, including 113 Europeans).
Rungwe District was so densely populated with humans that it
was rare to see large wild animals there. Wildlife in Iringa District
was much more plentiful and much more varied. I had never seen
an elephant, a lion, a giraffe, a wildebeest, a python or an ostrich
in Rungwe District.

In Iringa District I saw all of them from time to time. In 1952,
the rainfall in Iringa was less than 27 inches. In Tukuyu it was
over 110 inches. Towards the end of the dry season, Iringa
District was always parched and yellowish-brown. In Rungwe,
the countryside was always green. My house in Rungwe had a
glorious view. My house in Iringa did not.

There were also contrasts between the townships of Iringa and
Tukuyu. Iringa was an important stopping point on the Great
North Road, which ran for more than 800 miles from the northern
to the southern borders of Tanganyika. Tukuyu was on a branch
road which came to an end when it reached Lake Nyasa, about
fifty miles beyond Tukuyu.

The amenities in Iringa township were not sophisticated by
British standards, but even so they were much more sophisticated
than those in Tukuyu. Iringa had a piped water supply, electricity,

two banks, two hotels, two garages, a cinema, a grade 1 aerodrome and many reasonably well-stocked shops. Tukuyu did not.

Both districts did have one feature in common during the time I worked in them. Teddy Kingdon and Geoffrey Hucks had both been promoted to the rank of Senior District Officer, and were wise, experienced, honest, and totally dedicated to their job. Like Teddy, who had been the captain of his college boat club at Oxford, Geoffrey had been a successful college oarsman in the late 1920s, when he had rowed in a crew which won the coxed fours at Cambridge.

Some people found Geoffrey's wife Aline rather formidable. She was a very able teacher who had been even more successful at sport than her husband. She was well over six feet tall, and had been an outstanding swimmer and tennis player, representing Great Britain in one sport and her university in the other. She was by far the best tennis player, male or female, in Iringa at the time I was there. Geoffrey and Aline had three delightful children, two daughters and a son. Their son John was still a schoolboy when I first met him, and he did not stop growing until he was about 6' 10" tall. It took me a bit longer to become close friends with Geoffrey and Aline than with Teddy and Dorothy, but I was extremely lucky to serve under two such District Commissioners in my first tour, and they and their wives all remained lifelong friends.

The other District Officer at Iringa, Geoff Bullock, was closer to my age than to Geoffrey Hucks's. He and his wife Anne and their two young sons also became very good friends. My house was next to Geoff Bullock's and opposite Geoffrey Hucks's, and we saw a lot of each other both at work and socially.

Neither Geoffrey Hucks nor Geoff Bullock had been in Iringa for very long when I arrived, though Geoff was nearing the end of his tour of service, having spent a year or so in Njombe District before being posted to Iringa in response to an emergency. None of us had been in Iringa when a scandal occurred which had rocked the whole of East Africa, and had even been reported in the national press in Britain. Shortly before I arrived in Tanganyika, the cadet then stationed in Iringa had been imprisoned for offences connected with ivory. I never met the man concerned, but I was told that he had a lot of charm, a quick wit, an unduly high opinion of his own ability, a wife with expensive tastes, and not much integrity.

Poaching ivory was not uncommon. Ivory commanded a high price, and hunters often killed elephant illegally and sold their

tusks on the black market, but this case was considered much more serious than simple poaching. An official with responsibility for law and order had devised a plot to defraud the Government, and in doing so he had induced a hitherto blameless Game Scout to act as his accomplice.

The task of protecting the lives, houses, and crops of peasant farmers from marauding elephant was normally carried out by uniformed Game Scouts. The tusks of all elephants shot by Game Scouts were brought in to the Boma and weighed, marked with an official stamp and number, and registered as 'Government Trophies' under the supervision of a responsible official. The tusks were then placed in a locked strong room, and were later sold by auction, the proceeds being paid into revenue. The value of tusks was usually linked to their weight, but disproportionate prices were always paid for extremely large tusks.

The tusks of elephant shot by Game Scouts to protect crops were usually quite small, but one day a Game Scout arrived in the Boma accompanied by porters who were carrying a pair of really enormous tusks from an elephant that the Game Scout had shot in the course of his job.

The cadet should have followed the standard procedure, but instead he arranged to hide the huge tusks in his own house, which was the same house that I later occupied. He then took out a Game Licence in his own name, and persuaded the Game Scout to provide another set of tusks to register as Government Trophies, thus accounting for his having engaged porters to bring them in to the Boma. The cadet's plan was to make a big profit by selling the very large tusks as if they were his own. It was a nasty little crime with greed as its motive.

The affair caused a lot of anger and bitterness. Some people thought the crime was a petty one which did not warrant a sentence of imprisonment, and claimed that Tom Skinner, Geoffrey Hucks's predecessor as District Commissioner, had been disloyal to his subordinate. He had failed to warn him of the likely consequences of his actions before he had gone too far to avoid prosecution. Others regarded the crime as outrageous, and appeared to think that if one District Officer was a criminal, then none of the others could be trusted either.

Relations between those who held opposing points of view about the case remained acrimonious for a long time. The cadet's decision to appeal against his conviction and sentence may well have prolonged the controversy, because when he appealed for the first time the High Court greatly increased the sentence imposed by the lower court. He appealed again, and the Court of Appeal for Eastern Africa reduced the sentence determined by the High Court, although it remained more severe than the original sentence imposed by the trial magistrate.

Whether they regarded the handling of the case as too lenient or too severe, many of the Europeans living in Iringa District criticised the entire Provincial Administration for the affair, and were less than friendly to any District Officers, even those who had not been in Iringa District when the crime was committed

On my first Saturday evening in Iringa, I accompanied Geoffrey and Aline Hucks to a dance at the Club. Geoffrey proposed me for membership, and he knew which people he could rely on to support my application. I met some new colleagues who welcomed me and offered me a drink, but I found the general atmosphere rather chilly.

Not everyone was frigid in the way they received me, however. Towards midnight a plump middle-aged lady with an upper-class accent, came up to me at the bar and introduced herself. She whispered in my ear that if I came out with her on to the golf course she would give me a very good time. I was told later that she was totally promiscuous, and 'threw herself at anything in trousers'. She had inherited a large fortune from her father, and lived outside Iringa with her husband, who had retired on a pension. It was alleged that her husband was only allowed to receive his extra pocket money from his wife if he let her have sex with anyone she fancied. I had heard rumours that such goings-on were quite commonplace among the 'Happy Valley' crowd in the Kenya Highlands, but this was the first time I had come across anything like it in Tanganyika. I spent the rest of the evening trying to avoid her attentions by inviting a series of other women to dance with me.

As in Rungwe, membership of the Iringa Club was exclusively for Europeans, but Iringa had a considerably larger membership and was better equipped. The Iringa Club even had water-borne indoor sanitation. There were fewer attractive picnic spots in Iringa District than in Rungwe, so recreation for Europeans consisted largely of tennis, golf, drinking in the Club, visits to the houses of friends, or visits to the cinema or one of the two hotels in the town. Some of my colleagues in Iringa liked classical music, but there were no weekly sessions devoted to listening to records as there had been in Rungwe.

The contrasts between Rungwe and Iringa even extended to the actual tasks we did, and the way in which duties were divided between the District Commissioner and his two District Officers. In Tukuyu, where the complement of Government officials was comparatively small, several specialist departments, for example the Forest Department and the Labour Department, did not have a senior officer stationed in the District. This meant that the task of supervising the work of those Departments had to be carried out by District Officers, who had all undergone a training course aimed at making them reasonably competent jacks-of-all-trades. In Tukuyu, I had to deal with forestry and labour matters, and with the supervision of the Cash Office. In Iringa, there was a Revenue Officer, a Forestry Officer, and a Labour Officer who were responsible for certain functions which I had carried out in Rungwe District.

In Iringa District, the duties of the District Commissioner and District Officers were distributed not on a functional but on a geographical basis. There was only one Paramount Chief for the whole Hehe tribe, but he had ten sub-chiefs, each of whom presided over a Native Court, and the responsibility for overseeing the whole range of activities in each of the sub-chiefdoms was allocated to one designated member of the Provincial Administration. Geoffrey Hucks and Geoff Bullock between them dealt with the hilly southern part of the District, which included many tea estates, tobacco farms managed by non-Africans, a private sector preparatory school for European children, a Government secondary school for African boys, and several Trading Centres with Indian-owned shops.

As the junior member of the team, I took over from my predecessor the responsibility for the arid low-lying northern part of the district, and for dealing with whatever might crop up in Pawaga Sub-Chiefdom, on the road which led northwards to Dodoma in Central Province, and Mazombe and Mahenge* Sub-Chiefdoms, which were on the road to Kilosa, in Eastern Province. There were steep escarpments a few miles outside Iringa on both the Iringa–Dodoma and the Iringa–Kilosa Roads, and the climate in my part of the District was significantly hotter than in the township or the highland areas to the south of it. At first I thought my part of the District was unattractive, but in due course I came to like it.

The Hehe of Pawaga Sub-Chiefdom

One of my new responsibilities involved regular monthly visits to Pawaga Sub-Chiefdom to pay cattle-owners for the milk they had supplied to the Uhehe Native Creameries. Cattle played an important part in the social and economic life of the Hehe tribe, and small creameries had been set up at various villages in Pawaga to enable villagers to sell their milk. In a hot climate it was hard to deliver milk from a rural producer to a town-dwelling consumer before it went sour, but clarified butter, or *ghee* as it was commonly known, lasted much longer, and was widely used for cooking, especially by Asians. Ghee was prepared by pouring the milk into a separator that removed the cream, which was then churned into butter. This was then melted over a slow fire to clarify it. It was then put into a big tin can in which it was sold to traders. The skimmed milk was returned to the supplier if he wanted it.

Each creamery was run by an operator, with an assistant to fetch firewood. In addition to processing the ghee and keeping the machinery spotlessly clean, the operator was required to issue every month a small card known as a *kipande* to each supplier on which the amount of milk he supplied was recorded daily. The suppliers included some with very peculiar names, for example, Japanizi s/o Zanzibaa, which means exactly what it sounds like, or Kaswende s/o Mpumbavu, which means Syphilis son of Simpleton. The operator also had to record the total amount of

Note: The Sub-Chiefdom of Mahenge in Iringa District is not the same place as the minor settlement of Mahenge, the Headquarters of Ulanga District in Eastern Province, where I was later posted and spent an entire tour of service.

Uhehe Creamery

milk purchased from the cattle owners and the total amount of ghee produced. There were plenty of opportunities for dishonesty, either by suppliers who could add water to their milk, or by the operator who could sell a proportion of the ghee on the black market and pocket the proceeds for himself. One of the important tasks of the Creameries Head Clerk, John Kasuga, was to monitor the amount of ghee produced from each gallon of milk in each creamery, and to make sure that the productivity levels were satisfactory. John also made the preparations for the monthly pay parade, and compiled the payment vouchers for each creamery, but he did not pay out the cash himself. I was given that task, with John Kasuga witnessing my signature as the paying officer.

It sometimes worried me that the Uhehe Native Creameries were said to be running at a small profit when no account was ever taken of the hidden subsidy provided by Central Government in the form of my salary and travel expenses while I was working on behalf of the creameries. I came to accept, however, that subsidies are often needed for a few years after a small commercial enterprise has been launched. In the case of the creameries, some years later government officials ceased to be directly involved, and John Kasuga managed them successfully on his own.

I drove Teddy Kingdon's car on my first visit to Pawaga. As in

Rungwe District, I was accompanied by Lameck and my dog Susan, but on this occasion there were two new colleagues travelling with me in the car, John Kasuga, who only came with me when I visited Pawaga, and my District Office Messenger, Ayubu Farjallah, who came with me on every safari I did in Iringa District.

The apparent contrasts between Abel Seme, my messenger in Rungwe District, and Ayubu could hardly have been greater. Abel was a jovial, roly-poly man with exceptionally black skin. Ayubu was very thin, very reserved, and the colour of his skin was very light. However, both men had in abundance those qualities that gave District Office Messengers such a good reputation throughout Tanganyika. They were intelligent, honest, extremely knowledgeable about local history, and totally loyal to the officers they served.

I had frequently heard comments from some of the Europeans in Tukuyu comparing the argumentative Nyakyusa unfavourably with the brave and respectful Hehe, who were said to be outstanding warriors, and were well represented in the King's African Rifles. I was therefore unprepared for what I found when I arrived at the village of Kimande, where the sub-chief of Pawaga had his headquarters.

I had already written to the Sub-Chief to let him know my plans to visit his area, and when I arrived in Kimande I expected the sort of celebratory welcome which visiting officials were normally given in Rungwe District. Instead I was received by a sleepy-looking Sub-Chief and a few apathetic village elders, the Native Court clerk, and the Sub-Chief's messenger. There were perhaps a dozen grubby and emaciated old men and a few tick-infested mongrel dogs waiting in the courthouse, which was in poor repair, with its roof and walls damaged by termites. The old men were wanting me to give them permanent exemption from poll tax on the grounds of old age and poverty. I told them I would hear their petitions as soon as I got back to the courthouse after I had walked round the village to inspect the school, the dispensary, the market, and the trading centre.

The Sub-Chief and his Village Elders accompanied me round the village, and I felt surprised and disappointed that, in comparison with most Nyakyusa villages which were clean and well-maintained, the first Hehe village I visited looked like a slum. Attendance at primary schools in Rungwe District was normally excellent, but the school registers showed that attendance at Kimande school was very poor. It was not yet midday, but the

The DO inspects the primary school

market and the dispensary had already finished their work for the day, and the Native Authority employees were being paid for a full day's work while only working for half a day or less.

What disgusted me most of all was that everywhere I went in the village I saw unburied human excrement lying close to the footpaths. Not surprisingly, the dispensary records showed an alarming level of hookworm and other parasitic infestations, but the dispensary itself had no latrines for the outpatients to use while awaiting treatment. None of the villagers' houses appeared to have latrines either.

When I got back to the courthouse, I asked the Sub-Chief when the rest of the people would arrive, and he told me that everyone he expected was already present. I waited no longer, but began to make an unrehearsed speech on two themes. I talked first about the need for children to learn to read and write if they were to have successful lives and make a useful contribution to the future development of their country. I said that I was very sad that the children of Kimande were not taking full advantage of all the help they could get from regular attendance at their school.

I then began to talk about hygiene. I tried to explain as simply as I could, and in terms which I was quite sure that the Nyakyusa would have understood, that hookworm infestation was transmitted through infected human excreta, and that people who walked barefoot were at serious risk if they used footpaths which were as polluted as all the footpaths in Kimande. I told them that if they took steps to improve their health they would feel fitter, they would become more productive farmers, and fewer of their children would die. I said that the first step towards a better future would be to build two pit latrines near to the dispensary, one for men and the other for women.

There were very few people in the courthouse to hear what I said. However, when I concluded my speech the audience applauded politely, but asked no questions. The Sub-Chief then replied with every sign of enthusiasm to what I had just said. He expressed the view that the new District Officer was full of splendid ideas, and that he and his people would always be glad to take my advice in future on every important matter. He himself would make sure that the latrines which I had recommended were erected at the earliest opportunity.

I thought I had achieved an immediate success in Pawaga with very little effort. I remembered my first safari to a packed court in Busokelo to talk to the Nyakyusa about soil erosion, and the opposition they had at first expressed to my proposals there, and I misguidedly believed that working with the Hehe would be less contentious than working with the Nyakyusa had sometimes been.

I inspected the area surrounding Kimande, and spent the night in the government rest-house there. It was seldom necessary to take a tent on safaris in Iringa District. Next morning I continued my journey to the remaining creameries where I was to make payments, and I returned to the Boma in Teddy Kingdon's car a few days later.

Teddy's leave came to an end, and he told me he was returning to become the District Commissioner of Singida District, in Central Province. I returned his car to him with my sincere thanks, and with the balance of the allowance I had received when using the car on official business. My mother had already written to tell me that Teddy had travelled from Dorset to the Isle of Wight just to meet her and tell her how I was settling in to my new job, and when Teddy returned to Tanganyika he let me know how my mother was coping without my father, and how she was settling into her new job as a doctor working in a sanatorium in Ventnor.

Having driven Teddy's car for a few months, I felt I wanted to have a car of my own, and I decided to buy the second-hand car of a colleague in the Public Works Department, Mervyn Willers, whom I trusted and who did not let me down.

On my second visit to Kimande, I arrived in my own Ford V8 Pick-up, feeling very proud of it. I asked the Sub-Chief to show me the new latrines he had promised to have built. He seemed rather hurt that I should have remembered his undertaking and taken it at face value.

On my third visit, I started to lose patience, and told the Sub-Chief that if the latrines were not ready by the next time I came, his wages and those of the village elders would be held on deposit in the Native Treasury until the latrines were completed. For a few more months nothing happened, and I eventually decided that I would remain in Kimande for as long as it took a group of Hehe men to dig two new pit latrines. The Sub-Chief reluctantly conscripted a gang of men, as tradition entitled him to do, and the job was completed quite quickly while I watched. Before I set off to visit the other creameries on my itinerary, I was quite pleased to see two immaculate latrines ready for use by the villagers. The Sub-Chief and his Elders were also quite pleased to receive their back pay.

The following month I noted that the latrines were still immaculate. They remained immaculate for the whole time I was stationed in Iringa. Nobody ever used them.

I had made the fundamental blunder of trying, with the best possible intentions, to impose my own ideas for progress on a group of very conservative peasants. I was under the impression that I had explained the reasons for using latrines, and the Sub-Chief had indicated his full agreement to my suggestion. However, I had not discussed the matter adequately with the villagers themselves. Most of them had not attended the Court when I gave my talk on education and hygiene, and they rejected completely an innovation that a European stranger was trying to introduce. The villagers of Kimande did not appear to accept that I was genuinely trying to help them to become healthier and more prosperous, and had no personal axe to grind.

The Paramount Chief Comes Home

Chief Adam Sapi

I felt disappointed about the Hehe tribe in general when I first visited Pawaga, but I soon discovered that other parts of Iringa District were administered by much more dynamic sub-chiefs. I had already heard many of my colleagues saying that the paramount chief of the Hehe was greatly respected, not just in his own District but in the whole of Tanganyika. As soon as I met Chief Adam Sapi Mkwawa, I realised that his outstanding reputation was well deserved.

At the time of my arrival in Iringa, Adam was on a study tour in Britain, organised, I believe, by the British Council. When he returned, there were innumerable celebrations all over the district to welcome him home, and I was invited to attend a huge tea-party, with guests from all races, held in the town's social welfare centre. It was a happy occasion, with many speeches. Some speeches were short and to the point. Others went on for a long time and were very boring. All expressed pride and pleasure at Adam's safe return after his long journey. It is not always easy to detect the real motives of a speaker who flatters the guest of honour, but I formed the impression that all those who spoke were completely sincere in the praise they lavished on the Chief.

At last it was Chief Adam's turn to reply. When he stood up, I was struck by his magnificent physique, his friendly smile, the twinkle in his eye, his humour, his fluency in both Swahili and English, and his courtesy to everyone, rich or poor, young or old, male or female, African, Asian, or European.

He was generous in his thanks to those who had arranged his study tour, to those who had arranged the party for his return, to those who had deputised for him while he was abroad, and to those who had just said kind things about him. He then talked about what he had learnt in Britain.

Many of his audience had never travelled outside Iringa District. Chief Adam's fascinating descriptions of things which I had always taken for granted, for example, of underground railways running along tunnels under the streets of London, escalators on tube stations, high-rise buildings, lifts in hotels and department stores, doors that opened and shut automatically, indoor flush toilets and bathrooms with running hot and cold water in the homes of quite ordinary British people, all had his audience convulsed with laughter.

The laughter was slightly more subdued when he told his audience that in Britain not every white man was rich, and that many of the menial tasks that in Tanganyika were done only by Africans, for example cleaning the streets and disposing of garbage, were often done in Britain by white men. Being born with a white skin was not a certain key to wealth and privilege in Britain. Success in every country depended on education, skill, and hard work. Britain was technologically far more advanced than Tanganyika, but the same human qualities which had brought developmemt over a period of years to Britain could do the same for Tanganyika as well.

I joined in the enthusiastic applause for Chief Adam's speech. I did not yet know him well, but I came to respect and like him more and more as I got to know him better. I was delighted, a few years later, when he accepted an invitation to come to my wedding in Dar es Salaam.

Adam was intelligent, energetic, and honest. He was also of noble birth. Hereditary titles and rank are now less highly valued both in Europe and in Africa than they used to be, but at that time most Hehe tribesmen still thought that the main reason to honour Chief Adam was that he was the head of a family of brave warriors, and the grandson of Chief Mkwawa, who had been a heroic leader of the resistance against the German forces who ruled the country from 1885 to 1918.

It seemed to me, and to my colleagues, that Adam was an outstanding example of the type of African leader on whom British officials still relied for the successful implementation of the policy of 'Indirect Rule'.

Indirect Rule

The concept of Indirect Rule was brought to Tanganyika by Sir Donald Cameron, who was the Governor from 1925 to 1931, and had previously served in Nigeria under Sir Frederick (later Lord) Lugard. After serving in Tanganyika, Cameron himself returned to Nigeria as Governor in 1931.

While he was in Tanganyika, Cameron introduced a system

which was modelled on the methods of administration which Lugard had implemented in Nigeria. Any country may conceivably be forced into submission by a ruthless tyrant with superior power and resources, but the philosophy of Indirect Rule acknowledged that a country could only be governed in a humane way if it had the consent of the people being governed.

In 1930, Cameron issued a Local Government Memorandum setting out the aims and methods of indirect rule. This memorandum includes the following paragraphs:

The mandatory power is under a solemn obligation so to train the natives that they may stand by themselves, at least as part of the whole community of the Territory, and we cannot discharge that obligation if we do not train the people in the art of administration. It must be plain that in any such training we must first teach the people to administer their own affairs, and it seems obvious that in doing the latter, the wise course, if not the only practical course, is to build on the institutions of the people themselves, tribal institutions which have been handed down to them through the centuries. If we set up artificial institutions, these institutions can have no inherent stability, and must crumble away at the first shock which they may receive. It is our duty to do everything in our power to develop the native politically on lines suitable to the state of society in which he lives. Our desire is to make him a good African, and we shall not achieve this if we destroy all the institutions, all the traditions, all the habits of the people, superimposing on them what we consider to be better administrative methods and better principles, but destroying everything that made the administration really in touch with the thoughts and customs of the people.

The system adopted by the Tanganyika Government for this purpose is based on the principle known as Indirect Rule, that is the principle of adapting for the purposes of local government the institutions which the native peoples have evolved for themselves, so that they may develop in a constitutional manner from their own past, guided and restrained by the traditions and sanctions which they have inherited (moulded or modified as they may be on the advice of British Officers) and by the general advice and control of those officers. It is an essential feature of this system that the British Government rules through these native institutions which are regarded as an integral part of the machinery of government, with well defined powers and functions recognised by Government and by law, and not dependent on the caprice of an executive officer.

The study tour which Chief Adam had just completed in Britain was one practical example of the way British administrators sought to create an elite chosen from among the traditional leaders of the country, by giving them a privileged education and by providing them with special training courses in Britain designed to help them to a better understanding of the principles of good government.

The policy was not always successful. Later, when I was stationed in Tabora District, I had the task of recording the sworn statements of witnesses in the case of a hereditary African ruler who had received a privileged education and special training, but was corrupt and tyrannical, and committed suicide when he was was about to be arrested for serious crimes against his own people.

Chief Adam, on the other hand, was one of the success stories of the policy of indirect rule. He graduated at a British university, and used his talents for the benefit of the Hehe people, but he did not confine his interest to the Hehe. He shared an example to those who were striving to unite the nation.

His personality and ability enabled Adam to retain the confidence and respect of his people when a new class of political leader was emerging. This consisted not of hereditary rulers but of well-educated people who wanted to introduce parliamentary democracy on the Westminster model, with the real power lying not with aristocrats but with commoners. Chief Adam managed to bridge the transition successfully. While the country was still being administered by Britain, he was appointed as a Member of Legislative Council, then of Executive Council. After Independence, he was for many years the Speaker of Tanganyika's democratically elected Parliament.

Adam Sapi Mkwawa was not the country's only aristocrat with exceptional intelligence, vision and charisma. Julius Nyerere, the country's first elected President, was also the son of a Chief, albeit of the Zanaki tribe, a much smaller and less prominent tribe than the Hehe.

The Sleeping Giant Stirs

From the time that Cameron introduced it until the last few years before Independence, the system of Indirect Rule was probably the only practical way for Britain to govern such an enormous territory.

Tanganyika is some 740 miles long and 760 miles wide – as big

as France, Belgium and Germany combined. The distance from
the north-west to the south-east corners of Tanganyika is similar
to the distance from London to Warsaw. Within its borders, it
contains every variety of soil and climate, from the humid heat of
the coast to the permanent snows of Mount Kilimanjaro.

During the period of British rule, the population consisted
mainly of peasant farmers whose loyalty was to their tribe rather
than to a country created arbitrarily by powers from Europe.

There were more than a hundred tribes in Tanganyika, and
many tribesmen had never travelled outside their own tribal
areas. The chiefs were content to go on ruling with the support of
the colonial regime. So long as the tribesmen all accepted their
traditional rulers, the system might have continued indefinitely.

The 1950s were a time of very rapid and profound social and
economic changes, however, and the system of Indirect Rule was
not well equipped to deal with them all. Several factors combined
to bring about change. A growing number of British politicians
appeared to be losing faith in Britain's role as an Imperial power,
and to regard the Empire as an unnecessary expense. India,
Pakistan, and Ghana had gained their Independence since the
Second World War, and what those countries had achieved
others could aspire to copy.

There were also factors inside Tanganyika itself which were
tending to promote change. After years of apparent stagnation, a
new Governor, Sir Edward Twining, appointed in 1949, gave a
fresh impetus to economic development. A road-building
programme meant that villages which had previously only been
accessible on foot could now be reached by car, bus or lorry. Even
though many earth roads became impassable during the rains,
the improved roads made it much easier for peasant farmers to
sell their cash crops. This was good for the economy. The roads
also provided the opportunity for adventurous young people to
travel to other districts and other countries, where they came into
contact with new ideas, some of which tended to threaten the
establishment. As levels of literacy of Africans gradually
improved, a growing number of young commoners began to
challenge the authority of traditional rulers, some of whom were
less well educated than the commoners themselves.

Tanganyika lacked the resources of cash and trained staff to
meet the demand for improved education and health-care.
Improvements would cost money, so the policy of the government was to encourage farmers to grow more. Staff of the
Department of Agriculture at every level played a major part in

the campaign to increase crop yields, either through improved methods of farming or by cultivating a larger acreage.

In Rungwe District the density of the population limited the chance for farmers to cultivate larger areas. In Iringa District, however, there was still plenty of unused land available in the 1950s. In sparsely populated areas like Uhehe, land was not bought or rented. A Hehe farmer only needed to seek the approval of his headman or village elder before starting to clear an unclaimed patch of land to use as a *shamba**. The main factor which limited output was the effort and time that it took to cultivate each acre of land manually with a hoe.

Much bigger areas could be cultivated by using a plough drawn by trained oxen, and still more with a tractor. Before I got to Iringa, arrangements had been made for loans to be made available to enable the best farmers across the country to buy ox-ploughs or tractors. The number of applications greatly exceeded the number of loans available, however, so most applications were refused, and loans were offered only to those regarded as likely to repay them.

One of my tasks was to investigate and make recommendations on applications from the part of the District for which I had special responsibility. Security was an important aspect of the application, and those who already owned a large number of cattle were more likely to get a loan than other people.

Some officials thought that a loan made to a group of farmers was more likely to be repaid than one made to a single individual, but this proved a fallacy. The seasons were the same for everyone, so all the borrowers in a group wanted to use their tractor at the same time. If the group's tractor broke down while one farmer was using it, arguments arose about who should repair it. Some of the implements bought by groups of farmers were not maintained regularly, and quickly became unserviceable. If one member of the group became ill or died, the question then arose of who, if anyone, should replace him, and how his share of the outstanding loan should be repaid. Experience showed that it was normally better for loans to be offered to individuals rather than to groups of farmers. In business terms, this made good sense, but it had unforeseen social consequences.

Farmers with tractors cultivated more and more land year by year. However, when the time came to harvest the crop, rich farmers could not do the task alone. They therefore employed

shamba: area of cultivated land/smallholding.

other Africans to help them, usually on very low wages. The system of agricultural loans led to an increase in the volume of crops produced, but it also led to the creation of a few rich capitalist farmers and a much larger number of poor labourers. Many of the labourers working in Iringa District were Gogo tribesmen from Central Province.

The main reason for labourers from Ugogo seeking work in Uhehe was that the rainfall in Ugogo was very unreliable, and the crops of maize, millet and sorghum often failed there, leaving the people dependent on cassava*, which is neither appetising nor nutritious, although it survives well in arid conditions.

There was a famine in Ugogo in 1953 and 1954, and Chief Adam showed his exceptional qualities by persuading his own tribesmen to come to the help of their hungry neighbours. I travelled down from Iringa to a village on the border between Ugogo and Uhehe, sitting beside the Chief in the cab of an Uhehe Native Treasury lorry that was loaded with several tons of maize contributed by Hehe farmers. Other chiefs may previously have shown such compassion to their neighbours, but I never heard of any.

Some supporters of capitalism claim that, when an entrepreneur becomes rich, part of his wealth will trickle down to the rest of the community. Many comparatively wealthy Africans helped to support members of their own extended families, but I saw little evidence to suggest that the wealth of a few entrepreneurs made any real difference to the lives of the people at large, other than to excite their envy.

Africans in remote villages still seemed content, but elsewhere, particularly in urban areas, there were signs of growing dissatisfaction and desire for change. This led, among other things, to the creation of the Tanganyika African National Union (TANU).

TANU was founded in 1954. Its leader, Julius Nyerere, recognised that rivalries between different tribes, and their different laws and customs, were hindering the formation of a nation state. He believed passionately in equality, and detested elitism and greed. His socialist rhetoric was aimed at the poor, who greatly outnumbered the rich. Nyerere's objective was to transform a colony made up of a large number of tribes, each of whom had its own laws and customs, into a nation state ruled by an elected majority. The ruling majority would, of course, consist of Africans. A policy aimed at creating a few rich entrepreneurs was not what Nyerere wanted at all.

cassava: a root crop.

After the country became independent and Nyerere became its first Prime Minister and later its first President, he set about destroying what he regarded as a manifestation of greed and ambition. Early in the 1960s, the new parliament enacted a law restricting the acreage any individual farmer was allowed to cultivate. This was bitterly resented by those African entrepreneurs who had benefited from the loan system.

Some years after I left Tanganyika, I was sad to hear a story about one of the Hehe farmers who had received a loan in the 1950s. He had made a commercial success of it, and by the 1960s he was cultivating a very large acreage, and was extremely rich. When the government enforced the new law, the farmer protested to Iringa's Regional Commissioner. When his protests were rejected, the farmer took his shotgun and killed the Regional Commissioner. I am not sure about the accuracy of the details I was told, but I believe that the killer was one of the people whom I had myself recommended as suitable to receive a loan.

Julius Nyerere's qualities were respected across the world. The contrast between him and some of the ruthless dictators who have misruled other newly-independent African countries is obvious. Even Nyerere's most fervent admirers now acknowledge, however, that his economic policies were definitely not a success. When he retired voluntarily as President in 1985, his country was as poor as, if not poorer than, it had been when Independence was achieved in 1961.

Law and Order and the Death Penalty

Every Administrative Officer was a magistrate, and a high proportion of my time in the Boma at Iringa was spent in the District Court, which had a big case-load but did not have a Resident Magistrate.

There were a few women in the Provincial Administration. Most of them were extremely able and hard-working, but they were not called District Officers. They were given the title Woman Administrative Assistant. I suspect that the reason for this discrimination was probably male chauvinism on the part of officials either in Dar es Salaam or the Colonial Office. The excuse given, however, was not that British officials anywhere were chauvinist, but that Muslim men would object to being tried in a District Court by a female magistrate. I thought this a feeble excuse, but it meant that women who served in the Provincial

Administration were not given magisterial powers, and could never aspire to becoming District Commissioners.

Cadets were required to pass examinations in Swahili and in law before being 'confirmed in permanent pensionable appointment' at the end of a two-year period of probation. Before I left Tukuyu I had already passed the Lower and the Higher Swahili examinations, but I had not yet sat the law examination, and I resolved to take it at the first opportunity after I reached Iringa.

The examination consisted of papers on the Penal Code, the Criminal Procedure Code, Civil Procedure, Local Laws, and Applied Laws. Candidates were required to obtain a pass in each subject. Those who did well enough were awarded a credit and the results were published in the *Tanganyika Gazette*, published by Government.

The Penal Code was a very bulky volume which contained page after page of numbered paragraphs defining a wide range of criminal offences. These definitions enabled trial magistrates to distinguish between offences which were similar but not identical, for example murder and manslaughter, rape and indecent assault, simple theft and more serious property crimes such as stealing by a servant, housebreaking, burglary or robbery, and to make sure that the charge was appropriate to the circumstances of the case.

The Criminal Procedure Code was almost as bulky as the Penal Code. It set out the rules on matters such as explaining the charge to an accused person at the start of a trial, the limits to the jurisdiction of different classes of magistrate, the maximum sentence which could be imposed for specific offences, the procedures for remanding in custody, confirmation by the High Court of certain severe sentences imposed by magistrates, and provisions relating to appeal.

There was also a provision under which, during the absence of the District Commissioner, the next senior magistrate present on the station could temporarily assume the powers of a first-class magistrate. This meant that serious cases did not have to remain pending until the DC returned to the station. It also meant that second- or third-class magistrates sometimes heard cases which they would not have been able to deal with if the DC had been present in the Boma.

District magistrates did not normally spend very much of their time on civil cases. These only arose rarely in most up-country stations. Such cases as did arise usually involved debt by non-natives, and I confess that I felt I had many more important tasks to do than listening to arguments about whether a trader's bill had or had not been paid. The litigants in civil cases were often represented by lawyers, and what the plaintiff stated on oath was frequently denied on oath by the defendant. Judgment was given on the basis of which litigant sounded more plausible rather than on the principle which was followed in criminal cases that an accused person is presumed innocent until proved guilty.

There were several locally enacted laws relating, for example, to taxation, the control of natural and mineral resources, road traffic, game licensing, liquor licensing, and a multitude of other subjects about which the country's Legislative Council had decided to make a new law.

The term 'applied laws' referred to laws which had been enacted in another country but were incorporated into the legal system of Tanganyika. The most important of these was probably the Indian Evidence Act. This Act contained many provisions which were similar to the law of evidence in Britain, but there was one major difference. In Britain, subject to certain safeguards, statements made to the police by a person in custody can be taken down and used in evidence. Indian legislators recognised that some over-zealous policemen might seek to obtain confessions from unsophisticated or illiterate people by improper methods like trickery, promises of leniency, threats, or even torture.

In India, it was thought that magistrates were less likely than investigating policemen to resort to such methods, and the Act included a provision to the effect that a confession made to a policeman, or in the presence of a policeman, by a person in custody was not admissible as evidence. The need to protect unsophisticated people is just as great in other countries as it is in India, and this law was applied in its entirety in Tanganyika.

The practical effect of this was that magistrates often had to spend time recording statements made by people who later pleaded guilty before the High Court. The law also seemed to imply that policemen were not always trustworthy. However, I believe that recording statements of people in custody was a justifiable use of a magistrate's time. I do not remember any case in Tanganyika where an accused person who had had a statement recorded by a magistrate later retracted his confession or claimed that it had been obtained in an improper way.

Candidates were allowed to have access to their textbooks when they took the law examination. I thought this was sensible, as magistrates trying cases always had access to their books. What separated the sheep from the goats was not simply the amount of law a candidate had memorised. That was fairly important, but no one expected a cadet to be familiar with every paragraph of every law. What mattered more was the speed with which he could find his way round the textbooks and discover the correct answers to the questions in his law examination, or any legal problems which might arise during the hearing of a case.

Each magistrate was issued with a personal copy of a set of the Laws of Tanganyika, and he was supposed to keep it up to date, either by entering amendments in manuscript or pasting printed amendment slips on to the appropriate page. I had been very remiss about this requirement, and when I was about to take my examination Geoffrey Hucks asked if I would like to borrow his volumes of the laws, which he had amended scrupulously. I was very grateful for his kindness, as there were several questions in which I would have given the wrong answer if I had relied on my own unamended copies of the laws. As it was, when the results were published I was awarded a credit.

Most of the cases which I tried were quite simple. Some involved petty theft, others traffic offences, others wilful neglect to pay tax. I always tried to determine sentences fairly, and to award the same punishment in cases where the facts were very similar. However, there were problems about which our training had given us little guidance. How much more severe should a sentence be for someone with previous convictions than for a first offender? Should the sentence for a person employed in a responsible position in the public sector be heavier than for a peasant farmer, on the grounds that public servants should set an example of integrity, or should it be more lenient on the grounds that dismissal from one's job and the loss of one's pension rights was in itself a severe punishment? Should a fine be heavier for a rich man than for a poor man who had committed a similar offence, and if so, how was the magistrate to carry out a means test? What allowance should a magistrate make for the family circumstances of an accused person? How could a magistrate find out all the relevant facts in a country which had no social workers and very few probation officers? Should those who saved the Court's time by pleading guilty be treated more leniently than people who contested the case?

One day a woman was brought before me charged with offences against the liquor licensing laws. Many people brewed traditional native beer for sale without purchasing a licence, and hoped they would not be detected. The distilling of potentially lethal illicit spirit was a much more serious offence, however, and this woman had been caught selling rot-gut in a very disreputable bar at an enormous price. She was charging her customers the equivalent of a labourer's daily wage for half a glassful of her witch's brew. Chief Inspector Pereira demonstrated to me the effects of the brew by pouring a little on to a piece of varnished wood, where it hissed and foamed and eroded the varnish. I hate to think what it did to the digestive systems of human beings. The woman had distilled several bottles of the stuff, and the bar was full of aggressively drunken customers when it was raided by the police. She was clearly making a big profit from her trade, so I thought a deterrent sentence was needed, and imposed the maximum fine which the law allowed for this offence.

Exactly two weeks later, Chief Inspector Pereira brought the same woman before me a second time, charged with precisely the same offence as before. This time I told her that as she had not been discouraged by her recent conviction and sentence, on this occasion I had no choice but to send her to prison. She was rather upset about this, and told me she had five young children to look after. I said that their father would have to care for them while she was inside, but she replied that all the fathers were unknown, and that she had become pregnant repeatedly in the course of her business.

I remained obdurate, and did not comply with her request to impose another fine, but I did give her time to go back under escort to her bar and try to make arrangements with her neighbours for the care of the children. I also asked Liwali Said-el-Abry, the Town Headman of Iringa Township, to make sure that no harm came to them while their mother was in gaol.

Another case brought before me involved another woman who was charged with brewing native liquor without a licence. She pleaded guilty, and I recorded her plea on the case file and proceeded to convict her. I then asked the prosecuting detective constable to tell me the facts of the case. He apologised profusely for his mistake, and told me that after her arrest a valid licence had been found, and that although she had pleaded guilty she was in fact not guilty of any offence whatsoever. The Criminal Procedure Code did not give any guidance on what a magistrate should do in such a situation, so I took it upon myself to tear up the first case file and to open a second one in which I recorded that the police had withdrawn the prosecution.

I then asked the woman why she had pleaded guilty to a crime of which she was innocent, and she replied, so softly that I was barely able to hear what she said, 'I cannot argue against the Government.'

I have often wondered, but I will never know, how many timid and unsophisticated people have been wrongly convicted and sentenced simply because they were too frightened to speak up in their own defence.

The options available to a magistrate when dealing with female offenders were very limited. Some prisons had a small block, separate from the main part of the prison, where female convicts could be held for the duration of their sentence, but imprisoning a woman often involved recruiting temporary female warders to guard just one convict. The women's cell was usually unoccupied. An institution for delinquent boys existed north of Dar es Salaam, but there was nowhere to send a delinquent girl. The law also totally prohibited corporal punishment of females of any age. Fortunately girls behaved better than boys, and I never had a young girl charged before me during the whole time I spent in Tanganyika.

Young girls were sometimes the victims of crime, however. A Hehe man in his twenties pleaded guilty in my court to raping a little girl of seven. The Medical Officer's report on her physical injuries made shocking reading, and I have no doubt that she was psychologically shattered as well.

I had myself been caned twice at school, and I thought it a sadistic and degrading form of punishment. However, the law allowed corporal punishment in addition to a custodial sentence for those convicted of raping a child, and I felt that this crime was a particularly brutal one. I therefore decided, albeit with some hesitation, to sentence the rapist to imprisonment and also to corporal punishment. The sentence needed to be confirmed by the High Court, which it duly was.

The rules concerning corporal punishment were strict. The sentence could only be carried out after a medical examination had confirmed that the culprit was physically fit to receive his punishment. The caning could only be carried out in the presence of a magistrate. A cloth soaked in disinfectant had to be placed over the convict's buttocks. He was to be held by the wrists and ankles while the beating was being administered. The caning was to be stopped at once if the convict began to bleed. It so happened that I was the magistrate who had the unpleasant task of witnessing the sentence which I had myself imposed.

The nature of the crime showed clearly that the prisoner was sexually abnormal, but I was appalled to see that what most people would have regarded as an excruciating punishment was, for him, another erotic experience, providing him with a new kind of sexual gratification. After that case, I never again imposed a sentence of corporal punishment on any sex offender.

The Criminal Procedure Code listed those offences which could only be tried by the High Court, for example murder and manslaughter. Most of the homicide cases which I committed for trial seemed unpremeditated. Some people were killed in drunken brawls. Others died when domestic quarrels got out of hand. I only remember one case where the murderer had an obvious financial motive, and planned his crime in advance.

A comparatively prosperous peasant farmer living alone in one of the villages in Mazombe Sub-Chiefdom was owed quite a lot of money by another villager. When the debt had been outstanding for a long time, he asked the debtor to pay without any more delay, and said that if he did not get his money back quickly he would sue the debtor in the Native Court. The conversation was heard by a number of witnesses.

A few days later, the creditor's house was destroyed by fire in the middle of the night. Neighbours tried unsuccessfully to rescue the houseowner, and when the charred body was brought out the following morning it was generally thought that his death had been an accident, although the matter needed to be investigated further. The post-mortem examination revealed, however, that the dead man had suffered a severe blow to the head, and had a fractured skull before the fire started. Forensic evidence also showed that the fire had been caused deliberately. Suspicion fell on the debtor, who had been seen close to the victim's house shortly before the fire was spotted. He had not returned to his own home until dawn the following day. A empty can which had previously contained petrol was found in his hut.

The debtor was charged with murder, and at the next High Court Sessions the Judge found that the evidence was conclusive, and convicted the prisoner and sentenced him to death.

Before any convicted murderer was executed, the Governor had to decide whether to exercise the royal prerogative of mercy and commute the sentence, or whether to go ahead and sign the prisoner's death warrant. Before reaching his decision, the Governor consulted the Attorney General and the other members of Executive Council, and together they considered the Court record of the case, and any comments the Judge may have made when passing sentence. They also considered a report prepared by an Administrative Officer stationed in the District where the crime had taken place. There were detailed guidelines concerning the drafting of such reports by Administrative Officers, who were required to describe as fully as possible the life and character of the prisoner, and the attitude of the Chief, tribal leaders and local tribesmen to the offence. Special mention was also to be made of any possible extenuating circumstances, such as traditional hostility between the tribes of a murderer and his victim, or possible fear of witchcraft, or a degree of provocation which was not serious enough to reduce the charge from murder to manslaughter, but which might nevertheless persuade the Governor to reduce the sentence. The report never raised any doubts about the guilt of the prisoner, as the trial Judge had already reached his decision about that.

I happened to be the officer who prepared the usual report for the Governor in this case. The prisoner's previous record was appalling. He had previous convictions for violent crimes and crimes of dishonesty, and nobody in his village had anything to say in his favour. Chief Adam Sapi Mkwawa and Sub-Chief Mwachengula of Mazombe both said, 'This was pure murder. The prisoner is a thoroughly evil man who planned his crime to avoid paying his debt. There are no extenuating circumstances at all.' I concluded my report by saying that I was in full agreement with the comments of the Chief and the Sub-Chief. My report was accepted, the death sentence was confirmed, and a date fixed for the execution.

For as long as I can remember, I have always been opposed to the death penalty. I accept that many decent people disagree with me, but it is my view that capital punishment cannot be reconciled with a belief in the fundamental human right to life, and I know of no conclusive evidence to prove that capital punishment has a deterrent effect on violent crime. Judges are not infallible, and there have been miscarriages of justice where innocent men have been convicted. It is always possible to order the release of a prisoner whose conviction is later discovered to have been wrong, but it is never possible to give life back to someone who has been executed.

The only arguments that I accept in favour of the death penalty are that it costs less to execute a murderer than to imprison him for the rest of his life, and that a murderer cannot repeat his offence after he has been hanged. However, I suspect that, if a Government is seen to be taking the lives of its own citizens in the name of the law, this may encourage its citizens to become more tolerant of all forms of violence.

On the night before the execution, I slept extremely badly. The following evening, I went to the Iringa Club feeling guilty and miserable. I decided that I needed a few strong drinks to cheer me up, but the more I drank the more morose I became. I never once doubted that the prisoner was guilty and that he was a thoroughly bad man, but even so I was appalled to think that my report was probably a factor in causing the death of a man who might still be alive if I had made a different recommendation. It took me some weeks before I was able to get the execution out of my mind and to concentrate once again on my ordinary tasks.

All God's Children

When giving evidence in a District Court, witnesses were required to repeat a form of words to the effect that they would tell the truth, the whole truth, and nothing but the truth. Before they did this, however, the magistrate always noted the witness's religion on the case record. Those who claimed to be Christians swore on the Bible to tell the truth, whereas Muslims, Hindus, and those who adhered to traditional African religions merely affirmed that the statements they were about to make would be true.

I got the impression that roughly a third of the Africans in Tanganyika during the 1950s described themselves as Christians, a third as Muslims, and the remainder said they had no religion, although the beliefs of so-called pagans often played a very important part in their lives.

The distribution of Christians, Muslims, and pagans varied enormously from place to place. Near the coast and in the areas which lay close to the routes followed by slave traders before the abolition of slavery, Arab influence was strong, and the great majority of Africans called themselves Muslims. Some were devout, others less so.

The proportion of people described as pagans, not surprisingly, was highest in the very remote parts of the country which had not been influenced by slave traders in the nineteenth century nor by missionaries in the twentieth. Hardly any well-educated Africans called themselves pagans.

By the time I reached Tanganyika, a wide variety of Christian Missions were active in many parts of the country. There were four Anglican dioceses: three controlled by the Universities Mission to Central Africa and the fourth by the Church

Missionary Society. The UMCA was generally regarded as a high church organisation, whereas the CMS was more evangelical. Most UMCA missionaries came from Britain, whereas the CMS recruited many of its missionaries in Australia.

The Roman Catholic Church had established missions served by various parent bodies, including Benedictines, Capuchins, Consolata Fathers, Holy Ghost Fathers, and White Fathers. Roman Catholic missionaries came from a very large number of countries in Europe and elsewhere.

In addition to Anglican and Roman Catholic missions, there were others run by the Danish Evangelical Lutheran Church, the Swedish Evangelical Lutheran Church, Seventh Day Adventists, Moravians, and the American Inland Mission, to name but a few.

Many of the Christian missionaries whom I met were saintly men and women who gave a wonderful example to the people among whom they lived and worked. Their contribution to the spiritual lives of individuals and to health, education, relief of poverty and famine, and overall social welfare of the tribes they served, are worthy of the very highest praise. It saddened me, however, that not all missions were as admirable as the best.

There was one feature which the good missions seemed to have in common. They made their education, health, welfare, and famine relief services readily available to all who asked for them, regardless of the needy person's religious affiliation. If that led to the recipients of those services asking for more information about Christianity, so much the better, but thorough instruction was given before a potential convert was baptised. Fellow Christians of whatever denomination were regarded as potential allies in the war against poverty, disease, ignorance, and superstition.

There were certain other missions which adopted policies that I found deplorable. They seemed to regard other denominations as rivals, and to measure their own success or failure simply by the number of baptisms they performed. That was, in their view, more important than the effect which becoming a Christian had on the spiritual lives of new converts. They also insisted that the dispensaries and schools which they controlled should be available only to members of the congregation, or else used as a negotiating tool to apply pressure on unsophisticated people to get baptised, even before they had received proper instruction about what baptism really meant.

I never asked missionaries what they were paid, but most lived very frugal lives. A very small minority, however, enjoyed an opulent life-style which seemed to me quite incompatible with the teachings of the Bible. One American woman missionary carrying two Leica cameras round her neck justified this display of wealth by saying, 'If you're doing God's work, you've got to have the best tools!'

Some months after I came to Iringa, Chief Adam Sapi and Sub-Chief Mwachengula came into my office in the Boma, and asked me to visit a village in the Mazombe area as urgently as I possibly could. They feared that a crisis there might lead to bloodshed. They had done their best to restore peace, but they did not have the jurisdiction to settle the matter without the help of a District Officer, since the case involved two European missionaries. As Mazombe was in the part of the District for which I had responsibility, they came to me.

The facts of the dispute were quite simple. It was very unusual for any village to have more than one mission, but Itete village on the road between Iringa and Mazombe had two, one Roman Catholic, the other Swedish Evangelical Lutheran. The Father Superior of the Roman Catholic Mission was an excitable and poorly-educated Italian with a very shrill voice. The Swede was obesely fat and extremely lazy. I had met him from time to time, once when he waddled into my office to complain that the Catholics were stealing the pupils from his school, another time to say they were stealing the patients from his dispensary. I had not pleased him by saying that people were free to seek schooling or medical treatment wherever they liked, and that, if they preferred the Catholic school and dispensary, there was no reason for me to interfere.

Two or three years previously, the Swedish mission had successfully applied for permission to set up a bush school in a small village about an hour's walk from the road leading from Itete to Mazombe. The villagers there had no bush school, and they all supported the idea of getting one. Bush schools taught literacy to a very rudimentary standard, but were not part of the primary school system which lasted for four years and prepared pupils for the Standard IV examination.

Unfortunately, having obtained approval for his scheme to open a bush school, the Swede did absolutely nothing about it, so the Italian, without asking anyone's approval, hired labourers to put up a small schoolhouse and appointed a catechist to teach there.

This spurred the Swede into unprecedented activity. He hired his own workers who put up a second school a matter of yards from the first one, and appointed an Evangelical Lutheran as its teacher.

What worried Adam and Mwachengula was that Teacher A had received a dried-up twig with a letter attached to it which said, 'If you do not go from here, you will dry up as this twig is dry.' Teacher B had then received a bag containing decayed human bones and various articles connected with witchcraft. This had been nailed to the door of his house during his absence. Each teacher suspected his rival of responsibility for the threats which Adam, Mwachengula, and the villagers all took very seriously.

I drove to the Native Court at Mazombe, and was met there by Adam and Mwachengula. We went as far as we could by car, then walked together to the village where we saw the two new schools. Both the missionaries had been told of my visit and were already waiting for us, with a crowd of about two hundred people.

The Italian put his case first, fortissimo – con molto espressione. There had been no school until he had provided one. Many pupils had hurried to enrol there, and it was absurd to interfere with a thriving school just because of the jealousy and spitefulness of the Lutherans. Roman Catholics greatly outnumbered Lutherans in the village, and in the previous months he had himself carried out four hundred baptisms there.

This prompted the intervention of the Village Elder, who introduced himself by saying that he was a pagan and was therefore quite impartial in the dispute. He went on to explain that the total population of the whole village was less than two hundred, and that carrying out four hundred baptisms did not mean that there were now four hundred Roman Catholics. The Father Superior had given everyone who had been baptised a reward of a shilling, and many people had returned two, three, or even four times to get a bigger share of the available cash. The Father Superior had not recognised the faces of the people concerned.

There were various statements corroborating what the Village Elder had said, and then the Swede replied. Due to unforeseen circumstances, he explained, the opening of the Lutheran school had taken longer than expected after he had been given permission to set it up, but the school was now there and it had a teacher. If the unauthorised school were closed immediately, all the children could transfer to the Lutheran school, and this would justify its retention.

While he was talking, the Father Superior's face got redder and redder until he could stand it no longer, and screeched in Swahili,

'Ever since the time of Luther they have always been stirring up trouble like this.'

The Swede then astonished me. He was sitting on a flimsy-looking wooden chair, with his bottom wobbling like a jelly over the edge. With one convulsive movement he turned the chair, with himself still sitting on it, through ninety degrees, presenting his back view to the Father Superior. As he did so, he muttered, also in Swahili, a colloquial expression which, while not actually obscene, was certainly not complimentary.

I gave everyone who wanted enough time to have their say, and then I delivered my judgement. The village wanted its own bush school, but there were not enough children to fill two schools, so I had to decide which of the two should stay. The Lutheran school had taken a regrettably long time to be set up, but it now existed and had its teacher. The Catholic school had been built before the Lutheran school, but it had been put up without permission. If one school was to go, it had to be the one which had not been authorised. The kind of threats which both teachers had received were unlawful, and anyone found guilty of making such threats concerning the school or of performing any act of violence would be punished very severely indeed.

I tried to sugar the pill for the Father Superior by promising that if he made an application to set up another bush school somewhere else where the villagers wanted it, this would be treated sympathetically. As far as I know, he never put in such an application.

After the case was settled, I walked back towards Mazombe with Adam, who was a Muslim, and Mwachengula, who described himself as a pagan. On the way I quietly asked them what they thought about missionaries who came to Tanganyika to bring a message of loving one's neighbour, and then behaved in the way we had just seen. They both unhesitatingly replied, 'We just laugh.' I felt deeply ashamed.

***

Most church-goers in whatever country expect the services which they attend to be conducted in their own language. In Tanganyika, however, few British expatriates lived within easy access of a church where services were conducted regularly in English.

I sometimes heard people comment that missionaries neglected the pastoral care of European families. I do not think this criticism is completely fair. Missionaries had come to Tanganyika primarily to bring Christianity to Africans, and they probably did not regard it as the best use of their time to make long journeys by car in order to conduct services in English that would probably be attended by only a very small congregation. Those expatriates who wanted to go to services in Swahili in their own stations were always made welcome by the priest and the congregation, but very few Europeans ever attended such services.

Iringa had one feature which I did not come across anywhere else. There was a small but pleasantly-appointed Protestant church standing just behind the Revenue Office. I understand that it had been built with funds bequeathed by a wealthy former resident who wanted to endow a Protestant church of no particular denomination. For some reason which was never explained to me, he had insisted that it should be used only for services conducted in English, but his legacy did not provide enough money to pay for an English-speaking priest.

The language condition was ignored when a British engineer married the daughter of a Greek tobacco farmer, and the wedding was conducted mainly in Greek, but while I was in Iringa no services in Swahili were ever held in what was commonly referred to as the 'European Church'. I found this title offensive, as it suggested that the church condoned apartheid, which was not the case. An African from Nyasaland attended our services regularly, as he understood English better than Swahili.

Before I arrived in Iringa, a number of officials and their wives had expressed a wish to have a service every Sunday in the church, and two volunteers, William Burkitt, one of the two Medical Officers, and Bill Carmichael, the Forestry Officer, had offered to take turns to conduct services of Morning Prayer. Bill was a Scotsman who followed the Church of Scotland tradition and preached rather long but well-prepared sermons. William was not only an able and dedicated doctor, he was also a sincere speaker, a very competent pianist, and played the church harmonium well.

After I had attended services regularly for a few Sundays, Bill and William both asked me one morning if I would be willing to share with them the responsibility for taking services. I agreed, as I felt that a team of three would be stronger than a team of two.

The size of the regular congregation grew to between twenty and thirty people on most Sundays, and many more at Christmas and Easter. Many of the church-goers wanted to take communion from time to time, so we wrote to Bishop Alfred Stanway, an Australian who had recently been consecrated as Bishop of

Dodoma, to ask if he could arrange for an Anglican priest to come to Iringa periodically to take a communion service. We undertook to reimburse the priest's travelling costs and to provide free overnight accommodation for him.

There was an anecdote circulating at that time in the Iringa Club, that at his consecration service in Dodoma Cathedral on the day after Christmas 1951, Bishop Stanway had started his sermon with the words 'Today is Saint Stephen's day.' His Australian accent was so strong that the African interpreter thought he had said 'To die is Saint Stephen's die', and had translated his words into Swahili as 'Death is the death of Saint Stephen'. The congregation had been puzzled. I believe the tale is true, but I never asked the Bishop to confirm it.

The Bishop replied favourably to our letter, and we were told to expect a visit a few weeks later from a young Australian priest working in Kilosa District. When he arrived, I thought he looked more like a film star than a priest. He had an excellent bass voice, and we hoped that services taken by him would be inspiring.

Unfortunately, the priest was bone idle. He never paid any pastoral visits to any of the congregation. He normally arrived at about midday on a Saturday, ate a very hearty curry lunch at the house of whoever happened to be putting him up for the weekend, then slept all Saturday afternoon. He then enjoyed Saturday evening as a guest in the Iringa Club, where members bought large numbers of drinks for him, but he never offered to stand any of his hosts a drink in return. None of his hosts asked to be repaid for the costs of putting him up, which they paid from their own pockets.

After taking a communion service early on Sunday morning, he always had breakfast and set off at once to return to Kilosa. When he got back, he submitted his travel claim by post to our Church Treasurer.

Unfortunately, we had not agreed in advance an appropriate rate of mileage allowance, and his claim was for two or three times the amount that he would have received as a government official doing the same journey in the same type of car.

The congregation contributed quite generously week by week, but each visit from the priest cost as much as the church's total income for several months. Eventually, on the advice of the Church Treasurer, we wrote to tell the Bishop that we could no longer afford to pay for further visits from the priest. Services of Morning Prayer continued to be taken by laymen until after I had left Iringa.

I suspect that the Church Missionary Society may have formed the same impression about their priest as we had. Shortly after his last visit to Iringa, we heard that he would no longer be working in Tanganyika, and was returning to Australia. The news did not distress us much.

One Lingua Franca or Many Tribal Languages

There were about 120 recognised tribes in Tanganyika, the largest of whom, the Sukuma, numbered nearly a million, and the smallest only a few hundred. Swahili, or Kiswahili to give the technically correct title of the language, as distinct from the territory or the people, was already the lingua franca which Africans used when talking to members of other tribes, and which was generally used in official correspondence and in schools. Expatriate officials whose jobs involved face-to-face dealings with Africans were normally required to become proficient in Swahili before being confirmed in their appointments.

The importance of Swahili was increasing steadily, due largely to the spread of education, radio, and the growing number of rural Africans seeking employment in big towns or on large estates, where they worked alongside people who came from other parts of the country. However, many tribes still used their own vernacular languages in their home villages. The Government recognised that an official would be able to communicate more effectively with peasant farmers if he could speak to them in their own language, so it provided an incentive to learn those languages by offering a lump sum bonus of £100, and an allowance of £5 per month for as long as he remained in the district where the tribal language was spoken, to any expatriate officer who obtained a government interpretership in the local language.

I had taken a degree in French and German, and knew that I enjoyed studying foreign languages. My work involved spending several days on safari each month talking to Hehe farmers, so as soon as I heard that I had passed my Law Examination I applied for permission to study Kihehe, the language of the Hehe tribe. My application was approved, and I asked John Kasuga, the clerk who dealt with the day-to-day business of the Uhehe Native Creameries and who always came with me on my monthly safari to pay the suppliers of milk, if he would be willing to teach me. He agreed with immense enthusiasm, saying that it would be a great honour for all his tribe if a District Officer were to learn their language. He categorically refused to accept any payment for the lessons he gave me.

I formed a very high regard for John's competence at his job, his personality, and also his teaching skills. My opinion was shared by Chief Adam, who a few years later appointed him to be the Sub-Chief of Kalenga, where the Chief's own headquarters were situated, and where, in the nineteenth century, the Hehe had fought a ferocious battle against the German forces.

I had not found Swahili particularly difficult. I had a grammar-book, a dictionary, and a number of paperbacks, many of which were published with the assistance of the East African Literature Bureau. Some were traditional folk stories, others dealt with technical or religious subjects. It was possible for me to study on my own, and I had practice every day in my office when I used the language at work drafting letters, or in conversation with Africans and with those Asians who did not speak English.

Kiswahili and Kihehe are both Bantu languages. The word *bantu* means 'people', and Bantu languages are those in which the word for 'a human being' ends with the syllable *-tu* or *-nu*. In Swahili, the word for people was *wa-tu*. In Kihehe it was *va-nu*. Although there were some similarities between the two languages, and indeed between all Bantu languages, I found Kihehe much more difficult to learn than Swahili.

The first problem was the lack of a good textbook. The only book I ever came across which purported to teach Kihehe was a very shabby little volume contained in the District Office archives. It had been published towards the end of the nineteenth century, and it was in German. The author was a missionary who had worked near the border between Iringa District and Njombe District, where the main tribe was the Bena. The title of the book was *Bena–Hehe Grammatik*, and it was not much use to learners of either dialect, as the author never indicated which words or structures were Kihehe and which were Kibena. The style was like that of an indifferent tourist phrase-book, giving a literal translation of a standard question like 'What is your name?', but not explaining how that form of words could be adapted in such a way as to ask, for example, 'What is his name?'. John Kasuga knew no German, and we quickly decided that we would make more progress on our own than by using such an unsatisfactory textbook.

My first lessons taught me the common forms of greeting and saying goodbye, ways to make a request, and how to express thanks. I liked the courteous way in which the Hehe normally replied to the word meaning 'thank you'. This was to say 'I thank you for being pleased.'

I prepared my own list of the words which I found particularly useful in Swahili, and I asked John to tell me the equivalents in Kihehe, which I then wrote down in my notebook and memorised.

After I got past the very elementary stage of learning single words, I started to try to form sentences in Kihehe. The normal pattern of these lessons was that I asked John to translate a short English or Swahili sentence into Kihehe, and I then tried to work out for myself the basic rules of Kihehe grammar contained in that sample sentence. At first there seemed to be no rhyme or reason to it at all. Even when I had worked out a few rules, for example about forming the plurals of various classes of noun, or about the different tenses of verbs, I was still bewildered by the complexity of the syntax of the language. John described to me more than twenty tenses for an active verb and the same number for the same verb in the passive. There were different tenses, for example, to describe actions that are happening at this very moment, habitual actions, actions that took place five minutes ago, actions yesterday, actions a week ago, actions last year, and actions that took place so long ago that they are almost forgotten. Similar complications arose in tenses referring to the near or remote future.

In Kihehe and Swahili, there was no equivalent to the English word 'not', and in order to change a sentence from positive to negative, the prefix and the probably the suffix of the verb had to be changed. There was also a special tense which story-tellers used in order to denote a narrative sequence of past events – 'and then the lion ate the rabbit'. There were special tenses which did not involve the use of a conjunction like 'if' to denote that the verb was conditional. In both languages, the sentence 'If you had not annoyed me, I would not have hit you', could be translated in as few as two words, but the construction of those two words was complicated in Swahili, and still more complicated in Kihehe.

Even in Swahili, the vocabulary of words to describe abstract ideas was quite small, but it was considerably larger than the equivalent in Kihehe. This was probably because Swahili had borrowed a number words of Arabic origin to convey abstract ideas, but Kihehe did not make much use of Arabic words. There were exact translations in Kihehe for a few very common English adjectives like 'big', 'small', 'good', or 'bad', but there was no way to distinguish 'hot' from 'warm' or 'wet' from 'damp' in one single word. One had no choice but to qualify a simple adjective by using a word like 'very', or 'a little bit'. Most English adjectives had to be translated by using a familiar noun as an example, 'like the colour of sand', or 'like fire'. There were verbs which referred to simple actions like 'to eat', 'to write', or 'to drink', but none, as far as I could discover, which corresponded to English words like 'to nibble', 'to scribble', or 'to tipple'.

Counting was very laborious, as I found on pay parades for the Native Creameries. Swahili had borrowed many numbers from Arabic. There were no words in Kihehe for numbers between ten and a hundred, although, in contrast to their normal practice, the words imported from the Arabic for 'a hundred' and 'a thousand' were also used in Kihehe. Numbers between ten and a hundred had to be expressed as multiples of ten. Thirty-seven, for example, had to be translated as 'three tens and seven'.

In both Swahili and Kihehe, nouns, verbs and adjectives were made up of the root of a word, combined with prefixes or suffixes to indicate the class of the noun, whether it was plural or singular, and the subject, tense, and object of the verb. In Swahili, the root of the word seldom varied, and it was not very hard to distinguish 'a beautiful book' from 'beautiful books', or 'I have beaten him' from 'he has beaten me', or 'I will beat him' from 'he will beat me'. There were very few irregular verbs in Swahili, and foreigners learning the language did not have to memorise interminable lists of the principle parts of verbs comparable to 'go-went-gone' or 'eat-ate-eaten', which are a nightmare for foreigners trying to learn English.

As far as I know, Kihehe also did not have many verbs that were irregular, in the sense of not following the normal rules. However, the normal rules were so obscure that just about every verb seemed to me to be as difficult for a learner to use correctly as irregular verbs are for students of English.

The main difficulty was that the consonants in the root of a verb were variable, and changed in accordance with the prefixes and suffixes which preceded or followed them. For example, the root of the verb 'to beat' was *-tov-a*. The prefix denoting the first person singular was *n-*, and the suffix for the past tense was *-ile*, but instead of the past 'I beat' being translated by *n-tov-ile*, as would have seemed logical, the actual form the Hehe used was *nof-ile*. In combination with the prefix letter *n*, the letter 't' of the root just disappeared, but it reappeared in the third person singular, 'he beat', which was *a-tof-ile*. When the root began with any other consonant, the combination with the prefix *n* varied in different ways from letter to letter. The prefix n- when followed by -l, for example, became nd-, followed by '-b' it became mb-.

I gave up trying to get the formations of verbs right, and I usually compromised by translating verbs in the past by using the appropriate form of the word 'to finish' followed by the root of the verb, and the future tense by using a similar technique with the Kihehe word for 'to want'. I learnt to understand Hehe speakers when they spoke their language correctly, and they seemed to understand my attempts to communicate with them in a sort of pidgin Kihehe. Even the Hehe themselves sometimes had problems with the past and the future. They used exactly the same word for 'yesterday' and 'tomorrow'. It meant 'the day next to today'.

It is often said that Eskimos have an extremely large number of words for 'snow', as snow is very important for them. Similarly, there were some words in Kihehe which described very specialised things that particularly interested African cattle-owners, but would not feature in any phrase-book for tourists or students. For example, one single word would be used to describe a brown heifer with white spots, and a different word would describe a white heifer with brown spots. I found it much simpler just to describe them all as cows.

John worked very hard to teach me his tribal language, both on safari to the creameries in Pawaga and also in my house in Iringa after the office closed for the evening. When at home, we would have a cup of tea and some biscuits, and I would invite him to stay on, after the lesson was over, to listen to some of my gramophone records. In contrast to the Nyakyusa, most Hehe seemed unmusical, but John loved classical music. His favourite of my records was a Violin Sonata by Bach, played by Yehudi Menuhin and Gerald Moore, which made his face light up every time he heard it.

Towards the end of my tour I got my interpretership. The examination consisted of a written and an oral test. The examining board was made up of three people: Geoffrey Hucks, Chief Adam, and the District Court interpreter, an unsmiling man called Eleuter Nzali. Eleuter was well-educated and competent, but I did not warm to his personality at all.

Geoffrey Hucks did not know Kihehe, but I believe that Chief Adam and Eleuter had worked together to set the written test, and had prepared their own model answers beforehand to enable Geoffrey Hucks to judge whether or not my answers were correct. For the oral test, I was given the task of actually trying a real case against a Hehe tribesman accused of theft. I had for several months been using Kihehe in my court whenever possible, and, fortunately for me, in this particular case the accused pleaded guilty. I was able to repeat the forms of words which I had already used in trying other cases, and did not have to go through the business of taking detailed evidence from witnesses, where the gaps in my knowledge would have become obvious.

Geoffrey and Adam both congratulated me warmly on passing the test, and I think John Kasuga was genuinely delighted at my success. That evening I went to the shops and bought him a 'thank you' present of a pillar-box red portable gramophone of the same model as mine, only mine was a sober black. His pleasure was an additional bonus for me.

The following day he came to me looking much less cheerful than usual. He asked me not to recommend him to any other Europeans as a Kihehe teacher. He did not say who had criticised him, though I suspect that it was Eleuter Nzali, but he told me that he had been threatened with severe consequences if he taught any other Europeans to speak Kihehe. He had been warned that, if Europeans understood Kihehe, the Hehe would then have no more secrets from the Government.

As far as I know, I was the only British official ever to obtain an interpretership in Kihehe, and after I left Iringa District I never came across any Hehe tribesmen who did not also understand Swahili. However, I enjoyed studying the language, and I was pleased that most Hehe peasant farmers seemed to appreciate my efforts to get to understand them better and to talk to them in their own language.

The future of minority languages gives rise to some difficult practical and moral problems. Language is constantly developing and changing, and some ancient languages died a natural death simply because people stopped using them, or children learnt a different language from that of their parents. There are at present many political leaders who are content to let minority languages die. They argue, with some evidence to support them, that having more than one language in a country is inherently divisive, and that conflicts often arise between groups who do not speak the same language. They also maintain that it is absurd for any country, especially an economically poor one where many tribal languages are spoken, to provide education in each of them, or to allow every member of a national parliament to speak in the language of his or her own constituency, which other members of parliament do not understand. Whether or not one accepts these arguments, I do not regard it as an infringement of human rights to let minority languages die of their own accord when they have ceased to serve any useful purpose, and it would require outside intervention and resources in order to prolong their lives artificially.

Adopting actively a policy of killing off minority languages is quite a different matter. History provides examples of autocratic rulers who have taken legislative measures, some of which were enforced ruthlessly, to kill off minority languages in their country. Repressive measures aimed at preventing members of minority groups from using their own language seem to me to be a flagrant abuse of human rights. One recent example of such abuse occurred during the Franco regime in Spain, when the Government prohibited the use of the Catalan language in all aspects of life, with the sole exception of oral communication in the privacy of one's own home. Fortunately this policy failed to achieve its objective, and Catalan is once again thriving, but there are many other languages which are threatened by policies still being implemented by unsympathetic Governments.

During the 1980s, long after I had struggled to learn Kihehe, I was a Whitehall civil servant, and I represented the British Government on the Working Group which drafted the United Nations Convention on the Rights of the Child. I was reminded of Kihehe when we were drafting Article 30 of that Convention, which sets out the right of a child, in states where linguistic minorities exist, to 'use his or her own language'. I regard any infringement of that article as an abuse of a human right.

However, there are some members of linguistic minorities who are not particularly interested in their own or their children's right to go on indefinitely using their own language. They feel that by learning a lingua franca they, and future generations, are likely to improve themselves socially and economically. The right to be educated in a language which will enable them to communicate with people from other tribes and other countries, and to have access to a wider range of information than is available in any minority language, is of much greater practical importance for them and their children than the right to use their own language.

If the children of a particular tribe do not want to use their own tribal language, then the prospects for the survival of that language are very bleak. Whenever a language is spoken only by adults, its days are certainly numbered, and the threat to minority tribal languages in Africa, and in many other parts of the world, is now serious. I cannot even guess how many of Tanganyika's 120 tribal languages are already extinct or in danger, as I have seen no estimates on that subject which relate to individual African countries, but some experts have predicted that perhaps as many as half of the world's languages are in danger of becoming extinct by the end of the 21st century. Alongside the demise of minority languages, those widely-spoken languages which are sure to survive will probably become stronger and stronger.

If that is the case, then it seems likely that Kihehe will be one of the casualties, and that Swahili will become, if not a world language comparable to English, at least the lingua franca for a large part of the African continent.

Languages are a part of human diversity and culture, and mankind is a little bit poorer whenever a language dies. However, it is not realistic to hope to preserve all moribund languages by artificial methods. Compelling children against their will to use the same language as their grandparents seems to me just as unacceptable as forbidding them to do so, in the way that Franco tried in Catalonia.

I believe that many languages will die, just as many endangered species of wildlife will become extinct in the next few decades. Before they are all lost without trace, however, I think it would be worth the cost and the effort if as much information as possible, both about Kihehe and about the other minority languages now in peril, could be stored in data banks, using technology which is now available. This needs to be done as a matter of urgency, as each year reduces the number of sources of relevant information. Future generations of minority groups should at least have an opportunity to hear recorded examples of the various languages used by their ancestors.

Coronation Year

A few months after I arrived in Iringa, Geoff Bullock and his family went on leave. Geoff's successor was a bachelor called John Cawthra, who had served in the Navy during the war and won a medal for actions which he never talked about. He seemed rather shy, but he was also able and hard-working, and I found him a pleasant colleague. We worked together for the better part of a year in Iringa.

The work and way of life of District Officers gave us all the opportunity to get to know our colleagues extremely well. It sometimes happened that officers who worked together on the same station did not get on with each other, and came to dislike one another cordially. I even heard of one District Commissioner on a very lonely station who hated his District Officer so much that he only communicated with him by sending him written messages by the hand of a District Office messenger, but that sort of situation was quite exceptional. It was much more common for colleagues to become lifelong friends.

Geoffrey Hucks encouraged the growth of team spirit between those who worked directly under his supervision. Every Monday morning we began the week with a few minutes sitting in his office, when everyone was at liberty to tell colleagues about matters of interest, or to seek their informal views and advice about problems. In this way, we were kept informed about what was taking place in those parts of the district which we did not visit regularly. We nicknamed the gatherings 'Geoffrey's prayer meetings', but they were not at all solemn.

One of the people I met when I went to Pawaga on creamery payment safaris was a South African crocodile hunter called Pienaar. He was married to an Afrikaans-speaking woman who was almost illiterate. They had about ten children and lived in abject squalor in a ramshackle and smelly mud hut near the Ruaha River. I visited their hut on one occasion, and saw that the children were being fed almost entirely on strips of sun-dried meat and tins of imported condensed milk. There were no signs of any fresh milk, fruit, or vegetables. I do not know whether African farmers refused to sell their produce to him, or whether Pienaar refused to buy anything grown by them, but the children all looked undernourished, unwashed and very frail.

One morning, Pienaar barged into my office a little unsteadily, smelling strongly of drink, and announced, for no apparent reason, 'I'd like to line a million of these black buggers up against a wall and shoot every bloody one of them – and I wouldn't call it murder because I'm a superior race.'

I told him I would never allow anyone to express sentiments like that in my office, and I ordered my office messenger, Ayubu Farjallah, to eject him, using force if necessary. Pienaar left voluntarily. He then went immediately to the Revenue Office. Eric Kenny, the Revenue Officer, was not in his office when Pienaar walked in, and his secretary, Angela Moores, an English girl still in her teens, asked him what he wanted. He told her he was about to make love to her. Fortunately Eric returned just in time to rescue her from a fate worse than death, and he himself chucked Pienaar forcibly out of his office. I think Pienaar stopped coming into the Boma after that episode, and I certainly did not waste my time on making any further visits to his hut when I was on safari in Pawaga.

***

There was always plenty of work for a District Officer to do, but in 1953 we had an additional task which took precedence over our other routine duties. Queen Elizabeth II had acceded to the throne on the death of her father King George VI on 6th February 1952. Her coronation took place in Westminster Abbey more than a year later, on 2nd June 1953. During the months leading up to the coronation, every British Commonwealth country, including Tanganyika, made its own plans to celebrate the occasion as joyfully as possible.

In Tanganyika, the main festivities took place in the capital, Dar es Salaam. I was told that they were magnificent and attended by huge crowds, but I was in Iringa and did not see them. In up-country districts, District Commissioners were given the responsibility for coordinating the local arrangements.

Geoffrey Hucks was meticulous in everything he did. He and a small group of officials discussed plans with all the attention to detail of a military operation. Responsibility for particular tasks was delegated to officials who had appropriate skills, and large numbers of volunteers of all races offered to help in any way they could to make the occasion a success. I believe that some rich traders, and others who were not so rich, contributed from their own pockets towards the cost of transporting, sheltering, feeding, and providing liquor for the thousands who came into Iringa from the outlying parts of the district. People of every race, colour, and creed joined together to honour the handsome young white woman who lived in a palace in London, and was now regarded as the mother of all her subjects in every Commonwealth country.

During the weeks just before the coronation, people began to decorate the streets and their own houses and places of business with bunting, posters of the Queen, and flags.

If one commercial establishment put up an impressive display, its rival would then try to put up a bigger and better one. It was hard to judge whether the White Horse Inn or the Iringa Hotel looked more festive. In the main shopping street, every shop seemed to seek to outdo its neighbours. Even in the high density residential areas where most of the inhabitants were poor and which normally looked very dreary, the appearance was transformed. Each little mud hut was adorned either with man-made decorations or with flowers, fronds, or branches of greenery picked from many kinds of tree.

Coronation Day itself provided, from dawn until long after sundown, an abundance of activities to gladden the hearts of an already blissfully happy crowd. Christians, Muslims, and Hindus all offered prayers in their own places of worship to seek blessing on the reign of the new queen. The local contingent of police gave a drill display which included the Royal Salute. Various dignitaries made loyal speeches that were amplified by public address equipment, but were hard for the audience to follow because the words were drowned by noise of singing and dancing. Children from the band of the local Ismaili Community School gave a unique rendering of *God Save the Queen*.

European ladies all put on their best clothes. Many wore rather startling hats which they never used on other occasions. Asian ladies wore the brightest of their saris. African ladies wore bright new lengths of printed cloth fabric. These were known as *kangas*, and were of every conceivable colour, decorated with appropriate slogans in English or Swahili, with a suitable illustration, usually a picture of the queen, printed in the middle.

Most European and Asian men wore their best suits, with collars and ties. The District Commissioner and his District Officers wore uniform, and I put on for the first time a khaki drill uniform which a tailor had made to measure for me, and a hideously uncomfortable khaki helmet. The tunic had brass buttons and the helmet a brass badge, each adorned with the representation of a giraffe's head.

Most of the African schoolchildren wore smartly pressed school uniform, many with ribbons of a particular colour to identify the school from which they came. Some African adult men wore European style dress, but most wore either long-sleeved white calico gowns called *kanzus*, or the elaborately adorned ceremonial robes of Hehe warriors.

One of the most memorable features of the day was the way in which Africans of every age danced and sang and beat their drums for hours on end without appearing to get tired. By the time evening came many were tipsy, but as far as I am aware there were no arguments or violence of any kind. The whole crowd behaved impeccably, and were very, very happy.

In the evening there was a party in the Iringa Club. I thought of it as my own birthday party, as I had reached the age of twenty-five just three days before the coronation, but had been too busy to hold a party of my own on 30th May. It added to the general spirit of elation when we heard that Edmund Hillary and Sherpa Tenzing had successfully reached the top of Mount Everest at the end of May.

By Dhow to Zanzibar

Not long after the coronation, I went on local leave. I spent the first few days with Teddy and Dorothy Kingdon at Singida, in Central Province, where Teddy had been appointed District Commissioner after his return from home leave. I was delighted to see them both again, but I thought Central Province was much less attractive than Southern Highlands. It was arid and infertile, and the Nyaturu tribesmen of Singida District had a tradition of anointing their hair with what I believe was rancid ghee. I thought it smelt horrible, but flies as big as bluebottles loved it.

Teddy took me on a one-night safari towards the Wembere Plain with the Veterinary Officer, Keith Thomas. In the evening, when the work of the day was over, Keith shot a gazelle which was then skinned and roasted over a log fire. It provided a hearty meal for the three of us and for all the African helpers who had come with us.

It was the dry season, and there was no chance of any rain falling, so we did not need to shelter in a rest house or a tent. After a late meal of fresh but rather tough meat washed down with a few glasses of Tusker beer, Teddy, Keith and I chatted and watched the stars. When at last we felt it was time to go to sleep, we lay under our mosquito nets in the open air. The camp fire was kept alight the whole night, partly to keep us warm and partly to discourage predatory animals whose sounds were audible all through the night.

I had hoped that my old friend Geoff Thirtle would still be working in Singida District when I stayed with the Kingdons, but he had recently been transferred from Singida to Kongwa. My plan was to visit Zanzibar for the second half of my local leave, and it seemed a good idea to call and see Geoff on my way by car and rail down to the coast.

Kongwa was a dreary place. After little or no preliminary research to discover whether it was a suitable place to cultivate groundnuts, it had been chosen as one of the main centres for the Groundnut Scheme (see Chapter 4). When the scheme failed, the groundnutters went away, leaving Kongwa looking like a ghost town. Geoff seemed to find the place as depressing as I did, but he had to live there. I thought at first that his generosity with the bottle was just a way of welcoming a fellow-oarsman, but it later became clear that he was drinking more than was good for him. Geoff 's subsequent career in Tanganyika and Britain did not do justice to his exceptional ability and very likeable personality, and he was still quite young when he died.

Baobab tree

Geoff owned an elegant Siamese cat, and during the night I spent in Kongwa the cat discovered the canvas hold-all in which I was carrying my baggage, and peed in it. Before I got on the train the next day, Geoff's dhobi cleaned the bag and tried to get rid of the smell of cat urine, and I set off on the train to Dar thinking all was well.

I had a sleeping compartment to myself on the train, but there were two married couples travelling in the first-class carriage with me, neither of whom I had met before. Griff Farr was a senior Medical Officer, and he and his wife Betty were also travelling to the coast to spend local leave in Zanzibar. Tony Richards was the Commissioner for Social Development, and he and his wife Babs were returning to Dar after an official visit to Western and Lake Provinces. They were the most delightful travelling companions, and I enjoyed the train journey immensely. By the time the train reached Dar, Tony Richards and his wife had invited me to stay with them in Dar for a few days on my way back from Zanzibar to Iringa, and Griff and Betty Farr had arranged to meet me as soon as I reached Zanzibar.

The Farrs made the last part of their journey from Dar to Zanzibar by steamer. I had the hare-brained idea that it would be more fun to make the crossing by dhow from the old coastal town of Bagamoyo, about 40 miles north of Dar. I travelled from Dar to Bagamoyo by bus. The road was bumpy and the bus decrepit, but we arrived safely, and I confirmed my passage on a dhow scheduled to leave for Zanzibar around midnight.

I then went to the Boma to pay a courtesy call on the District Commissioner, Patrick Duff. I intended to spend the evening at what was really a hotel, but called itself the Bagamoyo Country Club. However, Patrick Duff would not hear of my spending the evening alone at the Country Club, and insisted on taking me back to his palatial house to meet his wife Betty.

The Duffs quickly discovered that I was fond of music, and we spent the evening chatting and making music together. Patrick had a very good tenor voice, and twenty years later he and I were both members of the Treasury Singers in London. Both of us had become Whitehall civil servants, though neither of us was in the Treasury.

At midnight Patrick came with me to Bagamoyo beach, and then he returned to his house while the other passengers and I hung around sitting on the sand for nearly two hours waiting for the crew to allow us to embark. When at last the dhow was ready to sail, all the passengers had to wade out to it through water about two feet deep. Most of the African passengers were Nyamwezi women from Western Province. Many had never seen the sea before, but they were travelling to join their husbands who were employed on the clove plantations in Zanzibar. I was told that ever since the time of the slave trade, the Nyamwezi had had a tradition of travelling to the coast to work, and that a high proportion of the work force on the islands of Zanzibar and Pemba were Nyamwezi from Western Province.

The inside of the hull of the dhow was strewn with coconut palm leaves. I have never tried to sleep on them, but they look harsh and scratchy. However all the African women passengers lay down on the leaves without complaining. The *nahodha* (skipper) invited me to sleep on the deck, as it would not be fitting for me to go below with the other passengers. Whether his attitude was based on racial or sex discrimination I do not know, but I did not object to his ruling. The hold looked murky and

S.N.Goddard.

overcrowded, and made me think about the horrors which the victims of the slave trade must have had to endure on their long journeys into captivity.

Arab dhows, known locally as *jahazi*, look very graceful, but distance lends enchantment. The stench from the hold was indescribable, and the smell in the open air was not much better. For a prolonged period, shark flesh had been laid out to dry on the timbers in the sun, and it had left a pervading odour of rotten fish. I tried to get to sleep lying on the bare boards of the deck, using my canvas holdall as a pillow. The dhow was not entirely to blame for my sleepless night. Geoff Thirtle's dhobi had done his best, but had not managed to get rid of the smell of cat's piss from my canvas bag.

The sea was very calm, but nearly all the mothers got terribly seasick and all the babies were screaming. At about three o 'clock, even if I had managed to get to sleep, I would have been woken by vociferous shouting by the *nahodha* and his crew.

There are sandbanks in the channel between Bagamoyo and Zanzibar, and one crew member had been posted in the bows holding a long pole. As the dhow made its slow progress east-wards, he prodded the pole down to the bottom of the sea to keep the skipper informed about the depth of the water. For some minutes he had been murmuring 'shallow water', but nobody had appeared to take any notice. Then he announced more loudly 'shallow water', and just after he gave this warning there was a gentle scraping noise as the keel of the dhow became embedded in the sand.

Chaos ensued. Women started screaming even louder than their babies. The crew members began to argue furiously about whether or not to lower the sail. At last the skipper's orders prevailed, the sail was lowered, and a huge boulder tied to a frayed rope was thrown into the sea to serve as an anchor.

The dhow remained motionless until dawn. Some crew members then climbed down into the sea and managed to push it off the sand. We completed the rest of the crossing without any more trouble, though I saw one exhausted mother vomit over the head of her baby whom she was trying to suckle. We were supposed to reach Zanzibar soon after sunrise, but it was nearly midday by the time we got there.

I was delighted to see Griff and Betty standing on the shore waiting for the dhow to arrive. They greeted me, and we arranged to meet up again for lunch in an hour or so, after I had checked in at my hotel, had a shower, and left my hold-all there.

My troubles were not over. I had been told that there would be no problem about getting a room in the Zanzibar Hotel, which had a good reputation, but when I arrived there and asked to book a room I was told that the whole hotel had been fully booked by the cast and film crew of an adventure film about ivory poaching. I remember seeing two films which were very popular in East Africa in the 1950s. One was called 'West of Zanzibar' and the other 'Where no Vultures Fly', and I think it was the latter which was being made on location when I reached Zanzibar.

The only place I could get a room was a very grotty little shack called the *Mnazi Mmoja* (one coconut-palm). The proprietress looked very disagreeable and rather dirty, and I must have looked pretty grumpy myself when I joined up with Griff and Betty and told them of my predicament.

As soon as he heard what had happened, Griff came to the rescue. He was a member of the Dar Club, which had reciprocating rights with the Zanzibar Club. He took me to the Zanzibar Club and introduced me to the Secretary, who proposed me as a

candidate for temporary membership. To my surprise, the
formalities, such as they were, were completed on the spot, and I
was given a comfortable and clean bedroom, although I was
asked to have my dinner that night somewhere else, as the Club
dining-room was booked for a party.

Glamorous film stars in expensive clothes were a rare sight in
Tanganyika, but Zanzibar at the time was full of them. The hero
who was preventing the poaching was immaculately dressed. His
girlfriend was radiant. The villains were fat slobs who all looked
as if they came from a particularly corrupt country somewhere in
the Middle East, but their clothes were richly embroidered. Most
of the Africans acting the parts of porters or hunters came from
Zanzibar, and were not provided with special clothes, but the
African who played the 'sergeant-major' type role came from
West Africa. He was very tall, handsome, well-built, and had
splendid teeth. He was dining one evening in the Zanzibar Hotel
and I happened to be at the adjacent table. A European greeted
him in Swahili, '*Jambo Bwana!*' The West African film star looked
annoyed, and replied loudly, 'I don't speak that *silly* language!'
After finishing his meal, he left an ostentatiously large currency
note as tip for the waiter. The pleasure his generosity might have
given was probably undermined when he shouted at the waiter
in English, in the most offensive tone of voice, 'You keep it, you
boy!' I may have misjudged him, but I believe that his behaviour
was intended to humiliate the waiter and to demonstrate his own
superiority over other people. I did not take to him.

Zanzibar is a beautiful island. It is small, and much more
densely populated than the mainland of Tanganyika. It has such
a good supply of fresh water that large ocean-going liners regularly call there. The stone town of Zanzibar has many impressive
old buildings of different pastel colours which align the sea-front.
The houses built by Arabs from the profits of the slave trade have
splendid carved doors, and often enclose a shady courtyard
which offers some protection from the heat and humidity. Some
streets are so narrow that driving is difficult, if not impossible.
When I visited it, Zanzibar was still ruled by a Sultan. Most of the
population are Muslims, although an Anglican Cathedral was
built over the site of the former slave market in the 1870s, and St
Joseph 's Roman Catholic Cathedral was built in the 1890s.

The direction of the wind during the monsoon in June and July
meant that, even if I had wanted to, I could not have returned to
the mainland by dhow. I sailed back to Dar on a steamer called *Al
Hathera* (the Green One – the Arabic name for the island of

Pemba, a few miles north of Zanzibar). The ship was owned by the Sultan, and we had no problems on the voyage back to the mainland. Tony Richards met me when the ship landed, and I spent a very happy weekend with him and his wife.

Many people are fascinated by Zanzibar, but I was very glad to get back to Tanganyika. It may have been a figment of my imagination, but I felt that the atmosphere of Zanzibar was oppressive, and still brought memories of past cruelties and decadent rulers.

Tanganyika achieved its independence in 1961 with no violence whatsoever. Two years later, when Zanzibar became independent, there were gruesome reports about a revolution and appalling bloodshed. The Sultan was deposed, and African rebels attacked their former Arab masters with shocking ferocity. Estimates at the time put the number of people killed at over 10,000, including many women and children.

I never went back to Zanzibar, and I have never had any wish to do so, even though, since 1964, the island has been politically linked to Tanganyika as part of a new united republic called Tanzania.

***

A few weeks after I got back to Iringa, I met the Governor for the first time. Sir Edward Twining was on a safari which included a lightning visit there with his wife and his personal staff. As was usual on Governor 's safaris, he and his wife stayed in the District Commissioner 's house, the Private Secretary in the house of one of the District Officers, and the ADC in the house of the other.

Twining recognised the great value of the work done by specialists in the other departments, but he had himself been a District Officer in Uganda, and he always had a particular rapport with officers of the Provincial Administration. On the night that Twining spent in Iringa, the two District Officers were both invited to dinner with him at the DC's house, and I had the chance to talk to him. I had already heard about his humour and his ability to motivate, to charm, to encourage his officials to speak frankly to him, and to listen attentively while they told him about what they hoped to achieve in their Districts. I was not the only young officer who felt inspired by Twining's charismatic personality. His style of leadership meant that, even in uncongenial stations, the DC and his team would always be encouraged by a visit from the Governor, and feel that he appreciated their work and took a real interest in what they were doing.

The main reason for his visit to Iringa on this occasion was to discuss with Chief Adam the arrangements for the return to the Hehe people of the skull of Chief Adam's grandfather Mkwawa, which had been taken to Germany in the nineteenth century. I was no longer in Iringa in June 1954, when the skull was returned. I was present, however, when Twining paid a later visit to Iringa, and I then saw for myself what the return of Mkwawa's skull meant to the Hehe, and the veneration which they showed for the Governor who had worked so hard to achieve it. (The story of the return of Chief Mkwawa's skull is told more fully in Chapter 5.)

On the Sick List

One day early in 1954, I was about to set off in my car on safari to a rather inaccessible part of the district when I suddenly vomited. I had not felt any symptoms of nausea, but I had been suffering for some weeks from what I thought was indigestion, and it seemed to be getting worse. I did not want to become ill in a place where medical help was not available, so I decided to consult the Medical Officer, Charles Runciman, before I left Iringa. Charles gave me a thorough examination, and then insisted on admitting me to Iringa Grade 1 Hospital for treatment and further tests.

Iringa had a complement of two Medical Officers. It also had two hospitals, a general hospital for patients who were treated free of charge, and a grade 1 hospital for patients who either paid for their own treatment, or whose terms of service entitled them and their families to grade 1 facilities. Many of the patients in grade 1 hospitals were Europeans, but Africans and Asians were not excluded.

Doctors were just as liable as officials in other departments to be transferred in the middle of a tour of service, and during the year and a half that I spent in Iringa, it had five different Medical Officers. Four were really competent and caring. The other was not.

The idle doctor was an amusing raconteur and was very frank about his shortcomings. He told me that he had previously been a ship's doctor, but had lost that job as a result of a complaint by one of the passengers. He did not stay very long in Iringa.

In every occupation there are some people who do their job better than others, but most people of average ability seem to get by moderately well, without being either conspicuously good or conspicuously bad. That generalisation seemed not to apply to Medical Officers in Tanganyika.

I believe the main reason for the contrast between the very good and the very bad doctors probably lay in the motives which had induced them to apply to join the Colonial Medical Service. Some doctors had found it hard to pass their examinations, and then had difficulty in getting jobs in the National Health Service or as doctors in the armed forces. They eventually applied to join the Colonial Medical Service as a last resort. They knew that there were too few doctors in Tanganyika, that they would not be working under close supervision from other doctors, and that they were not likely to be sacked, however lazy and incompetent they might be. They would have steady employment, with a pension when they reached retirement age.

Other doctors felt a strong vocation to relieve suffering, to heal the sick, and to prevent disease. There was more unmet need for health care in Tanganyika than in wealthier countries, and even at a very early stage in their careers young doctors would have the opportunity to carry out forms of treatment which, in the National Health Service in Britain, would only be undertaken by specialists with many years' experience.

When I arrived in Tukuyu, I had felt less confidence in the highly qualified but lazy District Medical Officer, who was coming to the end of his tour of service, than I had in the Indian Sub-Assistant-Surgeon. When I got to Iringa, I met a District Medical Officer called William Burkitt, who was totally dedicated to his work. He was a quietly-spoken and earnest bachelor, who was the moving force in establishing regular church services in English there. My respect for him grew when I saw his response to a serious road accident on the Iringa–Kilosa road.

One Tuesday afternoon, a bus which was licensed to carry forty-eight passengers, but was in fact carrying fifty-four, was approaching an escarpment where the road descended steeply from the plateau on which Iringa stood, over 5,000 feet above sea level, to the plains where the altitude was only about 1,600 feet. The bus driver, a man of mixed race called Jack Hamilton, stopped at a beer-club a few miles before reaching the escarpment, and, according to the survivors who gave evidence against him, remained drinking beer for about three hours before setting off again. He was determined to make up for lost time by driving very fast, but he failed to negotiate one of the hairpin bends on the escarpment. The bus hurtled to the bottom, killing six passengers and seriously injuring more than thirty. Jack Hamilton was just sober enough to jump clear of the bus before it left the road.

The injured were brought into Iringa general hospital, and

William Burkitt spent the next five days and nights caring continuously for his patients. He did not emerge from the hospital until the following Sunday morning, when he took an hour away from his patients in order to conduct a service in church. I was horrified by his haggard appearance. With the support of Joy Taylor, a dedicated and very pretty nursing sister, I managed, with some difficulty, to persuade him to take a few hours' rest, as we both insisted that it would not help his patients if William were to collapse. He returned to his patients that evening however, after resting for just a few hours. Thanks to his skill, care, and the example which he gave to his junior staff, nearly all of the injured patients eventually recovered.

A year or so later, William became so frustrated at working under a bureaucratic Provincial Medical Officer, who regarded paper as more important than patients, that he resigned from Government service, and began to work instead for a Mission Hospital, at a much lower salary.

Charles Runciman, William Burkitt's successor, was South African. He had much more sense of humour than William, but he was no less able and caring. While I was an in-patient in Iringa hospital, Charles did everything he could, given the limited facilities at his disposal, to make a diagnosis and to cure my condition. There was no X-ray equipment in Iringa, and some of the techniques he used were not very pleasant. I had a tube stuffed up my nostril and into my stomach. It was attached to a milk drip, and for days on end I subsisted entirely on milk. It eased the burning sensation in my stomach slightly, but I was not sorry when he decided to pull the tube out again, and to send me to the Ocean Road Hospital in Dar es Salaam for an X-ray examination as soon as he thought I was fit to make the journey.

One morning, Charles came in to my ward on his rounds, and showed me a telegram he had received from Dar es Salaam. An American called Patrick Hemingway, the son of the author Ernest Hemingway, lived in the Sao Hill area of Iringa District, and the telegram came from the great man himself, announcing that he was planning to visit his son, and would be arriving by plane in Iringa on the next flight from Dar. He said he needed to be met by ambulance at the airport. The telegram said nothing about the medical condition which required the use of an ambulance.

The airport was situated a few miles north of the town, and passengers were normally transported to or from the airport in a car provided by East African Airways. Charles assumed that Ernest Hemingway must be unwell, and he arranged for the

Medical Department Landrover to meet him, with a nursing sister to escort him.

The following day, Charles was seething with indignation when he came to visit me in my ward. He said that Hemingway had been in good health when he flew from Dar, but had asked for an ambulance to meet him as he wanted to receive preferential treatment over more humble passengers. I said I thought such behaviour was outrageous, and Charles decided that Hemingway ought to be made to pay the cost of what the Medical Department had spent on an unnecessary call-out.

That afternoon, at Charles Runciman's request, I prepared the first draft of a detailed invoice for him to submit to Hemingway. It included every item that had been wasted as a result of his self-ishness. I calculated to the nearest cent the cost of so many hours and so many minutes of the time of a nursing sister and a driver, a mileage charge for the exact distance travelled by the four-wheel drive ambulance, and I included even very trivial items like the cost of a thermos of tea, of heating the water in a hot-water bottle, the cost of a telegram sent to Dar confirming that Hemingway would be met by ambulance as he requested, and a hire charge for a stretcher, blankets, and sundry bits and pieces which were normally kept in the ambulance.

Charles and I were both slightly uneasy about the exorbitant prices we were proposing to charge for each item on the bill, but we felt that Hemingway could afford to pay, and needed a lesson. The Medical Department could always find a good use for the extra money. I never met Ernest Hemingway myself, but Charles told me that he paid the bill without a word of complaint.

A few days later I flew to Dar with two seriously ill female patients, and we were all taken by ambulance to the Ocean Road Hospital. Charles requested the hospital to let him know the result of tests which he did not have the equipment to do himself, and he also mentioned that my mother was a doctor, and asked the hospital to prepare an extra copy of their report for her. That request was ignored.

The Ocean Road Hospital was a lovely building in a magnifi-cent position overlooking the sea, but its reputation was not good. I arrived not long after a very senior official had had a heart attack on the afternoon of New Year's Day, but his family had been unable to get prompt treatment for him because it was a public holiday and the doctor who was on call had gone sailing in the harbour. The next few doctors to be called were either not available or else too drunk to attend to any critically ill patient, however senior. When at last a doctor responded to an emergency call, the patient was dying. The only action taken against the doctor who should have responded to the call was to transfer him to a very remote district where it was assumed that he would not have to deal with such senior patients.

I was put in a ward with ten or twelve beds in it, and each morning a doctor with a hairy chest and the physique and finesse of a second-row rugger forward strode round the ward, spending a few seconds by each bed while he gave instructions to a bored-looking nursing sister. He seldom spoke directly to any of the patients.

I found the heat and humidity of the coast oppressive, and felt much worse than I had done in Iringa. It took several days to arrange the X-ray examination, which involved standing up and taking a barium meal. This did not reveal what was wrong with me, and the morning after my X-ray, a woman doctor called Catherine Pike, whom I had not met before, came to me and asked me a lot of questions and really seemed to be genuinely interested in finding a cure for my condition. She told me she was prescribing a new form of treatment, and asked me to tell her if it made me feel any better.

Later that day, the burly doctor came and actually said a few words to me. He said that the hospital had finished with me, and that I could go back by the first available train and bus to Iringa. I told him what Dr Pike had said, and he dismissed her suggestion very curtly.

My discharge from the hospital was itself symptomatic of the attitude of its staff. I asked the sister in charge of my ward if I could telephone the Secretariat to ask them to prepare a travel warrant for my journey back to Iringa. She replied that in-patients were not allowed to use the phones. I then asked if a messenger could take a written message, and for paper to write it on. She said that was not possible, but did not give me any reason. I asked her whether I was expected to walk to the Secretariat and to the Railway Station to make the necessary arrangements, as I did not yet feel quite up to it. She walked off in a huff, as if I had made an improper suggestion. The problem was only solved when John Samuels, a Crown Counsel whom I had met during the High Court Sessions in Iringa, came to visit me in hospital, and offered me the use of his car and a driver, and I was able to make the arrangements for my journey back to Iringa.

Charles Runciman was not pleased when he got the report about me from the Ocean Road Hospital. It had been signed by the burly doctor, and seemed to imply that I had been malingering. Charles advised me to apply immediately to go on leave to Britain and get treatment there, and told Geoffrey Hucks what he had recommended. They both thought that a sea voyage would do me good, so I travelled back to England in April 1954 on board the *Kenya Castle*, one of the single-class liners which had replaced the *Llanstephan Castle*.

I was disappointed to have to leave Iringa just two months before the ceremony when the Governor was expected to return the skull of Chief Mkwawa to the Hehe tribe, but I could not persuade Charles or Geoffrey to let me stay on until June.

My mother was working as a resident doctor in the Royal National Hospital in Ventnor, in the Isle of Wight, when I arrived on leave, and I stayed as a paying guest in a farm-house next to the hospital. Arrangements were made for me to be given another X-ray examination in a hospital in Ryde, and it took only forty minutes for them to make a diagnosis. They gave me another barium meal, and then tipped me up so that my feet were higher than my head. This had not been done in Dar, but it revealed that I was suffering from a 'large sliding diaphragmatic hernia'. I was referred to a consultant surgeon in Southampton Chest Hospital, who told me that if I did not have an operation my discomfort would continue, and I might not live much beyond the age of forty. I later heard that other doctors were not quite so pessimistic about the outlook for patients with diaphragmatic hernias, but I immediately gave my consent for the operation.

Even in 1954, there were already waiting lists in Britain for operations on the National Health Service, and I had to wait until September before I could be admitted to Southampton Chest Hospital. I am still reminded of my operation by a scar eighteen inches long between my ribs.

I have nothing but praise for the care which I, and all the other patients in the surgical ward, received in Southampton. My convalescence took time, however, and my leave had twice to be extended for a total of four extra months before the medical authorities in the Colonial Office decided that I was fit enough to return to Tanganyika. I had spent nine months on leave before starting my second tour of service in January 1955.

Techniques have changed enormously since the 1950s, but the qualities that distinguish good hospitals and good doctors from bad hospitals and bad doctors still remain the same.

Chapter 4

Southern Province

(January–April 1955)

Port Peanut

While I was on my first tour I had formed a number of preconceived ideas about where I would like to be posted for my second tour. I was reconciled to the thought that there were several districts that were less attractive than Rungwe or Iringa. As long as I avoided Southern Province, which was generally regarded, for many reasons, as the Cinderella Province, I would be glad to get back to work in any District Office.

It was also a normal part of a District Officer's career pattern to spend a tour in the Secretariat. I did not much like the idea of working entirely with paper and having very little face-to-face contact with Africans, but even the Secretariat had its compensations. One became an expert in a specialised aspect of Government policy, and the recreational facilities for expatriates in Dar es Salaam were more varied and extensive than anywhere else in Tanganyika.

The job which I wanted at all costs to avoid was the job of Staff Officer to a Provincial Commissioner. This was almost entirely a desk job, and it had none of the advantages of working in the capital. I was therefore not at all pleased when I received notification of my posting. I was to be the Staff Officer to the Provincial Commissioner in Mtwara, the new Headquarters of Southern Province, also known as 'Port Peanut'.

Until 1953, the Provincial Headquarters of Southern Province had been situated in the attractive coastal town of Lindi, and the District Office of the area in which Mtwara was situated had been in a picturesque old village called Mikindani. A new harbour with a deep water berth had been constructed at Mtwara, and a new township had been established there on what were described as 'the most up-to-date planning lines, allowing plenty of room for expansion in the future'. What that actually meant was that the houses of most government officials were about two miles from their offices, and that a vast square earmarked as the town's future trading centre was an ugly open space. The proposal to develop Mtwara as a major port had been one of the targets of the Groundnut Scheme.

That scheme was itself a part of the grand vision of the Labour Government elected in 1945, with Clement Attlee as its Prime Minister. In the late 1940s, Attlee's Government enacted a series of famous pieces of legislation such as the National Health Service Act, the National Insurance Act, and the National Assistance Act. These laid the foundations for the Welfare State, and implemented recommendations contained in a report by Sir William Beveridge, published in 1942, for tackling the problems of want, disease, ignorance, squalor and idleness. Many Labour Members of Parliament had seen in their own constituencies the effects of such problems.

Another problem which the Attlee Government wanted to tackle was malnutrition. Proposals had been made in 1946 for a scheme covering a total area of some three million acres, mainly in Tanganyika, which would be planted with groundnuts in order to relieve the shortage of margarine fats. In 1948, the year when most of the social welfare legislation came into force, the Government also enacted another piece of legislation which is now almost completely forgotten. The Overseas Resources Development Act created the Overseas Food Corporation, with a capital of £50 million.

The OFC assumed charge of the Groundnut Scheme in April 1948, and the decision was taken in London that the scheme should be directed not by the Colonial Office, whose officials included some with experience of tropical agriculture, but by the Ministry of Food. An army general managed the scheme for its first year, and fostered the attitude among the mainly ex-service expatriate personnel employed by the OFC that urgency, regardless of cost, was paramount. Pilot schemes and agricultural experiments took time, and work had to be started at once. Quantities of second-hand machinery were bought wholesale from War Disposals, without verifying beforehand whether tanks, for example, could successfully be converted into tractors, whether there were facilities to deliver tractors to Southern Province, whether there were enough skilled mechanics and spare parts to maintain the machinery, or whether it would be suitable for tropical conditions. Certain areas were chosen for the planting of groundnuts on the basis of inappropriate rainfall figures recorded on gauges situated at a different altitude, with a significantly higher rainfall, than the areas selected for planting.

The site chosen for growing groundnuts in Southern Province was in Nachingwea, over a hundred miles inland from the port of Mtwara, and a railway line to deliver groundnuts from Nachingwea to the coast was built before it was known whether there would be enough groundnuts to justify the cost. It had been estimated that from 1952 onwards more than 400,000 tons of groundnuts would be exported annually from Southern Province. but I have no idea of the evidence on which that figure was based.

A deep-water berth was constructed at Mtwara. This was big enough to accommodate the largest cargo ships. I was told that work on building the deep-water berth had been started before tests were made on the suitability of the available fresh water for use in ships' boilers. By the time it was eventually discovered that the water contained a chemical which made it unsuitable for ships' boilers, it was already too late to reconsider the decision about the siting of the harbour.

The auditing and accounting procedures of the scheme were no better than the planning. When the scheme collapsed in the early 1950s, it became clear that a high proportion of the money and equipment lost had been the result of negligence or malpractice, although how tractors could disappear without trace in a sparsely populated country without a developed communications system remains a mystery to me.

The Groundnut Scheme collapsed in 1950–51, and its place was taken by a far less ambitious scheme under the control, not of the Ministry of Food but the Colonial Office. The Overseas Food Corporation ceased to exist in 1954, and was converted into a new body with the title 'Tanganyika Agricultural Corporation'.

The early planners of the Groundnut Scheme appeared to have been living in a dream world, but some of them did at least mean well. Relieving other people's hunger is not a discreditable motive for one's actions, however misguided those actions may be. Unfortunately, the scheme recruited a number of expatriates who were generally regarded as unscrupulous buccaneers. Most of them had already left Southern Province by the time I got there, but I was told that they had shown no interest whatsoever in the welfare of Tanganyika and its people, had treated their labourers in the way that a bullying drill sergeant sometimes treats a squad of new recruits, had behaved badly in a great variety of ways, and had damaged Britain's reputation with Asians and Africans.

The township of Mtwara bore witness to the failure of the Groundnut Scheme. The town had originally been planned to cater for a population of many thousands, and it covered a huge area. Plans for building a thriving town with amenities like a library, places of worship for all religious groups, schools, cinemas, and even, it was suggested, an opera house, became inappropriate when the expected economic boom failed to materialise.

In 1954, it was estimated that there were only about 100 Europeans, 50 Asians, and 700 Africans living in Mtwara township. The Europeans were nearly all Government officials and their families, who had been posted to Mtwara and had no intention of staying there any longer than they had to. The Africans also included a high proportion of people working for the Government, but most of them came from other districts, and had no plans to settle in Mtwara. The Asians were mainly shopkeepers, who had been persuaded to set up businesses in Mtwara by suggestions that they would get rich quickly if they had already established their shops before the influx of potential customers began.

Other traders were more cautious, and were afraid to apply for rights of occupancy and building permission in Mtwara while the authorities still persisted in their grandiose vision of creating a town full of magnificent buildings. People applying for rights of occupancy in the town were required to comply, within a prescribed period, with covenants which insisted on more costly developments than an entrepreneur setting up a new business could reasonably afford to pay. As the future of the goose that had been expected to lay the golden eggs became more and more uncertain, fewer and fewer businessmen wanted to set up their businesses in Mtwara.

Provincial Commissioner's Pup

I was posted to Mtwara to replace a Deputy Provincial Commissioner called Bryan Dudbridge. The difference between a Deputy Provincial Commissioner and a Staff Officer was that a DPC could himself take any decisions or action which a Provincial Commissioner had the power to take, but a Staff Officer could not take any real initiative himself. He had to comply with instructions from his boss, and the main part of my job consisted of countersigning routine returns and papers going backwards and forwards between District Commissioners and the Secretariat in Dar, via the Provincial Office, and sending reminders to District Offices concerning routine documents that were overdue. The only real excitement came when a cobra about seven feet long slid between the front legs and the back legs of my office chair while I was sitting in it.

It did not take me long to discover that, until I arrived in Mtwara, Donald Troup, the Provincial Commissioner, had done very little work. Every important initiative had been taken by Bryan Dudbridge, who was extremely able and conscientious and later became the Head of the Provincial Administration for the whole of Tanganyika. Donald Troup, a former Oxford rugger blue who had gone badly to seed, was himself aware of how Bryan Dudbridge had carried most of the work-load of the office, and he seemed to dread a situation in which he might actually be required to do a bit of work himself.

Before he had even met me, he had engaged in an acrimonious correspondence with Frederick Page-Jones, who was at that time the Head of the Provincial Administration in Dar, insisting that it was absolutely out of the question to send a mere second tour greenhorn to such an important place as Mtwara. The replies from Dar were quite gratifying for my vanity, as they insisted that I was competent and had been very well reported on in my first tour, and that, whether Troup liked it or not, he would just have to put up with me. I thought that the correspondence about me ought to have been confidential, but it was filed on an unclassified file, and, like everyone else in the office, I was free to read all that it contained.

It was not only from that file that I learned that my superiors had said nice things about me. When I returned from leave, I was handed an envelope containing a hand-written letter from Geoffrey Hucks. He had addressed it to me, c/o my bank in London, as I had not known when I left Iringa what my address in England would be. Geoffrey had marked the envelope 'to await arrival'. The Westminster Bank was not particularly efficient. They failed to notice the instruction on the envelope, and redirected it back to me 'c/o the Secretariat, Dar es Salaam', where an alert clerk did notice the instruction, and held on to the letter from April until the following January. Geoffrey thanked me for the work I had done in Iringa, and wished me a speedy recovery and a pleasant leave. He ended the letter by telling me that he thought I was the best cadet he had met in the 24 years he had served in Tanganyika, and that he had reported officially to that effect.

There were some very congenial and able people in Mtwara, but few of them regarded it as a happy station. During the years between 1953, when it became a District Headquarters, and Independence in 1961, there were six expatriate District Commissioners in Mtwara. Five of them had marriages that broke up while they were actually stationed there. The only DC not to be involved in a divorce was a bachelor. Mtwara had a Club for European members, but it was a cheerless place and the atmosphere there was often unfriendly.

When I arrived in Mtwara, I was told that I would be sharing with a recently appointed cadet called David Connelly the house which Bryan Dudbridge and his family had occupied. David was a very congenial companion. He was already married, but had not been allowed to bring his wife out to join him until he passed the appropriate examinations.

I regarded this policy as deplorable. Couples in their early married life do not enjoy being separated for months, and anyone with any perspicacity at all would quickly have concluded that Audrey Connelly would prove an ideal wife to support her husband in his career as a District Officer. There were other cadets with admirable wives who were in a similar position to David's. It did not save any money to pay for a wife to join her husband after he had already been in Tanganyika for some months, and most husbands would gladly have undertaken to refund the cost of the fare of their wives if they themselves failed to complete their first tour of service satisfactorily.

I suspected that one possible reason for the inflexibility of senior officials concerning the rules about wives coming out with their husbands on first appointment was that their own generation had come out to Africa when there were still few good prophylactic drugs to prevent malaria and other tropical diseases. They had themselves been advised to leave their families in Britain while they served in an unhealthy climate, so they wanted the new generation to put up with the same sort of hardship which they themselves had had to endure when they were still young. There were some married cadets who came out with me on first appointment and brought their wives with them, but I think they were given specially favourable treatment because they had served in the forces during the war. Even that concession stopped short of letting the wives share a cabin on board ship with their husbands.

Audrey arrived as soon as possible after David passed the necessary examinations, and I offered to move into a smaller quarter to let David and Audrey live together in a well-built house. This offer was rejected, even though I was still a bachelor, because I was senior to David. He and Audrey moved into a sub-standard quarter built of mud and wattle, with a thatched roof. I think it was also infested with creepy-crawlies, but I never heard either Audrey or David complain.

I disliked Mtwara, and did not have much opportunity to visit the inland districts of Southern Province to find out whether my prejudice against the whole province was justified. However, I did have one opportunity to get out of Mtwara for a couple of days while I was stationed there. I was appointed to be a member of the Higher Standard Swahili Oral Examining Board, which was convened to meet in Lindi to examine a District Officer from Kilwa and another from Nachingwea. I stayed as a guest in the house of Tony Golding, who was the DC of Lindi District at that time.

I thought the town of Lindi was delightful. It was situated beside a bay with an extensive sandy beach, palm trees waving in the breeze, and waves breaking gently on the shore. The DC's house overlooked the bay. It had been built in the time of the German regime, and the ground floor had been the Provincial Office and the upper floor the Provincial Commissioner's quarters before the Provincial Office had been moved to Mtwara. The top part of the building was now the DC's residence and what had been the Provincial Office had been converted into accommodation for guests. Whatever the defects of the Germans in administering their African colonies, they could certainly put up lovely buildings which had very thick walls and remained reasonably cool throughout the year.

It saddened me that the Groundnut Scheme, which cost the British taxpayer millions of pounds and did a lot of damage to Britain's reputation as a colonial power, led to the establishment of a hideous town like Mtwara and to the down-grading of two attractive old towns, Lindi and Mikindani.

I was shocked one day to see the file copy of a reply which Donald Troup had sent to the Secretariat. This concerned the public reaction to the proposal to close the District Office at Mikindani and move it to Mtwara. He was asked whether there had been any representations from members of the public on the subject of the proposed closure, and he had stated quite unambiguously that there had been no such representations. The decision taken in Dar to close the Boma in Mikindani was based on misleading information, however. The file which contained a copy of Donald Troup's letter also contained dozens of written complaints, mainly from traders in Mikindani who feared that their businesses would go bankrupt. I at first thought that Troup was merely idle, but that file convinced me that he also had very little regard for the truth.

***

Television had not reached Tanganyika by 1955, and I did not have a radio set. What I learnt of the news from the outside world came from the *Times Weekly Airmail Edition*. For many years the rowing correspondent of the *Times* was a former Oxford Blue called Richard Burnell, who had won a gold medal for Great Britain in the 1948 Olympic Double Sculls. He was very knowledgeable about rowing, and his forecasts were usually reliable. There was one race about which his judgement was not quite so trustworthy, however. Year after year, in the weeks leading up to the University Boat Race, one could be pretty certain that he would report that the Oxford crew were outstanding, and that Cambridge were rubbish. He did this in 1955, and Donald Troup gloated over me concerning the ignominious defeat Cambridge were about to suffer. I said I was not too downcast, since I did not trust the forecasts I had seen in the newspapers. Donald Troup then challenged me to place what was, on my salary, quite a large sum of money as a bet that Cambridge would win. I accepted the challenge, and was more than pleased a week or two later to hear that Cambridge had won by no less than sixteen lengths, one of the largest margins in Boat Race history. Troup did at least pay his debt of honour, but as he gave me my winnings he said he hoped they would choke me.

My worst argument with Troup arose when he stormed into my office shaking some papers under my nose. I had given the Provincial Education Officer and the Provincial Agricultural Officer orders to make an official journey by air, and Troup shouted at me that I had no right to give James Clegg and James Stewart such orders, as they were both far senior to me. The rule about officials flying on duty was that they could only do so with written prior approval either of their Head of Department in Dar, or of a Provincial Commissioner. An urgent matter had arisen which required James Clegg and James Stewart to fly at once to the other end of the Province. Troup was not in Mtwara at the time, and it was much too late to get the relevant documents signed in Dar and returned to Mtwara. I had therefore been requested by the officers concerned to authorise their flight on behalf of the Provincial Commissioner, and I had done so without the slightest hesitation.

While Troup was shouting at me, I explained that I had not given the order of my own initiative, but that I was complying with two requests that had seemed entirely reasonable in the circumstances. I asked Troup what he wanted me to do if the same circumstances were to occur again. He did not bother to give me an answer, but stormed out of my office huffing and puffing. Fortunately, I never had to deal with a similar situation again.

I had no respect for Donald Troup, and one of my failings is my inability to conceal my feelings when I work under a boss whom I do not respect. I have no doubt that Troup disliked his impudent young staff officer just as much as his impudent young staff officer disliked him.

One Thursday afternoon, I heard the telephone ring in Troup's office, and Troup answered. When the conversation ended, he came into my office and said, 'Go home and pack your boxes at once. You're leaving.' I asked him to explain the reason, and he told me very brusquely that I was to be the Governor's next Private Secretary, and was to report to Government House in Dar on Monday. He declined to congratulate me or wish me success in a posting that I, and most of my colleagues, regarded as something of an accolade.

It was normal for a District Officer to employ more than one domestic servant, but I was told that I could only bring one servant to work for me at Government House. My cook Lameck had followed me from Tukuyu and Iringa, and he was a very good cook whom I liked and trusted. He had no experience of

Government House

washing and ironing clothes, but Hassan, my houseboy-dhobi, was someone I had only engaged at Mtwara and I was not very satisfied with his work. Lameck was quite elderly, but he was very keen to come with me even if it involved learning a new kind of work, so I paid off Hassan. Lameck tried very hard when he was with me in Government House, but he never became as good a dhobi as he was a cook. He stayed on with me after I left Government House, but he went back to the job he did best – cooking.

I was overjoyed to leave a place I disliked and to see the last of an uncongenial boss, and work which I found boring. I was also delighted that Sir Edward Twining had chosen me to be his Private Secretary. The bad news was that I had to pack all my personal effects between Thursday afternoon and Saturday morning, when the steamer which plied up and down the coast between Mombasa and Mtwara was due to sail north from Mtwara on its monthly journey, calling at every port including Dar es Salaam. I had far more breakages in that one move than in all the others during my whole time in Tanganyika.

To this day, I have never discovered a reason to explain to my satisfaction why those responsible for selecting officers for promotion chose an idle, untruthful and disagreeable man like Troup in preference to Teddy Kingdon or Geoffrey Hucks, both of whom were actually older than Troup, and would have made excellent Provincial Commissioners.

I also regarded it as insensitive of the authorities in Dar, when they knew that Troup was so opposed to having a mere Provincial Commissioner's Pup to replace a Deputy Provincial Commissioner, that he was not told until the very last minute that my posting to Mtwara was only to be temporary, and that my successor later in the year would be another Deputy Provincial Commissioner, with similar powers to those of Bryan Dudbridge.

Chapter 5

Private Secretary – Government House

(April 1955–April 1956)

His Excellency, Sir Edward Twining

My posting to Government House came as a complete surprise. Both my predecessors as Sir Edward Twining's Private Secretary had been retired army officers, one a brigadier, the other a lieutenant-colonel. It had never occurred to me that Twining might appoint any serving district officer to be his next private secretary when Colonel Tom Leahy completed his contract of service, much less that he would choose me.

In Britain, a young and promising Whitehall civil servant, male or female, can be appointed as private secretary to a minister, and this does not normally involve a great change of life-style. He or she will go on living at home and travelling into the office in the morning and home in the evening, except when accompanying the Minister on formal visits. In Whitehall, a private secretary might or might not be married.

Working as Private Secretary to the Governor of Tanganyika was quite different. The Governor's Private Secretary was expected to be male and unmarried. He was provided with his own bed-sitting-room in Government House, but hardly ever used it during the day, as he lived *en famille* with the Governor and his wife. During normal office hours, the Private Secretary worked in an office adjacent to the Governor's office. The Twinings always had breakfast alone, but the Private Secretary normally had lunch and dinner with them in the main dining room, and was in attendance in the drawing room before and after meals.

The cost of my board and lodging was met from special allowances paid to the Governor, and my salary continued at the rate I had been getting before, so I was able to make some modest savings while I worked for Twining. More than the financial advantages of secondment to Government House, however, I valued the opportunity to get to know a very remarkable man with a gift of inspiring devotion from those who worked for him.

Edward Francis Twining was born in a vicarage in London in 1899. His father, the Reverend William Twining, was the vicar of St Stephen's Church in Rochester Row, in Westminster. His mother, Agatha Twining, to whom he was devoted, was twenty years younger than her husband. I at first found it rather puzzling that someone whose name was Edward was always called Peter by his wife and close friends. I was told later that Twining's parents had both wanted to call their son Peter, as he was born on St Peter's Day, but that the baby's great-uncle George, the sub-dean of Salisbury Cathedral, who christened him, was an eccentric clergyman who disliked the name Peter, and had insisted on giving him the names Edward Francis instead.

Twining's early years did not give much indication that he would end his career as a distinguished colonial governor, and that after his retirement he would be included in the first list of life peers created under the Life Peerages Act of 1958. His school career began at a preparatory school near Bournemouth, from which he went on to Lancing College on the Sussex coast, where he was considered to be a pleasant boy with a sense of humour but not much claim to academic ability.

In 1917, he took the entrance examination for the Royal Military Academy at Sandhurst. His name was not included in the first list of successful candidates, but he was eventually admitted because some of the candidates who had done better than him in the academic tests had either failed their medical examinations or else withdrawn for other reasons. He completed the course at Sandhurst and was commissioned as a second lieutenant in the Worcestershire Regiment. He served in Ireland, and was awarded the MBE for his work there. On his return to England, he was posted to Dover, where he found the work dull, so he decided to apply for a secondment to the King's African Rifles.

His application was successful, and in September 1923 he left England to start his journey to Uganda. While he was serving as a KAR officer in Uganda, he was visited by two women, Evelyn du Buisson and her cousin, Helen Mary du Buisson, who was always known as May. The du Buisson family were old acquaintances of the family of Agatha Twining, and after a slow courtship Peter Twining and May du Buisson became engaged, and were married in July 1928. They had two sons, John, who later followed his father into the Colonial Service in Uganda, and William, who got a first-class degree in Law at Oxford, and became a Professor of Law at a very early age.

Like my own mother, May Twining had qualified as a doctor at a time when women doctors were rarer than they are now. She was intelligent, quiet, shy, and determined. She lacked the charisma and sense of humour of her husband, but her kindness and her tireless work for the advancement of women, especially in the context of a voluntary organisation known as the Tanganyika Council for Women, won her the respect and affection of many friends.

Twining was not a typical army officer, but he had himself made the decision that he wanted to join the army. I never heard Lady Twining speak disparagingly of the army, but I formed the impression that she probably played a major part in persuading her husband that a career in the Colonial Administrative Service would be more constructive and satisfying than the job of a soldier. Whatever the reason, Twining left the army, and in spite of his lack of academic qualifications he was selected for the Colonial Administrative Service and offered a post in Uganda, subject to completing satisfactorily a preliminary course at Oxford University. The course he took was broadly similar to the course which I myself completed more than twenty years later at Cambridge.

Twining's career as a District Officer in Uganda provided him with a chance to show some unusual qualities. He served not only in remote districts but also in the Secretariat and as Staff Officer in a Provincial Commissioner's office. He continued to find examinations uncongenial, however, and for nearly ten years he failed to pass the language examinations which were essential to a successful career in Uganda. He therefore decided to seek another occupation in a different country, and applied for the post of Deputy Head of a new Department of Labour in Mauritius. He travelled to Mauritius in February 1939. The Second World War started a few months later, and Twining's responsibilities came to cover a wider field than labour. His work in Mauritius was so successful that he was awarded the CMG in 1943.

In 1944, he was appointed Administrator of the Caribbean island of Saint Lucia, and remained there until 1946, when he was appointed Governor of North Borneo. Before he left North Borneo in 1949, his name was included in the New Year's Honours list, and he became a KCMG.

In 1949, he was offered the governorship of Tanganyika as the successor to Sir William Battershill, who was retiring on grounds of ill-health.

Twining had already been the Governor for nearly five years when he appointed me to be his Private Secretary. During that period he had managed to inspire the affection of officials, especially those in the Provincial Administration, and to stimulate the political and economic development of an enormous country in ways which his immediate predecessors had failed to achieve. He built up warm relationships with many leaders in the European, Asian, and African communities. He never spoke Swahili fluently, but he got on particularly well with the tribal chiefs on whose cooperation the success of the policy of Indirect Rule depended.

His exuberant personality was reflected in the kind of music he enjoyed. On Sunday mornings he retired by himself to his private study in Government House and listened, at full volume, to long-playing records of such works as Verdi's *Requiem* or Berlioz's *Grande Messe des Morts*. The music was audible in other rooms as well, and I enjoyed it. In fact I was so impressed that the first long-playing records I ever bought for myself were a complete set of the Verdi *Requiem*.

Twining had two pedigree miniature dachshunds, Titus and Berenice. He used to call Berenice 'Very-nice', which was giving her the benefit of the doubt. There was no scope for doubt at all about Titus. I do not think I have ever met a less attractive little dog. If one was walking, he would nip one's ankles. If one was standing still, he would lift his leg and pee over one's shoes, or, still better, over the bare feet of domestic servants. Whenever Twining's gramophone was playing, Titus would sit outside the door of the study and raise his head and howl fortissimo until the music ended.

I had been allowed to bring my crossbred dog Susan and her daughter, Wol, who had been born while I was in Iringa, to Government House with me. They spent much of the time quietly in my bed-sitting-room, although I took them for walks at regular intervals along the beach or in the grounds of Government House. When I accompanied the Governor on safari, however, my dogs were boarded in kennels run by a local animal welfare organisation in the suburbs of Dar. Susan and Wol were never rude to Titus or Berenice, but they were selective about the dogs they made friends with. They did not worry about aristocratic pedigree, and treated Titus and Berenice with total disdain.

Sadly, as Twining approached retirement, he seemed to be out of sympathy with the aims of political leaders who were seeking an end to colonial rule before he thought the country was ready for it. The Tanganyika African National Union (TANU) had been set up by Julius Nyerere a few months before I was posted to Government House, and I got the impression that Twining regarded the new political party, with its emphasis on 'Africa for the African', as inherently racist. He valued the part that many Asians and Europeans played in the economic development of Tanganyika, and tried to encourage the development of a multi-racial political party, the 'United Tanganyika Party' (UTP), whose aim would be to combat racism and to encourage peaceful co-operation between all communities.

I met several people who later stood as UTP candidates in Tanganyika's first democratic general election at the end of the 1950s. I thought some of them meant well, although there were others whose motives for joining the party seemed less praise-worthy. However, I did not meet any who appeared to have the drive or ability to become an effective political leader. No UTP candidate was elected to Legislative Council, and the party had very little influence on Tanganyika's progress towards independence.

Working in Government House

I flew from Mtwara to Dar es Salaam with little idea of what the Governor's Private Secretary was expected to do. The Colonial Service course which my colleagues and I had done at Cambridge before going to Tanganyika had been designed to train cadets for jobs in District Offices. While we all knew that colonies were governed by Governors, no one had thought it necessary to tell us that Governors all had personal staff, or what the personal staff were required to do.

The responsibilities of the Private Secretary were just as varied as those of a District Officer, but they were very different. Twining himself once told me that the most important task of a Private Secretary was to ensure that Government House ran like a well-oiled Rolls Royce engine, but he did not go into detail about how this objective was to be achieved.

By the time I arrived in Government House, my predecessor, Colonel Tom Leahy, was already on the point of returning to Britain, and he did not have enough time to brief me adequately about the job. However, I knew that I would be nominally in charge of all the staff working in Government House. Much of what I learned about my own duties came from asking the people who would be working under my supervision to describe their own jobs to me. It soon became clear that there were several distinct aspects to the job of Private Secretary. These included the general management and financial control of Government House; helping the Governor to entertain guests and make them feel welcome; escorting him on ceremonial occasions and deputising for him at rehearsals for formal parades; and accompanying him on visits to up-country stations.

The Private Secretary had no responsibility for policy matters, which were dealt with by the Governor himself, assisted by an Executive Council which was broadly comparable to the Cabinet in Britain. However, documents which officials in the Secretariat wished to submit to the Governor were normally addressed to 'PSGH' (Private Secretary Government House). The Private Secretary then endorsed them with the letters 'YE' (Your Excellency), and passed them through to the Governor. As soon as he had read the file, the Governor would make his comments in manuscript in red ink, and the file would then be returned to my office. This gave me an opportunity, although I was not involved in decision making, to see for myself how high level decisions were reached.

I also saw the case papers of a number of murder trials where the accused had been convicted and sentenced to death. Before I arrived in Government House, I had got the idea that convicted murderers were nearly always executed. Twining and his advisors on Executive Council were compassionate men, however, and did their utmost to find features in the life of the prisoner or the circumstances of the crime that would justify the use of the prerogative of mercy. Whenever he did reluctantly sign a Death Warrant, Twining was in a bad mood for days on end.

I thought Government House was a beautiful building. It was surrounded by extensive lawns which were green for most of the year, though they became parched and discoloured during the dry season. I had never visited an Arabian country, but its architecture suggested to me the kind of white castellated palace which a cultured oriental potentate might choose to live in. It was designed to catch whatever breezes came in from the sea, and even at the hottest times of the year it was never unbearably hot inside the building. It was not air-conditioned, but every room had one or more ceiling fans. The Governor's office and all the main public rooms on the ground floor and the bedrooms on the first floor had splendid views over the Indian Ocean.

The main entrance to Government House was from the direction of the town centre. Just inside the gate which separated the garden from the public highway there was a guard room. In front of the guard room was a wooden structure that looked like a sentry-box. The visitors' book was kept there, and those who wished to pay their respects to the Governor could do so without having to enter the main building. The grounds also contained extensive quarters for the African staff, who were often required to work late at night in order to wait at table at formal dinners or to serve drinks at sundowner parties.

I was at first rather shocked by the number of people on the complement of staff in Government House. Tanganyika was a poor country, and it seemed almost immoral to employ so many people on various tasks designed to create an image of affluence and to enable the Governor and his guests and retinue, including myself, to live in luxury. I felt guilty about the sumptuous standard of my bed-sitting-room, with its superb view over the Indian Ocean, and furnished far more lavishly than the quarters normally allocated to expatriate officials.

Criticism of the affluent life-style of diplomats and heads of state has grown in recent years, but in the 1950s, soon after the austerity of the Second World War, I think that most people of all races living in Tanganyika took great pride in pomp and ceremonial, and, if consulted, would have expressed the view that penny-pinching would be quite inappropriate in Government House.

There were seven Europeans and about thirty Africans working for the Governor. The Private Secretary and the ADC/Assistant Private Secretary, who at the time I arrived was Twining's young nephew Sam, both lived on the premises. Sam and I each employed one personal servant, whose wages we paid ourselves.

One other European who lived in Government House was the resident housekeeper, Mrs Watt, an elderly Scottish widow. She lived in a flat in one of the outbuildings of Government House, and supervised all the domestic arrangements very competently.

Four other European officials, Phyllis Merrick, the social secretary, Marjorie Sharp, the Governor's personal stenographer, Major Walker, the cypher officer, and Sylvia Rogers, the assistant cypher officer, all lived in quarters in the town of Dar, and came in to work at Government House each morning.

A very experienced African clerk, Stephen Mzinga, worked in the general correspondence office. He retired while I was in Government House and was succeeded by another exceptionally able and loyal clerk, Harrison Kachingwe, who was the first African clerk I met who knew shorthand. Harrison's father had himself been a clerk in Government House before the outbreak of the Second World War.

In addition to the office staff, there were numerous houseboys, cooks, laundry boys, messengers, and gardeners, half a dozen drivers, and one police constable who was the governor's personal bodyguard. Apart from Police Constable Saidi, who wore the normal uniform of a police askari, all the African manual workers were provided with special uniforms with brass crowns on their fezzes and their tunics. They were all exceptionally good at their jobs, and took an immense pride in their work and in their appearance.

The most outstanding members of this respected group of retainers were probably the drivers. The Head Driver, Salehe Msigara, was a former Regimental Sergeant Major of the King's African Rifles, whose skill as a driver, a mechanic, and a leader earned him a medal not normally awarded in Britain, the Queen's Certificate and Badge of Honour.

African staff were usually addressed by name, and I was sometimes afraid that a visitor who understood Swahili might draw the wrong conclusion when he heard the Governor calling one of his drivers Mtumwa and another one Mjinga. These were their real names, but *mtumwa* is the Swahili for 'slave' and *mjinga* for 'fool'.

The work-load of each individual varied from day to day, depending on the Governor's programme. For example, if he was hosting a sundowner or dinner party, or travelling with all his retinue on safari, or holding a meeting with important guests staying in Government House, this would involve extra work for some or all of the staff.

At times the junior staff were extremely busy, but at other times they seemed to be getting their wages for doing very little. Everyone working in Government House had to have security clearance, which meant that temporary staff could not be taken on at short notice to cope with sudden emergencies. Staff who were known and trusted were sometimes required to work for very long hours, but they never complained about this. They knew that they were sure of keeping their jobs even when there was not very much for them to do.

Overseeing the work of the other members of the Governor's household was not a very arduous task, as they all knew their jobs and wanted to please the Governor without needing to be motivated by me.

One staffing crisis took place while I was in Government House. Sir Edward Twining was on home leave and the Chief Secretary, Robert Stapledon, was the 'Officer Administering the Government'. One morning he called me into his office immediately after breakfast, and told me that it had come to light that the cypher officer was deeply in debt, and was regarded as too much of a security risk to be allowed to go on handling incoming and outgoing messages classified as secret. This meant that Sylvia Rogers had to take over the running of the cypher office, and that I had, in addition to my other duties, to act temporarily as her assistant until a suitable replacement could be found. Fortunately it did not take very long to appoint Valerie MacKenzie, the wife of a very senior police officer, to the vacancy. She was far more competent at encoding and decoding messages than I.

Responsibility for the financial management of Government House involved, among other things, seeing that the approved expenditure votes were not overspent. That was a task I was already used to in District Offices, but in Government House it could cause problems. When information reached the Governor that Princess Margaret was planning to pay a Royal Visit to Tanganyika, Lady Twining decided that many of the curtains and carpets were too shabby for such an important guest, and needed to be replaced immediately. I had the delicate task of trying to discourage her from going on a shopping spree until I had received formal approval for supplementary expenditure.

Possibly as a result of the years he had spent as an army officer, Twining liked dressing up in the full cermonial uniform of a colonial governor, and his appearance in uniform was very impressive. However, the star of the show usually did not appear until the actual performance. When rehearsals for a formal parade were thought necessary, as they usually were, it was my job to deputise for the Governor, and take the salute on his behalf, and inspect the askaris on parade. The rehearsals were nearly always held in the early morning, before the heat of the sun beating down on an open parade ground became unbearable.

My first serious gaffe in Government House occurred at one such rehearsal. I had planned to get up at six o'clock, but I overslept and arrived on the parade ground about half an hour late, without having shaved. I got out of the gubernatorial car and the troops gave the Royal Salute. I then inspected the askaris and left the parade ground, got back into the car again, and was driven back to Government House.

None of the army officers or the very senior civilians whom I had kept waiting made any comment to me about my lateness, although if I had been in their position I would have been extremely irritated if the Private Secretary had kept me and a host of other senior officers and askaris waiting so long.

As soon as I got back to my office, I wrote about a dozen manuscript letters of apology to the people whose time I had wasted, and I sent messengers to deliver them urgently.

At about ten o'clock, Twining called me into his office, looking less than pleased with me. He had been told about my blunder, and ordered me to write to those whom I had inconvenienced. I told him I had already done so, and his mood changed at once. He told me in a friendly way to return to my office and to make sure that nothing like it ever happened again.

Later that day I received a phone call from a senior and highly respected official in the Secretariat called Hugh Elliott. I hardly knew him, but he thanked me for my letter, forgave me for my lapse, and invited me to come to his home that evening for a drink with him and his wife Elizabeth, whom I had not previously met. I never forgot their kindness, and we became good friends.

After Twining discovered that I understood German, he sometimes asked for my help in translating German documents that he wanted to refer to in a book which he was writing, *A History of the Crown Jewels of Europe*, which was published in 1960. He never allowed my work on the translation of German to interfere with my official duties as his Private Secretary, but I eventually became quite interested in the subject of crown jewels, and did not begrudge the time I spent on this work. When the book was published, it was very highly praised by expert critics, and it also made a slight profit for its author.

The Governor's Guests

Colonial Governors were expected to get to know and be known by the people they governed, and one way to achieve this was to invite guests to meet them socially. It would have been unreasonable to expect Governors to meet the cost of official hospitality out of their own pockets, however, so they were paid a special allowance in addition to their salaries. Twining was an exuberant personality who enjoyed meeting people and building up friendly relationships, and he made full use of his entertainment allowance.

The hospitality which he offered varied according to the guests he was receiving and the reason for their visit. Distinguished guests who were coming to Tanganyika to take part in discussions of national importance were often invited to stay for a few days in one of the guest rooms in Government House. They had their main meals in the dining room with the Governor and Lady Twining. Such guests were not necessarily Twining's personal friends, but most of them were friendly as well as being experts in their field. One of the privileges of working in Government House was that I met several eminent people whom I would not have met anywhere else.

Nearly all of Twining's house guests behaved impeccably, but some did not. He himself told me of his clash with one British politician who had accepted an invitation to Government House and then made a series of offensive remarks about the oppressive way the colonies were ruled. Twining had put up with this behaviour until the guest made a gratuitously insulting remark about the late Queen Mary. Twining then told him that if he spoke like that again he would be asked to get out of Government House and stay in a local hotel.

I still find it odd that a politician who was not a fool should behave so rudely to his host and hostess. At first I wondered why he had accepted Twining's invitation at all when he was so prejudiced against colonial governors and what they represented. Perhaps the reason was that he was hoping to gather scandalous material to include in future books and speeches criticising Britain's policies in Africa.

I never met any other of Twining's house guests whom I suspected of being motivated by malice, but there were one or two who were haughty and domineering. The arrogance of the wife of an army General was very trying. She spoke extremely loudly, with an affected upper-crust drawl, and had come with her husband to attend a ceremonial parade of the Sixth Battalion of the King's African Rifles. During the evening after the parade, the officers and their guests held a party in the Officers' Mess, and the askaris were celebrating in their own lines. The General's wife came up to me and demanded that I should drive her in a Government House car to look at the askaris. The battalion commander had particularly requested us to let the soldiers celebrate on their own, without being interrupted by visits from Europeans, and I reminded her as forcefully as I could of the colonel's request. She replied that she was not going to be told what to do or not to do by anybody, and persisted in ordering me to be her chauffeur. I reluctantly obeyed.

When we got to the soldiers' lines, there were a large number of very happy and slightly tipsy African askaris, singing and dancing. Many of them were Hehe tribesmen who recognised me from my time in their home district of Iringa, and they came up to the car wanting to greet me and shake my hand. A few greeted the General's wife as well, but most of the soldiers took no notice of her. However, she appeared to be utterly terrified of the horrible drunken louts threatening her life and her honour, and screamed at me that she wanted to be driven back at once. On this occasion I was only too glad to comply with her orders.

The Twinings waited until the General and his wife had left Government House before they made any comment. When at last they did, it was quite clear that they had found the behaviour of the General's wife just as objectionable as I had.

When there were house guests staying at Government House, Twining often took the opportunity of inviting to dinner people who were likely to be involved in the discussions or negotiations which the house guests were having with the Governor. The meals were always delicious. The conversation was sometimes very witty and sometimes very serious, but it was never dull.

Many of the functions at Government House involved dressing formally, and Twining told me to get the best tailor in Dar to make me a black tail coat of the appropriate pattern, with dark blue velvet lapels, light blue silk lining, and large gilt buttons with the insignia ER II on them. I thought the tail coat was too thick to wear in the hot and humid climate of Dar, and the cost was much more than I could afford, but I was not required to pay for it myself. I also had a white drill tropical uniform made, with drain-pipe trousers and a tunic with a very tight collar. I bought a white helmet, a second-hand sword, gilt buttons, and badges of rank from an official who was retiring. The buttons were embossed with a giraffe's head, the national emblem of Tanganyika. The white uniform was horribly uncomfortable, whatever the temperature.

Twining's hospitality involved a large number of evening functions, but he also regularly invited a mix of about a dozen guests of all races to have lunch with him in Government House. These could include senior officials or business leaders, but he also often invited much younger guests, many of whom he did not know personally, but whom he wanted to meet. Lunches were less formal than dinners, but sometimes the guests were shy and said very little. Guests of whatever race were normally invited with their wives, but in the 1950s many Asian and African women were less sophisticated than their husbands, and were not used to eating with formal settings of cutlery for each place at the table. Some of the guests also spoke little English, and I some-times tried to reassure diffident African women by talking very softly to them in Swahili. However, some of the guests may well have felt that an invitation to a meal at Government House was an ordeal rather than an honour. Even so, it was clearly right for Twining to include wives in his invitations to such functions.

The invitation lists and table seating plans were prepared by Phyllis Merrick, the social secretary. She kept a record of every-one who had signed the Governor's Visitors' Book, and those who had attended recent functions, and she kept herself informed about anyone planning to visit Dar whom Twining might wish to entertain. She maintained close liaison with Mrs Watt, the house-keeper, and they always managed to ensure that the food offered to guests did not include anything which their religion did not allow them to eat. Phyllis Merrick and Mrs Watt both did their jobs excellently.

From time to time, when Twining wanted to entertain more guests than could be seated together around the dining table, he invited them to a large sundowner party in Government House. He was very firm about the time when his sundowner parties were to finish and all the guests return home. Even though the parties did not go on until late at night, by the time they came to an end several of the guests had managed to put away a fair amount of alcohol, and were laughing very loudly at one another's jokes. I did not greatly enjoy these parties, partly because the ADC and I were expected to converse with as many guests as possible, and could not spend a lot of time chatting to those whom we found most congenial.

One aspect of life as Private Secretary which I disliked was the way in which one or two ambitious officials and their even more ambitious wives thought it would improve their chances of being invited to Government House if they ingratiated themselves with the governor's personal staff. One couple in particular invited me repeatedly to dine with them even though we had very little in common. When I told Twining that I had been invited to dinner with them yet again, he asked me whether my would-be host was a B.Sc. I misunderstood the question, and said he was a lawyer, not a scientist. Twining laughed and told me that he had used the initials BSC, not to mean 'Bachelor of Science' but 'Bloody Social Climber'. He was a pretty shrewd judge of character.

Although some formal dinners at Government House were intended to provide an opportunity for senior officials to have discussions with visiting experts or politicians, most of the invitations to other functions were issued without much regard to seniority. This was not always understood by people who set great store by their own positions in the hierarchy.

In 1955, the number of unofficial members of Legislative Council, the Tanganyikan equivalent of Parliament in Westminster, was enlarged, and three women, one African, one Asian, and one European, were appointed. The morning after a large sundowner party, the newly-appointed European woman member wrote to me asking me to bring to the Governor's notice the blunder he had made by failing to invite her to his party when there were many guests who were junior to her. I felt uneasy about passing on to the Governor a letter which I was sure would annoy him, but the explosion of fury when he read it surpassed my expectations. He called me into his office and instructed me on the exact words I was to use in my reply. I was to tell the woman that, as she had requested, I had referred her letter to His Excellency, who considered it a piece of gross impertinence, and had ordered that her name should be deleted from the list of those eligible to receive invitations to Government House. Furthermore, His Excellency demanded an immediate explanation of why, when she had not been invited to the sundowner, she had nevertheless attended it. I had not spotted her among all the other guests, but Twining had.

Later that day I had a telephone call from a sobbing and hysterical woman. She implored me to ask the Governor to allow her to make her apology to him in person. I was non-committal, but promised that I would let the Governor know of her request. To my surprise, he agreed to see her, and when she was admitted to his office she again started to howl and grovel on the floor in front of him. It was not a dignified tragic performance, but it was partially successful. Twining relented to the extent that he told her that her name could be reinstated on the list, but as far as I know she was never actually invited to any subsequent functions which Twining hosted.

The Governor's social engagements were still more hectic when he was on safari up-country than they were when he was in

Dar. Even on a whistle-stop visit to a remote district, Twining
would make a point of meeting officers of the Provincial
Administration at a meal, and also of meeting as many as possible of the local community leaders at a drinks party, which might
be held either at midday or in the evening. The ADC and the
Private Secretary always attended these events, and were
expected to play an active part in making the guests feel welcome
and helping to make the occasion a success.

   Being a member of the Governor's retinue gave me the chance
to visit every province, to see more than forty of the fifty-plus
districts in Tanganyika, and to meet thousands of the country's
leaders. I found it very exciting, but there was one slight disadvantage. If one arrived in a strange place together with the
Governor and his wife, all the people on their own home ground
were able to identify the Governor's Private Secretary, especially
if he happened to be conspicuously tall. I continued to find it
embarrassing, several years after I had left Government House, to
be greeted by name by people I barely recognised and whose
names I did not remember, and possibly had never even known,
who told me that they had met me when I had come with the
Governor to the district where they were stationed.

Travelling with the Governor

When Twining took up his appointment as Governor, the first thing
which impressed him about Tanganyika was its size. It is about four
times as big as Uganda, the first colony where Twining served, and
more than 1,500 times the size of Saint Lucia, the Caribbean island
where Twining had been Administrator.

   Unlike some previous governors, Twining was not the kind of
man to administer any country simply by giving instructions to
subordinates without ever having seen the places or met the
people who would be affected by his policies. He also paid many
follow-up visits to check on whether his instructions had been
properly carried out. All through the nine years he served in
Tanganyika, he visited every province and district regularly,
including many quite remote places which had not been visited
by a governor for years. Twining's relationship with senior officials of the Provincial Administration was very close, but that did
not mean that he relied exclusively on them to supply him with
information about their problems or about the success of the
measures taken to solve them.

On the other hand, Twining did not waste his time on routine tasks which he knew he could safely leave to other people. He decided on where he wanted to go and the main objectives of the safari, and he then left it to his staff in Government House to consult those who had local knowledge and to work out with them a draft detailed programme, and then submit it to him for his approval.

This was quite a complicated task. The programme always had to be formulated weeks or even months in advance of the visit, so that the people whom Twining wanted to meet or who wanted to meet him could be informed and make their own arrangements. Officials from every department needed to be told of the Governor's plans, so that they could prepare their own reports of their problems and achievements. Telephone services were so rudimentary in the 1950s, however, that it was always difficult and sometimes impossible to speak from the capital to discuss plans with people in up-country provincial or district headquarters, let alone tribal chiefs living in villages which had no telephones.

The staff in Government House did not usually know the names or backgrounds of local community leaders, so the Provincial Commissioner or District Commissioners were always asked to make a list of suitable guests to be invited to parties hosted by the Governor in the stations he visited.

Planning the timing of a safari was particularly difficult. Estimates of how long a car journey would take were very inexact, as even so-called 'territorial main roads' often became flooded and even impassable during the rains, and conditions on village roads in rural areas were still more unpredictable. Bridges could also be washed away in tropical rainstorms. Nearly all safaris were undertaken during the dry season, but even when the weather was dry, a convoy of cars could easily be delayed by a mechanical breakdown or a burst tyre.

Twining recognised the value of keeping in touch with the people he governed, but he did not want to spend more time than necessary on travel. He always tried to avoid returning by car over exactly the same roads that he had taken to reach his destination. In some cases this involved planning the itinerary to cover a circular route. In others, a fleet of Government House cars was sent off in advance. The drivers were given instructions to meet Twining and his retinue a few days later, when they arrived either by air or by train.

There were three main forms of transport which Twining used on safari. The Government had a two-engined plane, a Percival

'Prince', which could also be used for other work such as aerial survey. The Governor had his personal train, but this could only be used to get to places on the Central Line to Kigoma, or on the Mwanza Line. It was not used on the railway line from Tanga to Moshi, in the northern part of the territory. There was also a fleet of Government House motor cars consisting of Chevrolets and Landrovers, with load carrying vehicles to carry all the drinks and provisions needed at parties hosted by the Governor. An ancient black Rolls Royce was only used on tarmac roads in the capital.

The ADC had special responsibility, among other things, for motor transport, and for ensuring that the cars were all maintained in a roadworthy condition. Twining was sometimes criticised for using American cars. The reason for his preference was that not long after he arrived in Tanganyika a British saloon car in the Government House fleet had come to bits on what was, for Tanganyika, quite a good main road. The bodywork and the engine had gone their separate ways, and Twining decided that Chevrolets were more reliable on Tanganyikan roads than Humbers.

When major repairs were needed on any of the Government House cars, these were done by the Public Works Department, but the Government House drivers were themselves excellent drivers and also very skilled mechanics, and could be relied upon to deal quickly on the spot with the kind of minor breakdowns which often occurred on unsurfaced roads.

Lady Twining always accompanied her husband on safari, but sometimes she would herself visit places concerned with social services while the Governor was involved with other matters. Her quiet kindness won her many friends. It was typical of her interest in other people that, whenever we were planning to go on safari, she asked me to let her know the names of all the District Commissioners and District Officers stationed in the districts we were intending to visit. She had a little notebook in which she kept details of those she had already met. She even made a note of the names and dates of birth of their children, so that she could bring appropriate presents when she arrived at their parents' home. People sometimes suggested that Lady Twining's generosity lacked spontaneity, but very few up-country stations had shops which stocked toys at all, and the choice was always much wider in Dar. She always took great trouble to find something which was likely to give real pleasure to the specific child for whom she bought it.

As I had seen when I was stationed in Iringa, the prospect of a Governor's safari involved a lot of extra work for a District Commissioner and his team, but a visit from Sir Edward Twining gave them enormous pleasure and did wonders for their morale. They felt that Twining really cared for them, appreciated the work they were doing, and listened carefully and sympathetically to whatever they told him.

Southwards with the Stapledons

The normal tour of service for expatriate officials in Tanganyika was about thirty months, but Governors went on home leave more frequently. This may have been partly to protect their health in a stressful job when they were nearing retirement age, but, no less important, Governors needed to keep in touch regularly with Ministers and senior officials in the Colonial Office.

Not many months after I arrived in Government House, the Twinings went on leave for a few weeks, and the Chief Secretary, Robert de Stapledon Stapledon, became the Acting Governor. He and his wife Sue remained in their own house adjoining Government House, together with Sue Stapledon's unmarried elder sister, Bunty Radford, who was friendly and polite to everyone. Stapledon himself was a very pleasant and able man who went on to become Governor of Eastern Nigeria and, later, of the Bahamas.

Sue Stapledon had, in her youth, probably been a very pretty woman, but by the time I knew her she often had a petulant expression on her face and she made little attempt to conceal her boredom when she had to entertain guests at Government House. At the end of one sundowner party where she was the hostess and had been wearing long white gloves, she compared the immaculate whiteness of her left glove with the grey colour of the glove which she had worn on her right hand when shaking hands with the guests. I was shocked by the contemptuous way she spoke, very loudly and in the hearing of everybody around her, about the people whose grubby hands she was expected to shake in the course of her duty.

Not very long after Stapledon took over as acting Governor, he went on a long safari by car through Southern Province and parts of Eastern Province. We flew from Dar to Songea, an old station situated to the east of Lake Nyasa. It was nearly 4,000 feet above sea level, and the Boma had been built by the Germans. Some people liked Songea, but I was not one of them.

We then drove through mile after monotonous mile of what was known as *miombo* woodland. Miombo is a sort of scrubby bushland and thicket, much of which is uninhabited as it is infested with tsetse-fly, which carry sleeping sickness. This can be fatal to human beings as well as to cattle. We stopped at each of the District Offices situated on the road which gradually dropped down towards the coast at Mtwara. At each of the places we visited I silently offered thanks that my stay in Southern Province had been so short.

When we reached Mtwara, I stayed in the house of George Baker, the officer who had taken over from me in the Provincial Office. When I was going to bed, I asked about a mosquito net, as I had always used one while I was in Mtwara, and I did not see one in his guest room. He answered that there was no need to worry, as the room had been sprayed with insecticide and the doors and windows were all protected with wire gauze. During the night, however, I was kept awake by the continuous high-pitched hum of mosquitoes, and eventually switched on the bedroom light. I clapped my hands and squashed about half a dozen mosquitoes, all of which were gorged with blood which I assumed to be my own.

Driving northwards from Mtwara along the coast road through Lindi and Kilwa was a great improvement. Lindi and Kilwa were both attractive old towns, and many of the beaches along the Indian Ocean were lovely.

After we crossed the Provincial border into Rufiji District, we met one of Tanganyika's most unorthodox District Commissioners. John Young was a very rich bachelor who was said to own a fleet of fishing trawlers, and did certainly own the best hi-fi equipment which I had ever seen.

One of Stapledon's tasks in Rufiji District was to present the Queen's Certificate and Badge of Honour to the Liwali,

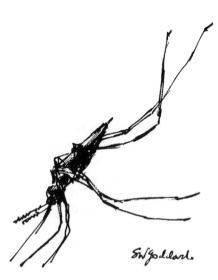

SW Goddard.

Anopheles Mosquito

or headman, of a village called Mohoro. I acted as his interpreter when he delivered a eulogy. The Liwali had played an important part in a strange affair that I still do not fully understand.

The facts of the case were very unusual, even in a country where witchcraft was commonplace. A number of men living in Mohoro village had simply disappeared, and the investigations by the police had not been successful either in tracing the men or in finding their bodies. At the suggestion of the Liwali, John Young, who had no great regard for the skill of his policemen, invited a well-known medicine-man from outside the Province to come and solve the mystery. When he arrived in Mohoro, the medicine-man, who later gave sworn evidence in the High Court that he had never been to Mohoro in his life before that day, walked round the village accompanied by a large crowd which included the Liwali, several policemen, and, I believe, John Young himself.

The medicine-man ordered a constable to climb one particular mango tree, and when he got almost to the top the constable found a human skull hidden in the branches. The medicine-man continued his walk, then pointed to a place in the ground and ordered another policeman to dig just there. That policeman uncovered a few more human bones. The medicine-man continued on his inspection of the village until several more parts of the bodies of three male victims had been found.

The medicine-man then asked the Liwali to order all the villagers to assemble so that he could try to identify the murderer or murderers. He then indicated three women, one of whom turned out to be the wife of one of the victims. When the women were medically examined, it was reported that they had all concealed human teeth in their own genitalia. I was not present when the women were tried and convicted of murder, but it was a horrifying crime, and the Governor agreed with the advice of Executive Council not to commute the three death sentences.

Very few murders in Tanganyika ever got mentioned in the national press in Britain, but it annoyed me that some British newspapers reported the case under the headline 'Witches executed in Tanganyika'. This was misleading. The women were executed for murder, not for the practice of witchcraft.

The last station which I visited with Stapledon on this safari was Mahenge, in Ulanga District, where I later served for a full tour. Here Stapledon also presented the Queen's Certificate and Badge of Honour to a respected African. The Head Boma Messenger, Kilosa Mhali, could not read or write, but he was a man of great integrity with immense knowledge of the whole district. I again interpreted for Stapledon. As he was speaking, the faces of the crowd seemed to be getting larger and smaller in front of me and the Boma compound to be swaying to and fro, and I thought I was going to collapse.

After the ceremony, there was a small party in the District Officer's house, and a man whom I did not know came and sat beside me. He told me he was Dr Butler, the Medical Officer, and said he was taking me at once to hospital for tests. He diagnosed malaria, and refused to allow me to travel back by road to Dar until the fever had subsided. He prescribed twice the normal dose of medication, as I was so much larger than the average patient, and I went back to Dar two days later, after my colleagues had already returned. Simba, the deputy head driver, stayed behind with me and drove me back to Dar as the only passenger in one of the Chevrolet cars.

In 1958, when I was posted to Mahenge, I loved it. I never associated it with my first experience of malaria, but my illness while I was on safari with the Stapledons reinforced my strong prejudice against Mtwara.

Sam Twining completed his contract of service as ADC soon after that safari, and a young Assistant Superintendent of Police called Don Ring took over from him on a temporary basis until the Twinings came back from leave. While he was in England, Twining had appointed a young man called David Suckling to become his new ADC and Assistant Private Secretary. David had had a distinguished career at school and had just completed his national service as a second lieutenant in the Royal Signals, the same corps in which I had myself been commissioned on national service. He was able and hard-working, and got on extremely well with the Twinings and with everyone else. I found him a delightful colleague and a very good friend.

The Wildlife of Northern Tanganyika

Not long after Sir Edward Twining returned from leave, he decided to pay another visit to Northern Province, which he had already visited several times. There were plenty of good reasons for him to pay special attention to Northern Province. The Chagga tribe, who lived on the foothills of Mount Kilimanjaro, were diligent and progressive coffee-growers, and were more responsive than some other tribes to encouragement to increase their productivity and the prosperity of their own area and of the country as a whole.

There was also a political aspect to his safaris to the northern part of Tanganyika. During my first tour of service, when I was still in Southern Highlands Province, I had never heard an African mention the Mau Mau rebellion which began among the Kikuyu in Kenya in 1952. Tukuyu and Iringa are both a very long way from Nairobi. Northern Province, on the other hand, was in direct contact with the Kenya border, and Twining had already taken prompt and effective action to deploy a very small group of Tanganyikan soldiers and police to remove suspected ringleaders of the rising, and to prevent the bloodshed and violence of disaffected Kikuyu tribesmen in Kenya from spreading southwards into Arusha and Moshi Districts. He wanted to retain the loyalty of Chagga and Arusha tribes. He also wanted to reassure those European farmers who lived in Northern Province that the Government had not forgotten about them, and would continue to do its best to protect them and their families in any emergency. He travelled frequently to Arusha and Moshi to make sure that the measures which he had planned were being implemented effectively. Arusha also had a small lodge where the Governor and his staff could stay without causing inconvenience to other people.

The programme of our safari on this occasion included visits to the main National Parks and Conservation Areas in the north of Tanganyika. Twining got great pleasure from watching wildlife, and he also wanted to see what progress was being made in improving the existing roads in the Serengeti, and the construction of a new road down the south side of the Ngorongoro Crater.

The Serengeti National Park is one of most famous wildlife sanctuaries in the world. It provides a habitat for vast numbers and an immense variety of large and small game animals. It has herbivorous mammals such as elephant, rhino, buffalo, giraffe, zebra, wildebeeste, impala, and gazelle. The biggest animals can generally protect themselves from attack by other living creatures, with the exception of man, but the smaller ones provide food for killers like lion, leopard, cheetah, and for reptiles such as pythons and crocodiles. Certain other carnivorous animals such as hyenas are scavengers, who subsist largely by capturing and sharing amongst themselves the carcasses of animals which they have not themselves killed.

The magnificent television films made in recent years by such people as David Attenborough have helped to make viewers in

Wildebeest

Britain aware of the incredible beauty of wildlife in Africa, and also of the cruelty which exists in the animal world. Nowadays, whenever I watch such films, I always find myself sympathising with the victim. I feel relief when a zebra escapes from a lion. I admire the grace of a mother cheetah, who uses her amazing speed to capture a gazelle with which to feed her cubs, but is then deprived of her kill by a group of marauding hyenas. I feel sorry both for the dead gazelle and the hungry cheetah cubs, and, while I accept that it is absurd to sit in moral judgement on animals, I tend to regard the behaviour of the hyenas as unsporting.

The struggle between animal predator and animal victim has gone on from time immemorial. Until comparatively recently, some sort of equilibrium was generally maintained, but human beings are now capable of upsetting the balance.

There is always likely to be controversy when the interests of humans conflict with the interests of animals. In contemporary Britain, there are

Impala

clashes between animal rights supporters and those who favour blood sports. My own view lies somewhere in between the two extremes. I am not a vegetarian, but I have never owned a gun and I regard killing animals simply for pleasure as wrong.

In East Africa, wildlife plays a far more important part in the lives of rural farmers and nomadic cattle-owners than it does in Britain. Traditionally, a typical rural African regards a wild animal either as a valuable supplement to a poor diet, or as an enemy who invades his plantations, destroys his crops, and sometimes even kills his cattle or his children. He has no qualms about killing wild animals, and the courage and skill of a good hunter is admired by the rest of his tribe. So long as the hunters were armed only with spears or bows and arrows and did not seek to make money by selling trophies, hunting did not seriously affect the numbers of wild animals.

When firearms became more common and more sophisticated, the situation changed. Those people who enjoyed killing could get their excitement at little risk to

Hyena

SnKpaddard.

Cheetah

themselves by using guns. I once heard an elderly American missionary boasting of how, in the days before the game laws were tightened, he 'once killed ninety zebra in one day, and just couldn't get too tired of shooting them'. He was not the only one who got pleasure from killing.

Others killed wild animals for profit, selling the trophies to black market traders who exported them illegally. Rhino horn is said to restore virility. Ivory, and the skins of animals such as leopard, are also sold for very high prices. During the time when the game laws were not very strict and were hard to enforce, with too few Game Scouts patrolling too large areas, the numbers of elephant, rhino, and leopard plummeted. Rhino, in particular, faced the danger of extinction.

That sort of mass destruction of animals brought about a change in public opinion world-wide. People began to accept that, unless effective measures were taken to protect animals, there might in the foreseeable future be no more animals left to protect.

Quite apart from the ethical isssues involved, tourism was another factor which helped to curb the slaughter of wild animals. Development of air travel was likely to raise the number of tourists, and the Government regarded this as desirable, and accepted that people from prosperous developed countries would want to visit Africa to see animals living in their natural habitat. Wild animals would therefore bring in more money to a poor country if they were alive.

In 1951, a new Fauna Conservation Ordinance was enacted to protect Tanganyika's wildlife. Before this change in the law, Africans had been permitted to hunt most of the commoner forms of game animal without a licence, but that concession was subject to serious abuse, and, under the new Ordinance, Africans were required to obtain a licence from their local Native Authority. Non-Africans paid varying fees to hunt different types of animal, and the numbers they were allowed to shoot were more severely restricted than before.

The results of the new law were generally beneficial, though it did not eliminate poaching completely. Organised gangs responded by investing in more equipment, including fast four-wheel-drive vehicles, and by putting up their prices. Illicit trophies became harder to handle and involved a greater risk of prosecution, but the principle of conserving game for the benefit of future generations cut no ice with those who made money from poaching or by selling trophies on the black market.

Even the growth of legitimate tourism also led to controversy. The Government had to make difficult decisions about how the revenue from the sale of game licences should be distributed. It could be spent for the development of the country as a whole, or to improve the local infrastrucure of roads and campsites in order to attract more tourists, or to compensate the local nomadic tribesmen, such as the Masai, who had traditionally been allowed to graze their cattle in areas that became designated as Game Reserves.

The problem was not just one of how to spend the revenue from game licences. Income from tourism depends on the economic situation in other parts of the world over which Tanganyika had no control, and on the competition from other tourist countries. The economy is improved by a thriving tourist industry attracting many visitors, but critics claim that the traditional character of a game park is harmed when it is full of four-wheel-drive vehicles all clustering round the herds of animals, with tourists clicking away at their cameras as fast as they can. Many of the tourists are wealthy enough to expect to camp in very luxurious conditions, but an unspoilt environment can easily be damaged by creating the kind of amenities which such tourists require.

Wild animals, of course, do not make any organised protests, but they all need to be adequately protected if they are to continue to flourish, and, incidentally, to give joy to future generations. People are gradually becoming aware of the number of species which are endangered, but there are still too many people who are not bothered if some rare and beautiful species become extinct.

Naturalists have identified about a hundred different species of mammal in Tanganyika's National Parks and Conservation Areas. Many exist in enormous herds, but comparatively few of them are brightly coloured. It is in the interests of both predators and their victims to remain as inconspicuous as possible.

The number of species of bird is considerably larger. There are more than three hundred different species of bird to be found in one park alone, the Lake Manyara National Park. Like mammals, birds can generally be divided into one of four main categories, based on what they eat. There are birds which eat only seeds and others

Leopard

which eat insects. Larger birds of prey, such as eagles, eat animals which they have themselves killed. There are also some unlovely birds such as vultures, which can be compared to hyenas, and eat the remains of animals which other predators have already killed.

Many of Tanganyika's birds, both large and small, are brilliantly coloured. Their dazzling colours – emerald green, scarlet, white, pink, golden yellow, violet, sapphire blue – help them to attract mates. They certainly give delight to bird-watchers from all over the world.

Our tour through Northern Province included visits to all the best known of Tanganyika's Game Reserves and Conservation Areas – the Serengeti Plains, Lake Manyara, the Ngorongoro Crater and the Ngurdoto Crater. The Serengeti is the largest and probably the most famous, stretching over vast open plains with rocky outcrops, and providing a habitat for huge numbers of zebra, wildebeeste, gazelle, elephant and lion. Lake Manyara National Park is much smaller, but the terrain is so varied that it provides a home for an even greater variety of wildlife than the Serengeti. The Ngorongoro Crater is now designated separately as a Conservation Area, but when I visited it with the Governor it still formed part of the Serengeti National Park. It covers about 100 square miles, and the crater is about 2,000 feet deep. The approach road from Arusha and Lake Manyara runs along the edge of the crater, mostly at a height of over 7,000 feet. When we visited it, a new road was being built down the south side of the crater but it was only passable, with extreme care, for four-wheel-drive vehicles. The Ngurdoto Crater is the smallest and probably the least well-known of the Game Reserves we visited. The crater is only one and a half miles across, and there is no access to human beings, who can observe the wildlife below from various vantage points along the rim of the crater.

I had never seen anything to compare with the wildlife in the Tanganyikan Game Reserves, and I will never forget the glorious

days we spent there. Perhaps
the sight which impressed
me more than any other was
when I looked down on the
animals in the Ngurdoto
Crater and saw a mother
rhinoceros with her new-
born baby. Rhinoceroses are
not renowned for grace,
beauty, or intelligence, but
this mother and baby were
completely secure in their
environment, and each
seemed to show for the other
a kind of love which I found
incredibly moving.

We spent each night in the Safari Lodge, where the altitude
made it very cold. In countries near the equator, the sun always
sets throughout the year at about six o'clock. After darkness fell,
we spent each evening chatting for an hour or two round the big
log fires in the Safari Lodge before retiring to bed in our cabins,
with umpteen blankets to keep us warm.

I have never returned, but I can quite understand why so many
tourists regard the wildlife sanctuaries of Tanganyika as being
the best place in the world to spend a holiday.

The Governor's Train

All forms of transport have their advantages and disadvantages.
The best way to visit the wildlife sanctuaries in the hilly parts of
northern Tanganyika is by four-wheel-drive car, but they are not
luxurious, even for passengers of average size. For someone as
tall as me, a long journey in a Landrover can be extremely uncomfortable.

I am not very fond of air travel either. I prefer to watch the land-
scape at ground level rather than looking out from the window of a
plane over the tops of clouds. I regard single-engined planes with
great suspicion, but I also had little confidence in the two-engined
Percival Prince which the Twinings used from time to time. It
bounced alarmingly in turbulent conditions, and even when it was
calm I still found the legroom cramped. My faith in the plane was
shaken further one day when I was sitting beside Twining at the

front of the aircraft and he asked me to fetch him a file from a dispatch box at the back end of the plane. The sudden shift of my weight caused the plane to climb much too steeply, and then to stall. When I returned to the front of the plane carrying the file, the plane started to dive. It seemed to take a very long time to resume its normal pattern of level flight, and when we eventually landed safely at our destination, the government pilot, Frank Cadwallader, an outspoken Cornishman, used some graphic language to tell Twining how crazy it was to send someone as heavy as me from one end of the plane to the other while we were airborne. He said that if we had been flying at a lower altitude, he might not have been able to prevent a crash.

Although many of the most spectacular parts of Tanganyika could not be reached by rail, travelling in the Governor's train was without doubt the method of transportation which I enjoyed more than any other.

Within a few weeks of their return from leave in Britain, the Twinings started to make plans for another safari, this time to parts of Eastern, Central, Western, and Lake Provinces. For this journey we would not be entirely dependent on cars, but would travel most of the way on the Governor's special train.

I had greatly enjoyed the journey I had made as a first-class passenger on an ordinary train from Dar to the village of Itigi when I was travelling to take up my appointment in Tukuyu, but the Governor's train was incomparably better.

The Governor's Train

The train was pulled by the smartest engine that East African Railways and Harbours could provide, a wood-burning Garratt locomotive in a class named after East African Governors. Our train was pulled by an engine called the 'Sir Edward Twining'. When the Governor was on board the train, the front of the engine was decorated with two Tanganyikan flags, one on the left side and the other on the right, and in the middle was a shield decorated with the national emblem, a giraffe. The train travelled no faster than ordinary trains, as most of the track, for safety reasons, was subject to a speed limit of 20 mph. The train was exceptionally long. It had carriages for the Governor and his wife. These put me in mind of pictures of the trains that Queen Victoria had used in the nineteenth century. The accommodation for the Governor's personal staff and various senior officials who had been invited to accompany His Excellency was almost as luxurious. At the rear end of the train was an observation car. There was an extremely comfortable dining car, with a galley next to it. The train also had second and third-class carriages for a nucleus of Government House domestic staff, postal staff to receive and dispatch documents for the Governor and any officials who might be accompanying him, for the engine driver and his assistant, and for the askaris of the Tanganyika Police Band. There were also a number of open trucks to transport the cars that were needed for local travel.

Many of the country's over fifty District Headquarters were situated on or close to the railway line between Dar es Salaam, Kigoma, and Mwanza. At places that were regarded as important, the train usually stopped for hours or even days while Twining and his retinue greeted the crowds and then travelled by car to visit the establishments included in the safari programme. There were also many railway stations in tiny villages where the train had to stop. The engine used wood fuel, and at every halt the railway staff needed to replace stocks of firewood and water. Even at the villages which consisted of just two or three mud huts and a grubby little shop, the train had to stop for at least half an hour. At even very small stations, the Police Band marched up and down the platform playing military music until the train was ready to continue its journey. Twining always took advantage of the opportunity to walk about and greet the people who had come to welcome him.

At bigger stations we were always met by large crowds, which included government officials, local leaders of every community and race, peasant farmers, their wives, and hordes of children.

Dancers danced. Drummers beat their drums. Their wives trilled the traditional noise which African women make to welcome distinguished visitors. A few local drummers gave up trying to compete against the Police Band, and stopped their drumming when the band struck up, but others took it as a challenge to drum even louder than before. The noise everywhere was so loud that conversation became impossible, but the atmosphere was always exhilarating. If a local chief presented him with a gift of the skin of an animal, a shield, or a tribal warrior's headdress, Twining took great pleasure in wearing them all as he walked about in the crowd.

I have, since my childhood, been fascinated by steam-engines, and at several of the smaller stopping places I slipped away from the crowd to watch the work of the engine driver. After I had done this two or three times, the engine driver saw that I was interested, and we started to chat. He explained what he was doing and he then invited me to come up on to the footplate and travel with him for the next part of the journey. This was an invitation I did not want to refuse, and I went and asked Twining whether he would need me during the next hour or so. When the train moved off, I was not in the observation car but on board the engine. A few minutes later, the driver invited me to take over the controls of the engine while he supervised what I was doing.

It is difficult to find words to describe the excitement of driving a real engine over the plains of Central Tanganyika. The sense of power I felt was something I had never experienced until then, and have never experienced since. When I looked back along the train, it thrilled me to see all the carriages that we were pulling. Looking forward, the vast expanse of open country with a single track railway line running through it provided a view which the ordinary railway passenger does not see from the windows on the side of the train. From time to time, we spotted a few giraffe and smaller mammals beside the track, and the driver told me to sound the whistle. I was not very good at this. The whistle was controlled by a cable with a handle at the end, reminiscent of a nineteenth-century lavatory chain. When I pulled it, nothing at first happened, but the driver nevertheless told me to release the handle. I was not keen to run over any giraffe, and held on to the knob until the whistle started to make a noise. Unfortunately, the blast of the whistle then continued for the same length of time that I had held the knob down, albeit several seconds later, and the driver reproved me for making so much unnecessary noise. I failed to learn my lesson, and nearly every time we saw children, cattle, or other animals near the railway line I again blew a blast on the whistle which lasted much longer than I had intended.

As the sun went down, I thanked the driver for letting me have an experience I will never forget, and I returned to my companions in the observation car.

The Governor had invited two members of Executive Council, the Member for Local Government, Jim Rowe, and the Member for Lands and Mines, Andy Pike, to accompany him on his safari. Andy Pike's wife was the only doctor who had impressed me favourably when I had been an inpatient in the Ocean Road Hospital in Dar the previous year. Margaret Twining, the Governor's niece and the sister of his former ADC, Sam, also came with us while she was spending a few weeks' holiday in Tanganyika.

After sundown each evening I was asked to join Twining, Jim Rowe, and Andy Pike for a game of bridge. The routine was always the same – I partnered Twining and Jim Rowe partnered Andy Pike. We played for very small stakes, and we were quite evenly matched. One evening, Jim Rowe and Andy Pike would win a few shillings, the next evening Twining and I would get our revenge. Twining always played his cards very well, but he had a tendency to overbid extravagantly. The other three players were rather more orthodox. It was agreed at the start of the journey that whoever won would give his winnings to Lady Twining for the benefit of her favourite charity.

Each evening I kept the score. I was asked to combine the winnings or losses of that particular evening's play with the balance carried forward from previous evenings, and to calculate a running cumulative total of who was up or down since the safari began. It was a pleasant and inexpensive way to spend our evenings.

When we reached Mwanza, Twining and I were just a few shillings up, and Jim Rowe and Andy Pike prepared to pay their gambling debts directly to Lady Twining for her to pass on to the Tanganyika Council for Women. However, Lady Twining was not at all pleased that we had kept a running total rather than giving her money in respect of each evening's winnings separately. She accused us all of behaviour on a par with stealing money from the church collection. Lady Twining had many excellent qualities, but a sense of humour was not one of them, and it infuriated her even more when Twining himself thought the situation extremely funny, and told us emphatically not to pay each evening's debts separately, although Jim Rowe, Andy Pike and I all volunteered to do so.

We left the train at Mwanza, and the Twinings stayed for a few days in the house of the Provincial Commissioner, Stanley Walden, while I stayed with Hans Cory, the Government Anthropologist, and his wife Lily, whose house was directly adjacent to Stanley Walden's.

The Twinings decided to spend a quiet evening, and I was given the pleasant task of escorting Margaret Twining to a party hosted by the Deputy Provincial Commissioner, John Bradley, and his wife.

The party was due to start at seven o'clock, but at about six o'clock Lady Twining asked me to go back to the station to collect something which she needed but had left on the train. When I got to the train, it was all locked up, and I had to find someone with a key to unlock it before I could get what Lady Twining wanted.

I was still tying my black tie and buttoning up my trousers when I heard Twining bellowing in Hans Cory's garden, 'Where's my bloody Private Secretary?' Hans Cory's dog was not used to strangers making that sort of noise on his territory, and growled ferociously at Twining, who got even angrier. He shouted at me that I was totally useless and would be returned with ignominy to the Provincial Administration the following day. He forbade me to take Margaret to the Bradleys' party, and told me I was to spend the evening by myself in Hans Cory's guest room.

I thought Twining was treating me most unfairly, but I did not say so, and crept back to my bedroom as ordered. A few minutes later, Stanley Walden came over from his house and told me to ignore the orders I had been given by Twining and take Margaret to the party as originally planned. I was very uneasy about disobeying the Governor when he was already in such a foul temper, but Walden told me that a good officer always complied with the last order given to him, even if it countermanded a previous order given by someone else. I eventually let myself be persuaded, and took Margaret to the party. It was not her fault that I did not enjoy it at all.

I had a miserable night. The next morning, before my own servant Lameck came to call me, Ali, the Governor's personal retainer who had been with Twining for over 20 years, knocked on my door and handed me an envelope addressed to me in Twining's handwriting. I opened it with trepidation, dreading what I thought it might contain. The opening words reassured me. Twining asked me to forgive him for the appalling way he had spoken to me, and said that, if I could manage to forgive him for such behaviour, he would like me to stay on as his Private Secretary. The choice was mine.

I had been totally unprepared for Twining's outburst the previous evening, but it surprised me just as much that a man in his position of power should have had the humility to make such a contrite apology.

I got dressed and went over to have breakfast in the Provincial Commissioner's house. Stanley Walden was waiting for me in his front hall, and asked me to come into his study for a moment before I greeted Twining. He said that he thought I would find Twining very different now from how he had been the previous evening, but he wanted to give me a word of advice: 'You are His Excellency's Private Secretary, not Lady Twining's.'

If Twining had carried out his threat to get rid of me, I think I would have felt very bitter about it, but the episode actually deepened my affection for him. I came to see that the great man did have outbursts of rage, but was honest enough to admit it. I was also very thankful that Stanley Walden had had the courage to stand up to the Governor by coming to the defence of a junior colleague.

The following evening the Governor was the guest of honour at a lavish party held in the house and garden of an Asian lawyer called Chopra, who was also a prominent Member of Legislative Council. I occasionally heard comments by a few jealous people who criticised Chopra for having become rich simply through the patronage of a diamond miner who had struck it lucky. Negative remarks like that failed to acknowledge Chopra's personal contribution to the success of Dr Williamson, who owned the Diamond Mine at Mwadui. Chopra had supported Williamson financially for a long time before the mine became profitable, and his business acumen, legal expertise, integrity, and unfailing loyalty made an incalculable contribution to the success of Williamson's Diamonds Ltd. It was not surprising that Williamson, who had no family of his own, eventually repaid Chopra by making him a very rich man.

The party went with a swing. Chopra's lawns sloped gently down to Lake Victoria, and the moon reflected in the lake looked lovely. The Police Band had been engaged to play gentle background music in the garden, and all the guests were enjoying a delicious buffet supper with abundant alcoholic or non-alcoholic drinks.

Suddenly a spotlight came on, focussed towards the top of a tall rocky outcrop in the garden. On the top of the outcrop a police bandsman was standing alone, with the light reflected by the polished brass buttons of his uniform and the polished brass of his instrument. He put a posthorn to his lips, and began to play with a beauty of tone and a technical virtuosity which I found astonishing. Years later, I was reminded of his playing when I heard a recording by the young American trumpeter Wynton Marsalis of Haydn's *Trumpet Concerto*. I was already aware of the fact that many Africans were naturally talented musicians, and I suspected that some policemen joined the police band because they wanted to play an instrument well, but could not afford to buy a good quality musical instrument for themselves. Even so, I wondered who had taught this young soloist to perform so brilliantly.

A few of the guests listened to him in rapt silence, but many more just went on chattering. They guffawed uproariously, and seemed not to notice that a superb musician was giving a performance which would have been applauded rapturously by concertgoers anywhere in the world. Such performances of live music were extremely rare in Tanganyika, and this one failed to get the appreciation it deserved.

Not long after we had returned from Lake Province, I heard that there was to be a live concert of chamber music in Dar, and I arranged to go to it. A pianist, a violinist, and a cellist from Germany, forming a group called the Wiesbaden Trio, were to perform works by various composers whose music I normally enjoyed very much.

The hall was full of people who, like me, were expecting a pleasant evening. There was no question of the musicians having to compete against chatter from people who did not want to listen to them, and the programme notes indicated that the performers were experienced and competent musicians. When they appeared on the platform, they were all dressed in formal clothes that would have been appropriate in Germany in winter, but were not the ideal garments to wear on the coast of tropical Africa in the weeks leading up to the hot season.

The playing of the first work they performed was mediocre, but I hoped it would improve as the evening wore on. Sadly, it did not. After the interval, the one work on their programme was Beethoven's *Archduke* Trio, which I already knew quite well from a historic recording made by Cortot, Thibaut, and Casals. Unfortunately, the hall was not air-conditioned, and the three German performers were unable to cope with the heat and humidity. They played more and more wrong notes, and, by the time they reached the finale, they had abandoned any attempt to play in time with one another. They were so sodden with sweat that they looked as if they had just clambered out of a swimming pool. The evening failed to live up to my hopes, and gave me far less pleasure than the police bandsman's splendid performance beside Lake Victoria.

Love at First Sight

The climate on the coast in Tanganyika is quite pleasant during the months from about June to September, but towards Christmas each year the temperature steadily rises to over 90° fahrenheit, and the humidity becomes oppressive. Expatriates start to feel listless and uncomfortable, and many, myself included, suffer from prickly heat, an itchy skin condition caused by blockage of the sweat glands.

During the 1950s, those expatriates who were able to do so liked to escape to a hilly and more temperate part of the country. Twining and his family and staff took advantage of the tradition that Governors used to spend the weeks before and after Christmas each year at a lodge in the Usambara Mountains in Tanga Province, nearly 5,000 feet above sea level. When we set off from Dar, I felt sorry for my colleagues who would have to endure the discomfort of working in the Secretariat.

The Governor's Lodge was a mile or two outside the small town of Lushoto. It was built in the Dutch colonial style, and had a lovely garden and magnificent views over the surrounding countryside. Lushoto itself was generally regarded as one of the most attractive stations in the whole country, and there were several hotels where expatriates liked to spend their local leave.

As in Government House in Dar, there was a wooden sentry box with a visitors' book at the bottom of the drive leading to the lodge. Each morning Twining was given a list of the names of those who had signed the book the previous day. Sometimes he decided to invite those who had signed to come to a meal, which was usually much more informal than meals at Government House.

A few days before Christmas 1955, Twining invited Jennifer Stevenson and her mother to come to lunch on Christmas Eve. Jennifer was a young English teacher working at the Government African Girls' Secondary School in Tabora, and she was spending two weeks' local leave with her mother at a nearby hotel called

The Governor's Lodge at Lushoto

the Magamba Country Club. Jennifer and her mother had not planned to sign the Governor's book, but one of the other guests at the Country Club, a Member of Legislative Council called Alec le Maitre, offered them a lift in his car to the shops in Lushoto. As they were passing the gate of the Lodge, Alec le Maitre and his wife insisted that Jennifer and her mother should both sign the visitors' book without delay.

I played no part in Twining's decision to invite Jennifer and her mother to lunch. When the two guests arrived, however, I happened to be the person who opened the front door of the lodge to welcome them, and as soon as I saw Jennifer I knew at once that this was the girl I was going to marry. She was extremely pretty, but it was not just her beauty which captivated me from the first instant I saw her. Her smile, her voice, and her sparkling eyes all combined to make me fall totally in love with her. I still do not understand how I was so sure about my feelings for her, but over lunch I had no thought for anything except the lovely girl I had just met.

I do not remember very much about the lunch party itself. Jennifer and her mother sat beside the Governor. Jennifer told me later that he showed real interest in the work she was doing at Tabora Girls' School. I was seated at the other end of the table beside Lady Twining, and I did not hear much of the conversation which Twining was having with Jennifer and her mother, but Jennifer also told me that Twining had happened to mention that his Private Secretary was 'intelligent, musical, and unpunctual', and Jennifer, half an hour after I had fallen in love with her, thought that a man with the qualities which Twining described would suit her admirably.

On Christmas Day, the Twinings went to the Anglican Church in Lushoto, and David Suckling and I accompanied them. Jennifer and her mother were also in the congregation, and after the service I wished them both a happy Christmas.

The congregation also included Muriel Pelham-Johnson. PJ, as she was generally known, was the Assistant Director of Girls' Education and Jennifer's boss. She happened to be spending a few days' local leave in Lushoto. I was told later, by several different people, that as soon as PJ got back to Dar she had complained bitterly to all and sundry that the Governor's Private Secretary was going to marry one of her best teachers. This would cause her a problem, because whenever a Woman Education Officer got married, this meant that she would accompany her husband wherever he might be stationed. This normally meant, for a teacher in a Government Secondary School, that she would have to resign prematurely from the Education Department. I have not the remotest idea how PJ spotted as soon as she saw us that Jennifer and I were already in love. It was less than twenty-four hours since we had met for the first time. However, PJ had plenty of experience of observing the symptoms, and her diagnosis was absolutely right.

Christmas also provided an example of how the Twinings took trouble to choose presents that would give pleasure to the recipient. I had bought an electric record player in Dar, but had very few long-playing records. I had happened to mention casually to Twining some months earlier that my favourite tenor was Jussi Björling, and he remembered and gave me a present of recordings of two complete operas with Björling in the leading role.

On the evening of Boxing Day, I was in my bungalow in the grounds of the lodge listening to my new records when I was visited by the District Officer, John Cooke. John had done the Colonial Service Course with me at Cambridge, and we had travelled out to

Africa together on board the *Llanstephan Castle*. We were very good friends. He invited me to join him for a drink at the Magamba Country Club. Knowing that Jennifer was staying there, I did not need much persuading. When John and I got there, I found Jennifer and spent the rest of the evening chatting quietly with her in a corner. Jennifer's mother had already gone to bed, and John did not take it amiss that I neglected him and left him talking with other friends who were drinking at the bar.

Marriages in any community always include a proportion which are unsuccessful, but the life-style of expatriates in the overseas civil service meant that the proportion of unhappy marriages was probably higher than in most other communities. One contributory factor was the very limited opportunities which officials, male or female, had to meet suitable potential partners while they were serving in small remote up-country districts. Sometimes the only bachelor on an up-country station became lonely, and found consolation in the company of the only spinster, usually the nursing sister, and drifted into marriage with her. The choice of potential partners was much wider in the Secretariat in Dar es Salaam or in a Provincial Headquarters, but that was not a factor which seemed important to those who had responsibility for the postings of unmarried expatriate officers. Whatever the reason, a high proportion of the wives of European officials had been nursing sisters before getting married. Their marriages were often successful, but sometimes after a year or two together the couple found that they had little in common, and drifted apart. When that happened, the whole expatriate community in the locality quickly heard about the situation.

What was still more likely to lead to an unsuccessful marriage was when a lonely bachelor went on home leave determined to woo and win an attractive bride while he was in Britain, and to bring her back in triumph to live with him in Africa. Bachelors on home leave for six months had plenty of opportunity to meet pretty girls. After two or three years spent living on his own in Africa with no family to support, a bachelor usually had enough money to entertain the lady of his choice in a fairly lavish way. Many of the women who met and married colonial service officials while they were on home leave had formed the mistaken impression that their admirers were fun-loving playboys who were only interested in their girlfriends. The girls who got married in such circumstances were often quite unsophisticated, and many had never left England before. When they accompanied their new husbands to Tanganyika, many of the young wives were shocked to find that their husbands had very demanding jobs which really interested them. The new wife was not the only or even the main interest in her husband's life.

A young wife newly arrived from Britain had other problems as well. Her husband had already been in Africa for at least one tour of service, and had got used to a life with African domestic servants who cooked for him, did his shopping, washed his clothes, and kept the house clean. Most employers managed to communicate with their domestic servants in Swahili, but a new wife who had not yet mastered that language had to rely on her husband to communicate with the servants and make the housekeeping arrangements with them. This undermined the self-confidence of many young expatriate women.

Even those who had previously prided themselves on being domesticated found that conditions in Tanganyika made the tasks of an expatriate housewife extremely difficult. There were a few towns which had electricity and a piped water supply, but most small up-country stations did not. Even in stations which had electricity, it was often unreliable and expensive, and cooking was nearly always done on a wood-burning stove in a smoke-filled and cockroach-infested kitchen which was built separately from the main part of the house. Drinking water had to be boiled and filtered, and in the dry season in many arid parts of the country there was too little water to have regular showers or to flush the lavatories. Lighting was usually provided by means of paraffin-fuelled pressure lamps which were not very easy to operate, and gave out more heat than light. A wife who had just arrived from Britain often found it very hard to get used to living without any of the modern conveniences which wives in Britain normally expect to have in their homes.

Some settled down magnificently, and supported their husbands in everything they did, but there were others who showed little interest in Africa or their husbands' work, and detested being left on their own when their husbands went on safari. It was not surprising that a proportion of the men who got married while on home leave retired prematurely from the colonial service when faced with the choice between their career or marriage to a wife who hated Africa.

For the first few days after I met Jennifer, I tried to tell myself that I was being every kind of fool, and knew next to nothing about the character or interests of the girl I was thinking of asking to marry me. My parents had not married in haste, but they certainly repented at leisure, and my mother in particular had repeatedly expressed the view that love at first sight was an illusion and could never last. However, every conversation I had with Jennifer strengthened my certainty that she and I agreed about all the important things in life.

We both loved our work in Africa. We had ourselves made the choice to work there. We both had a very similar level of education in independent single-sex boarding schools, where we had both been regarded as gifted academically, but where we were not particularly happy. Jennifer had gone on from school to get a good honours degree in English at St Andrews University and she had qualified with distinction on a postgraduate teaching course at Bristol University. While I was at university I had involved myself in the activities of my college's mission in a slum parish in South London. Jennifer had been asked by her university to take part in a research project which involved her living as a lodger in a council housing estate under the same roof as a multi-problem family in which the father eventually served a prison sentence for living off his wife's immoral earnings. Jennifer and I shared the same views about religion and politics, and our recreational interests were similar, although until we returned to England together Jennifer had not had any interest in sport, especially rowing. We both loved classical music and choral singing, and her collection of gramophone records exactly duplicated many of my own favourite recordings in the collection I had brought to Africa with me. She had even brought her piano out to Tanganyika with her.

A few days after Christmas, the Governor called me into his office and asked me, almost in the traditional words used by a concerned father, whether my intentions towards Jennifer were serious and honourable. I do not remember exactly what I said in reply, but Twining got the message. He then told me that he thought Jennifer was a lovely girl, and that if David Suckling would agree to carry out my routine duties until Jennifer returned to Tabora, I could take her out every day in my car, escorting a group of visitors who were staying at the lodge, while they were being driven on sightseeing trips by a Government House driver. David was happy to agree to this arrangement, and Jennifer and I are still deeply grateful to him for having done my work as well as his own for the next few days.

On the afternoon before Jennifer was due to leave Lushoto, it was raining quite hard, and she and I went for a walk together on our own, as the guests at the lodge did not want to get wet. Jennifer was wearing a raincoat and a waterproof hat which were useful rather than elegant, but her sensible clothes did not discourage me. I decided that, even though we had only known each other for ten days, I did not want her to go back to Tabora before I had asked her to marry me. For about an hour we walked together in complete silence. At last I said just four words, 'Will you marry me?' and Jennifer answered, 'Yes'. As proposals of marriage go, it could hardly have been shorter, but our marriage has now lasted for over forty years, and we cannot imagine any other partners with whom we could have been so happy.

We returned to the Magamba Country Club, and Jennifer told her mother that she had accepted my offer of marriage. When I got back to the lodge, I told Sir Edward Twining, and he immediately invited Jennifer and her mother to remain in Lushoto for a few more days, and to come and stay with him in the lodge as his guests. He undertook to explain to Jennifer's headmistress that he was personally responsible for her returning to school a few days late after her two weeks' local leave had come to an end.

The Countess's Daughter

As soon as Jennifer's mother heard of our engagement, she invited me to her room in order to congratulate me and wish us both well, to say nice things about me as a future son-in-law, and to tell me in private about Jennifer's background and the circumstances of her birth. Jennifer's mother, Frances Countess Lloyd George of Dwyfor, was exceptionally charming and intelligent, but I did not accept the accuracy of the explanation she gave me then, and what I have since learnt has not made me change my opinion.

Jennifer's mother was born in 1888. She was the daughter of a Scottish father, John Stevenson. Her mother was partly French and partly Italian. Frances was educated at Clapham High School, the same school that my own mother attended. Another pupil at the school was Mair Lloyd George, the oldest and favourite daughter of her father. Mair was a beautiful and sweet-natured girl who died at the age of seventeen, after an emergency operation for appendicitis.

Frances went on from school to take a degree in classics at Royal Holloway College, an attainment which was uncommon for girls at that time. After she graduated, she was employed for a short while as a teacher in Wimbledon.

In 1911, Lloyd George consulted the headmistress of Clapham

High School to ask her to propose a suitable person to become the private tutor of Mair's younger sister Megan. The young woman whom the headmistress recommended was Frances Stevenson. She was well qualified for the job, spoke fluent French, and was a talented musician. Megan in due course became Frances's bitterest enemy, but when she was a child she and her tutor got on well. Frances described Megan in her autobiography as 'an enchanting child'.

In 1912, Lloyd George, who was then Chancellor of the Exchequer and forty-nine years old, invited Frances to become his Private Secretary. She was an exceptionally competent and loyal Private Secretary, and was awarded the CBE at the end of the First World War in 1918. However, her relationship with Lloyd George was not just that of a private secretary to a cabinet minister. Lloyd George had told Frances that he was in love with her, and in spite of the difference in their ages she fell in love with him. Her feelings for Lloyd George were in conflict with her conventional Victorian upbringing, and at first she had been hesitant about accepting the post 'on his terms', which involved being not only his private secretary but also his secret mistress. Lloyd George made it very clear to Frances that he did not want his career to be ruined by the sort of scandal that had caused the downfall a few years previously of Charles Stewart Parnell, the Irish politician.

After Frances had taken the decision to accept Lloyd George's offer, she remained as his devoted private secretary for thirty years, having become his mistress at the beginning of 1913.

Lloyd George's first wife, Dame Margaret, who had spent most of her time in North Wales with her children while her husband was pursuing his political career in London, died in 1941. Two years later, on 23rd October 1943, Lloyd George married Frances quietly in a register office in Guildford. The following year, Lloyd George was created an earl, and his second wife became Countess Lloyd George. Lloyd George's family by his first marriage, and in particular Megan, never forgave Frances for her relationship with their father, and even vented their spite on Jennifer.

When I met Jennifer, I had already heard rumours about Lloyd George's sex life. I knew nothing about the relationship of Lloyd George and his private secretary, but I guessed that, as Frances had been called Stevenson before her marriage, and had given birth to her daughter Jennifer Stevenson in 1929, after she had been Lloyd George's private secretary for over fifteen years, she must have been Lloyd George's mistress as well as his private secretary. I assumed that Jennifer was illegitimate, and it did not worry me in the least. Whatever the sins of their parents, children should never be blamed for being born out of wedlock. I was therefore extremely surprised when Frances told me about what she described as 'my secret first marriage' to one of Lloyd George's political advisers, Colonel Thomas Tweed.

There are several facts which cast doubt on the explanation that Frances gave me of Jennifer's birth. Letters between Tweed and Frances indicate that they loved each other passionately, but Tweed was already married to another woman at the time Jennifer was conceived, and he was much too intelligent to risk his career and even his liberty by bigamously marrying anyone, especially the private secretary of the former Prime Minister. Jennifer's birth certificate is in the shortened form normally used for illegitimate children. In 1943, when Lloyd George and Frances were married in Guildford Register Office, their marriage certificate referred to Frances as a spinster, not as a widow or a divorced person. I have no doubt that Frances was married only once in her life, and that there is no substance at all to her claim to a secret previous marriage.

I still find the reason for her to make such a claim to me rather puzzling. Frances did not need to tell me about the circumstances surrounding Jennifer's birth, but if she felt that I, as her future son-in-law, really ought to know as much as possible about my fiancée, then I think she should have told me the truth. It has been suggested that Frances may have feared that I would be discouraged from going ahead with my engagement to Jennifer if I suspected that she was illegitimate, but if Frances genuinely thought that she could not have understood my feelings for her daughter.

I was not the only person who was told untrue stories by Frances. It is quite understandable that she did not want to jeopardise the career of Lloyd George by announcing publicly that she was his mistress, but Frances also tried to deceive Jennifer herself about her origins. The first explanation Frances gave her was the unlikely tale that Jennifer's real parents had been missionaries who had been killed in China. She then told Jennifer that she had promised not to tell 'the true story' until Jennifer reached the age of sixteen. Finally, when Jennifer was fifteen, shortly after Lloyd George had died, Frances told her the same trumped-up story that she later told me about her 'secret marriage' to Colonel Tweed.

At the suggestion of her solicitor, Frances legally adopted her own daughter while Jennifer was still a child. This adoption did not have any effect on the parental responsibility of Frances, but its aim was to provide an answer to potentially embarrassing questions.

Although Jennifer and I both accept that her parents were not married at the time she was born, the question of whether Lloyd George or Tweed was Jennifer's father is still open to doubt.

In 1915, Frances had written in her diary that she would be proud to have Lloyd George's child, and would be willing to suffer for it. She knew that this would jeopardise Lloyd George's career, however, so she had two abortions. By 1928, however, Frances had reached the age of forty, and had for some time been expressing an increasingly strong desire to have a child of her own before it was too late. Eventually Lloyd George agreed to comply with her wish. He spent Christmas 1928 with Frances, and remained with her until 12th January 1929, when he went to join his family on their winter holiday abroad. The period when Frances and Lloyd George were together covers the most probable date of Jennifer's conception. She was born on 4th October 1929.

After Lloyd George went on his winter holiday, Frances spent a few days at Torquay. On 1st February 1929, she wrote to Lloyd George from Torquay telling him that she thought she might be pregnant, and that this would 'put the seal and crown' upon their love. On 4th February, she wrote to him confirming that 'it really has happened this time, my love'.

The most obvious theory is that Lloyd George is Jennifer's father, but it is not completely certain. Unknown to Lloyd George, Colonel Tweed had also been having an affair with Frances, and he joined her in Torquay in mid-January 1929. It is just possible that he, not Lloyd George, was Jennifer's father. It is Jennifer's view that perhaps Frances herself did not know which of her two lovers was the father of her child.

Tweed could be Jennifer's father, and Frances told me that he was. However, if she told me a lie about Tweed having married her, it is of course equally possible that she also told me a lie about his being the father of her child. Many years later, after the publication of her autobiography in 1967, Frances was asked by Fyfe Robertson in a television interview whether she regretted never having had children herself, and, after a pause, she replied 'Lloyd George was my child'. Jennifer told me that she felt obliterated by her mother's apparent denial of her existence.

If we could now find out the truth about Jennifer's paternity, my preference would be for Lloyd George rather than Tweed to be her father. Lloyd George's behaviour to women was disgraceful, but he was a great Prime Minister, and he did love Jennifer's mother for a very long time. In due course he married her after his first wife died. Although he never admitted publicly that Jennifer was his daughter, he was terribly upset in 1932, when he discovered that Frances had had an affair with Tweed. Jennifer was without doubt Lloyd George's step-daughter, and he was a constant and loving figure in her life whom Jennifer always referred to as 'Taid', the Welsh for grandfather. When Lloyd George died in North Wales in 1945, Jennifer was one of the members of his family who were with him at his bedside. In contrast, Tweed took very little interest in Jennifer, although he did not seem to take much interest in his legitimate children either.

Several respected journalists and politicians have commented from time to time on the close physical resemblance between Lloyd George and Jennifer. I never met Lloyd George, but I can also see the similarity between Jennifer and a bust of Lloyd George which now belongs to her. When I saw on television a photograph of Lloyd George's eldest daughter Mair, I thought at first glance that the photograph was one of Jennifer herself as a schoolgirl, not of a beautiful teenage girl who might or might not be her half-sister. If Lloyd George had also seen this resemblance between Jennifer and his beloved daughter Mair, who died more than twenty years before Jennifer was born, that might help to explain why he always showed so much love to Jennifer.

Frances tried to justify her affair with Lloyd George by dismissing his first wife, Dame Margaret, as 'a lump of flesh possessing, like the jellyfish, the power of irritating'. She appears to have been passionately in love with Tweed, but she never stopped loving Lloyd George, even at the time that she was deceiving him. When he eventually discovered her affair with Tweed, she promised that she would not repeat her lapse, and LG was magnanimous enough to forgive them both and keep them on his staff.

I do not trust people who tell lies to me, but I find it even harder to condone the way that Frances misled her own daughter about her origins. However, there may be some extenuating circumstances. Frances always put the interests of Lloyd George above everything else. She did not hesitate to tell lies to protect him and his career, and it is possible, though it cannot be proved, that she persuaded herself that, by having a second lover, she might protect Lloyd George from scandal if it ever became known that his private secretary had become a single mother.

Last Days in Lushoto

Jennifer and I were both blissfully happy during the days that she and her mother were guests at the Governor's Lodge. Frances continued to be as charming as ever, but Jennifer told me later of her amazement at hearing her mother say that she had not enjoyed staying at the Governor's Lodge. Frances said that being the guest of the Governor had reminded her of an aspect of her career with Lloyd George which she had found uncongenial. When she was with Lloyd George, everything in the household always revolved round him. At the lodge, everything revolved round Sir Edward Twining. After ten years of being the widow of a world celebrity, Frances had come to enjoy feeling free to make her own decisions, and she missed this sort of freedom when she stayed with Twining. She never made the comment to me, and I assumed that she was enjoying her visit as much as she appeared to be.

There was another aspect to my engagement to Jennifer which Frances mentioned in letters she wrote to her friends in Britain. My career was likely to keep Jennifer and me in Africa for the rest of our working lives. This meant that she would not see her daughter as often as she wanted, and that, if we had children of our own, as we intended, she would only see them intermittently, when we came home on leave or she visited us in Africa.

When the time came for Jennifer to go back to Tabora, I missed her enormously and wrote to her by every post, but the Governor gave me an unusual task which helped to take my mind off other things.

The Director of Public Relations in Dar had submitted for the Governor's approval a draft booklet by an experienced District Commissioner who was also a very good photographer. It purported to describe the life of an Administrative Officer in Tanganyika. Its aim was to get more recruits to apply to join the service, and Twining asked me to give him my frank opinion on the draft. He also asked his younger son William, who was on a visit to Lushoto, to do the same thing. William had just graduated with first-class honours in law at Oxford, and was planning an academic career. He was also a delightful companion with a great sense of humour.

William and I both read the draft independently, and let
Twining have our comments, which were similar. We both
thought that the photographs were excellent, but that the text, if
it attracted anyone, would attract exactly the type of candidate
the service needed to avoid. The emphasis was on the personal
prestige enjoyed by District Officers rather than on what they did
to earn that prestige. The booklet seemed to assume that anyone
wanting a career in Tanganyika would be interested primarily in
a secure job with a pension on reaching retirement age, varied
leisure activities in racially segregated clubs which provided
opportunities for expatriates to play golf and tennis, and that the
height of a District Officer's ambition would be to kill wild
animals. I was convinced that any intelligent undergraduate
thinking of applying to enter the Overseas Civil Service would
dismiss as ridiculous the descriptions of the great white boss
wisely dispensing justice under a mango tree to all his admiring
subjects. It seemed to me that the booklet ignored the fact that
most District Officers who entered the Provincial Administration
in Tanganyika during the 1950s were working primarily for the
improvement of the social and economic conditions of a very
poor country which would, in due course, aspire to the independence that countries like India, Pakistan, and Ghana had
already achieved.

When the Governor asked William and me if we could write a
better draft I replied, with complete lack of modesty, that we
could not possibly write a worse one, and Twining invited us to
collaborate on preparing an alternative version.

When our draft was completed, Twining seemed quite pleased
with it, but I heard that the Director of Public Relations was reluctant to offend the officer whom he had originally asked to do the
job. The text which was eventually printed, without the names of
the authors, included a lot of material which I would much rather
have omitted.

We were all less busy in the lodge than we had been in
Government House, and Twining was very generous about
agreeing to let David Suckling and me visit our friends whenever
we asked his permission. We never asked for an evening off if we
knew that there was an engagement at which our presence would
be required.

One evening when I was not required at the Lodge, John Cooke
took me with him to Lushoto School to listen to a recital given by
a young soprano who had trained in Nairobi and London. Sylvia
Kaufmann was the daughter of the manager of a sisal estate near

Tanga, and was about to continue her training in Munich, with a view to starting a career as an opera singer. Her recital, unlike the disastrous concert of chamber music performed by the Wiesbaden Trio in the sweltering heat of Dar, was a resounding success. Sylvia looked radiant and she sang quite beautifully. It did not take me long to spot that John had fallen deeply in love with her. When he visited me at the lodge a few days later and told me he had followed my example, I knew exactly what he meant. Sylvia and John got engaged three weeks after Jennifer and I did, but they got married three weeks before us. My only regret about the timing of our respective weddings was that we were all too busy with the arrangements for our own weddings to be able to attend anyone else's.

Fixing the date of our own wedding caused a slight problem, as Jennifer had already left Lushoto when Twining asked me to make a choice which also involved her. He told me that he would be pleased if I remained as his Private Secretary until mid-1957, when my tour of service would be due to end, and that Jennifer and I might decide to get married then. If we did not want to wait so long, we could get married earlier, provided I understood that I would not be able to continue as Private Secretary after I was married. I told him that I did not want to wait for more than a year, and that I was sure Jennifer felt the same. His response was typical of his warmth and generosity. He said that he would himself like to give Jennifer away at her wedding, that he and Lady Twining would also be happy to host the wedding reception for us in Government House, and that he would invite Jennifer's mother and mine to be his house guests at Government House for a few days before and after the wedding.

This splendid offer was subject to one condition. If I decided to leave Government House before the end of my tour of service, I was to advise him concerning my successor. He asked me to write, for his eyes only, candid pen-pictures of every unmarried District Officer in his second tour of service, and, based on my personal knowledge of my own contemporaries and of the job of Private Secretary, to make my recommendation. Some of my contemporaries were less able or hard-working than others. Some seemed to be well suited to work in an up-country station, but would not have enjoyed the social formalities involved in living in Government House and attending to the needs and foibles of distinguished guests. Some had no interest in art or music, which were important to Twining. I was brutally frank about one contemporary whom I regarded as arrogant and conceited, and wrote that I did not like him at all, and doubted whether Twining would either.

There was one colleague who seemed to me to have all the qualities needed to make a good Private Secretary to any Governor, but in particular to Sir Edward Twining. John Margetson had completed the Colonial Service Course with me at Cambridge, and we had shared with another colleague a three-berth cabin on board the *Llanstephan Castle* on our first journey to Tanganyika. He was highly intelligent and had been a scholar of his college. He had impeccable manners and a lively sense of humour. During his National Service he had been commissioned in the Life Guards, and would have no problem about escorting the Governor on ceremonial military parades. He was also very fond of classical music, and had brought his own clavichord out with him to Africa, though the instrument did not react at all well to tropical conditions. I was quite certain that Twining would find him both efficient and congenial, and I recommended him very strongly as my successor.

I was delighted when Twining accepted my recommendation, and appointed John Margetson to take over from me. Sadly for Tanganyika, John later resigned prematurely from the Overseas Civil Service in order to join the Foreign Service. He then had a distinguished career as a diplomat. When he eventually retired with a knighthood he was the British Ambassador to the Netherlands.

Twining's kindness to Jennifer and me sometimes showed itself in ways that I only learnt about after the event. He knew that Jennifer was an extremely good teacher, and that, in normal circumstances, if a woman secondary-school teacher married a serving officer, she would be expected to resign her appointment in order to accompany her husband, wherever he might be stationed. Tabora was at that time the only Government African Girls' Secondary School in Tanganyika. Twining knew that I would be returning to normal duties in the Provincial Administration, but he did not want the Education Department to lose Jennifer if this could be avoided. He therefore arranged with the Member for Local Government and the Provincial Commissioner of Western Province for me to be posted to the District Office at Tabora when I left Government House, and for one of the officers currently stationed in Tabora, Anthony Mayle, to be transferred to a neighbouring district. Anthony never seemed to bear me any ill-will for the inconvenience I caused him.

The Mandate of Tanganyika to Britain

From the last part of the nineteenth century until the end of the
First World War, Tanganyika was administered by the Germans,
and was known as German East Africa. After the German defeat
in 1918, representatives of the victorious allied powers met in
Paris to discuss the terms of what came to be known as the Treaty
of Versailles, and Britain was represented by the Prime Minister,
David Lloyd George, who was accompanied by his private secretary and mistress, Frances Stevenson.

In his book *The Truth about the Peace Treaties*, published in 1938,
Lloyd George includes a chapter about the German Colonies.
There was unanimous agreement that the colonies should not be
restored to Germany, and the discussion went on to consider the
question of their future disposal. In the course of this discussion,
which was opened by Lloyd George himself, the French Minister
for the Colonies outlined three possible solutions: 'internationalism pure and simple; a mandate given to one of the Powers by the
League of Nations; and annexation pure and simple by a
Sovereign Power'.

Lloyd George was opposed to internationalism, which had not
been successful in small countries like the New Hebrides, and
would be even less likely to succeed in large ones.

The Dominions and France raised strong objections to a system
which consisted of the appointment of a mandatory by the
League of Nations. This would involve empowering one nation
to act on behalf of another. Every mandate was revocable, and
continuity could therefore not be guaranteed. There would be
little inducement for countries to invest capital in a country
whose future was unknown. Another important question
concerned the country to whom the mandate should be given.
Little countries had no colonising traditions, capital, or men. On
the other hand, the presence of a large administering country
would be a danger to its neighbours, and might compel the
adjoining nations to organise for defence.

The system of 'annexation pure and simple' was the one
supported by France, on the grounds that it was the only one
which would promote the development of the country
concerned, and provide effective protection for the natives
during the period required for their development.

Lloyd George was successful in bridging the various difficulties of principle which had arisen, and the question of practical
detail then arose of which colony should be mandated to which

power. On 7th May 1919, the Supreme Council in Paris decided that the mandate for German East Africa should be held by Great Britain.

Belgium was furious about this, since they had played an important part in the conquest of that colony. However, in Lloyd George's own words, 'The resources of the British Empire were so engaged in reconquering Belgium for the Belgians that they had not enough men to spare for the minor fighting in German East Africa, and had to seek the assistance of the Belgian forces which garrisoned the Congo.'

The arguments put forward by Lloyd George prevailed, but as a result of the Belgian protest an arrangement was reached whereby Belgium was given the mandate for the neighbouring states of Ruanda and Urundi (now known as Rwanda and Burundi).

A document which was circulated by Lloyd George to other members of the Congress represents in substance the settlement of the question of the former German colonies, and was later incorporated in the Treaty itself. It includes the following paragraph:

The Allied and Associated Powers are agreed that advantage should be taken of the opportunity afforded by the necessity of disposing of these territories formerly belonging to Germany and Turkey, which are inhabited by peoples not yet able to stand by themselves under the strenuous conditions of the modern world, to apply to those territories *the principle that the well-being and development of such peoples form a sacred trust of civilisation, and that securities for the performance of this trust should be embodied in the constitution of the League of Nations.* [My italics]

By the time I arrived in Tanganyika, the United Nations had taken over the responsibilities of the League of Nations, but the territory was still mandated to Britain, and representatives of the UN visited it at regular intervals to satisfy themselves that the mandatory power was complying with all its obligations.

A UN mission which visited Tanganyika in 1954 caused controversy when its report was published, and the Chairman openly dissented from the views of the other members. The recommendation that the British should commit themselves in principle to the goal of independence for Tanganyika was not so contentious as the suggestion that a target date should now be agreed for independence within twenty-five years. The Chairman of the visiting mission, and the great majority of senior officials working in Tanganyika, thought that such a timetable was totally unrealistic. The country's infrastructure, it was claimed, would take much longer to develop to a level which would enable the people of Tanganyika to govern themselves. In the event, Tanganyika achieved independence in 1961, only seven years after the target date of twenty-five years had been generally regarded as impracticable.

I never once regretted that I was posted to a territory where the requirement on the administering power to govern in the best interests of the people being governed was spelt out so clearly and unambiguously. I still find it strange, however, that Frances Stevenson, who accompanied Lloyd George to Paris for the discussions about the Peace Treaties, never mentioned either to her daughter Jennifer or to me the important part which LG had played in the negotiations which eventually resulted in Britain's responsibility for the administration of Tanganyika.

Without LG's interventions in 1919, Jennifer and I, assuming that we both eventually decided that we wanted to work in an overseas territory, would probably have been appointed to other colonies, and we might never have met.

Others may not have quite such strong personal reasons for being grateful to Lloyd George as I do, but I think most of my colleagues who served in Tanganyika were glad that they were posted to that country rather than anywhere else.

Chief Mkwawa's Skull

My first active interest in the Treaty of Versailles was concerned with one specific provision, Clause 236, which the former Colonial Secretary, Winston Churchill, regarded as unimportant, but which Sir Edward Twining did not.

Throughout the period I worked as Twining's Private Secretary, I had plenty of opportunity to see for myself how his larger-than-life personality and sense of fun endeared him to peasant farmers and their traditional rulers. Every tribe welcomed him warmly whenever he visited their districts, but none were more enthusiastic than the Hehe of Iringa District, where I had served as a cadet. The reason for Twining's immense personal popularity among the Hehe was unique.

I formed a high regard for the skill of Germans in putting up buildings which were attractive to look at and comfortable to work in, but I did not like what I heard about the way they had governed the country. Very old men who remembered the days when the Germans had ruled them sometimes told me that their rule was extremely harsh, and that forced labour, whippings, and executions without trial were commonplace. They said they much preferred the way the country had been administered since the Germans left. Some people may question the reliability of informal statements by elderly Africans praising the British colonial regime when those comments are made to a British official, but I believe that the opinions expressed to me were genuine. Many similar criticisms of the brutality of German colonial rule were also expressed during the negotiations which led to the Treaty of Versailles. Certainly there were several rebellions against the German rulers, and such uprisings were not repeated in Tanganyika during the period of British rule.

The most famous revolt against the Germans was the so-called 'Maji-Maji' rising, which lasted from 1905 until 1907. It brought together as allies for the first time a number of tribes which had previously dissipated their strength by quarrelling with one another. The word *maji* means water in Swahili, and those who took part in the rebellion appear to have shared a common belief in the effectiveness of a concoction of water, maize, and sorghum seed, to protect themselves from the power of enemy bullets. Some reports say that the African warriors believed that the medicine would make European rifles spurt water instead of bullets, and others that they thought that the bullets would trickle off their bodies like water. The magic was not effective, however, and the Germans suppressed the rebellion ruthlessly, shooting the rebels, destroying villages and crops, and causing a famine which lasted for several years. One report estimates that some 75,000 Africans died as a result of the fighting and the famine. Another puts the figure at between 200,000 and 300,000.

The Maji-Maji rebellion was the most serious revolt against the Germans, but there were others which preceded it. One of these was led by Chief Adam's grandfather Mkwawa, Chief of the Hehe, who were then the most powerful tribe in the southern part of the country.

Mkwawa was an able military leader, and during the 1880s he had defeated many of the most important tribes whose lands were adjacent to his own. He levied tribute on the trading caravans passing through his lands, and his warriors attacked those caravans that tried to avoid payment.

In 1891, the Germans decided that it was time to stop Mkwawa doing this, and sent troops from Kilosa to enforce their orders. Mkwawa at first tried to negotiate, but the German forces fired on his envoys, and only one survived to let Mkwawa know what had happened. Mkwawa then retaliated by ambushing and virtually annihilating the soldiers sent by the Germans.

From 1891 to 1894, Mkwawa continued with impunity to raid caravans passing through his land, but in 1894 the Germans decided to send another stronger force against him. A battle took place a few miles south-west of Iringa, at the village of Kalenga, where Mkwawa had built a fortified position. The fortress was bombarded and captured after very fierce fighting, but Mkwawa himself escaped.

For the next four years, he lived as a fugitive, supplied secretly with food and information by his own tribesmen, but in 1898 General Liebert, the Governor of German East Africa, offered a reward of five thousand rupees for the head of Mkwawa. The bribe was successful, and an African traitor told the Germans where to find Mkwawa, who was lying sick in a remote village near the Ruaha river in the Pawaga area. The search party found Mkwawa and his servant. Both men were already dead, Mkwawa having first shot his servant and then taken his own life by shooting himself in the stomach. However, the search party feared that he might just be pretending to be asleep and leading them into a trap, so the German Sergeant-Major in charge made quite sure that Mkwawa was dead by shooting him in the head, which he then cut off. He returned the decapitated body of the dead chief to the Hehe for burial, and delivered the skull to his superior officer. It eventually found its way to the Anthropological Museum in Bremen.

The Hehe were desolated by the death of their leader, but their distress was made much worse by being compelled to bury his body without a head. Their grief found expression some twenty years later in Clause 236 of the Treaty of Versailles, which made provision for the return by the German authorities of Mkwawa's skull to the Hehe people.

The authorities in Tanganyika followed the example of Winston Churchill in regarding this clause as unimportant, and took no effective action to secure compliance until 1950, when Chief Adam Sapi, Mkwawa's grandson, brought the matter to the notice of the recently appointed Governor, Sir Edward Twining, who took promises seriously.

Not long after the Coronation of Queen Elizabeth in May 1953, Twining went in person to Bremen, where he believed that he might find the skull. He took with him details of the measurements of the heads of Chief Adam and other members of the family, as he had been told that the shape of Adam's head was similar to that of his grandfather. Twining also knew the calibre of the rifle which had fired the bullet that entered Mkwawa's skull.

After a prolonged search, during which he examined a large number of skulls kept in the Bremen Anthropological Museum, Twining, with the help of a forensic surgeon, found a skull which he thought might well be the skull of Mkwawa. Chief Adam was informed of the progress of the search. After considering all the evidence very carefully, Adam said that he was prepared to accept that the skull was genuinely that of his grandfather. The Curator of the Museum then agreed that it should be returned to the Hehe people.

When the Hehe heard that the skull was to be returned to them, they built a magnificent mausoleum at Kalenga to house it. On 19th June 1954, exactly 56 years after Mkwawa's death, Twining handed over the skull to Chief Adam Sapi Mkwawa.

I had myself been involved in some of the preparations made in the Boma at Iringa during the months leading up to the return of the skull, but had returned to England for medical treatment a few weeks before the ceremony took place. Those who attended it told me that the celebrations and the tribal dances had lasted for the rest of that day and for the whole of the following day, and that an estimated 30,000 people had attended.

Nearly two years later, when Twining visited Iringa again on safari, I was part of the retinue which accompanied him. He decided to make a speech on the large recreation ground in the middle of the town, and he asked me to be his interpreter.

This occasion was unlike all the other occasions when I interpreted for the Governor. He wanted his speech translated not into Swahili but into Kihehe. I protested that my knowledge of Kihehe had become rusty, and it had never been good enough to translate a complicated speech unrehearsed. Twining therefore agreed to let me have a copy of the draft text so that I could prepare a translation before he delivered his speech. However, when I saw what he was planning to say, I concluded that my knowledge of Kihehe was not up to translating it satisfactorily, however much I prepared it in advance, so I asked him if he would have any objection to my seeking help from Chief Adam himself. Twining agreed, and Chief Adam told me he was genuinely delighted that a speech by a Governor whom his tribe honoured more than any previous Governor was to be interpreted into Kihehe by the Governor's Private Secretary. We spent an hour or so working together on Twining's text, and Adam then wrote out in beautifully neat hand-writing a translation of the speech which I read out later to a crowd which was very large, though I do not think it numbered as many as the 30,000 who had attended the original ceremony.

The response of the Hehe was wildly enthusiastic. The only person who grumbled to me was Twining's bodyguard, Police Constable Saidi, who was a Sukuma tribesman from Lake Province. He told me he was very disappointed by the whole occasion. He spoke no English, so had not understood what Twining had said, and no Kihehe, so he had not understood what I had said. It is not easy to please everybody.

Chapter 6

Tabora District

(April 1956–September 1957)

Tabora Boma

The Biggest District in Tanganyika

When the Governor gave me the choice of staying on as his unmarried Private Secretary until the end of my second tour of service or of returning to work in a District Office in order to get married, I had no hesitation in choosing to get married as soon as possible. He invited us to select the date for our wedding, which would take place in St Alban's Church in Dar es Salaam.

Choosing the wedding day was not difficult. We wanted to get married on a Saturday, when as many guests as possible would be able to attend the wedding. We also wanted to get married during the school holidays, when Jennifer's absence on honeymoon would cause little inconvenience to Tabora Girls' Secondary School. The date we chose also needed to fit in with Twining's other engagements. This narrowed the field of choice. There was only one date which satisfied all these requirements, and that was 30th June 1956, so that was the date we chose.

When I left Government House in the middle of April, I knew that it would not be very long before I would see the Twinings again. Even so, I was sad to say goodbye to them. Before I left, the Governor asked me to walk round the gardens of Government House with him. He thanked me much more warmly than I deserved for all the help I had given him as his Private Secretary, and told me that I had already been spotted as likely to have a successful career in the Overseas Civil Service. Neither of us then had any suspicion of how short that career was to be.

I had already accompanied the Twinings on one or two short visits to Tabora, and I had met Denis O'Callaghan, the District Commissioner under whom I was now to serve. I had not formed a particularly favourable first impression either of the town or of the man.

Tabora was the Headquarters of Western Province, Tanganyika's largest province. Tabora District, with an area of 25,000 square miles, was Tanganyika's largest district, very nearly half as big as the whole of England. In the 1950s, the town of Tabora, with over 14,000 inhabitants, was Tanganyika's biggest inland town. Its population was only exceeded by the two ports of Dar es Salaam and Tanga.

In spite of its enormous size, the population of Tabora District as a whole was only 158,000, of whom about two-thirds were Nyamwezi tribesmen. The Nyamwezi were the second largest tribe in Tanganyika, and were the main tribe not only in Tabora but also in the adjoining districts of Nzega and Kahama, to the north of Tabora.

Tabora had originally developed as a staging post for caravans on the slave and ivory routes from Lake Victoria and Lake Tanganyika to the coast. In 1872, the year before he died, David Livingstone spent a month sharing a hut with Stanley at the village of Kwihara, close to the town of Tabora. When the Germans opened up the interior of the country towards the end of the nineteenth century, they constructed the Central Railway from Dar es Salaam to Kigoma, passing through Tabora.

After the end of the First World War, the British administration embarked on the construction of a new branch line about 235 miles long to connect the Central line with Mwanza. The junction was situated at Tabora, which thus became an increasingly important communications centre. An airport was later established a few miles out of the township.

Tabora is situated 4,150 feet above sea level, and its climate is not so oppressively humid as on coastal stations nor so arid as in the neighbouring Central Province. However, the rainfall is unpredictable, and while I was stationed in Tabora the water supply was inadequate, and drinking water usually tasted disgusting, even after filtering.

Apart from the capital, Dar es Salaam, the town of Tabora had more non-Africans than any other district in which I served. According to censuses taken in 1948 and 1952, there were nearly 400 Europeans, 2,000 Indians, and 600 other non-Africans in Tabora in the early 1950s. Not surprisingly, there was quite a wide range of amenities for expatriates.

The town had electricity, even though the supply was unreliable. There was a reasonable telephone service, which smaller stations usually lacked. Some of the quarters occupied by expatriate officials, including mine, had telephones. Tabora only had one 'European-style' hotel, but it was, by local standards, a very good one. I was told that it had been built by the Germans before the First World War as a Hunting Lodge for the Kaiser. It was managed by East African Railways and Harbours, and was quite large. It had a good reputation for comfort, cleanliness, and the quality of the food it served. The town had a General Hospital, used mainly by African patients, and also a Grade 1 Hospital.

Tabora had two clubs exclusively for Europeans. Snobbery was much more obvious in large than small stations, and the Tabora Club was sometimes thought of as being comparable to an army Officers' Mess, and the Tabora Railway Club to a Sergeants' Mess.

There were various places of worship, including a large Roman Catholic church, an Anglican church without a resident priest, a Moravian church, and a number of mosques and temples.

The shops in Tabora were expensive, but those which catered primarily for expatriates were reasonably well stocked. There was also a branch of the Standard Bank of South Africa. There was even a cinema. The owner, an Asian entrepreneur, had served a gaol sentence for illicit diamond trading, and on his release he had used his ill-gotten gains to set up a cinema which he cheerfully called 'The Diamond Talkies'.

Virtually every Government Department had an office in Tabora with an expatriate in charge of it. In addition to the members of the Provincial Administration working in the Provincial or the District Office, representatives of all the major departments were normally stationed there. These included the agricultural, education, forest, game, labour, lands and surveys, medical, mines, police, prisons, public works, tsetse control, veterinary and water development departments. Tabora also had its own resident magistrate, and was one of the towns where sessions of the High Court were held regularly.

Even before I met Jennifer, I knew that Tabora was a particularly important centre for education. It had two large Government Secondary Schools for African pupils, one for boys and one for girls. They were generally regarded as the best in Tanganyika. The boys' school had originally been set up in 1925 to educate the sons of hereditary tribal leaders in order to equip them for the tasks of ruling their tribes in an enlightened way, but it gradually admitted a bigger proportion of pupils of very high intelligence but humble birth. The girls' school never concentrated on attracting pupils from high ranking families. I presume that this was because, whatever their level of education or birth, girls were not expected to inherit or be appointed to positions of political power. The girls who were admitted to the secondary school got their places on the basis of academic merit, and when they completed their secondary education they generally aspired to qualify for skilled professional jobs. In addition to the Government Secondary Schools, there was a Roman Catholic Secondary school run by the White Fathers, a seminary for the training of priests, two Indian schools, a small European nursery school, a training school for prison warders and another for railway apprentices.

The town was dominated by the Boma, a large and impressive fort built by the Germans on the top of a small hill. This contained not only the offices of the District Commissioner and his staff but also many other departmental and local government offices.

I did not dislike Tabora as much as I disliked Mtwara, but in spite of my being near to Jennifer and our approaching wedding, and the fact that I was working for a regime which was much more humane than the German regime had been, when I was in Tabora I often found myself thinking of the appalling human suffering caused by the slave trade. The enormous numbers of mango trees which grew in or near the town were a reminder that they had grown from stones of fruit which Arab traders had given to their captives whom they were taking to the coast in chains to be sold into slavery. Places which have been the scene of atrocities often seem to retain an aura of evil long after the atrocities have ceased. I cannot explain the reason for my feelings, but I thought the atmosphere in certain parts of the District was very sinister.

The Wedding

My house in Tabora was about a hundred yards from the Boma, and, until we got married, Jennifer continued to live in half of a large bungalow in the grounds of the Girls' School, a mile or so outside the town centre. The other half was occupied by Peggy Fowler, who taught domestic science and later became the head of domestic science teaching in the whole country. She was an ideal neighbour for a bride-to-be in Tanganyika, because she had the expertise to make wedding cakes in old-fashioned wood-burning ovens. After the ingredients had been mixed, the three sections of the cake each needed to be baked. This involved rotating them from time to time by hand in order to make them cook evenly. Peggy started putting the mixture in the oven one day at twelve noon, and did not finish the baking until five o'clock the following morning. She iced the cake a few days later in the kitchens of Government House.

The plans for our wedding were complicated. Jennifer's mother, my mother, and Jennifer's aunt, Muriel Stevenson, all wanted to attend, and they flew out from England for the occasion. They stayed in Tabora for a few days before travelling down to Dar by train. While in Tabora, my mother stayed with me, and Jennifer's mother and aunt stayed with her. I at least had met Jennifer's mother at the same time as I met her, but Jennifer did not meet her future mother-in-law until just a few days before our wedding.

The Twinings had invited our respective mothers and Jennifer herself to stay at Government House over the wedding, but Jennifer needed to arrange accommodation in Dar for her aunt and also for the friend she had asked to be her bridesmaid, Margaret Smith, a lovely, gifted, and very absent-minded biochemist, who had been her closest friend when they were undergraduates together at St Andrews University and then on their postgraduate courses at Bristol. While Margaret was staying in Dar, she got the news that Bristol University had awarded her a doctorate of philosophy.

There were three categories of people to whom Jennifer and I wanted to send invitations. We had many friends and relatives living in England who would not be able to travel to Tanganyika, but we thought they would nevertheless like to be invited.

We had too many friends in Tabora to invite them all to come to Dar, so we decided to ask them instead to a large sundowner party which was nominally hosted by our mothers, but was held in my house the week before the wedding. Only our closest friends in Tabora came both to the sundowner and the wedding.

We were particularly pleased that Joseph Sawe and his wife Dinah were able to come to both. Joseph was a Chagga from the Kilimanjaro area. He was a graduate of London University and had completed the same course as Jennifer at Bristol. He was an Education Officer at the Boys' Secondary School, and it was he who had persuaded Jennifer to apply to work in Tanganyika rather than in any other African country. Apart from the fact that we both liked Joseph and Dinah very much, we felt that we both owed him a special debt .

While working in Government House, I had got to know a large number of colleagues in both the public and the private sectors. I assumed that most of my friends and acquaintances who lived in Dar would accept an invitation from the Governor to attend our wedding and a reception in Government House. However, Jennifer and I were rather hesitant about including certain rich and distinguished people with whom I had got on well, but whom I only knew slightly. We did not want to appear to be fishing for expensive wedding presents. Jennifer and I had actually discussed between ourselves whether or not to include the head of the Tanganyika Sisal-Growers' Association, Sir George Arnautoglu, and his wife in our list of invitations, and we had decided against it. We ought not to have worried. Just before our wedding day, John Margetson, the new Private Secretary, advised me to get an invitation sent to them as quickly as possible, as they had already bought us a beautiful present, and had expressed to him their disappointment at not yet having received an invitation. Their generosity, and that of all our other friends, took us both by surprise.

The fortnight before our wedding was hectic. Jennifer's mother was nearly seventy, and mine nearly sixty, and they were not used to the African climate. Neither of them wanted to feel exhausted before they made the journey by train from Tabora to Dar, so we tried to limit the number of engagements they had in Tabora before they started on another round of celebrations in Government House.

The whole wedding group had a very comfortable train journey to Dar. After my mother had resumed full time work as a doctor, she usually preferred to be known as Dr Longford rather than Mrs Longford, but when I booked a berth for her, I referred to her as Mrs Longford, so that the railway staff would know that she was a woman when they allocated berths in sleeping compartments designed for two people.

Our wedding was due to take place on a Saturday morning in St Alban's Church, and we planned to spend our honeymoon motoring in parts of the Congo, Ruanda and Urundi, which were then all administered by Belgium. Jennifer and I booked seats well in advance on the weekly flight operated by Sabena Airlines from Dar to Usumbura, in Urundi. This was scheduled to leave every Sunday morning, and we arranged to spend our wedding night in the Country Club in Bagamoyo before returning to Dar in a hired car to catch the plane.

We had already left Tabora when I received a telegram from Sabena (whose critics sometimes alleged, rather unfairly, that the initials stood for 'Such A Bloody Experience – Never Again!') informing me that, in order to suit the convenience of many passengers travelling on pilgrimage to Mecca, the departure time of the plane had been put forward by twenty-four hours. I replied that we did not want to disappoint our guests by setting off on honeymoon before the wedding had taken place, and cancelled our air booking. We arranged to stay for two more days in Bagamoyo and then to travel by train from Dar to Kigoma, and from there by lake steamer to Usumbura, where we would collect my new Peugeot 203 car which we had already sent off by freight train from Tabora.

The wedding service was conducted by the Archdeacon of Dar, Edmund Capper, who later became the Bishop of Saint Helena. Jennifer was given away by Sir Edward Twining. I had asked John Margetson, David Suckling and Randal Sadleir to be the ushers at the service, and the guests had already started to arrive and the ushers were showing them to their seats when someone discovered that they had forgotten to bring the printed Order of Service cards to hand out to members of the congregation. John left the church at full speed, and was driven back to collect the boxes containing the cards. He reached Government House just in time to let Twining and Jennifer know of the problem, and to advise them to delay their arrival at the church for long enough for the cards to be distributed to all the guests. Jennifer later told me that Salehe, the Head Driver, had driven the ancient black Rolls Royce very slowly twice round the golf course with Twining and her in the back seat before they drew up outside the west door of the church.

The service went well, though I remember not a word of Archdeacon Capper's address. The regular organist was on leave, but his replacement played beautifully. Jennifer's mother had arranged for a dressmaker in England to make the wedding dress and the bridesmaid's dress, and both looked lovely, especially, in my opinion, the wedding dress. My colleague Geoff Thirtle, the best man, and I wore morning dress hired from a firm in Nairobi and sent by post to Dar. I was surprised that a hire firm in Kenya should have in stock formal clothes that were large enough to fit me perfectly, but they were not suited to a tropical climate. While I was standing in the church, I sweated so profusely that some kind person wiped my face with the towel normally used for wiping the chalice, and huge drops of sweat fell on to the stone floor in front of me.

During the service, Salehe removed the Governor's flag from the bonnet of the Rolls Royce. After the service was over, I joined Jennifer in the back seat of the car, and Salehe drove us to Government House, where the Twinings hosted a splendid reception for us.

That was the beginning of a marriage which has already lasted over forty years, and has given us both the greatest happiness. It has also provided us with a wonderful family of three children and seven grandchildren.

Honeymoon in Countries under Belgian Rule

When we reached Dar Station on the Tuesday after our wedding, Jennifer and I had another unforeseen problem. The station authorities, with commendable efficiency, had remembered that the Mr Longford and Mrs Longford who had made the journey from Tabora to Dar a few days previously had been mother and son. They therefore used their own initiative, and put Mrs Longford in a sleeping compartment with Miss Rourke, another teacher at the Girls' School, and Mr Longford in the same compartment as a Roman Catholic missionary.

The train appeared to be very heavily booked. There were several more first-class passengers than usual, due partly to the number of people returning to Tabora after our wedding. However, I explained to the guard and to the stationmaster that this Mrs Longford was not my mother but my new wife. The stationmaster apologised for the misunderstanding, and somehow sorted the problem out. He managed to provide a compartment for Jennifer and me without putting Patricia Rourke into the same compartment as the White Father.

When the train was about to leave, a good friend, John

Mitchell-Hedges, the government photographer, ran on to the platform carrying a parcel under his arm. It was an album containing the photographs he had taken of our wedding. The photographs and the album in which he had mounted them were of very high quality, and we were extremely touched that he had spent his weekend developing his films and then putting the enlargements into an album for us. It was a very personal wedding present which only he could have given us.

Many of the other guests at our wedding had brought presents to Government House. We had not taken them with us to the Bagamoyo Country Club, and David Suckling had looked after them for us over the weekend. He brought them to us at Dar Station, and they were loaded on to the train. We did not want to take a large number of bulky parcels on our honeymoon with us, so when the train reached Tabora, Peggy Fowler took charge of the situation. She arranged for all the presents to be taken off the train and stored safely in her house until we got home nearly three weeks later.

Jennifer and I enjoyed being married. We also loved the train journey to Kigoma, but the journey by an ancient steamer on Lake Tanganyika was even better. East African Railways and Harbours ran a service up and down the eastern shore of the lake, calling at Kigoma and Usumbura (now called Bujumbura), the capital of Urundi, and all the little ports to the north and the south of Kigoma.

The lake steamer was called the *Liemba*. She provided accommodation for twenty first-class and a number of second-class passengers, and she also towed several barges loaded with freight. The *Liemba* dated from the period when Tanganyika was still a German colony, and was originally called the *Götzen*, after Count von Götzen, who in 1894 was the first European to explore the area west of Lake Tanganyika and Lake Kivu. The *Liemba* had sunk in Kigoma harbour at the beginning of the 1914–1918 war,

Lake Steamer Liemba

but she had been salvaged and reconditioned in 1924. There was no doubt that she was old fashioned, but both Jennifer and I found her comfortable and extremely romantic.

The ship's captain had a pet dog of unusual shape and talents. The captain himself told us that, like so many dogs in East Africa, his dog had been fathered by a dachshund. The mother was an exceptionally large German Shepherd bitch. The pup which was born to these parents inherited the large and heavy body of his mother and the very short legs of his father. My own dog Susan had very short legs too, but they were in proportion to the rest of her body. The captain's dog looked frankly grotesque, but it was affectionate and intelligent. Jennifer and I stared in amazement when we saw him climbing up companionways which were almost vertical. We failed to ask the captain whether, once the dog had reached the top deck, he needed help to come down again, or if he could manage to climb down ladders as well as up them. However, Jennifer and I discussed between ourselves the question of whether the dog descended companionways head first or tail first. We never discovered the answer.

When we reached Usumbura, I was glad to see that our car, which we had sent on ahead of us, was waiting for us on the quayside. My pleasure soon gave way to irritation when I discovered that some things had been stolen on the journey. We had been told that we could safely leave small items in a locked car, and the car was still locked when we recovered it, so I presume that the thief must have been someone in a position of trust with access to the key. I blamed my own stupidity, and concluded, without a shred of evidence to show where the theft had actually taken place, that someone in Urundi must have been responsible. I had never had such an experience in Tanganyika!

One of the friends I had made in Dar was the Belgian Consul-General, Mr van Gorp, and I had asked his advice about planning our honeymoon in the Belgian Congo and in Ruanda–Urundi. He had made many very helpful suggestions. He particularly recommended us to book a room for a few nights in a hotel called the Résidence Royale in the beautiful town of Bukavu, formerly Costermansville, overlooking Lake Kivu. We took his advice, even though the hotel was nearly five times as expensive as any of the best hotels in Tanganyika. We did not begrudge the cost, however, as the rooms were so comfortable and the service so good. The food was absolutely delicious – far better than anything I had ever eaten in post-war Britain or in Tanganyika, even at formal dinners in Government House which I had thought were of a high standard.

It was not surprising that the hotel was so luxurious. The whole town centre seemed affluent. The main shopping boulevards were lined with shops displaying goods that rivalled the best one could buy in Harrods or Fortnum and Masons. Jennifer and I got the impression that all the food consumed by Belgian residents had been flown in from Europe, and that expatriates seldom bought locally-grown fruit, vegetables or meat from African farmers.

We did not see any Rolls Royce cars in Bukavu, but nearly all the cars driven by Europeans were expensive gas-guzzling American cars which were uncommon in Tanganyika. Having been rather proud of my new Peugeot 203, I realised that my car was certainly too small and too cheap to be regarded by Belgians as a status symbol, even though it was reliable, easy to drive, and economical.

Some of the roads around Bukavu were being repaired, and there were signs indicating diversions off the road we had expected to use. The side-road we were obliged to follow when we left the town took us through the African quarter of Bukavu. This consisted of the most appalling slums, including a labour camp made up of shabby little huts, many built of grass, which were crammed within inches of each other. Most Africans used firewood for cooking and paraffin for lighting, and one spark could have started an uncontrollable fire endangering the lives of all the inhabitants, especially the elderly or very small children. Open drains loaded with excreta ran alongside the huts, and the stench was indescribable. Even if the Belgian administrators were as indifferent as they seemed to be to the living conditions of the Africans on the outskirts of the town, Jennifer and I felt that self-interest should have made the prosperous residents of the tree-lined boulevards recognise that slums like that were a public health hazard not just to the slum-dwellers but also to themselves.

A mile or so outside Bukavu, we joined the main road along the western shore of Lake Kivu, and headed towards Goma, just on the Congo side of the border with Ruanda. The road passed through some magnificent scenery. The lake was incredibly blue, and the lake shore was covered with brilliantly coloured tropical vegetation. Coffee and banana plantations alternated with dense wild forests. The road was extremely hilly, with the lake to the east and a range of volcanoes to the west. Jennifer and I were fascinated by the bubbling hot streams, and slightly uneasy at the rumbling noises we heard above us. We did not greatly care for the smell of sulphur in the volcanic region, but thought it less obnoxious than the stink of the drains in Bukavu. We still use in our bathroom now a pumice stone which we picked up from the side of one of the volcanoes.

When we reached Goma, we stayed for a night or two in a hotel where we met another guest who got into conversation with us as soon as he found out that Jennifer and I were not Belgian, but both spoke reasonable French. He was a very well-dressed, very tall, very self-confident, very black Tutsi tribesman who owned a bright red Ford V8 pick-up truck.

The Belgian public relations system made much of the claim that Africans who made the grade could become *évolués* (advanced), and that there were no limits to the wealth and status an African designated as an *évolué* could achieve by his own diligence and enterprise. I innocently asked our colleague about being an *évolué*, and his reply amazed us. He was a not an *évolué* at all. He was just a very successful businessman. He had not bothered to seek any change to his formal status. The freedom allowed to exceptionally able Africans to succeed on their own initiative was, he asserted, used by a wealthy but unscrupulous colonial government as an excuse for not bothering about the health or education needs of the vast majority of ordinary peasant farmers.

It reflects some credit on the Belgian authorities that he felt able to express his opinions so freely. I had never at that time heard an African in Tanganyika speaking so disrespectfully to me about the Government. This might be due to politeness or timidity, and criticism of the Government certainly became much more common as independence came closer, but I also think that many intelligent Africans in Tanganyika acknowledged that their Government was genuinely attempting to improve the lives of every African, not just those of exceptional ability.

We travelled on from Goma into Kisenyi, in Ruanda, and stayed in a guest-house where the proprietress, a Belgian, was friendly. She asked us about our jobs in Tanganyika, and when we told her she immediately telephoned Monsieur Weber, the Belgian counterpart of a District Commissioner, to tell him that an *administrateur britannique* was staying in her guest- house with his wife. M. Weber was charming, and invited us both to spend an evening at his villa on the lake. He asked us many penetrating questions about our work in Tanganyika, and then told us how delighted he himself was to be serving in a country mandated to Belgium by the United Nations, rather than in the Congo itself. In Ruanda, the interests of

Africans were regarded as being of great importance. In the Congo, the only interests that were considered seriously were those of the Belgians themselves, particularly those who worked for the *Société Générale de Belgique* or one of the various mining organisations. He mentioned the problem of the long-standing hostility between the Tutsi aristocracy and the more numerous but lowly Hutu tribe. However, he did not appear to expect the kind of bloodshed which has taken place between Hutu and Tutsi in the years since Ruanda–Urundi achieved independence.

At the end of the evening, when we were about to return to our guest-house, M. Weber told us that he had arranged for a group of Tutsi warriors to give a performance of tribal dancing in honour of a very important British visitor, whose name he had forgotten, and he invited Jennifer and me to watch the dance as well. His assistant would collect us the following morning, and guide us to the place where the dance was to take place.

When Jennifer and I arrived with our guide at the village where the dancers were already assembled, I was surprised to see that the very important British visitor for whom M. Weber had arranged the dance was the General who had been the Governor's guest in Dar es Salaam for the ceremonial parade of the King's African Rifles. He was again accompanied by his wife. The General seemed quite pleased to see me, and greeted Jennifer warmly. His wife may have felt embarrassed that I had witnessed her arrogant behaviour in Dar a few months previously. Whatever the reason, she was icy to me, and barely civil when I introduced Jennifer to her.

I had enjoyed watching many tribal dances at various places in Tanganyika. Those who took part in a *ngoma* – the Swahili word means both 'dance' and 'drum' – usually had good reason to be proud of their skill, and also of their traditional costumes and accoutrements. In some tribes in Tanganyika, the dancers all wore similar costumes, but this was not always the case. Sometimes there would be as many different costumes as in a fashion parade. I never heard of a case where the dancers were provided with special uniforms by their Native Treasury or by tour operators. At weddings, funerals, or other celebrations, the dancers were often given beer, but I did not hear of ngomas where the performers received payment in cash. I formed the impression that most dances in Tanganyika were performed by enthusiastic amateurs.

In the dance we watched in Ruanda, the dancers were all dressed in identical costumes provided for them, I believe, by the counterpart of a Native Treasury in Tanganyika. The robes, head-dresses, spears and leather shields were all of the highest quality. The dances had all been arranged by a very sophisticated choreographer, and I was told that every dancer and drummer received a payment for taking part, although we, as guests invited by M. Weber, were not required to pay. After the performance was over, each dancer returned his costume, shield, and spear to the master of ceremonies, and the equipment was locked away in a big cupboard in the Native Court building. The Tutsi dancers seemed complete professionals.

Tutsi tribemen are very tall, and all the dancers we watched were used to being photographed by tourists, and knew exactly how to model for splendid action photographs. The General's wife erected a tripod and fixed her cine-camera to it and was filming away when one of the Tutsi warriors advanced towards her brandishing a spear and looking extremely fierce. It was obvious to Jennifer and me that this was part of his act, and that he had already done it to countless other spectators with cine-cameras. The film of his mock attack would have been a highlight of any home movie about the savagery of Africa.

The General's wife, however, was absolutely terrified. She let out a piercing scream, and lifted her tripod with the camera still rolling, tilted it at an angle of 45 degrees, and made a very hasty retreat to take shelter behind her husband. She was extremely upset by a performance which had been intended to give pleasure to us all.

I had never spoken previously to Jennifer about her, but when I saw how the General's wife had reacted to the dancer in Kisenyi, I told Jennifer about how she had behaved as a guest of Sir Edward and Lady Twining in Dar es Salaam. We came to the conclusion that her husband must be an exceptionally able man to have risen so far in his army career married to such an arrogant, disagreeable and cowardly wife.

We took our leave of M. Weber and his assistant, and next morning we drove northwards from Kisenyi to the Albert National Park, where we had booked a cabin for a couple of nights. When we arrived there, we made a disconcerting discovery. Unlike Tanganyika, where guests staying in Game Parks were allowed to watch the animals from their own cars without having to pay extra for the privilege, in Ruanda we were told that we could only watch the animals when escorted by a Game Scout and driven in an official Landrover, for which we would have to pay an additional fee.

Everything in the Congo and Ruanda–Urundi had cost much

more than we had expected, and the Belgian authorities were not willing to accept a cheque drawn on a Tanganyika bank account or even cash payment in East African currency. Jennifer searched through her handbag and I rummaged through my wallet and all my pockets looking for Belgian francs, and we just managed to scrape together the amount we were required to pay before entering the park itself. It was worth the effort.

We left our cabin just before dawn, and watched the pink sky as the sun rose slowly in the east. The Game Scout guided us to the top of a little hill overlooking a river bed, where there must have been at least forty hippos huddled together at the water's edge. Suddenly, without warning, every hippo evacuated its bowels, and, as it did so, twirled its tail furiously. The effect was like squeezing forty extremely generous cowpats through forty electric fans. Each hippo was covered with contributions from all its neighbours. Jennifer and I stared in amazement, and then burst out laughing. I suspect that the actions of the hippos were connected with staking out their own territory, but I still have no idea how or why they all managed to open their bowels simultaneously!

We thoroughly enjoyed sightseeing in the Congo and Ruanda–Urundi, but we were not sorry to cross the border into Uganda. The road towards Kabale was not so spectacularly beautiful as some of the places we had seen near Lake Kivu, but it was pleasant enough, and we were glad to be back in a country where East African currency was acceptable. We stayed at the White Horse Inn in Kabale, which was pretty and welcoming. The gardens were beautifully cared for, even though the hotel's sanitation was primitive.

We then drove back into Tanganyika, calling first at the town of Bukoba, on the western shore of Lake Victoria. When we reached Bukoba, Jennifer and I paid a courtesy call on Ian Woodrooffe, the District Commissioner, and asked his advice about a personal matter involving the District Officer, my old friend Bob King. Bob was a few years older than me, but we had been together at the same college at Cambridge and we had remained very good friends. Bob and his wife Margaret had already been in Tanganyika for some years when I arrived in Dar es Salaam on first appointment, and they had both welcomed me very warmly.

Sadly, a few months before Jennifer and I got married, Margaret King died suddenly. She had been playing tennis one afternoon, and by midnight she had died of polio, leaving her husband and two young daughters. Bob decided that he could not combine a job which involved frequent safaris with the responsibilities of looking after his daughters, and that it would be better for the children to go back to England to be cared for by their grandparents. He remained in Bukoba as a lonely widower. In normal circumstances I would not have hesitated to call on him when passing through Bukoba, but I was worried that it might be painful for him to entertain a friend who was enjoying his honeymoon while he himself was still suffering from his bereavement and his separation from his children. However, Ian had no doubts about advising us to call on Bob, who would be very disappointed if he learnt that we had passed through Bukoba without visiting him.

We took Ian's advice. After I had introduced Bob to Jennifer and we had both expressed our deep sympathy, we all started to chat about a wide range of topics, some sad, some joyful. Bob seemed really pleased to meet Jennifer, and he showed no trace of envy of our happiness.

Premature deaths of expatriates in Africa were much less common in the 1950s than they had been in the nineteenth century, but the suffering they caused to families was just as great. I was, if anything, sorrier for Bob's daughters than I was for Bob himself. They lost their mother and the home they were used to. They were separated from their father for reasons they were still too young to understand. They were returned to a far-away country where they were taken into the home of grandparents whom they had had little previous opportunity to get to know well, due to the distance which separated Britain from Tanganyika.

After we left Bukoba, we made our way back to Tabora

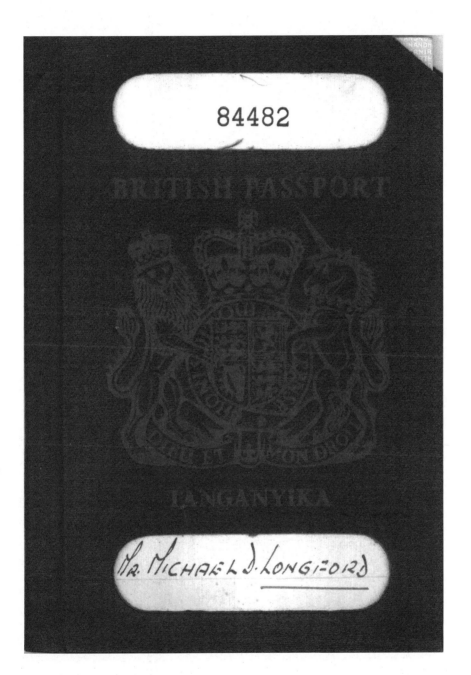

84482

BRITISH PASSPORT

TANGANYIKA

Mr. Michael d. Longford

The author's Tanganyikan passport.

Government House, Dar es Salaam.

Domestic workers at Government House.

Governor's Lodge, Lushoto.

Jennifer

Governor's Train bearing the Governor's Flag.

Tanganyika Police Band beside the Governor's Train.

The wedding of Michael and Jennifer, 30th June 1956.

The bride and groom leaving Government House.

Elaine Dyson
(Acting Headmistress,
Tabora Girls' School)

John Crabbe
(Headmaster,
Tabora Boys' School)

H.R.H.
Princess
Margaret

Senior pupils
of the
Girls' School

baby
John
Ramadhani

Peggy Fowler
(Head of Domestic Science,
Tabora Girls' School)

(The girl who is bathing the baby later qualified as a doctor.)

Princess Margaret visits Tabora School, 13th October 1956.

District Commissioner's House at Mahenge.

Ruth with Jennifer and Michael (and the dogs Susan and Wol)
in their garden at Mahenge.

Catherine on the beach at Lindi.

A Pogoro girl.

Kilombero Ferry in the rainy season.

The main Ifakara road in the rainy season.

Ngoma (drum, dance) at Malinyi in Ulanga District.

Ngoma (drum, dance).

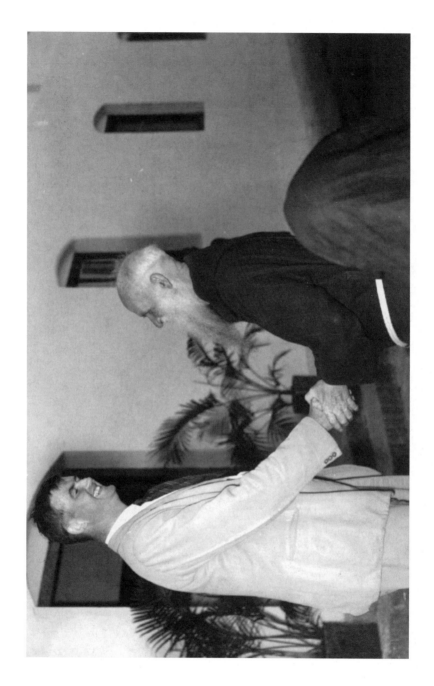

The author and Fr Gerard at Kasita Seminary.

Front row, from left to right: Osiah Mwambungu, Michael & Jennifer Longford, Dr Gary Butler (Medical Officer), Mrs Laurie Butler, Archbishop Edgar Maranta, Fr Gerard, Bishop Elias Mchonde, Mrs Anne Bullock, Geoff Butler (District Commissioner), C N U Nair (Cashier), Chief John Mlolere of Vigori Chiefdom.

Fr Gerard's Golden Jubilee at Kwiro, 22nd July 1958.

Catherine Longford, the author, Jennifer Longford carrying Philip, Ruth
Longford, Joan Christodoulou carrying Andrea, Stephanie Christodoulou,
Chris Christodoulou carrying Nicholas, Bishop Trevor Huddleston.

The christening of Philip Longford and Nicholas Christodoulou by
Bishop Trevor Huddleston at Lindi Anglican Church, 18th March 1962.

through Biharamulo, Kahama and Nzega. Jennifer and I would have enjoyed a honeymoon anywhere, but we were very glad we had chosen to spend the first weeks of our life together visiting so many beautiful places.

However, we did not like what we saw of Belgian administration, particularly in the Congo. For one colonial power to criticise another could be construed as an example of 'the pot calling the kettle black', and the way Britain administered Tanganyika was certainly not perfect. We made many mistakes. We did not, in my view, deal severely enough with the tiny minority of expatriate officials who were lazy, corrupt or tyrannical. A few older officials resisted change and may have wanted to preserve a privileged way of life for themselves.

However, when Jennifer and I compared what we saw of the ways that Tanganyika and the Congo were governed, we felt that the British system of administration was vastly preferable. Not all, but most British officials in Tanganyika seemed to be inspired to some extent by idealism and a genuine concern for the welfare of Africans. Jennifer and I did not stay in the Congo long enough to know that country well, but we saw no signs of altruism among any of the Belgians we met and spoke to there.

In 1903, Joseph Conrad, the author of *Heart of Darkness*, wrote that it was an extraordinary thing that the conscience of Europe, which, seventy years previously, had put down the slave trade on humanitarian grounds, still tolerated the Congo Free State as it was under the regime of King Leopold II. In the same year, the House of Commons in London agreed without a division a motion making reference to 'measures to be adopted to abate the evils prevalent in the Congo Free State'.

In 1908, the country's name was changed from Congo Free State to Belgian Congo, but the country continued in fact to be a commercial enterprise dominated by corrupt officials and based on the use of forced labour. The Belgians were able, somehow, to give the impression to world opinion that the administration of the Congo had improved radically, and that the country was now being governed well.

In 1960, however, when the Congo was hastily granted independence, many outsiders were astonished at the violence which followed, when ruthless and self-seeking African dictators took over power from ruthless and self-seeking Belgians. The crisis caused many of the expatriates living in the Congo to flee, and, because I spoke French, I was given a special temporary assignment in Morogoro to provide help and advice for refugees

travelling in overcrowded trains down to the coast in Dar es
Salaam, on their way back to Europe.

The trouble in the Congo in 1960 took many people completely
by surprise, but Jennifer and I had seen one corner of the country
four years earlier, and it did not surprise us in the very least.

A Royal Visit

Before leaving Government House in April, I had heard that
Princess Margaret was planning to visit Tanganyika in October.
When the details of her programme were announced, it included
a visit to Tabora. This was scheduled to last four hours on
Saturday 13th October, during which she would inspect a police
guard of honour on the town's main recreation ground, visit the
Government Boys' Secondary School, and have lunch with
important guests of all races at the Tabora Hotel before flying on
to Mwanza. Many residents of Tabora were disappointed that her
programme did not include an overnight stop there.

When Jennifer and I arrived back from our honeymoon in July,
the town was already agog with anticipation. Some senior people
of all races were sure to receive invitations for themselves and
their wives to attend the royal lunch. Others, including Jennifer
and me, were clearly not senior enough to expect an invitation. In
between, there were many middle level officials and private
sector managers from Tabora and other parts of Western
Province who might or might not be included on the guest list.

During my time as Private Secretary, I had disliked the way in
which certain people whom the Governor described as 'bloody
social climbers' manoeuvred in order to get themselves invited to
Government House, but what had been only a few isolated cases
of delusions of grandeur in Dar es Salaam became an epidemic
when the invitations that people were angling for involved a
lunch with Princess Margaret. Women seemed to be more prone
to the complaint than men, and several husbands were nagged
mercilessly by their wives for not trying hard enough to get
invited.

When the lucky ones heard that they were successful, the
husbands usually thought it would be sufficient if they got their
best suits pressed and their best shoes polished for the occasion,
but many of the wives took advantage of the opportunity to order
from abroad new and expensive frocks and hats of much better
quality than anything stocked by the shopkeepers of Tabora.

The town of Tabora was given a face-lift, but only to those parts of its face which the Princess would see. Government offices and quarters along the route she would follow had their corrugated iron roofs repainted, but only on the side of the roof which was visible from the road. A few metres at the top of each of the branch roads which joined the road to the airport were bituminised, but those parts that the Princess would not see were left untreated. The whole town was cheerfully decorated with flags and bunting.

At every town that the Princess visited, each detail of the programme had to be settled in advance. The time to be spent at each stopping point on the route had to be precisely noted. Those who would be asked to show their work to the Princess were required to rehearse beforehand exactly what they were going to demonstrate, and how long they would need in order to explain their jobs to the Princess.

The programme in Tabora was too short to include a visit to the Girls' Secondary School, but it was agreed that, when the Princess visited the Boys' School, she should be given the opportunity to meet girls as well as boys. She was therefore invited to watch a group of pupils from the Girls' School bathing little John Ramadhani, the baby son of an outstanding African graduate teacher on the staff of the Boys' School. The bowl the girls used as a bath for John was the same one that Peggy Fowler had bought to mix our wedding cake in earlier that year.

At the rehearsals of events on the Princess's programme, someone normally acted the part of the Princess herself. Elaine Dyson, the deputy headmistress, took on this role for the rehearsal of the bathing of the baby. She leant over to look at the baby being washed, and baby John was intrigued by the unfamiliar texture of her hair. He grabbed a handful and tugged it with all his might. This made everyone but Elaine laugh. However, it would have caused utter consternation if baby John had pulled the Princess's hair the following day, and suitable precautions were taken. As it was, one of the press photographers took an enchanting photograph of the Princess and the African baby which appeared in newspapers all round the world.

The tour went off very well, although there was sharp criticism of some of the press representatives. There were over 50 journalists and photographers accompanying the tour, and some of them behaved in an uncouth way. I was appointed as Press Liaison Officer for the few hours they spent in Tabora, and did not find the task a pleasant one. Sir Edward Twining himself described the journalists as 'the most impossible people'.

One particularly successful aspect of the royal visit, however, was the cordial relationship which Princess Margaret built up with Sir Edward and Lady Twining. Those who met the Princess all agreed that they had found her charming.

After the tour ended, most of the people who had put in so much effort to make it a success felt rather flattened by the prospect of returning to their routine tasks. I was chatting in the club one evening with Hugh Butterworth, who taught at the Boys' School, and Tony Mence, the Game Ranger, when Tony suggested that it would be fun to put on as a pantomime a new version of Cinderella, based on a visit by Prince Charming to Tabora. Tony was a very good game ranger, with a fondness for practical jokes which had caused him a few problems at university. When he told me the story of one particularly outrageous prank, he added that, when he later applied for a job in the Game Department, he had to provide references, and the Dean of his university had written about him 'I cannot think of anyone I would more gladly see in an overseas appointment'! The recruitment panel in the Colonial Office took this as a recommendation, and appointed him to Tanganyika.

Hugh and I thought Tony's idea was a splendid one, and we agreed to collaborate on writing the script in our spare time. We knew that there were several very talented people in Tabora who might like to take part or to use their special skills behind the scenes. The Health Inspector, Frank Knowles, was an outstanding amateur pianist. Muriel Forbes, the wife of the Regional Mines Officer, had been a professional actress in musical comedies before her marriage, and we hoped that she would agree to produce the show and take the part of the Principal Boy.

When Tony, Hugh, and I had completed the script, the Amateur Dramatic Society held auditions, and we were all delighted by the number of people who wanted to take part. Some members of the ladies' chorus were prettier than others, but they could all sing and dance reasonably well. The men's chorus were designated as 'The Press Gang', and were required to be as loutish as possible and to sing extremely badly. The parts of Cinderella and Dandini were played by very attractive women who could act and sing well. Muriel Forbes agreed to take the part of Prince Charming as well as directing the production. I was given the part of one of the Ugly Sisters, *Hakuna*. My sister *Hamna* was about a foot shorter than me. The words *Hakuna* and *Hamna* both mean 'there isn't any' in Swahili.

The script was full of references to Princess Margaret's visit, and also to the idiosyncracies of some of our colleagues, most of whom took the jokes in good part. However, the Provincial Commissioner, whose name was J C Clarke, was not amused by a rather feeble joke about how a mere clerk called Jaycee had been allowed to shake Prince Charming's hand.

We gave two performances in the Hall of the Boys' School less than four months after Princess Margaret's visit, and every seat was sold. A review of the production commented: 'in saying that the performances were excellent, it is not necessary to make any of the usual allowances and reservations. The entertainment was first class judged by any standards, and there was no doubt about the genuine appreciation of the audiences'.

Just after the end of the first performance, Anne Butterworth, Hugh's wife, gave birth to a son. Anne explained that she had gone into labour as a result of laughing too much.

The professionalism and leadership of Muriel Forbes were quite outstanding. She brought out skills which many of the actors had not known they possessed, and she also managed to organise the schedule of rehearsals to fit in with the safari commitments of members of the cast.

There was no television in Tanganyika in the 1950s, and amateur dramatics provided a very enjoyable form of recreation for the Europeans living there. However, they were only possible in the bigger stations. Small stations had too few expatriates to make up a cast, let alone an audience. Even in a place like Tabora, the population was always liable to change due to people going on leave or being transferred, but when a group of people stayed together long enough to put on a good performance it gave a big boost to the morale of the whole station.

Married Life

Jennifer had given up her quarter at the Girls' School when we got married, and she joined me in my house near the Boma when we returned from honeymoon. While we were away, our house had been looked after by Lameck, who had been my cook in Tukuyu, Iringa, Mtwara, and then my houseboy-dhobi in Government House. When we got to Tabora, he returned to cooking, the job he did best. Jennifer and I agreed that Asmani, a Haya tribesman who had been Jennifer's factotum in her house at the school, would continue to be employed by us, working as a

houseboy, and that Lameck, who was older and more experienced than Asmani, would be in charge.

This arrangement was not a success. Asmani had worked very
well for Jennifer. He was a reasonable cook, kept her house clean,
arranged flowers beautifully, laundered and ironed her clothes,
and did all her household shopping for her, riding into market
from school on a bicycle which he borrowed from Jennifer.
However, he resented my intrusion, and he resented even more
being under the supervision of Lameck, even though Lameck had
worked for me for nearly five years, whereas Asmani had only
worked for Jennifer for less than eighteen months. Jennifer told
me later that once when she asked him about a document she had
mislaid, Asmani had immediately replied that it was folded in
her cheque-book. He could not have known this unless he had
been prying among her personal papers while she was somewhere else. I myself had no good reason at that time to doubt
Asmani's honesty, but I neither liked nor trusted him.

Asmani left me in no doubt that he also disliked me. He never
smiled at me, and his words to me were polite but the tone in
which he expressed them was not. The Public Works Department
provided twin beds to furnish the quarters of all expatriate officials, married or single, and Asmani made Jennifer's bed very
carefully every day, but he took no trouble at all over mine,
which was always uncomfortable. After a few weeks of my
grumbling, Jennifer agreed that we should look for another
houseboy.

Early in October, just before the royal visit, we gave notice to
Asmani, but we did our best to find a new job for him. We
referred him to another couple who had told us they were
wanting to employ only one domestic servant who was versatile
and able to work by himself. They took him on, but dismissed
him after only a month. When he left, Asmani took his wages
from his employers, and then put all their dirty dinner plates
unwashed into a cupboard, and covered each pile with one clean
plate. For several months after he stopped working for us,
Asmani tried to retain Jennifer's bicycle, but Lameck eventually
managed, with some difficulty, to retrieve it on her behalf.

When we dismissed Asmani, I asked the Town Headman,
whose official title was the Liwali of Tabora, if he could recommend a replacement for him. The Liwali told me he knew one
really excellent houseboy, and would ask him to come for an
interview at our house as soon as possible. The man who arrived
that evening was a Manyema tribesman called Juma Farjallah. It

was sometimes said that the Manyema were the last tribe in East Africa to practise cannibalism, but Juma was a perfect gentleman. He brought three documents with him, his discharge certificate from the King's African Rifles and excellent references from his two employers. He had been a corporal, and had completed his military service with an exemplary character. He had then worked for two employers for a total of over twenty years. His most recent employer was a very senior police officer called Roland Wheeler, whose recommendation covered most of that period. Juma had only left that job when Roland Wheeler was posted as Commissioner of Police to a colony in West Africa.

Juma remained with us until we ourselves left Tanganyika six years later. I have never met, either in Tanganyika or in any other part of the world, a better or more loyal servant than Juma. Jennifer and I remained enormously grateful to the Liwali for recommending him to us. We were as devoted to Juma and his wife, Mgeni Jumanne, as they were to us. Mgeni was a smiling grandmother who moved extremely slowly and whose figure reminded us of pictures of Queen Victoria taken at the time of her Diamond Jubilee. We were particularly pleased that our own children's closest early contacts with adult Africans were with a couple who were liked and esteemed by everybody, and were regularly greeted by other Africans, even those in high-status and well-paid jobs, with the formal Swahili greeting of respect *Shikamuu* - 'I grasp your feet'.

The working hours in the Girls' School were not the same as in the Boma. Classroom teaching started very early each morning, and Jennifer had already left to go to school before I had my breakfast. I went to my office an hour or so later than Jennifer, but I returned for lunch in the middle of the day. Jennifer remained at school until mid-afternoon, by which time I had returned to the Boma to continue work until the evening. This meant that we only had lunch together at weekends or during the school holidays.

We had decided before we got married that we wanted children, and saw no reason to delay starting a family. I was overjoyed when Jennifer came back from seeing the Medical Officer, Karl Eckhart, and told me the good news that she was expecting a baby. The bad news was that she had a gynaecological problem which meant that she might have a miscarriage during the early months of pregnancy. The doctor was a bit prudish about letting junior clerks in the Education Department know that a young married Education Officer was actually pregnant, and in October he wrote on her medical certificate that Jennifer was excused from her normal duties as she was suffering from 'indigestion'.

Although the doctor told Jennifer about the end of October not to travel to the school for two or three weeks, a number of her pupils accepted her invitation to come to our house and be taught there. They often stayed on longer than normal school hours, and I got to know some of them quite well. It was obvious that any girl who obtained a place at the secondary school was very intelligent, but all Jennifer's pupils were charming as well. I can quite understand why Jennifer really enjoyed teaching them.

I was not so enthusiastic about my work in the Boma under Denis O'Callaghan, the District Commissioner. Jennifer was not a great admirer of his either. Before I reached Tabora, he had told her, in a way which she found unpleasant, that I would need to get my knees brown after my cushy existence in Government House. In common with her colleagues, she had disapproved of a request which Denis made to the expatriate staff at the school that they should report to him any criticisms of the Government made by pupils. Denis's contention was that such comments were seditious and had to be stifled. The school's teaching staff, on the other hand, thought that freedom of expression was a human right, and that it would have been very unprofessional to report any pupil to the authorities for speaking disrespectfully about the colonial regime.

Denis was a very small man who smoked evil-smelling cheroots and reminded me of the film star Terry Thomas playing the role of a confidence trickster. His wife Sybella was a large lady. Jennifer and I liked her much better than her husband, but we were a bit shocked when we hosted our first curry lunch party after our wedding, and Sybella shouted at Denis from one end of the dining table to the other that he was a bloody fool. I did not discover what prompted this outburst, but, whatever his other faults, I never considered Denis to be a fool. Sybella had a powerful voice, and exercised it regularly drilling a section of African women called the 'Walele Mama', who wore uniform and carried little wooden rifles on parade. She was eccentric but kind, and she was also a very talented artist. We still get pleasure from a painting by Sybella of a row of little shops in Tabora, which she gave us as a wedding present, and two water colours of Tabora district, which my mother bought and left to me when she died.

Tabora had an unusually large complement of Administrative Officers. The Provincial Office had a Provincial Commissioner and a Deputy Provincial Commissioner based in Tabora. The

District Commissioner of Kigoma District also had the status of Deputy Provincial Commissioner and moved to Tabora temporarily when the Provincial Commissioner was on home leave. The District Office had a District Commissioner and either two or three expatriate District Officers. It also had two Assistant District Officers (ADOs), who had been recruited in Tanganyika. From time to time, cadets on first appointment would spend a few weeks in Tabora before being posted to other Districts. Tabora also had a Woman Administrative Assistant (WAA).

Equal rights for women in the Provincial Administration were not given high priority in the 1950s. It was alleged that Muslims would resent being tried by magistrates who were women, so a WAA was given no judicial powers. However, the calibre of all the WAAs I met, both in Tabora and elsewhere, was extremely high. When I arrived in Tabora, the WAA there was an extremely able woman called Geraldine Bolton. Her successor, Beryl Lake, was just as able. She was the daughter of a former Provincial Commissioner, and she was, as far as I know, the only administrative officer of either sex to have obtained a Ph.D., though she never referred to herself as Dr Lake.

ADOs were usually Africans who had achieved promotion on merit from the clerical grades of the service. Tabora had one ADO who was an African, Herbert Gondwe. The other was an Indian, G N Nayar. Both of them were able, honest, hard-working, and very congenial colleagues.

Herbert Gondwe became a District Commissioner about the time of independence. He wrote to us at Christmas for several years after Jennifer and I had left Tabora, and even continued to write after we had returned to Britain. His letters regularly ended with a paragraph to the effect that God had blessed him and his wife with their umpteenth child – the last one we heard about was, I think, the seventeenth – and telling us the baby's name, and whether it was a boy or a girl. We had met several of their older children in Tabora, and they were all happy, healthy, intelligent, and well-behaved.

People in many European countries tend to think that only feckless and irresponsible parents have such huge families. In Africa, however, most parents were proud to have a large number of children, but the children of educated parents like Herbert Gondwe and his wife stood a much better chance of surviving into adult life than the children of illiterate peasant farmers. We did not hear of the Gondwes ever losing any of their children.

Many other ADOs of the calibre of Herbert Gondwe also went on to be promoted further to very senior positions, but I served later with one ADO who was lazy, incompetent, and seriously in debt, due to spending most of his salary on drink. Adverse annual confidential reports sometimes led to unsatisfactory officers being transferred, but unless they actually committed a criminal offence it was usually very hard to get them dismissed on grounds of inefficiency after they had been confirmed in their appointments.

Officers in the Provincial Administration were very frequently transferred from one district to another during a tour of service, but the number of transfers which took place while I was in Tabora seemed higher than the average for the rest of the country. Sometimes transfers were inevitable, but I do not think those who made the decisions about postings gave enough thought to the disadvantages of constant changes of personnel. The business of packing up one's household in one station and unpacking in another cost time and money which could have been used to better effect. Personal friendships were interrupted, and children in particular often found the loss of their companions upsetting. Perhaps the worst feature of the constant staff changes, however, was that the administrators and the local Africans whom they administered did not have long enough to get to know and trust each other. Officers with drive and initiative were often transferred before their ideas for social or economic development in a particular district could be properly implemented. Routine tasks continued to be carried out adequately by officers who had not yet become familiar with the district and its people, but little real progress was possible in such a situation. Some of my African friends commented to me that they felt that the turnover of district officers was too fast.

Philip Lousada, who had been the DO I when I arrived in Tabora, completed his tour and was replaced by Peter Hopkins, who was very able and energetic. Not long after Philip Lousada went on leave, Denis O'Callaghan himself went on leave, and Peter Hopkins took over as the acting District Commissioner. Another District Officer called Jim Mainwaring arrived. He was less effective than Alan Jones, who was posted to the Secretariat. Two cadets called Chris Gornall and Mike Ransome arrived on first appointment from the UK, and spent a few weeks in Tabora before being posted to other stations in Western Province.

While Peter and I had been DO I and DO II, we both regularly heard disturbing reports on the safaris we made to Unyanyembe

Chiefdom about the tyrannical way the Chief was ruling his area. We always told the District Commissioner of what we had ourselves been told, but the reply we got from Denis was always the same, 'We can't hope to govern Unyanyembe successfully without the cooperation of Chief Fundikira. Turn a deaf ear on any complaints you may hear about him.' Peter and I were very uneasy about the situation.

Strikes and political demonstrations were still rare at that stage in Tanganyika's development, but one day we received information that one of the newly-formed trade unions was planning to hold a demonstration the following day. Next morning, Peter and I arrived at the Boma at the usual time, and were shocked to find that Denis O'Callaghan had driven out to the Native Court at a village called Ndono, ostensibly to carry out a spot check of the cash in hand. There was no reason to suspect any irregularities at Ndono, and I reluctantly concluded that Denis's motive for going on a one-day safari without telling either Peter or me beforehand was in order to be safely out of harm's way if any trouble arose in the township.

Unfortunately, during the rest of my career in Tanganyika, I came across Denis both when I was serving in Ulanga District in Eastern Province, and later in Lindi District in Southern Province. He followed me to both Provinces, and the experience of serving under him again in two other places did nothing to change the impression which I formed of him in Tabora.

David Livingstone Slept Here

While the slave trade was flourishing, many Nyamwezi tribesmen adopted the religion of the Arab slave traders and became Muslims. Islam has been an influence in East Africa for much longer than Christianity. However, by the time European powers had embarked on the scramble for Africa during the second half of the nineteenth century, various missionary societies were already sending people to work in what a hymn-writer of that time described as 'heathen lands afar'. Probably the most famous of these missionaries was Dr David Livingstone.

David Livingstone was one of the great men of the nineteenth century. His work as an explorer was of immense importance, regardless of his great influence as a healer, evangelist, and campaigner against slavery. However, he would probably not have become so famous if a journalist called Henry Morton

Stanley had not been commissioned by the owner of the *New York Herald* to travel to Africa and find Livingstone, who had last been heard of near Lake Tanganyika, and had then disappeared for over three years in the equatorial forest.

Stanley set out from Zanzibar for the interior of Africa in March 1871, and in November he reached the village of Ujiji on Lake Tanganyika. When he found Livingstone there, Stanley greeted him with the remark which became familiar across Britain and the United States – 'Dr Livingstone, I presume.'

Stanley later wrote a book called *How I found Livingstone* which was over seven hundred pages long. The book was a success commercially, and several editions were published.

After the two men met, Livingstone and Stanley explored the north end of Lake Tanganyika together. They then returned together to Tabora in 1872, and lived for some months in a village called Kwihara, near to the Chief of Unyanyembe's palace at Itetemia. Stanley tried to persuade Livingstone to return with him to Europe, but Livingstone decided to stay on. He wanted to explore the waters around Lake Bangweulu. He became ill with dysentery there, and died on 1st May 1873. His faithful servants James Chuma and Abdulla Susi carried his body, together with his papers and instruments, down to the coast, and it was finally buried in Westminster Abbey.

The house, or *tembe* in Kwihara where Livingstone and Stanley lived was very solidly built, and had been preserved by the Government as a memorial. When I was posted to Tabora, it was being renovated, largely due to the enthusiasm of the District Commissioner of Kigoma District, Bryan Savory. He was an expert on the history of Tanganyika in general, and on Livingstone in particular. He seemed rather shy and retiring, and did not get the promotion I thought he deserved, but he was liked and respected by Africans and by those officials who served under his quiet leadership.

After the restoration work on the *tembe* had been completed, a few memorabilia were installed, and it was given the title Livingstone Memorial Museum. I found the exhibits rather disappointing and the hand-written documents difficult to read, but I hoped that the inauguration of the museum would encourage other people to provide items of interest to be put on display there.

The *tembe* was a large single-storey house built of mud walls about three feet thick. The roof was flat, and there was a broad verandah in front of the house. A huge carved door led into the house from the centre of the verandah. The building was designed to be as secure from attack as possible, and to provide a safe place in which to keep stores of food, survey instruments, weapons, ammunition, and documents.

It did not bother me greatly that the splendid carved door was not the original one that Livingstone had used. That had been sold during the period of German administration of Tanganyika, and was now in the Africana Museum in Johannesburg.

The first occasion on which Jennifer and I saw the Governor and Lady Twining after our wedding was when they paid a short visit to Tabora in January 1957 to take part in the formal opening of the museum. John Margetson and David Suckling stayed with Jennifer and me while the Governor was in Tabora.

The other distinguished visitor for the occasion was the Moderator of the Church of Scotland from Nairobi. He was invited because David Livingstone had been born in Lanarkshire, and was a member of the Church of Scotland, although he worked for the London Missionary Society. A large number of spectators of all races were also present at the ceremony, which took place a few weeks before Bryan Savory and his wife left Tanganyika on retirement.

I was given the task of interpreting into Swahili the speeches of both the Governor and the Moderator. I suspected from the wicked gleam in Twining's eyes that his speech would include something extremely difficult to translate, and I was absolutely right.

Twining started his speech innocuously enough, but I feared the worst when he looked pointedly at me as he referred to the fact that the new door was just a copy, and that the original was now in a foreign country. He added that many people might resent this, just as many Greeks resented the removal from the Parthenon of the Elgin Marbles. There is no Swahili word for 'the Elgin Marbles', and I had to think on my feet to work out a paraphrase that would convey Twining's meaning to Nyamwezi tribesmen.

As if that wasn't bad enough, Twining concluded his speech with a sentence which sounded stilted and bombastic, and quite unlike the style he normally adopted in his speeches. He said that he hoped the new museum would not be 'vandalised by icono-clastic introverts who wished to inflate their puny egos by scrawling their undistinguished signatures on the walls of historic buildings'. I think I managed to get his meaning across, and I was rewarded with a conspiratorial grin as soon as I finished translating.

Interpreting for the Moderator of the Church of Scotland presented a very different problem. Everything he said would have been quite easy to translate if only he had paused from time to time to let me get on with it. As it was, he gave an unscripted address which seemed to go on for ever. When at last he came to an end, he expected me to remember everything he had said.

I am sure I inadvertently left out large lumps of his speech, but I did not feel too guilty about it. Most Scottish preachers are reasonably eloquent, but this speech was incredibly boring, in spite of the exceptional circumstances surrounding the ceremony and the great public interest still inspired by David Livingstone's work and personality. I doubt whether any of the Swahili speakers in the audience objected to my leaving out some of the particularly forgettable passages in what the Moderator had said.

Interpreting Church Affairs

Jennifer shared my enthusiasm for learning languages, and even though she was employed to teach English at the Secondary School, and always used English in the classroom, her knowledge of Swahili improved steadily, and she passed the Government Higher Standard Swahili examination just before our first daughter was born.

My application to prepare for an interpretership in Kinyamwezi was approved, and Jennifer and I enjoyed being together as we both studied in the evenings. We had plenty of Swahili books for Jennifer to use, and I found Kinyamwezi much easier than Kihehe. The grammar was simpler, and there was a Kinyamwezi version of the New Testament which I could read in my spare time.

Pascal Shija, a clerk in the Native Treasury who came from Nzega District, in the northern part of Unyamwezi, agreed to be my tutor, and from quite soon after my arrival in Tabora I started using Kinyamwezi rather than Swahili in conversation with Africans, especially on safari.

African tribesmen often gave nicknames to European officials, though the officials themselves seldom got to know them. This was perhaps just as well, since some were not flattering, and described with merciless accuracy a particular idiosyncrasy like an ungainly way of walking or a laugh that sounded like a hyena. I was never told my nickname in any other district, but for some reason I was told that in Tabora I was called Masanja. This is quite a common Nyamwezi family name. I asked why people used it for me, and was told that the Masanja clan came from the north, and that they used that name for me because I spoke Kinyamwezi with a north-country accent. I had not been aware that I had a north-country accent, but I presumed that Pascal Shija from Nzega District was responsible.

Some officials, including the Governor himself, found it hard to master foreign languages, and I was sometimes asked to run spare-time courses for people who needed help to pass the Government Lower Swahili examination in order to be confirmed in their appointments.

As a general rule, missionaries tended to speak Swahili as well as or better than Government officials, but there were some who certainly did not. The Salvation Army ran a camp for destitutes a few miles north of Tabora, and one day the Australian captain who had been in charge of the camp for about twelve years came into my office and asked me to help him deal with a problem. I understand that in Britain those employed by the Salvation Army are normally given ranks that correspond to the titles of commissioned army officers, but that was not always the case in Tanganyika. This problem concerned a Salvation Army sergeant-major and a sergeant who were involved in a bitter quarrel. Unfortunately the captain's knowledge of Swahili was not good enough for him to understand what it was all about.

I was surprised that the captain could not follow what seemed quite simple to me, at least in linguistic terms. The sergeant's daughter was engaged to be married, but she was also pregnant, and the father of her unborn child was not the man she was going to marry. She nevertheless wanted a white wedding. The sergeant-major thought this inappropriate, and insisted that the sergeant and his daughter ought to show a little humility and arrange a very quiet wedding instead. The sergeant stuck to his guns. He wanted a slap-up wedding for his daughter, with as lavish a reception for all his friends as he could afford, and he was jolly well going to have one, whatever the sergeant-major said. I listened to them both without making any comment, but I tended to share the sergeant-major's view on the matter.

The sergeant-major then got angry. He told the sergeant that he and his sinful and immodest daughter should approach the throne of glory with true contrition and penitence. The girl's behaviour was a disgrace, and had brought shame and condemnation on herself, her family, and the Salvation Army as a whole.

This was too much for the sergeant. He shouted back at the

sergeant-major, 'You dare to talk about my family's shame when you have two sons in prison, two daughters who are prostitutes in Mbeya and two more who are prostitutes in Dar es Salaam.' The sergeant-major rolled his eyes and looked up to heaven, and replied, 'That is the cross which our dear Lord has been pleased to lay upon my shoulders.'

I summarised in English for the captain what the two men had said, but I declined to express any opinion about the merits of the case.

The next time I was asked to act as interpeter was shortly before Easter 1957. It also involved translating into English what an African said in Swahili, but this was a very different occasion.

Tabora had an Anglican Church which had regular services taken by laymen, but it had no resident Anglican priest. The town was in the Diocese of Central Tanganyika, and the headquarters of the diocese were situated in the town of Dodoma, in Central Province.

Priests visited Tabora from time to time, and we were pleased to hear that Bishop Yohana Omari, the Assistant Bishop of the Diocese, was planning to pay us a visit. An expatriate wife arranged a tea party at her house, and invited all the English-speaking members of the congregation. She was not a lady I liked very much. She had a habit of announcing to anyone she met that she never used lipstick because the Virgin Mary had not used lipstick. She nevertheless did not hesitate to use other technological innovations which had not been around at the time of the birth of Christ.

When Jennifer and I arrived at the tea party, we were shocked to see our hostess's pretty six-year-old daughter sitting with her face towards the wall in the corner of the living room. Her hair had been clumsily chopped off, and I thought she looked rather like a porcupine. There was a pile of her hair still lying on the polished floor underneath the hard chair on which she was sitting, and she was vainly attempting to mend the frock she was wearing, though she was far too young to be a skilled seamstress.

The mother could not wait to tell us the reason for her daughter's disgrace. The girl had been told to wear her smartest chiffon frock to welcome the bishop, and to be very careful not to tear it. However, while she had been playing in the garden waiting for the bishop to arrive, she had climbed a tree and unintentionally torn her frock. As a result, the girl was told that if she wanted to look ugly for the bishop, then she would be made to look very,

very ugly indeed, and would also be forced to sew her frock in front of all the guests, including the bishop himself.

I still feel shame that I was one of a group of churchgoers who were told with such gloating triumph about such an act of cruelty by a mother to her child, and that none of us offered a word of protest. I was thankful that when the black bishop arrived he managed to show great kindness to the unhappy little white girl. He did not say a word about her appearance or the task she was trying to perform.

Bishop Yohana Omari was the first black man to become an Anglican Bishop in Tanganyika. He did not speak English very well, so he asked me if I would translate his words from Swahili into English as he told us about how he had become a Christian, and the changes which his conversion had brought about for him and his family. I found it deeply moving to repeat in English words the story which he told us in Swahili.

Omari is a Muslim name, and Yohana Omari told us that he had been born into a Muslim family. He said that he had completed Standard X at school, and had become a Medical Assistant working in a Government Hospital. He had been no more and no less corrupt than all the other Medical Assistants, which meant, he said, that he had been very corrupt indeed. He had been keen to improve his education, wanting to read every Swahili book he could get hold of. Whenever a patient came into his ward who was too sick to guard his own personal belongings, the young Muslim Medical Assistant had stolen anything he fancied from the patient's locker. One day he had stolen a book which happened to be a copy of the Swahili New Testament.

When Yohana had started to express an interest in Christianity, his father had been furious, and had ordered all the other members of the family to have nothing more to do with him. Yohana had not abandoned his new-found faith. He had been baptised and changed his way of life. He had stopped beating his wife, and had begun to love his neighbour and to treat his family and other people with a new kindness. He had changed the way in which he bore witness to his love of God.

Not very long after his baptism, he had decided that people's souls lasted longer than their bodies, and that he would give up his work as a Medical Assistant in order to spend his whole life preaching the gospel.

He had became a candidate for ordination, and had served in many parishes before his consecration as a bishop.

He ended his talk by telling us that his father had not been converted from Islam, but that his family had eventually become reconciled to the situation, and were now on friendly terms with him.

As I listened to him and translated what he was saying, I wondered what average respectable churchgoers in middle-class parishes in England would say if their bishop told them that in the early years of his married life he had been a wife-beater, and that he had become a Christian as a direct result of breaking the commandment 'Thou shalt not steal'.

Shortly before Jennifer and I left Tabora, I was licensed as a Lay Reader. Before receiving a licence I had been authorised informally to take services in church, but I was delighted that the document which gave me formal authorisation to do so bore the signature of Bishop Yohana Omari.

The Fundikira Affair

Tabora District had three major chiefs. The titles of chiefs varied from tribe to tribe, but the Nyamwezi title was *Mtemi*. Mtemi Kitambi, who ruled in the northern part of the District, was an amiable man who did his job adequately but was not a very dynamic leader.

Unlike Kitambi, Haroun Msabila Lugusha, the Mtemi of Sikonge in the southern part of the District, was a man of exceptional ability and initiative. His qualities of intellect and personality were comparable to those of the Chief of the Hehe tribe, Adam Sapi Mkwawa. Both men had been appointed as African Members of Legislative Council at a time when few Africans achieved this distinction, and they were very highly respected by their own people and by people of other races as well.

Sikonge Chiefdom shared a boundary with Unyanyembe Chiefdom, where the Mtemi was Nassoro Saidi Fundikira. Unyanyembe was situated between Sikonge and the outskirts of Tabora township, and had been a focal point along the route followed by the slave and ivory traders during the nineteenth century. The Mtemi of Unyanyembe lived in a palace shaded by countless mango trees in an immaculate compound in the village of Itetemia. The family was an old aristocratic line. The Mtemi in the early part of the nineteenth century had also been called Fundikira.

Nassoro Saidi Fundikira had become the chief following the deposition of his father, Saidi Fundikira, who had been involved in some sort of corruption, and had been exiled by the British administration to Shinyanga District in Lake Province, where he was still living during the 1950s. I was not told the details of exactly what Saidi Fundikira had done, but he was generally thought of as a rather nasty man. I never met him.

The system of Indirect Rule, introduced to Tanganyika between 1925 and 1931, when Sir Donald Cameron was Governor, was probably the best way in which a colonial power with just a handful of expatriate officials scattered over a huge area of Africa could, with the consent of the people, rule effectively and maintain law and order. However, any system of Government is only as good as the people who administer it, and some powerful traditional rulers, and also the administrators who guided them, were inevitably better than others. It was bound to cause unrest when a traditional ruler abused his power so badly that the colonial government ceased to have confidence in him and decided to replace him with someone else.

Many people initially regarded Nassoro Fundikira as a great improvement on his father. He was a heavily built man with very strong horn-rimmed spectacles. He usually wore the traditional robes and ornaments of a great chief, with what looked like a very large piece of ivory fixed to the top of his head, and a very long cord of cowrie shells tied around his neck. He wore expensive leather shoes, and was always extremely smart in his appearance. He also measured up well to all the usual criteria by which officials tended to judge whether a chief was efficient or not. Taxes were collected promptly. The villages in the chiefdom were clean. School attendance was not bad. Peasant farmers seemed diligent. There seemed to be comparatively few delays in getting cases heard in Chief Fundikira's Local Court. If workers were needed to repair a road or a Local Authority building, the Chief's subordinates always enrolled enough men to complete the task quickly. A few years before I arrived in Tabora, Chief Fundikira had been awarded the OBE. Many chiefs were awarded the so-called 'Queen's Medal for Chiefs', but an OBE was an indication that someone in authority had thought particularly highly of Fundikira.

Nassoro Fundikira seemed friendly enough when I arrived in Tabora. On Christmas Day 1956 he even paid Jennifer and me a courtesy call at our house to bring us his greetings, though he himself was a Muslim. I began to have misgivings about him, however, when I travelled in Unyanyembe on safari, and a worryingly large number of Africans started coming to visit me

228 The Flags Changed at Midnight

secretly after dark in the villages where I happened to be camping, in order to make complaints to me about the actions of their Mtemi. Their complaints concerned a wide range of abuses, but the accusers invariably came alone and spoke in a whisper. I saw that they were very frightened, and always replied to them as softly as I could in case an eavesdropper was around. I reminded them that it was an offence to make false accusations to a government official, and that they needed other reliable witnesses to corroborate their allegations if they were to be taken seriously. However, I could not completely dismiss from my mind the possibility that they were telling me the truth, and that Fundikira really was brutal and corrupt.

Denis O'Callaghan completed his tour of service and went on leave in March 1957, but before he did so he arranged for Fundikira to be awarded a British Council travel scholarship to Britain at the same time so that he could show him around. Peter Hopkins took over as Acting District Commissioner.

As soon as both Denis and Fundikira were safely out of the District, a number of people who had been too frightened till then to make themselves heard came forward. Small groups of people came to Peter and me and repeated some of the stories which we had already heard secretly, from one accuser alone. They also told us about some other incidents as well.

Peter Hopkins and I discussed a plan of action with Charles Sutcliffe, the Provincial Superintendent of Police, and it was agreed that Charles should lead a specially selected team of non-Nyamwezi detectives to investigate the allegations against Fundikira, that Peter should be resonsible for dealing with the possible political implications of the affair, and that I should move from my normal office into a tiny room situated in a remote corner of the Boma compound, out of sight of the general public, and there record, in my capacity as a magistrate, the statements made on oath by those who wanted to accuse Fundikira. It was agreed that I ought to be the only magistrate involved in this task, as my knowledge of both Swahili and Kinyamwezi was good enough to enable me to record statements without needing an interpreter, and using an interpreter might endanger the confidentiality of what we were doing.

The sworn statements which I recorded related to three types of crime. Some people alleged that Fundikira had ordered the assassination of several of his enemies, though no one ever suggested that he had himself carried out the murders. Without any confessions by the killers or any statements from eyewitnesses who had heard Fundikira giving his orders to the killers, and with little reliable evidence about the causes of death so long after the victims had died, it seemed unlikely that the High Court would convict Fundikira on charges of conspiracy to murder.

Many fathers also claimed that Fundikira had raped their daughters, and produced the girls who said Fundikira had had sex with them without their consent. When I recorded those statements I had no reason to believe the girls were lying, but I thought that so long after the event, and without any form of medical examination, it would be extremely difficult to secure a conviction for rape if Fundikira defended himself by claiming that the girls had consented, even if eyewitnesses stated that they had seen the girls in Fundikira's bed.

The last accusation concerned a large cash box bequeathed to his heirs by a very rich Nyamwezi tribesman. The box was alleged to have contained about 88,000 shillings, an immense amount of money for any African at that time. The relatives claimed that Fundikira had taken the box away for safe keeping in his palace when the owner died, and that the lawful heirs had never received their share of the money, but had always been threatened by Fundikira when they asked him about it. The money was never recovered, and my belief is that it was used to finance an affluent life-style for Fundikira and his supporters. The statements made by the witnesses contained no discrepancies either on major issues or on matters of detail, and I thought that the case against Fundikira on this count was strong.

One of the people who had made a sworn statement to me was found dead a couple of days later. An investigation took place, but no one was ever charged concerning his death. It might possibly have been from natural causes, but it might have been caused by a vegetable poison which could not be traced. I suspect that the man was murdered, but I have no idea of how or by whom. It was clear that Fundikira himself could not be directly implicated in this death, as he was abroad at the time it occurred. Nevertheless, rumours about an investigation into his activities began to circulate, and the fear grew that, even though Fundikira himself might be in Britain, his henchmen were still around and were ruthless enough to take whatever steps they thought necessary to protect their boss's interests.

As soon as I completed recording the statements and got the deponents to sign them as a correct record of what they had said, all the papers about the case were sent to Dar es Salaam, and were considered by Executive Council.

I understand, though I was not present at their discussions, that the whole Executive Council agreed that Fundikira ought not to be allowed to continue to hold the post of Chief of Unyanyembe, but that the majority wanted the matter to be dealt with quietly and with as little fuss as possible. It would be expedient to deal with Nassoro Fundikira in a similar way to his father Saidi Fundikira, and simply depose him and exile him from Unyanyembe. However, at least one member of Executive Council expressed a different view. The recently appointed Attorney-General, a man named Cole, thought that law-breakers, however powerful and prominent they might be, were not above the law, and that it was essential for justice to be seen to be done. In his view, Fundikira should stand trial on a charge relating to the misappropriation of the money in the cash box. When he threatened to resign and make a public statement about his reasons for doing so, his view prevailed. Government lawyers prepared an arrest warrant to be served on Fundikira as soon as he returned in August.

All the officials concerned with the case tried to keep the investigation secret, but when he got home from Britain, Fundikira somehow came to hear the news that he was about to be arrested. While Charles Sutcliffe was knocking at the locked door of the Chief's palace in Itetemia with an arrest warrant in his hand, there was a loud explosion from inside the house. After the door was forced open, Fundikira's body was found lying on the floor. He had committed suicide by shooting himself with his elephant rifle.

I have very mixed feelings about the whole case. Fundikira's tyranny had caused terror and suffering to many of his subjects, and I agonised about whether a more prompt and determined response by expatriate officials, myself included, might have helped to protect some of Nassoro Fundikira's victims and encouraged Fundikira to mend his ways and rule his people justly.

However, the people of Unyanyembe did not seem to regard Nassoro Fundikira's death as rescuing them from oppression. I had never seen anything comparable to the scenes of hysterical lamentation and wailing throughout Unyanyembe which followed the news of his suicide. The colonial regime was widely blamed for driving a great national hero to suicide. Whatever they may have thought secretly, none of the people of Unyanyembe openly praised the Government for taking appropriate action in an attempt to bring a tyrant to justice.

Just before Jennifer and I went on home leave, Nassoro's younger brother Abdullah Fundikira was elected as the new Mtemi of Unyanyembe. Abdullah was a university graduate working for the Agricultural Department, and I felt confident that he would be an excellent chief and would clean up the corruption left by his brother. I did not remain in Tabora long enough to see for myself how Abdullah Fundikira ruled Unyanyembe.

Laws unto Themselves

The maintenance of law and order is an essential ingredient of good government throughout the world. Unfortunately, the methods of preventing crime and punishing criminals which are suitable for one type of country or society are not necessarily appropriate for another.

During the time that I served in Tanganyika, there were two distinct systems for the administration of justice. The supreme judicial organ was Her Majesty's High Court, headed by the Chief Justice, who was assisted by half a dozen Puisne Judges. Every Judge had obtained legal qualifications in Britain. I believe that they were all barristers.

The High Court was based in Dar es Salaam, but High Court Judges also presided over Sessions held at regular intervals in the more important up-country stations, including Iringa and Tabora. High Court Sessions were always held in English, and court interpreters were used as appropriate in order to translate the proceedings to and from Swahili or a tribal language. When the accused or a witness spoke only a tribal language, a Boma Messenger was usually called in to interpret from the tribal language into Swahili, thus doubling the chance of mistakes.

In every district, there was a Subordinate Court, established under the provisions of the Subordinate Courts Ordinance of 1941, which replaced earlier legislation enacted in 1930. There were about thirty Resident Magistrates, most of whom were stationed in larger District Headquarters. Every District Officer, even a Cadet, was a magistrate, but the extent of his jurisdiction depended on his seniority. Many cases were heard in Swahili. Special provisions existed for the supervision of the judicial work done by Cadets, and severe sentences imposed by any Subordinate Court had to be confirmed by the High Court. There was a right of appeal from Subordinate Courts to the High Court, and from the High Court to the Court of Appeal for Eastern

Africa. High Court Judges made use of assessors to advise them, but there was no provision for trial by jury.

Free legal aid was provided by the Government for those charged with serious offences such as murder or manslaughter, and who could not afford to pay for their own defence. The fees paid to defending lawyers were calculated on a flat rate-per-case basis. This may have encouraged some lawyers to save their own and the Court's time by persuading their clients to plead guilty in cases which could reasonably have been contested. Whenever an accused person pleaded not guilty, this involved hearing the evidence of all the prosecution witnesses, and it took much longer than dealing with a simple plea of guilty.

The High Court system had some features which distinguished it from the British system, but it also incorporated a number of elements which are regarded as essential ingredients of British justice. The balance of probability was acceptable in a civil case, but in a criminal case the prosecution had to prove the guilt of the accused beyond the shadow of a doubt.

It surprised me to discover that some laws enacted in India had also been applied to Tanganyika. One of these, the Indian Evidence Act, included a provision, aimed at discouraging over-zealous policemen, to the effect that a statement made in the presence of a police officer by a person charged with an offence was not admissible in evidence. This meant that confessions had to be recorded by a magistrate while the accused person was put in the custody of an office messenger. I was a witness in many High Court cases, and nearly all of them involved submitting copies of statements made by the accused which I had myself recorded.

Alongside the system of courts established by the British on lines that broadly resembled the English system, there was a system of indigenous tribunals. These were to be found in larger villages in every district, and were usually presided over by a chief or sub-chief, assisted by one or more court elders. Such courts had functioned for many years before the colonial era, but their existence was ratified, and the extent of their powers and jurisdiction was established, in the Native Courts Ordinance of 1929, which was replaced in 1951 by the Local Courts Ordinance. Two important features of these courts were that they could only deal with cases involving Africans, and no litigant could be represented by a lawyer. Nearly all the cases dealt with in chiefs' courts concerned what was referred to as Native Law and Custom, but the courts also had power to deal with infringements of certain other laws. Cases were heard either in Swahili or in a tribal language, but the cases were always recorded in Swahili by the Court Clerk, and all the documents used in Local Courts were printed in Swahili.

Native Law and Custom varied significantly from tribe to tribe. Some tribes regarded adultery, for example, as a criminal offence, while others did not. Each tribe had its own rules concerning such matters as inheritance, custody of children, divorce, and the disposal of the bride-price following a divorce. Local Courts could divorce couples who had married in accordance with Native Law and Custom, but they had no jurisdiction to grant a divorce to those who had contracted a Christian marriage.

Appeals from Local Courts were dealt with by special tribal Appeal Courts, and appeal from a Local Appeal Court lay to the District Commissioner, who might delegate this task to a District Officer. In the areas inhabited by some very litigious tribes, the volume of work generated by 'DC's Appeals' was enormous, but in the Districts where I served I was only rarely involved in hearing such appeals.

Most Local Courts were administered reasonably well, but the standard of justice in any judicial system depends greatly on the integrity and energy of the court holders, and a few Local Courts were not satisfactory. One element of a District Officer's job which I regarded as being particularly important consisted of the regular inspection of all Local Court records, both in the Boma and on safari, to make sure that cases were dealt with promptly, that the sentences imposed seemed reasonable, and that fines did not remain unpaid. Local Courts had power to imprison offenders, and all sentences of imprisonment had to be confirmed by a District Officer.

It is easy to criticise as racist a system under which indigenous people are subject to the jurisdiction of courts which have no power to try non-natives. However, the existence of Local Courts was consistent with the objectives of the policy of Indirect Rule. Long before the arrival of the colonial powers, it was already accepted that courts presided over by traditional rulers normally dealt with all civil and criminal cases within their own tribes. To change that system, and to insist that cases should be tried centrally by a non-native magistrate, would have seriously undermined the status of the chief or sub-chief. It would have created an impossible work-load for magistrates, and would have required them to become familiar with the laws and customs of many different tribes. It would also have forced litigants and witnesses to travel into District Headquarters to attend hearings which might take place many days' journey from their home villages. Whatever their defects in theory, in practice Local Courts were absolutely essential to the administration of justice with the consent of the people.

There was no direct link between Local Courts and the High Court. The only officials who were involved in the day-to-day operation of both systems were District Officers. They scrutinised the work of Local Courts, and their work as Subordinate Court magistrates was subject to the scrutiny of the High Court.

When I arrived in Tanganyika on first appointment, I had sworn a judicial oath in front of the then Chief Justice, Sir Herbert Cox. He had impressed me as a kindly old gentleman who appeared to subscribe to the view of the Lord Chancellor in Gilbert and Sullivan's operetta *Iolanthe* that the law was the true embodiment of everything that was excellent, that it had no kind of fault or flaw, and that he himself embodied the law.

I had no more dealings with him until I became Sir Edward Twining's Private Secretary. One morning, the Governor asked me to deal with a letter he had received from the Chief Justice, which was marked 'Personal'. The first page set out at some length Sir Herbert Cox's views concerning the separation of the judiciary from the executive, and the reasons which made him unwilling to give instructions himself to officials who were part of a separate hierarchy headed by the Governor.

His letter then went on to explain that the wood-burning stove in his garden which provided him and his household with hot water was not working satisfactorily, and that he would appreciate it if the Governor could take the necessary measures to get the boiler mended. The letter was politely but extremely pompously worded, and Twining simply passed it to me for action. I telephoned the Executive Engineer of the Public Works Department to let him know the Chief Justice's request. I asked him to let me know as soon as the repair was completed, and a few hours later I got a phone call to tell me the job was done. The Chief Justice could have saved himself and other people unnecessary trouble if he or one of his subordinates had telephoned the Executive Engineer, but that would have been beneath his dignity.

People were amused by the pomposity of Sir Herbert Cox, but I never heard anyone criticise his competence as a lawyer. A judge who attracted criticism for delivering verdicts which seemed incomprehensible and passing sentences which seemed idiosyncratic was Judge Derek Harbord, known to his less intimate acquaintances as 'Cardboard'.

As a young man, Harbord had, in the same period, been called to the bar and also ordained as a deacon. He had then served as an Anglican priest for several years, but had resigned to become a Roman Catholic. However, he could not become a Roman Catholic priest because he was already married, so he used his qualification as a barrister to practise at the English bar. He then joined the Colonial Legal Service and became a Resident Magistrate in Northern Rhodesia. In 1953, he was appointed a High Court Judge in Tanganyika, and soon became the subject of gossip wherever he presided over High Court Sessions. The main jokes concerned the leniency of the sentences he imposed on Roman Catholics and the severity of the sentences he imposed for arson. People suggested that he would have a breakdown if ever he had to try a Roman Catholic charged with arson. It was ironic that he was received back into the Church of England after more than twenty years as a Roman Catholic, and then became the rector of a church in London which was severely damaged when one of the drug addicts sheltering overnight in the crypt set fire to it.

Harbord had many likeable qualities. He was hospitable, friendly, and an amusing raconteur. One of the stories which I heard him tell on several occasions was about a radio show in which members of a team consisting of the Radio Cook, the Conductor of the London Symphony Orchestra, the Poet Laureate, and the Lord Chief Justice were asked to come up with their ideas for a collective noun similar to 'a pride of lions' to describe a group of prostitutes. The Radio Cook suggested 'a jam of tarts', the Conductor suggested 'a flourish of strumpets', the Poet Laureate suggested 'an anthology of pro's' and the Lord Chief Justice won the competition by suggesting 'a firm of solicitors'. The joke was always received with laughter. I suspect that Harbord was happy not just to be the centre of attention whenever he told it, but also, as a barrister, to repeat over and over again a joke which poked fun at solicitors.

His jokes did no great harm to anybody, but I felt sorry for those whom he sentenced to longer sentences in prison than other judges would have imposed. My first experience of this had been in Iringa. Among the accused people appearing before Harbord were a semi-literate African peasant and a bus driver of mixed race. The peasant had been swindled by an Arab trader, and wrote him an abusive letter in which he included a threat to kill him. He never attempted to carry out the threat, and the Arab did not appear to take it too seriously.

In an earlier chapter I have already mentioned the bus driver and the accident he caused by getting drunk a few miles before descending a steep escarpment on the Iringa–Kilosa Road. The incident was memorable because of the large number of dead and injured, and also for the dedicated care which the injured received from the Medical Officer, Dr William Burkitt. Another factor which made the case memorable was that when Harbord came to try the cases of the peasant and of the bus driver he imposed a much more severe sentence on the unsophisticated victim of a swindler than he did on the driver who had caused many deaths and injuries by driving his bus while drunk. My colleagues and I could not understand the reason for Harbord's decisions.

Some years later, when Harbord came to Tabora to preside over High Court Sessions there, he greeted me in a very friendly way, and asked me to sit in his Court with Tabora's two very intelligent Assistant District Officers, Herbert Gondwe and G N Nayar, both of whom were likely to be appointed as magistrates in the near future. He wanted me to explain to them both as much as I could about the procedure and working methods of the High Court. I said that I might have to leave the courtroom if it proved necessary for me to give evidence about statements which two of the people awaiting trial had made, and which I had recorded. Harbord was very affable about it, and said that that would be no problem at all.

The statements I had recorded both related to homicide cases. In one, a farmer had allowed his goats to stray into the maize plot of his neighbour, a lady who used very unladylike language when she saw what the goats had done to her maize. The owner of the goats had lost his temper when the woman insulted him, picked up a pestle (used for grinding corn) and hit her with it, rupturing her spleen. Before she died the following day, she apologised to her assailant for the filthy language she had used, he apologised to her for hitting her, and they forgave each other, saying that they would meet again in heaven.

In the second case, a road gang headman employed by the Public Works Department arrived home at the end of a working day to find his unweaned baby crying and his wife nowhere to be seen. He was told that she had deserted both her baby and her husband, and had gone off with her boyfriend, accompanied by her brother. The road gang headman had then gone to look for his wife, and when he found her and asked her to come home and breast-feed the baby, the brother and the boyfriend had both attacked him and said to him, 'Today you will die.' They had then begun to beat him. When he made his statement to me a day later, I made a note of all the marks of appalling violence on his body. The road gang headman told me that he had been forced on to his back by his two enemies, one of whom sat on his chest while the other beat him mercilessly. His hands had been tied together with rope, but he had somehow managed to get his left hand free, though he was not left-handed, and had taken the sheath-knife which he used every day to cut liana creepers in the forest, and had stabbed upward into the bottom of the lung of the man who was sitting on his chest. The man had died within a few minutes, and the road gang headman had walked about thirty miles through the night to give himself up immediately to the police in Tabora.

When I recorded his statement, I thought that, if other witnesses corroborated it, as they later did, it was an obvious case of killing in self-defence, and that the accused would be acquitted. Charles Rees, the Acting Resident Magistrate, told me that he agreed with my view, but had nevertheless committed the man for trial so that the decision to acquit would be taken by a judge rather than by himself. He said later that he bitterly regretted the part he had himself played in the case.

When the accused were asked to plead, no proper explanation was given to either of them about the distinction between murder, manslaughter, or justifiable homicide, and each admitted having killed his victim. In both cases, this was recorded as a plea of guilty to manslaughter.

In passing sentence, Harbord explained that the owner of the goats had killed a woman who had provoked him by using obscene language. The accused had apologised and been forgiven, and the case was, in his view, not serious. The accused had already spent four months in prison on remand awaiting trial, and the Court would therefore impose a sentence which would result in his immediate release from custody.

I and my two colleagues thought that Harbord must be in a good mood, and that the next case would also be dealt with leniently. We were quite wrong. He took no account of the fact that the accused carried a knife as a tool which he needed every day to do his job. He announced to the Court that the practice of carrying knives was quite intolerable, and that the accused would be imprisoned for seven years.

Herbert Gondwe and G N Nayar were both just as astonished as I was, and they asked me to explain the reasons which had made the judge impose a far more severe sentence for what seemed to be a less serious offence. I confessed that I too was completely bewildered. We therefore decided to approach the prosecuting Crown Counsel, to ask if he could seek clarification from the judge himself. The Crown Counsel replied that people never asked Harbord for an explanation of the reasons for the sentences he imposed. Harbord would probably take grave offence at such questions, which he would regard as implying criticism of his competence as a judge.

Sir Herbert Cox retired while I was stationed in Tabora. He was succeeded by a new Chief Justice called E J Davies, who happened to preside at the next High Court Sessions to be held there after Harbord's visit.

I gave evidence before Judge Davies in English about a statement made to me in Swahili by the accused, and as I was giving my evidence I noticed that the court interpreter had translated my words incorrectly to the accused. With the new Chief Justice's permission, I spoke in Swahili to correct what the interpreter had said, and I then carried on giving the rest of my evidence in English.

Charles Rees and his wife Celia had invited Jennifer and me and a few other guests to dine with them that evening in order to meet the new Chief Justice socially. Charles had previously been a District Officer, but he had serious heart trouble, and was no longer able to go on safari, so he had been appointed as an Acting Resident Magistrate.

Over dinner the conversation turned to legal matters, and someone referred to the problems that could arise when the person presiding in a court of law did not have any knowledge of the language which the accused and the witnesses were using, and the accused did not understand the language of the court.

I then mentioned that the terms 'murder' and 'manslaughter' and 'justifiable homicide' did not mean exactly the same in English, but that many interpreters, when they translated a charge, simply used the words 'you are charged with killing', and made no attempt to explain in Swahili the different types of homicide. The answer, 'Yes, I killed him,' was generally assumed to be a plea of guilty to manslaughter, and I said that I suspected that many people who had been convicted of manslaughter on their own plea of guilty might well have killed in self-defence, and would have been acquitted if they had really understood the charge and pleaded 'not guilty' instead.

Davies did not seem pleased at the tenor of the conversation, and said loudly and pompously, 'I have been a Member of Her

Majesty's Overseas Judiciary for over thirty years and I have never once learnt a single word of a foreign language, and I don't intend to start now.'

I replied, 'In that case the standard of justice administered in your court depends on the competence and integrity of your court interpreter, and in my experience those are qualities one ought not to take for granted in Tanganyika.'

It was very discourteous to my host and hostess for me to make such a remark at the dinner table, and it infuriated the new Chief Justice. The following day, I apologised to Charles and Celia for behaving so badly, but Charles said he agreed entirely with what I had said, and that someone needed to say it.

Conduct Unbecoming

When I was a boy, I was taught that people in positions of trust who committed crimes directly linked to their jobs deserved to be punished more severely than other criminals. My views about this were apparently not shared by everyone in the judiciary in Tanganyika.

When auditors visited the provincial depot of a Department shortly before I arrived in Tabora, they discovered that large quantities of timber and other materials were missing. Investigations were put in hand, and it became clear that the theft was an inside job, but the police were unable to get conclusive evidence linking the theft as a whole to any one individual. It was clear that the provincial head of department, a professionally qualified European, had been culpably negligent about enforcing the rules concerning security of Government property, but such inefficiency was not in itself sufficient to justify prosecuting him. However, the police also established that he had in his possession, and claimed as his personal property, certain items of furniture that had been made for him under his orders by carpenters paid from the funds of his department. The timber from which this furniture was made was proved to be government property, and the head of department was charged with theft. He was convicted of stealing a comparatively small amount of timber, and given a short sentence of imprisonment.

He elected to start serving his sentence immediately, but appealed against his conviction and sentence. The High Court allowed the appeal, ostensibly on the grounds that a prison sentence, however short, would also result in the loss of his job

and his pension rights, which was, in the opinion of the Appeal
Court Judge, a more serious punishment than the circumstances
of the case justified.

I was shocked by this reasoning, which meant that a man who
was known to be dishonest was allowed to go back to a position
of responsibility in the public service. I thought the judgment sent
out all the wrong messages, and could also be quoted as an
example by those who claimed that the law dealt more severely
with Africans than it did with Europeans.

Not every member of the judiciary was so lenient to British
people accused of crimes. Towards the end of 1956, there was a
case in Tabora District involving a European lawyer in private
practice, who had been charged together with two Asian bus
owners with various offences which included attempting to
pervert the course of justice.

The lawyer had previously been a Resident Magistrate in Tabora.
He had resigned from the public service and had set up in private
practice in Mwanza. I do not know the exact circumstances which
led to his resignation, but the Liwali of Tabora, whom I regarded as
a man of complete integrity, described him to me as *yule mzungu
mchafu* – 'that dirty European'. Since he had moved to Mwanza,
however, he appeared to be doing well for himself and his clients,
who included a number with doubtful reputations.

He was engaged to defend two Sikh bus owners who lived in
Tabora and had been charged with a number of traffic offences.
They had been found by a policeman called Wenceslas when they
were carrying passengers for reward in an unroadworthy bus. As
soon as the Sikhs engaged a European lawyer, he visited Tabora,
and questioned Wenceslas, with the aid of an Indian interpreter,
about his evidence.

Constable Wenceslas later stated on oath in court that the
lawyer had offered him a bribe of 25 shillings to change his statement, but that he had refused to do so, and had reported the
matter to his superiors. In addition to the charges relating to the
traffic offences, the bus owners and their lawyer were then
charged with various more serious offences.

The case was regarded as sufficiently important to justify
sending two exceptionally able and experienced lawyers to
Tabora to deal with it. John (later Sir John) Summerfield, a Crown
Counsel, prosecuted, and the case was tried by a senior resident
magistrate, Philip (later Sir Philip) Biron, who became a judge a
year or two later. Both Summerfield and Biron were highly
respected.

The trial took more than three weeks. Wenceslas gave his evidence without faltering, and when the court adjourned one Friday afternoon an Indian witness was still giving evidence to the effect that he had heard the lawyer making the offer of a bribe in English and that he himself had translated it into Swahili for Constable Wenceslas. He, too, initially stuck to his story under cross-examination.

Government officers worked on Saturday mornings, and the case was adjourned until the following day. Next morning, however, the Indian who had acted as interpreter could not be found. When he eventually turned up on Monday morning, he said that the statement he had made on Friday afternoon was untrue, and that he had not heard any offer of a bribe by the accused. He had only made his previous statement because the police had intimidated him into doing so.

I suspect that he was well paid for withdrawing his statement, involving as it did the probability that he would be charged with perjury and sent to prison.

While all this was going on, I was in the squash court which was part of the Boma compound and adjoined the Resident Magistrate's court. I was there to supervise the punishment of a juvenile delinquent with a string of previous convictions whom I had just convicted for his latest offence of shoplifting. He and his father had both begged for mercy on the grounds that the boy had been accepted for training in Pakistan as a religious leader, and an addition to his series of convictions for shoplifting might prejudice his chances of getting there. I was unmoved by this plea. The boy was a habitual thief, and, though it was no concern of mine, I did not think he had the qualities needed by a religious leader of whatever faith.

The options for dealing with juvenile delinquents in Tanganyika were very limited, and I sentenced the boy to six strokes with a light bamboo cane. The boy was medically examined, and the sentence was then carried out by a Boma Messenger in my presence. Any sentence of corporal punishment had to be carried out in the presence of a magistrate.

In my experience, the naughtier the delinquent, the louder he screamed, and this delinquent was very naughty indeed. I was told that his piercing shrieks were plainly audible in the magistrate's court, and that Philip Biron had looked down from his desk over the top of his spectacles and asked the prosecuting counsel, while the screams were still going on, 'Are the police taking another statement, Mr Summerfield?'

The case against the lawyer and the bus owners might have collapsed when the interpreter whom the police had called to corroborate the evidence of Wenceslas withdrew the statement which he had already made on oath. However, John Summerfield did not drop the prosecution. The case dragged on for a very long time. Some witnesses gave evidence which contradicted the evidence of other witnesses, and even the evidence which they themselves had already given. The case record covered more than a thousand pages of evidence, and, when Philip Biron gave his judgment, it took thirteen hours, from 8 a.m. till 9 p.m., to deliver. The bus owners and their lawyer were all convicted and imprisoned.

While Philip Biron was in process of delivering his judgment, the Indian interpreter was arrested and charged with perjury, and he too was later imprisoned in a separate case.

In August 1957, I was personally involved in another case concerning a European suspect. It was alleged that he had been the driver in a fatal traffic accident on the Tabora–Sikonge Road. All the Africans in the village where the accident happened had no doubt about who had caused it, but the suspect denied it, and because of legal technicalities that were understood in Britain but meant very little to Africans, no one was ever charged with causing an old woman's death.

Shortly before the accident happened, I had driven from Tabora to Sikonge Mission, with my Boma Messenger, Maulidi Omari, in order to take the oral part of my Kinyamwezi interpretership examination. I had already passed the written part the previous week. The examining board included the Mtemi of Sikonge, Haroun Msabila Lugusha, the Headmaster of the Boys' Secondary School, John Crabbe, and the doctor in charge of Sikonge Mission Hospital, Dr Arthur Keevill, who had spent many years in Unyamwezi, and spoke the tribal language fluently.

At the end of the test I was told that I had passed, and I began the drive back to Tabora. When Maulidi and I were passing through a small village on a straight stretch of sandy road, I was stopped by a group of villagers who showed me the body of a very frail old woman lying in the road. I was told that she was totally deaf, and had been walking with her five-year-old granddaughter when she had been knocked down and killed instantly by a small heavily-loaded ash-coloured Volkswagen car, and that the car had been driven by a European man who had a woman passenger in the front seat with him. Some villagers said the woman was holding a baby on her lap but others said they had not seen a baby. The villagers then showed me a point about fifty yards from where the body was lying, and said that the driver had stopped his car there, had got out and made a clear footprint in the sand, then got back into the car and driven away at very high speed, without returning to help the woman he had knocked down, or speaking to any of the villagers.

I had not seen a Volkswagen on the road between Sikonge and the site of the accident, and assumed that the driver was heading for Chunya, in Southern Highlands Province, south of Tabora District. I drove back as fast as I could to Tabora, and reported the accident to the Assistant Superintendent of Police, who radioed to Chunya Police Station to request them to stop any Volkswagen car and question the driver.

A few hours later, Chunya Police replied to the effect that they had stopped a suspect car and were detaining its driver, a European employed in the private sector in Lake Province, who was going on holiday in what was then called Southern Rhodesia. The police officer alleged that when the driver was stopped his wife had exclaimed, 'My God! It must have been that old woman,' but she and her husband later denied that she had made any such remark, or that they had been involved in any accident.

What initially seemed a clear-cut case proved to have some problems. The footprint in the sand became invisible and it was not possible to compare it with the shoe the suspect was wearing. There was not a single bump on the bodywork of the car, and it was thought that even though the dead woman was small and frail, there would have been a dent if she had been hit so hard that she died. The impact had apparently been on the off-side of the car, but a mark which looked as if it might be a blood stain was on the near side of the car, and forensic tests were not able to establish whether it was blood at all, let alone the blood of the deceased woman. The wife of the suspect explained the mark as having been caused by the remains of a tin of proprietary baby broth, which the baby had rejected while the car was in motion, and which she had thrown out of the window. Technically the weakest point in the case against the suspect was the fact that the only eyewitness had been a little girl of five. None of the villagers who ran out of their houses when they heard a noise had actually seen the accident happen, and when they saw the driver of the Volkswagen car, he had been too far away for them to identify him with certainty. The little girl picked out the suspect car without hesitation at an identity parade of scores of cars assembled in Tabora, including my own, but the Government lawyers in Dar decided that the evidence of a child of five was not strong enough to obtain a conviction in face of the denials of the suspect and his wife. Unfortunately, this case may have reinforced the view sometimes expressed in Tanganyika that Europeans generally escaped punishment in cases involving Africans.

There were more scandals in Tabora than in any of the other stations where I served, but even there most of the expatriate officials were honest, competent, hard-working men and women who were doing their best to promote the development of Tanganyika and its people. Sadly, just as when a prominent politician in Britain is found to have done something discreditable and his whole party becomes tainted with accusations of corruption and sleaze, so in Tanganyika the reputation of British officials in general suffered disproportionate damage because of the actions of a very small minority.

It's a Girl

Jennifer's pregnancy progressed quite smoothly, although we had to deal with a few minor domestic problems. One day our cook Lameck came and showed me a letter he had just received. It was written in Kinyakyusa, and told him that his brother had died and that he was now urgently needed back in Tukuyu to take care of all his brother's children. We were very sorry to lose Lameck, who was a good friend and an excellent cook, but we engaged another experienced elderly cook to replace him. It transpired that he was lazy and an indifferent cook, and though he remained with us until the end of our tour, we did not ask him to join us at our next station when we returned from leave.

Our superbly loyal and efficient houseboy, who stayed with us until we left Tanganyika, was called Juma Farjallah, and we had appointed as our laundry boy a young lad who was also called Juma. The cook we took on in place of Lameck was called Juma as well. The Swahili word for Friday is *ijumaa*, and I believe that most of the people given that name were born on a Friday, which is the Islamic holy day. Our three servants all called Juma had no problems about knowing which one we were speaking to, but Jennifer and I used to refer to them between ourselves as 'Big Juma', 'Little Juma', and 'Ancient Juma'.

Little Juma had started work as our garden boy, and when we promoted him to laundry boy we engaged a Nyamwezi tribesman called Omari Abdullah to work in our garden. Omari was extremely hard-working, a teetotaller, scrupulously honest, and sang very softly to himself all the time. He got on well with Big Juma, and stayed with us for more than five years.

Little Juma's promotion was not a great success. He scrubbed clothes with such boundless enthusiasm that they rapidly fell to pieces. The sheets and pillowcases that we had been given as wedding presents went into holes in a matter of a few weeks. When Jennifer asked him to try to wash clothes more gently, he thought this meant he was not getting them clean enough, and scrubbed them even more ferociously.

Jennifer reluctantly decided that it was just not possible to teach him the skills of a good laundry boy, so we offered him his old job in the garden at no reduction of pay, and we invited Omari to become our laundry boy. Omari accepted eagerly, but Little Juma was not willing to revert to his previous job, and ceased to work for us. Omari became an excellent laundry boy, and under Big Juma's tuition he also learned all the skills of a good houseboy.

Not long after he stopped working for us, Little Juma came to my office in the Boma and showed me a medical certficate which said that he was suffering from leprosy. He wanted me to help him get treatment, and I gave him a note to take to a leprosarium not far from Tabora. I gather that he never turned up there.

Jennifer had been told that her baby was due about the third week of April, but the month was already drawing to a close before she decided that it was time for her to be admitted to hospital. She went in early on 29th April, and when I arrived at the Boma that morning, Peter Hopkins, the District Commissioner, told me that he did not want to see me again until after the baby had been born, and that I was to remain with Jennifer through her confinement.

Jennifer was in labour for about 36 hours, and eventually gave birth on the evening of 30th April to a healthy daughter weighing a little over eight pounds. We called her Ruth Margaret. She was born exactly ten months after our wedding day.

Within an hour or two of Jennifer's admission to the maternity ward, our friend Dinah Sawe, the wife of Joseph Sawe, was also admitted. She had her baby son Andrew by Caesarean section, and he was born a few hours before Ruth.

The Islamic month of Ramadhan, when devout Muslims fast every day until sundown, fell in April that year, and the new moon which heralded Id-el-Fitr and the end of the month of fasting was sighted at the precise moment when Ruth was born. For the whole time that we remained in Tanganyika, Muslims always referred to Ruth as *Mwanaidi* – 'Daughter of the Festival', and treated her with particular affection and kindness. I did not ever need to tell African strangers that our daughter was often called Mwanaidi – they already knew.

Joseph and I were both thrilled at our wives and their new babies, and we gazed adoringly at the beautiful little white girl and the beautiful little black boy asleep in their cots side by side next to their mothers.

From the time they were a day old, both babies were moved back overnight into the labour ward to give their mothers a chance to sleep, and one night a Somali woman came into the hospital to have her baby. The midwife was rather contemptuous about the fuss that Somali women always made when they gave birth, but I do not think she realised that female circumcision was very common among Somali women, and that the pain of childbirth for them was even more excruciating than for women who had not been mutilated. The screams of the Somali mother were distressing for Ruth and Andrew, who both cried for the whole time that the Somali woman was in the labour ward.

One of the very rich Muslim traders in Tabora gave a party at the Tabora Hotel on 1st May to celebrate Id-el-Fitr, and Joseph and I were both invited. When we were there, we met a mission worker called Geoff Salisbury. We knew that Geoff's wife was also pregnant, but that there were rhesus factor problems. His wife had been advised to travel to Dar es Salaam to have her baby there, in case she needed treatment that was not available in Tabora. Geoff told us at the party that his wife had given birth to a son in Dar on the same day as Ruth and Andrew were born in Tabora, and that mother and son were both making excellent progress.

The food at the party was superb. Fresh salmon had been flown out specially from Scotland, and every kind of Asian and European delicacy was spread out in profusion on the tables. Our host was a Muslim, and no alcohol was being served, but the three new fathers all felt totally euphoric on fruit juice.

Not long after Jennifer and Dinah came out of hospital, Joseph invited us to dinner at his house. There were two other guests, an American called Elmer, who had been awarded a scholarship by a foundation in the United States to work temporarily as a teacher in Tabora Boys' Secondary School, and his wife Betsy Mae.

The first thing we noticed was that Little Juma was serving at Joseph and Dinah's table. I agonised for a moment before deciding that it would be grossly unfair to Joseph and Dinah to fail to tell them that Little Juma had leprosy, and was not a suitable servant to work in a household with a new baby. I did not mention it at the dinner itself, but told Joseph the next day, when I thanked him for his hospitality.

Even without that problem, the evening had its awkward moments. The American teacher was not very bright. He had majored at a university which I had never heard of in 'Algebra, Remedial English, and Ballroom Dancing', but he considered the work of Standard X in Tanganyika, which was the equivalent of two years before School Certificate, to be much more advanced than degree standard at the university he had attended.

Although he was supposed to be teaching at a secondary school for African boys, during the course of dinner he started to express his views about educating people of non-European origin. The gist of his argument was that educated Eskimos couldn't fish, and that it was therefore wrong to try to educate them at all, and that this applied to other non-Europeans as well. Such comments would have been very offensive anywhere, but when made to his African host who was an Education Officer and a graduate of a British University, I found them totally unacceptable. Joseph and Dinah were too well mannered to argue against him, but I felt no such inhibitions. I did not want Joseph and Dinah to think that Jennifer and I might share the views of Elmer and Betsy Mae.

Jennifer told me when we got home that my face had turned bright purple when I insisted that, whatever the limitations of educated Eskimo fishermen, none of whom I had ever met, educated Africans were far more productive than illiterate ones. I told Elmer that it was morally dishonest of him to accept the stipend paid to scholars for teaching Africans when he thought the way he did. I was even more outspoken than I had been when I had annoyed the Chief Justice over dinner at Charles Rees's house. I do not enjoy being rude to other guests at dinner parties, but on both these occasions I felt justified in behaving as I did.

John Crabbe, the Headmaster of the Boys' School, told us that the American was totally useless as a teacher, but that there had been one good result from his having been awarded a scholarship to teach in Tanganyika. The boys who failed to get a place at the University of East Africa at Makerere all stopped applying for places at obscure American universities, as they had no wish to continue their education at any place which produced such people as the only American they had met.

Soon after Jennifer returned from hospital with Ruth, Omari asked us to interview a relative of his, Pili Rajabu, who wanted to work for us as Ruth's ayah (nurse-maid). She seemed a pleasant girl, but before we took her on we asked her to undergo a medical examination. We were glad we did so. She returned from hospital with a note from the doctor saying that she was suffering from syphilis. We thanked Pili for her interest, and engaged an ayah called Cecilia John instead.

Both Jennifer and I were completely enchanted by our new daughter. We were convinced beyond a shadow of doubt that Ruth was the most beautiful, most loving, and most intelligent little girl in the whole world. I got into the habit of playing records and dancing up and down the verandah carrying her in my arms. The record I played more often than all the others was of some Hungarian Dances by Brahms which she seemed to enjoy greatly.

Ruth's arrival did not please every member of the household. Susan and her daughter Wol were never aggressive to Ruth, but were obviously jealous of the attention she was getting. Both dogs were normally impeccably house-trained, but one morning I came into our dining room to find that one of them had done something very nasty on the floor. The Archdeacon of Bukoba was staying with us as an overnight guest, and the mess had been deposited just beside his dining chair. I was not able to identify the culprit, so I just spoke very severely to both dogs. They looked suitably conscience-stricken, and the offence was never repeated.

At the request of Elizabeth Webber, her headmistress, Jennifer had not resigned from the staff of the school until the last possible moment. Maternity leave was not available to women in government service, and we discovered quite quickly that feeding three mouths on one salary was not so easy as feeding two mouths on two salaries. We therefore decided to do less entertaining than we had done before Ruth was born, but we were completely happy with each other's company and a new baby to cuddle.

When Ruth was only a few weeks old, Jennifer developed a breast abscess and had to go back into hospital. Ruth went with her, and I felt much lonelier than I had ever done as a bachelor. There was an outbreak of smallpox in several of the villages round Tabora at the time, and many patients had come into the hospital for treatmant. The doctor advised us to agree to Ruth being vaccinated immediately, even though she had not yet reached the age when babies were normally vaccinated.

Jennifer recovered from her abscess quite quickly, but a couple of months later, when she and Ruth were accompanying me on a safari in my car to a village called Ndono, Jennifer became very jaundiced and was extremely sick. She was suffering great pain, and we decided to go back to Tabora at once. She was again admitted to hospital, but this time the hospital was not able to diagnose what was wrong, and could not do much to help her. When she was discharged, the doctor ordered her to have a totally salt-free and totally fat-free diet. I chivalrously promised to eat the same sort of food that she was eating, but it had so little flavour that I was only able to keep my good resolution for two days before I reverted to eating the kind of dishes which Ancient Juma normally cooked. These were not very appetising, but at least they were not quite so tasteless as what he was preparing for Jennifer.

After we got back to England in the autumn, Jennifer had a recurrence of her illness, and was operated on in the Isle of Wight. The surgeons diagnosed that she had been suffering from a stricture of the bile duct, which was the same illness that Prime Minister Anthony Eden had had at the time of the Suez Crisis. Jennifer commented that it was not surprising that Eden had made errors of judgement about Suez if he had been in the same sort of agony as she had been.

Future Leaders

I got to know a number of pupils at both the Girls and the Boys' Secondary Schools well enough to form an impression of their ability and personality.

Before we were married, Jennifer had agreed to produce, for the Girls' School Open Day, a performance by some senior girls of a one-act play called *The Dumb Wife of Cheapside*. It is not as well-known as it deserves to be. It is not difficult to perform, and is hilariously funny. It had three major roles and enough supporting roles to give several other actors a chance to take part. Just as, at my own single-sex school, boys had played female roles in school plays, the girls at Tabora took male as well as female roles, and did it very well. The plot was the stuff of comic operas by composers like Rossini or Donizetti. A rich old man has married a pretty young girl who is, in every sense of the word, completely dumb. He consults a pompous doctor, who diagnoses that the wife is tongue-tied, and performs an operation to cure her. Unfortunately, this is too successful, and the wife, played in Tabora by a diminutive but very talented girl called Rhoda Christopher, starts chattering endlessly, and talks complete rubbish. This makes her husband even angrier than her silence, so he asks the doctor to restore his wife's dumbness. The doctor says he cannot do that, but he offers to make the husband totally deaf instead. The husband agrees, and his life becomes calm again. As the play ends, the husband is smiling contentedly while the doctor shouts louder and louder at him, 'My fees! MY FEES!!'

I often went with Jennifer to rehearsals and chatted to the girls taking part. They all spoke English extremely well, acted splendidly, and enjoyed the rehearsals just as much as the audience later enjoyed the public performance.

When I asked any of the girls what she planned to do when she left school, she usually replied that she wanted to train for a caring profession such as teaching or nursing. Particularly gifted girls usually aimed to get a place at Makerere University. Whatever their ambitions, they all wanted to make use of their own education to serve the community and to help their country to develop.

Jennifer continues to hear news of her former pupils, and their careers have been outstandingly successful. One became the Minister of Education. Another became the Attorney-General. Several became doctors or nurses. Many became teachers. One of these, after some years' experience, herself became the Headmistress of Tabora Girls' School. Others became church leaders, diplomats, or senior civil servants.

During the 1980s, when I was myself a Whitehall civil servant, I attended an international seminar organised by the United Nations in Vienna. Delegates sat in the alphabetical order of their countries, and the representative of the United Kingdom of Great Britain and Northern Ireland was placed next to the representative of the United Republic of Tanganyika and Zanzibar. My neighbour was a woman called Zara Nuru, a member of a Muslim family from Pangani District, on the coast near Tanga.

Zara was charming, and represented her country's interests superbly. Each morning she greeted me in Swahili, using the traditional way of showing respect to one's elders. She told me that she had attended Tabora Girls' School after Jennifer had finished teaching there. She had gone on to Makerere, and then to the University of Boston, Massachusetts. She had become a civil servant, and was now the Permanent Secretary of the Ministry in Dar which was responsible for social affairs. She said she owed her success entirely to Miss Paddy Hurley, her head-mistress when she was in Standard VIII at Tanga Girls' School. Miss Hurley had walked more than twenty miles in the humid coastal heat just to visit Zara's father in the hope of persuading him to let his brilliant daughter continue her education up to Standard XII at Tabora. Zara's father's attitude to girls' second-ary education was conservative, and he thought it unnecessary to keep Zara on at school any longer. Fortunately Paddy managed to convince him that his daughter really was excep-tional.

I am quite certain that Zara's gratitude to her former head-mistress was completely genuine. A few years later, I met Paddy Hurley for the first time in London, and told her what Zara had said about her. It made her very happy.

Tanganyika did not have the resources to provide secondary education for everybody, but I think the policy of concentrating those limited resources on just a few outstandingly able pupils, however unfair this might have seemed to those who were rejected, was justified. Some thought of education as a way to get rich, but most of the girls at Tabora School held the view, put into words some years later by Julius Nyerere, that 'some of our citizens still have large amounts of money spent on their education, while others have none. Those who receive that priv-ilege therefore have a duty to repay the sacrifice which others have made.'

I got to know a selection of pupils at the Boys' School in a different context. I broke the provincial record for discus-throwing, and was selected to represent Western Province in the territorial athletics championships as a shot-putter and discus-thrower in Moshi in 1956 and in Mwanza the following year. In the evenings before the championships I used regularly to go to the school's playing field to train with pupils from the Boys' Secondary School who had been selected for the track and jumping events. John Crabbe, the Headmaster, had himself been a successful athlete at Cambridge, and he gave the team encour-agement and skilled coaching. The boys whom I got to know, with one exception, seemed to want to do well for their team rather than for themselves.

The exception was a boy called Christopher. He was the fastest sprinter in the School, and indeed in the whole country. He wore very ostentatious spectacles with brightly-coloured frames, and

I doubted whether he really needed them. I got irritated by his habit, before every race, of writhing and groaning as if he were in great pain, and announcing to his colleagues, 'I cannot race today. My whole body is paining me.' I would willingly have let him drop out of the team, but all his colleagues gathered round him to persuade him that he just had to run. When the Headmaster came to join the boys in begging Christopher to do his bit for his team, Christopher would put on a face like a martyr going to the stake, and then win his race very comfortably. I was pretty certain that his melodramatics were sheer vanity. As soon as he had safely won the race and was being congratulated by his colleagues, he abandoned any pretence of being in pain.

The other athletes were all exceptionally gifted, but they were also quite unassuming. The team included two boys, Sam Haggai and Alexander Nyirenda, who broke the territorial records for their events and were the first Africans from Tanganyika to be selected for training at the Royal Military Academy at Sandhurst, where they also broke the record for their events. Alexander was the young subaltern who, five years later, raised the new national flag on the top of Mount Kilimanjaro on the night his country achieved its independence. Other boys went on to Makerere University. Many trained for skilled professional careers, mainly in traditionally male forms of employment such as agriculture, engineering, medicine, and veterinary science. Like the girls, they were a great credit to their school.

There was another factor which made me keen to learn as much as I could about how schools ought to be run. When Twining had visited Tabora for the opening of the Livingstone Memorial Museum, he had briefly mentioned to me that plans were being made for a multi-racial secondary school to be opened near Iringa. He then said that a multi-racial preparatory school to feed it, and possibly some independent schools in Britain as well, might also be opened in Rungemba, a very lovely house owned by Lady Chesham in the Sao Hill area of Iringa District.

Twining asked me if Jennifer and I might be interested in becoming the joint heads of Rungemba school. I said that we would think seriously about it, but could not give an immediate reply.

When Jennifer and I went home on leave to Britain, we got in touch with headmasters of various preparatory schools, who showed us round their establishments, and we asked several public school headmasters if they might agree to accept one or two boys from Rungemba whose parents had been late in entering their son's name for any school in Britain.

We flew from Tabora at the end of our tour. Many friends came to see us off at the airport, including the Liwali, who gave us a huge bunch of dates. We were very touched by his generosity, but not so keen on East African Airways, who charged us an exorbitant fee for carrying the dates as excess baggage.

We had a disappointing leave in Britain. We spent half the time at Jennifer's mother's house in Surrey, and the other half in my mother's house in the Isle of Wight. Our mothers squabbled over which was seeing the most of us. Jennifer spent a month in hospital, and I became temporarily a 'single parent' looking after Ruth. Our enquiries about the Rungemba project were not encouraging, and we were not sorry when the time came for us to go back by ship to Africa to start a tour in Eastern Province.

Chapter 7

Ulanga District

(March 1958 –October 1960)

Mahenge Boma

The Back of Beyond

When Jennifer and I disembarked in Dar es Salaam from the Union Castle liner *Kenya Castle*, we stayed for a few days with Eric and Doris Kenny and their young son Julian. Eric and I had worked together in Iringa, where he had been the Revenue Officer. He had resigned from government service to take up an appointment with the Tanganyika Electric Supply Company, TANESCO. His new job involved business trips to every station which had electricity, and he had stayed with us from time to time in Tabora. We still enjoy using the pair of candlesticks that Eric and Doris gave us for our wedding. The Kennys were delightful hosts, and Julian and Ruth got on extremely well together. Their flat had a lovely view over the sea, and was of a higher standard than the accommodation normally provided to expatriate government officials in Dar.

Before leaving Dar to travel to my new station, Mahenge, in Ulanga District, I requested a meeting with a senior official of the Education Department called Spencer. I wanted to discuss with him the proposals for a multi-racial preparatory school at Rungemba, to let him know of the disappointing results of the contacts I had made with a number of headmasters while on leave in England, and to ask him for clarification of some important points that Jennifer and I were still uncertain about.

I had visited Rungemba when I had been stationed in Iringa, but Jennifer had never seen it. I knew that the site and the building made a lovely home, but felt that several alterations would be needed to adapt the house for use as a school, and it was not clear to me who would be responsible for this. The school was to be financed largely by contributions from rich donors who were in sympathy with the concept of multi-racial education, but we did not know who had promised to contribute, or how much. We believed that some pupils would pay fees, and that those who could not pay the full fee would be given assisted places, but we did not know how this means-testing would operate.

Jennifer and I wanted a firm assurance that pupils completing up to four years of their primary education in a school organised on European lines would not then have to go on to a secondary school where, however good the academic standards might be, the material living conditions for pupils were of a lower standard than they would have got used to at Rungemba, and where a language other than English predominated. We were also uneasy about the plans for staffing the school. We had been told, without being ourselves consulted, that our assistants would be a couple called George and Barbara Spring, who had teaching experience. We had met the Springs and liked them very much, but their qualifications seemed to be a replica of our own. Like us, they were both graduates in arts subjects, and we thought the school would need a specialist to teach maths and science.

George and Barbara also had a young family, and we wanted to be sure that the school would have a big enough complement of teachers to go on functioning satisfactorily if both Barbara and Jennifer became pregnant at the same time, or to deputise when either the Springs or we ourselves went on long leave to Britain. We thought we would need a matron to supervise the health of

the pupils. We were also anxious about the provision of appropriate moral and religious instruction for pupils who were not
Anglicans. The school was likely to accept pupils of other reli-
gions and other Christian denominations, so it needed to cater for
their needs as well as those of Anglican pupils. We did not know
whether the committee planned for the school to develop gradually, with one new class opening at the start of each year, or
whether every class would start to function simultaneously as
soon as the school opened.

I asked for an assurance that I would not be expected to resign
from my pensionable appointment in the Provincial Administration in order to take up an appointment as headmaster of
Rungemba, and that a secondment would not affect my pension
rights when I reached retirement age.

Spencer attempted to satisfy me on all these points. He said
that there was no question of pupils having to go on to African or
Asian schools when they left Rungemba, and I understood him to
say that all of our concerns were already being examined closely
by a committee that included representatives of all the races and
communities in Tanganyika who had an interest in the project. I
was not completely reassured, however, as the members of the
committee whose names he mentioned all seemed to be better
known for their involvement in politics than for their knowledge
of education policy and practice. However, Spencer explained
that the school would not be ready to open for a year or more,
and that Jennifer and I could rest assured that all the unresolved
problems would be sorted out in that time.

Jennifer had been looking after Ruth while I was talking to
Spencer, but I told her what he had told me. She felt as uneasy as
I did about reassurances that seemed rather too glib, but she was
glad that I had had the chance to discuss the Rungemba project
before we set off for Mahenge.

It was the normal practice for friends to look after dogs when
their owners were on leave. We had looked after Peggy Fowler's
dog Jill while Peggy was on leave, and Peggy reciprocated by
looking after Susan and Wol for us. When our leave ended, Peggy
had sent them by air from Tabora to Dar, for us to collect from
kennels run by a local voluntary organisation. Our car and boxes
were sent by freight train from Tabora to Morogoro, and Juma
and Omari travelled there by passenger train. We had paid
retainers to both of them while we were in England, and when
they travelled to our new station to rejoin us at the end of our
leave we also had to pay the fares of them and their families, but

we thought this cost was fully justified if the servants were as loyal and efficient as Juma and Omari. We arranged for the lorry that was taking our baggage from Morogoro to Mahenge to take Omari and his family and Juma's wife as well. Juma travelled with us in our car. When driving with a wife and young child on earth roads in Tanganyika, it was always a good idea to travel either in convoy with another car or with a trusted servant to help in any emergency.

G T Bell, the Provincial Commissioner of Eastern Province, was not in Morogoro when we arrived, but I was very warmly welcomed by his Deputy, G N Clark.

Geoff Bullock, who was now the District Commissioner in Mahenge, had already sent us a very friendly letter which had reached us on the ship in Mombasa. It contained an invitation for us to stay with him and his wife while we were settling in to our own house. G N Clark confirmed that we would spend the first few months of our tour in Mahenge. How long we stayed there would depend on the progress of the Rungemba project, but even if that did not materialise, he thought I would probably be posted somewhere else after about six months. He told me that Geoff Bullock, with whom I had worked in Iringa, had particularly requested that I should be posted to Mahenge.

I was much more pleased with my discussions with G N Clark than with Spencer. Mahenge was the place where I had gone down with my first attack of malaria when I was on safari with the Acting Governor, Robert Stapledon, but the mosquito which infected me had bitten me in Mtwara, and I had liked what I had managed to see of Ulanga District. I also looked forward to working once again under a boss I knew I liked very much.

I suppose being told that one's posting is only temporary should never be taken as a promise. We expected to stay in Mahenge for about six months, but it proved to be the only station where I completed a full tour of two and a half years. Fortunately Jennifer, Ruth and I all loved it, although we had a number of crises while we were there.

The main feature about Mahenge was its remoteness and inaccessibility. It was about 200 miles from Morogoro, the Provincial Headquarters, and about 160 from Kilosa, the nearest station on the Central Railway Line, and was situated on a massif which rose to a height of between 3,000 and 4,000 feet above sea level. Under German rule, Mahenge District and Songea District had formed a single province, with its headquarters in Mahenge, but Mahenge had become part of Eastern Province and Songea part of Southern Province, and the road between the two places had become completely impassable.

Mahenge was too small to be designated as a township. In the 1950s, the so-called 'minor settlement' contained about 500 Africans, 14 Asians, and 17 Europeans. Most stations in Tanganyika were much bigger. The population of Tabora Township, for example, was more than twenty-five times that of Mahenge. Between 1905 and 1907, Mahenge had been an important centre of the Maji-Maji rebellion, but, after the rising was crushed, many of the rebels and their families died as a result of German reprisals, and the area continued to be sparsely populated.

The Boma was an impressive fort built by the Germans at the top of an escarpment. In addition to the Government Offices, it housed the local prison. The walls of the Boma still bore the marks of bullets fired during the rebellion.

Mahenge itself and its immediate surroundings were pretty and well-watered. Europeans found the climate pleasant throughout the year, and warmed their houses with log fires in the evenings during the cool season. There were masses of brilliantly-coloured tropical trees, flowers, shrubs, birds and butterflies.

Mahenge also had many viewpoints from which one could look out northwards over the huge expanse of the valley of the Kilombero River and its tributaries. Viewed from a distance, the valley looked very attractive, but the climate there was hot and humid, especially just before the rains started. The villages close to the river were all infested with mosquitoes, and when we went on safari to the low-lying parts of the district, we always slept under mosquito nets, though we did not use them in Mahenge.

Ulanga District covered an area of 16,094 square miles, and had a population of about 124,000 people, including about 280 Asians and 150 Europeans. The Europeans were mainly Capuchin Missionaries, most of whom came from Switzerland. Much of the district was uninhabitable due to infestation by tsetse fly and the risk of sleeping sickness. Another large portion of the District formed part of the Selous Game Reserve, where human access was prohibited except for a very few people specially authorised by the Game Department.

Unlike the districts where I had served previously, where one important tribe predominated, the African population of Ulanga was made up of seven different tribes, each with its own chief or sub-chief. There were 56,000 Pogoro living on the Mahenge Massif, and 20,000 Ndamba, 15,500 Bena, 10,500 Mbunga, 10,200

Ngindo, 5,500 Ngoni, and 4,500 Hehe living in or near the flat-lands of the Kilombero Valley.

Soon after I was posted to Ulanga, I applied for permission to study Kipogoro for an interpretership, but this was refused on the grounds that if I learned the language of one tribe all the others would be jealous. However, throughout my time there, I was paid a bonus of £5 per month for the interpretership in Kihehe that I had obtained in Iringa. This was because there was one Hehe sub-chief, Nduna Pius, and a few Hehe tribesmen living in Ulanga District. I was glad to receive the bonus, but my knowledge of Kihehe was of no real value at all, as all the Hehe tribesmen living on the Ulanga side of the border with Iringa District used Swahili, even amongst themselves.

I understand that, some years after Tanganyika had become independent, Ulanga District was divided into two separate districts, with the northern part being renamed Kilombero District, but at the time I served there it was one big district, and comprised the south-west corner of Eastern Province. It adjoined Iringa and Njombe Districts in Southern Highlands Province to the west, and Songea District in Southern Province to the south. However, the only access by motor road into Ulanga District was from the north, either from Kilosa or Morogoro.

In order to reach Mahenge by motor vehicle during the dry season, one had to cross the Kilombero River by a pontoon ferry near the minor settlement of Ifakara. This was the main trading centre in the district, and had a bigger population and many more shops than Mahenge. It also had a Catholic Mission Hospital which was far better than the Government Hospital in Mahenge. There was an old German cemetery near Ifakara, and Jennifer and I were shocked to see how young the Germans buried there had been when they died. Nearly all the graves were of men who had died between the ages of nineteen and twenty-five.

The ferry, which was operated by the Public Works Department, consisted of a raft which used empty oil-drums to provide the necessary buoyancy to carry two small cars or one lorry across the river. The raft had no engine, but was attached to a wire rope, and a team of burly Africans pulled on it to get the raft from one side of the river to the other.

This was adventurous at the best of times, but the ferry did not operate during hours of darkness. When the river flooded, as it always did between the months of March and June, the ferry had to be taken out of service. For about three months every year, Mahenge was totally inaccessible to motor traffic. The only way to reach it or leave it by car was to take one vehicle to one side of the Kilombero River, and use a different vehicle to continue the journey on the other side. A dug-out canoe was normally used to carry passengers across the river during the rainy season. When travellers reached the south bank of the river during the months that the ferry was out of service, most people had to make the last part of their journey to Mahenge on foot, as public transport was rarely available.

There were only three Indian shopkeepers in Mahenge. Gulamali Mohamedali Gulamali supplied most of the Europeans and salaried African officials with a limited range of food, drink, and household supplies like paraffin. Another trader was also called Gulamali. Africans gave Gulamali Somji the nickname 'Gulamali *Magendo*' (the Swahili word for black-market) to distinguish him from his namesake. The third shop was owned by a man called N G Gokhale. Milk was obtainable from the Capuchin Mission at Kwiro, which also sold meat one day a week. Fruit and vegetables could be bought from the market, and people coming up to Mahenge from the river often brought fresh fish with them, which they distributed to colleagues.

In addition to his poorly-stocked retail shop, Gokhale owned a canvas-covered lorry which he had converted into a bus by fitting it with hard wooden seats for passengers. He had a contract to carry the mail once a week between Kilosa and Mahenge. During the dry season, his bus normally arrived in Mahenge on a Thursday evening, and left the following morning. This meant that all the expatriate officials in Mahenge used to spend each Thursday evening in their own homes answering the letters they had just received from their families in Britain.

During the rains, Gokhale's bus could not get beyond Ifakara, and porters were engaged to carry the mailbags on their heads between Ifakara and Mahenge. The journey by foot took three days each way.

There was no electricity and no telephone system in Mahenge. There was a primitive telegraph line which could transmit messages in morse code between Mahenge and Ifakara, but it was very unreliable. The flimsy telegraph poles and the wire were subject to all the usual hazards such as falling branches or theft of the wire, but in addition they were frequently knocked down by elephant. It usually took the line mechanic some days to locate the fault, and during that time there was no connection between the Post Office in Mahenge and the Post Office at Ifakara, or anywhere outside the District.

I never thought that Tanganyika was likely to have bloodshed similar to what had occurred in Kenya at the time of the Mau-Mau troubles, but if there had been any sort of uprising in Mahenge, the line would certainly have been cut, and government officials there would have been unable to call for help from outside. We therefore pressed hard for our Police Station to be provided with a reliable radio transmitter–receiver set to give us a link to Provincial Headquarters. We were very glad when it eventually arrived after some anonymous bureaucrat in Dar had argued that Mahenge was much too insignificant a station to deserve such costly equipment.

The earth road from Ifakara was the only route to provide access by car to the Boma at Mahenge, but there were also two other roads which branched off that road and led westwards. These were even worse than the Ifakara–Mahenge road. One went from Ifakara along the valley to the north of the Kilombero to areas inhabited mainly by Mbunga, Ndamba, and Hehe tribes and the villages of Mchombe, Chita, and Merera.

The other road started at Lupiro, a village mid-way between Ifakara and Mahenge, and ran along the foothills of the Mahenge Massif towards areas occupied by Bena, Ngindo and Ngoni tribes. This road passed through the villages of Mtimbira and Malinyi, and came to an end at the Ngoni village of Kilosa-kwa-Mpepo (not the same as Kilosa), about a hundred miles west of Lupiro. There was a footpath beyond Kilosa-kwa-Mpepo leading, eventually, to a village called Matumbi, where there was a Local Court. The walk from Kilosa-kwa-Mpepo to Matumbi took five days. When the road between Lupiro and Kilosa-kwa-Mpepo was closed, the journey by foot between Matumbi and Mahenge took sixteen days each way.

The banks of many of the tributaries to the south of the Kilombero were very steep, and the simple wooden bridges across the river beds were regularly washed away by the rains year after year. It was a constant complaint from the officials working in Mahenge that the Public Works Department were so inflexible about a rule that did not allow them to leave on site, in the custody of a responsible person such as the village headman, any of the timber and equipment that would be needed in order to rebuild those bridges after the rains ended. This unwillingness to leave equipment in situ during the rainy season meant that work on the second bridge on the road leading west from Lupiro could only start after work on the first bridge had been completed, and so on. By the time that all the bridges had been rebuilt, the rains were always just about to start again. The result of this rule was that the road was only passable by car up to its terminus at Kilosa-kwa-Mpepo for about one or possibly two months each year. This was totally inadequate to stimulate any economic development in those areas that the road was designed to serve.

Rules were not always carved in tablets of stone. Local Courts in Tanganyika were normally required to submit their revenue and court records to the Boma at least once a month, but if the court clerk at Matumbi had been required to comply rigidly with that general rule, he would have had no time to do his real job. Permission was therefore given for Matumbi to submit its tax and other revenue once every three months. This was obviously sensible, but the example cut no ice whatsoever with the officials of the Public Works Department.

When he briefed me in Morogoro, G N Clark had asked me to arrange to break my journey in Ifakara in order to meet Geoff Bullock, who would be waiting for me there. Anne, his wife, was expecting her third baby and was about to give birth in the Roman Catholic Mission Hospital in Ifakara, which had an outstanding reputation.

When we reached Ifakara, Geoff greeted us with the news that Anne had had another son, Timothy, but that the baby was underweight and the doctor was rather worried about him, and had advised Anne to stay in hospital for a few more days, and for Geoff and their elder sons John and Peter to remain near her. A very promising young cadet called Simon Hardwick, whose place I would be taking, would be ready to welcome us in Mahenge. Jennifer, Ruth and I would sleep in the DC's guest house, and Simon would provide us with our meals.

We did not want to keep Geoff from his family for too long, and we were ourselves anxious to reach Mahenge before night-fall, so we did not stay very long in Ifakara. I was delighted to see Geoff again, and Jennifer, who had never met him before, liked him as much as I did.

The sun was setting by the time we reached Mahenge, but Simon Hardwick was there to greet us. I was sorry that he would be leaving Mahenge before we had time to get to know him well, as he seemed to deserve all the nice things Geoff had said about him. He gave us a very cordial welcome, and helped us to unload Ruth and our overnight luggage from the car. Ruth had not enjoyed the bumpy last few miles of the journey, and we felt that our first priority was to feed her and put her to bed. We decided that it was too late to try to unload the heavy crates, so we left them on the back of the lorry in the driveway in what was to become our garden.

Soon after midnight, we realised that we had made a bad mistake. There were brilliant flashes of lightning, and the heavens opened. Torrential rain penetrated all our crates and soaked the contents. The worst of the damage was to our books, whose colour ran onto whatever happened to be next to them in the boxes. Three inches of rain fell between midnight and dawn.

When we opened the crates the following morning, we laid out all our property to dry. Jennifer was not very pleased to discover that a colleague on the staff of the Girls' School had failed to return the piano which she had begged to borrow when we went on leave. It did not reach us until after the ferry reopened at the end of the rainy season.

We then made a tour of inspection round what was to be our home and garden, and forgot about our damaged possessions and missing piano, completely enchanted by what we saw.

The house had a large sitting room with an open fire-place in one corner. There was a dining room, one small and two large bedrooms, a storeroom, and a bathroom and WC. Behind the house was a verandah and covered passageway leading to the kitchen and the quarters where Juma and Omari would live. In front of the house, there was a lovely open verandah with a superb view over the Kilombero Valley, with what looked like clouds in the distance. It was several days before we noticed that the outlines of what we had assumed were clouds never changed, and that in fact we were looking at the Uluguru Mountains, more than 100 miles away.

The feature which delighted us most of all was the garden, which had clearly been tended with great skill for many years. At the back of the house there was a well-maintained and well-stocked fruit and vegetable garden with a pretty little stream flowing through it. It contained oranges, limes, grapefruit, mulberries, bananas, guavas, paw-paws, and strawberrries, as well as peas, beans, cabbages, and tomatoes. The front garden was on three levels, separated by gentle flights of steps. The borders were a mass of ornamental flowers and shrubs, including roses which appeared to flourish better in Mahenge than anywhere else in Tanganyika. On each level of the front garden, there was a big lawn where Jennifer and I later spent many happy hours playing with Ruth and the dogs. The top lawn caught the sun, but the lower lawns were shady, and a perfect place to rest or play when the sun shone too brightly.

Birds thrived there, and Hugh Elliott, a friend who visited us later and was an expert ornithologist, identified twenty-four species of bird in our garden before breakfast.

Colleagues, Friends and Enemies

When Jennifer and I moved into our new home in Mahenge, we spent a day or so being introduced to the people who would be our colleagues and neighbours. This did not take very long, because so few government officials were stationed there. There were four European married couples and two bachelors. The District Commissioner, the Medical Officer, the Sleeping Sickness Settlement Officer and I were all married. The Field Officer (Agriculture) and the Field Officer (Tsetse) were not. My predecessor, Simon Hardwick, who was also unmarried at the time, left Mahenge soon after Jennifer and I arrived.

Not all of our European colleagues were complete strangers. Jennifer and I had served in Tabora with the Sleeping Sickness Settlement Officer and his wife, Ken and Mavis Pouncett. Even though Jennifer had not met Geoff and Anne Bullock before, I had worked with them in Iringa, and was already on very friendly terms with them. I had briefly met the Medical Officer, Gary Butler, when he had treated me for malaria when I was accompanying the Acting Governor on his safari to Mahenge.

The complement of expatriate officials fluctuated. Sometimes we had a Game Ranger or a Geologist, for example, posted to the district for a temporary assignment. Mahenge was also often visited during the dry season by representatives of other Departments who were stationed either at Provincial Headquarters in Morogoro or in Kilosa, but were required to keep an eye on the work of their Departments in Ulanga District as well. There was no hotel in Mahenge, and the rest-house was not luxurious, so visiting officials were normally invited to stay with one of the families who lived there. Jennifer and I enjoyed having guests to stay, and some of our regular visitors like Tom Moore, the burly Assistant Superintendent of Police stationed at Kilosa, became close friends.

We also had two Asian officials in Ulanga, a cashier who came from South India, and a Sikh District Foreman. Africans who held positions of responsibility included the Senior Inspector of Police, the Head Clerk of the District Office, the Head Tax Clerk, the

Treasurer of the Local Treasury, the Chief Prison Warder, and two Medical Assistants.

Juma and Omari, who had both worked so well for us in Tabora, had already joined us in Mahenge, but we had decided not to go on employing the indifferent cook who had replaced Lameck in Tabora, so we wanted to engage a new one. We also wanted to employ an ayah to help look after Ruth.

We interviewed a number of applicants for the post of cook, and much the most suitable candidate was a Pogoro tribesman called Mohamed Nganga. He and I were both born in 1928, but we did not know which of us was the older. Registration of birth for Africans was not compulsory, and he had never been told the month in which he was born. Most Pogoro were of slender physique, and Mohamed was particularly small, weighing less than half as much as me. His head seemed large for such a small body, but he played the guitar, and local girls found him irresistible.

We had a slight problem about employing Mohamed. He had worked for the Butler family, but had just been sacked for asking for an increase of wages from the equivalent of £3 per month to the equivalent of £3.25 per month. Jennifer and I were perfectly happy to give him the wage he asked for, which was lower than the going rate for cooks in Dar or Tabora, but when Gary Butler had described Mohamed's strengths and weaknesses to us, he particularly asked us not to pay him more than he had received from them, as he said this would send the wrong message to the other domestic servants still working for the Butlers. I thought that the wage that Jennifer and I paid to our employees was a matter for ourselves and the employees concerned, rather than a previous employer, but secrets did not remain secret for long in a small station, and we did not want to annoy Gary so soon after arriving in the District.

Our solution satisfied everybody. Gary told us, and Mohamed himself confirmed it, that he was a very good cook when sober, but occasionally had a bit too much to drink. We offered to employ him on the same basic salary that he had got from the Butlers, but to pay him in addition a retroactive bonus of five shillings each month if he had remained sober, or had asked us for time off before going to the beer-club. He only once forfeited his bonus for being drunk in charge of the cooking pots. He remained in our employment for the next four years, until Jennifer and I left Tanganyika. He got on very well with Juma and Omari, and, on the comparatively rare occasions when he asked

for time off to visit a beer-club, the others were always willing to
deputise for him. Mohamed had only attended school to primary
level, but he was very intelligent.

I discovered later that he enjoyed reading and that his handwriting was neat and legible. He was also very good at changing
the wheels of my car whenever we had a flat tyre, which was
quite often on Tanganyikan roads. After Jennifer and I left
Tanganyika, Mohamed obtained a junior office job working for a
Saudi Arabian airline company in Dar es Salaam.

We had no trouble in finding a suitable ayah, Innocentia Paulo
Livuga, generally known as 'Ina' to distinguish her from the
Butlers' ayah who had also been christened Innocentia. Ina was
the widow of a carpenter who had worked for the big Roman
Catholic Mission at Kwiro, a few miles from Mahenge. The
missionaries at Kwiro recommended her to us very warmly. She
had five children of her own, and wanted to earn enough money
to pay the fees for her older children to attend Middle School. Her
youngest child was a toddler of about the same age as Ruth. Ina
and Ruth became devoted to each other. Ina did not speak
English, and as Ruth learnt to talk she became nearly as fluent in
Swahili as she was in English, sometimes mixing up the two
languages in the same sentence.

Just before Ruth's first birthday, a large group of African
Muslims came to our house on the festival of Id-el-Fitr and lined
up in front of our verandah to pray for blessings on our daughter
Mwanaidi. They had come because they knew she had been born
at the exact moment when the moon was seen at the end of
Ramadan the previous year, and they lifted their hands towards
heaven and then bowed their heads to the ground. Ruth astonished us by imitating their actions. She lifted her arms to heaven
and then bowed down as the Africans were doing. Ruth clearly
enjoyed their visit, and Jennifer and I were very touched that they
should have honoured our daughter in this way so soon after we
had arrived in Mahenge.

Friendships formed on a happy small station tend to last a long
time. After we had returned to England, we continued to get
letters from both Juma and Mohamed. We remained in touch
with Geoff Bullock and with his successor, Michael Dorey. The
Field Officer (Agriculture), Robin Blackall, was a bachelor when
he was in Mahenge, but he later got married and his elder daughter became my goddaughter, and Jennifer and Ruth became the
joint godmothers of Robin's son. Every Christmas for many years,
we went on getting cards from what began as a large number of

the Capuchin Fathers, but sadly the number dwindled as the elderly Fathers became ill and died. Instead of greetings, we got cards with black edges and a photograph, telling us of the death of someone who was not the same nationality or denomination as ourselves, but who had remained our life-long friend.

What gave us as much pleasure as any of the cards and letters we received was a personal visit to our home in England by the former cashier at Mahenge, Mr C N U Nair, who was the best cashier I ever worked with. When he reached retirement age some years after independence, he returned to his birth-place in South India, and I never expected to see him again. In the summer of 1998, however, he paid a visit to Britain to stay with relatives who lived in Croydon, and came with his cousin's family to visit us at our home near Guildford. Jennifer and I paid a return visit to Croydon. Nair's cousins were all successful in skilled professional jobs and had varied careers of their own, but they seemed perfectly happy to listen while Nair and I reminisced about our time together in Mahenge. It was forty years from the last time we had seen each other, and Nair was within a few weeks of his eightieth birthday. His hair was as white as snow, and he was rather deaf, but his ebullient laugh and his sense of fun were completely unimpaired. It was a joyful reunion.

We chatted about mutual friends, in particular the Bullocks, and about two episodes which had concerned us both. The first involved the trial and imprisonment of an evil and corrupt Head Tax Clerk. The second was where my absolute confidence in Nair's integrity led me to risk my own career by ignoring the rules about the financial control of government cash offices.

The Ulanga District cash office normally operated in the Boma in Mahenge, but it opened for a few weeks each year at Ifakara, so that anyone living in the northern part of the district could renew licences and pay fees to Government without the need to make a difficult journey into the Boma. One of the villagers of Kiberege, an African shopkeeper called Shabani Rashidi, came to the temporary cash office to renew his annual Trading Licence. Nair was always attentive to detail, and spotted that the licence being submitted for renewal bore the signature of a clerk who had been transferred from Mahenge two years previously. The licence also appeared to have an alteration of the date of issue from 1956 to 1957. A search through the counterfoils of old trading licences confirmed that the original licence had been issued in 1956, and Nair asked Shabani to explain. Shabani, who was intelligent but almost illiterate, said that he had not forged the licence himself.

He insisted that had handed the fee of £1 to his cousin, the Head
Tax Clerk, Ali Athmani. Shabani added, not unreasonably, that if
he had forged his licence in 1957 he would have done the same
thing again in 1958. If the licence he had just submitted for
renewal was in fact a forgery, then the guilty person could only
be his cousin, Ali Athmani, who must have stolen the money
which Shabani had entrusted to him to pay for a new trading
licence.

Shabani was asked to produce any evidence to support his
allegation against Ali Athmani. Many poorly educated Africans
have a habit of holding on to all their letters and documents,
and Shabani went home under police escort to look for the letter
which would prove his innocence. Luckily for him, but not so
luckily for his cousin, he was able to produce from a shabby
wooden box a letter in Swahili in what looked like Ali Athmani's
handwriting, and bearing his signature. The letter, dated 1957,
apologised for losing the licence that had already expired, and
said that the attached new licence was all that Shabani would
need in order to continue trading. The Senior Inspector of Police
in Mahenge, Antony Sarota, sent this letter to Headquarters in
Dar es Salaam, where it was examined by Superintendent Ray
Brothers, the police handwriting expert, together with an
acknowledged sample of Ali Athmani's handwriting. Ray
Brothers reported that both examples were written by the
same person, and Ali Athmani was charged with forgery and
theft.

I was the magistrate who tried the case, which was hotly
contested. Ali Athmani insisted that it was all a conspiracy by
people who hated him for no reason, and that all the prosecution
witnesses were lying, including Ray Brothers, who had travelled
from Dar as an expert witness for the prosecution. Ali Athmani
made a very long statement in his own defence, and called
several defence witnesses, none of whom cast any doubt on the
case for the prosecution. The case file ran to 105 pages of manuscript, and the trial went on for four days, arousing immense
interest in the whole District.

On the second afternoon, while I was sitting in court, I
suddenly felt extremely unwell, and thought I was going to
collapse. I did not interrupt the hearing of the case, and after a
few minutes I felt better again. That evening, the prosecuting
officer, Antony Sarota, asked me if I had noticed two ugly old
women sitting below my desk in court. I told him I had, and he
remarked that they were two witches from Mtimbira Village

whom Ali Athmani had engaged to bewitch me. I said I intended to call them and tell them I did not want them to be in my court the following day. Inspector Sarota was completely horrified at this suggestion. He undertook to make sure they did not return to the courtroom while the case was in progress, and told me very solemnly that if I spoke to them myself it would increase enormously their power to harm me.

I gratefully accepted Sarota's advice, and when I got home I told both Jennifer and Gary Butler, the doctor, of the unpleasant experience I had had. Gary took it very seriously indeed, and said that if I felt at all unwell again he would arrange for me to be rushed immediately to Morogoro Hospital, as he thought it would be dangerous to try to treat me in Ulanga. Jennifer said that, at precisely the moment when I had felt so ill in court, she had had an experience of near panic that something dreadful and evil was happening to me. She had never felt anything like it before, and never had the same experience again, even at times when I was genuinely ill.

When all the witnesses for the prosecution and the defence had given evidence, I went home to write my judgement without being disturbed. I promised to return to court later that evening, as soon as I had completed it. It took longer than I expected, as I did not want to make any mistakes which might enable Ali Athmani to get off on a technicality.

It was already dark when I returned to the court, carrying my papers and a paraffin lamp. The whole Boma compound was still packed with a crowd of silent spectators. Men and women were sitting on the ground, but they moved out of my way to let me pass.

I convicted Ali Athmani on three counts: forgery, issuing a forged document, and theft of £1. I sentenced him to a total of eight months' imprisonment, subject to confirmation by the High Court, which confirmed the conviction and sentence.

Next day I drove from Mahenge to Kwiro Mission on other business, and the whole way along the road I was greeted by jubilant Africans dancing and waving their arms, and singing and ululating joyfully. My Messenger, Abdullah Likomiti, was with me, and commented, 'They are thanking you for removing an ulcer.'

After Ali Athmani was imprisoned and dismissed from his job as Head Tax Clerk, he had to be moved from prison to prison. He eventually completed his sentence in a prison in the far north of the country, because in all the prisons in Eastern Province there were other convicts who had been his victims. They ganged up on him, and beat him up so badly that his life was thought to be in danger.

I was told over and over again of reasons why the man was so feared and hated. Many people told me about his habit, when he met a woman he fancied, of ordering her husband to produce his tax ticket, which he was legally entitled to do, then tearing it up, which was not normally part of the job of a tax clerk. He then charged the husband with wilful neglect to pay tax, giving perjured evidence in court if ever the husband dared to deny the charge. Ali Athmani then used the opportunity to commit adultery with the wife while her husband was serving an unjust prison sentence for a trumped-up charge of failure to pay poll tax.

Ali Athmani seemed to be much richer than could be explained by his salary. He appeared to enjoy an unusually high standard of living, and he owned a shotgun and a motor cycle. I suspected that, in addition to forcing his attentions on attractive young women, he also extorted money from unsophisticated farmers, but no one ever made a formal complaint to the police or to a magistrate about this side of his corruption.

I was often told an even more shocking story about him. One day, at the Local Court in a village called Chera, he had allegedly taken a rope to bind the ankles of an old man. He then tied the rope to his motor cycle, and dragged the old man round and round the court building, tearing the skin off his back and causing injuries from which the old man died while still attached to the motor cycle. The villagers who had witnessed the event were then ordered by Ali Athmani to 'bury this filth', but no one ever dared to make a complaint to the authorities. Whenever I heard the story, I asked to be given more details about exactly what had happened, but I was always given the same reply, 'Yes, we all know he did it, but I was not there myself and did not see him kill the old man.' Even after Ali Athmani went to prison, the people of Ulanga were still too terrified to testify against him.

I believe that sentencing Ali Athmani to gaol did as much for my reputation among Africans in Ulanga as anything else I ever did there, but the case would never have come to light if C N U Nair had not been so observant and quick-witted.

I also reminded Nair about another episode which had taken place when I had been in Mahenge for nearly four months. The cash balance in the Government cash office was checked daily, and neither Geoff Bullock nor I had ever spotted a single mistake when Nair was the cashier. The end of each month was a particularly busy time, as the clerks of Local Courts brought their court records and cash into the Boma for checking, and we always tried to complete the task as quickly as possible, so that the clerks could go back to their chiefdoms rather than hanging around in the Boma. The end of June was even more hectic than other months, as the government financial year ran from 1st July to 30th June, and a plethora of annual returns had to be submitted to the Accountant General's office as soon as the financial year ended. These were supposed to be checked and certified as correct by an administrative officer.

At the end of June 1958, I had to spend two nights unexpectedly on safari on urgent business, and I did not get back to Mahenge until after dark on the last day of the financial year. When I arrived at the Boma, I found Nair waiting for me with a paraffin lamp and a mass of annual returns and accountable documents, all neatly arranged, and piles of currency notes and silver and copper coins.

It was my second wedding anniversary, and I wanted to get home to Jennifer as soon as I could. I was completely certain that, however long I might spend examining the books and counting the cash, I would not find anything wrong with any of them. I asked, 'Is everything correct, Mr Nair?' and he replied, 'Yes, Sir.' I then signed all the appropriate documents as being correct, without having checked any of them.

I would have been in serious trouble if there had been any cash or accountable documents missing, but, as I expected, everything turned out to be in perfect order. While I was signing, I remarked to Nair that this was the first time I had ever certified that documents and a cash balance were correct, simply on the basis of someone else's word. I added that it was the greatest compliment that could ever be paid to him. He replied, 'I agree. I appreciate it very much.'

A New Governor

A more important event also took place in June 1958. Sir Edward Twining left Tanganyika on retirement. He had been Governor for nine years, and under his leadership Tanganyika's economy and infrastructure had improved greatly. While I had been his Private Secretary, I had seen for myself the gift that Twining had for inspiring personal devotion among people of all races. During the farewell tours which he made round the country before he left for Britain, huge crowds gathered to say goodbye to him and Lady Twining, and to present them with gifts, many of which were splendid examples of tribal craftsmanship.

Shortly after his retirement, Twining was one of the first group of distinguished people to be created life peers. He took the title of Baron Twining of Tanganyika and Godalming in the county of Surrey.

In spite of the love he felt for his people and many of his people felt for him, there were some who thought that Twining had been Governor for too long. He was sincere in his wish to bring about gradual peaceful political development, with independence in a multi-racial state as the eventual target. However, the rate of progress which he thought appropriate was too slow to satisfy the aspirations of African political leaders, who hated the colonial system and for whom multi-racialism held little appeal. Twining, on the other hand, regarded the 'Africa for the African' policy of the Tanganyika African National Union (TANU), founded in 1954 and led by Julius Nyerere, as inherently racist. With hind-sight, however, it now seems obvious that Twining's efforts to counter the influence of TANU by encouraging the development of a rival party called the United Tanganyika Party (UTP) were bound to fail.

Not many Africans joined UTP, but the few who did had nearly all been members of the elite during the colonial era. They included a number of hereditary chiefs whose authority was being challenged by TANU. The non-African members of UTP were mainly businessmen or estate owners. They could all be portrayed by their opponents as reactionaries who simply wanted to preserve their own privileged positions, and had no sympathy for the aspirations of ordinary people.

Julius Nyerere

The UTP also lacked a leader with political acumen or magnetism. Its Chairman, Ivor Bayldon, was a well-meaning car dealer who owned a successful garage in Mbeya. I had first met him socially in Southern Highlands Province, and when I met him a few years later in Government House I did not change my view that, if there was anyone who could inspire voters to support UTP, Bayldon was not that man. His command of Swahili may have been adequate for business purposes, but he was not capable of explaining the aims of his party in a convincing way to audiences consisting mainly of Africans.

Nyerere, on the other hand, was articulate, intelligent, honest, and comparatively moderate in his demands. He had immense personal warmth, charisma, and a great sense of humour. He was a graduate of Edinburgh University, and could make speeches equally well either in Swahili or in English. The leaders of local branches of TANU included a number of self-seeking and ambitious people, some of whom had criminal records or who preached a message of hatred, but Julius Nyerere himself was respected, even by many of his opponents. Long before Twining left, it seemed certain that TANU would win the forthcoming general election.

Twining was succeeded by Sir Richard Turnbull, who had been Minister for Internal Security in Kenya at the time of the Mau-Mau troubles, and then had served as Chief Secretary in Nairobi for three years. Turnbull was regarded by those who knew him as very able, and I was favourably disposed towards any new Governor who spoke Swahili well, had been a keen oarsman at university, and was reputed to be fond of classical music.

Soon after Turnbull arrived in Dar, he made a speech to Legislative Council which was transmitted by the government-controlled broadcasting station. Jennifer and I listened to it in Mahenge on our little battery radio. Not all that Turnbull said was clearly audible through the interference on our radio, but we heard enough of the speech to have mixed feelings about it.

We were pleased to hear Turnbull's undertakings to speed up political progress towards independence, but were dismayed by the thinly veiled criticisms that he made about his predecessor. We regarded them as disloyal and unjustified. They were presumably intended to curry favour with the growing number of Africans who were supporting TANU. Without ever having met him, Jennifer and I formed the impression that our new Governor was clever, shrewd and calculating, but not very likeable.

He had acquired the reputation of being a tough guy in dealing with the Mau-Mau crisis in Kenya in 1953, but he was intelligent enough to see which way the wind was blowing in Tanganyika in 1958. My affection for Twining may cause me to be less than fair in my assessment of Turnbull, but I still wonder how far his actions as Governor were motivated by a sincere wish to see Tanganyika become independent, and how far he was actuated by expediency and a wish to advance his own career by playing on the winning side. Whatever his motives, however, I have nothing but respect for the skill he showed in bringing constitutional advance to Tanganyika in a peaceful way, and in building up a better personal relationship with Tanganyika's first President, Julius Nyerere, than Twining had ever managed to do.

I had very little contact with Turnbull in Tanganyika. The first time we really spoke to one another was after we had both left Africa. We then met for several successive years in the months of June and early July during the 1970s, when we were both coaching crews that were training for Henley Regatta. Even after his retirement, he looked slim, energetic, and very fit. Oarsmen and ex-colonial civil servants are usually quite friendly people, and Turnbull and I had plenty of common interests. However, I seldom saw him smile, and he seemed dour and austere. I may be quite wrong, but I formed the impression that anyone who had been close to Twining was suspect in Turnbull's eyes. Whatever the reason, even though Sir Richard Turnbull proved a successful Governor, I never regarded him, either in Africa or on the towpath of the Thames, as a personal friend of mine.

Tanganyika's First African Cadet

Soon after the Kilombero Ferry reopened after the end of the rainy season, and a few weeks after Sir Richard Turnbull became Governor, news reached Mahenge that a young African graduate of London University, who had just completed the Overseas Civil Service course at Fitzwilliam College, Cambridge, was about to take up his appointment as a District Officer (Cadet), and that his first posting would be to Ulanga District. His name was Osiah Mwambungu, and he was a Nyakyusa from Rungwe District. Another African cadet was also appointed at the same time, but he was posted to the northern part of the country, and I never met him.

I was delighted that there was to be an an addition to the team of administrative officers. Ulanga District had been out of sight and out of mind for a long time, and I thought that the work-load was too heavy for Geoff Bullock and me on our own. I was sure that the District would progress more rapidly if the number of

District Officers was increased. In fact, by the time my tour of service ended in 1960, Ulanga's complement had increased to a District Commissioner and three District Officers, one of whom was based in a sub-station at Ifakara. I thought this was adequate, but not excessive.

I felt that the appointment of African cadets was long overdue, and it also gave me particular pleasure that the first one should be a Nyakyusa. Many expatriate District Officers remembered with special affection the tribe with whom they had served on their first station, and all through my time in Tanganyika I had a particularly soft spot for the Nyakyusa.

When Ozzy, as he asked all the Europeans officials in Mahenge to call him, arrived, it was clear that he was very intelligent and very sophisticated. He was a handsome bachelor. His English was faultless. He was always beautifully dressed, and had impeccable manners. Before Ozzy arrived, the wife of one of the expatriate officials had expressed racist views about fraternising with an African at parties hosted by European officials, but she quickly discovered that no one else supported her. When Ozzy actually arrived, she seemed just as hospitable and friendly as the rest of us.

It may perhaps have been a factor in the posting of Ozzy to Ulanga District that there was no segregated club in Mahenge, so there was no possibility of controversy about amending the club's constitution in order to allow Africans in senior positions to become members. From Ozzy's point of view, however, his posting to a very small station like Mahenge meant that he had no African colleagues of comparable education to his own to befriend him there.

When Ozzy had been in Mahenge for a few weeks, he asked Jennifer for her advice. He told her that he was the best-educated bachelor Nyakyusa, and he wanted to get married. While at University in England he had fallen in love with a Ghanaian girl, but no girl from a rich West African country would marry a man from a poor country like Tanganyika, so he would presumably have to marry a Tanganyikan girl. He would therefore choose the best educated unmarried Nyakyusa girl in the country. He decided that there were only two suitable candidates, and he thought that Jennifer was in a good position to advise him, as she had taught at Tabora Girls' Secondary School, where both the girls whom Ozzy was considering had been educated. Jennifer had herself taught only one of the girls, Blandinah Robert. The other, Victoria Mwanjisi, had been at the school a little earlier.

The decision was not a simple one for Ozzy. Victoria's father was progressive, and was willing to follow new trends, and allow his daughter to be married without a bride-price from the bridegroom, provided that her husband-to-be was highly educated, in a secure job, and would be able to support her well. Blandinah's father was not so modern in his views, and wanted his daughter's groom to pay a larger than average bride-price because of Blandinah's high level of education.

Ozzy explained the problem to Jennifer succinctly. He preferred Blandinah, but she was expensive, whereas Victoria was available free. Jennifer replied that for someone on a salary like Ozzy's the amount of bride-price demanded was not the most important issue. She advised him to choose the one whom he liked best and who seemed to return his affection for her. This happened to be Blandinah. Ozzy later married her. Sadly, the marriage was not a success, and I understand that they divorced after a few unhappy years.

Shortly after he arrived in Ulanga, Ozzy went on safari with other government colleagues to visit the Local Courts along the Lupiro–Malinyi road. When they all got back, I was told by Ozzy's companions that the peasant farmers in Malinyi had been extremely rude to him and had, among other things, called him a *mzungu mweusi* – a 'black European'. Ozzy had then burst into tears in public at being spoken to so impolitely. I was not present on that safari, but Ozzy himself on his return to the Boma spoke to me very disparagingly about the primitive and uncouth people with whom he would be working.

On paper, Ozzy was very competent. He was thorough in the way he checked cash books and Local Court records. He drafted official correspondence in excellent English or Swahili. He also got on well with the expatriates in Mahenge. Where he failed badly was in his personal relationships with unsophisticated peasant farmers. He did not try to conceal his contempt for them, and seemed to dislike them as much as they disliked him.

He was also extremely vain. He did not have many ornaments or personal household items, but there were more than a dozen framed photographs of himself, including many studio portraits taken professionally in England, and no photographs at all of anyone else, hanging on his living room wall.

He had not yet learnt to drive, and soon after his arrival, he was given special permission to take out a provisional driving licence, and have driving lessons from Francis, the Boma driver, using the Government Landrover.

One of the tasks of District Officers in those Districts which had no police officer of the appropriate rank was to act as examiners in driving tests, and this task regularly fell to me in Mahenge. When Francis had been teaching him for a month or two, Ozzy told me he was now ready to take his test, and I fixed a time to go out with him. There was not a big choice of routes that were suitable for driving tests, and I usually asked candidates to drive along a flat stretch of road along the Mahenge Massif as far as Kwiro Mission, then to turn right into a lane which led down to the bottom of the escarpment on the Mahenge–Ifakara road, and then to drive back up the hill into Mahenge. On a straight stretch of road near Mahenge, I normally asked candidates to reverse for a short distance, keeping the car travelling in a straight line.

Being driven by Ozzy was a terrifying experience. He drove like Toad of Toad Hall, ignoring pedestrians and potholes. He was totally unable to negotiate the junction from the side lane to the bigger road at the bottom of the escarpment. I got out of the car, ostensibly to warn any vehicles that might be descending the escarpment that the Boma Landrover was blocking the road, and the driver could not move it, but the real reason was pure cowardice on my part. At last he managed, with my guidance, to negotiate the bend and get on to the road leading back into Mahenge. When we reached the straight stretch of road near the top of the hill, I then asked him to reverse the car without leaving the carriageway. All four wheels mounted the grass verge along the roadside.

When we got back to the Boma, I told Ozzy that I could not truthfully sign a document certifying that he was competent to drive, and advised him to go on with his lessons with Francis for a bit longer. Ozzy was unable to conceal his fury at my decision.

He only remained in Ulanga for a few months. The rest of his career was disappointing. I was told that in due course he was transferred from the Provincial Administration to the Co-operative Development Department, which was concerned with the collection and marketing of cash crops such as coffee produced by African farmers.

I never saw Ozzy again after he left Ulanga, but I heard that he died while still quite young. The stories I heard about the other African cadet who joined the Administration at the same time as Ozzy were just as disappointing.

Some people might claim that the fact that the first two African cadets did not fulfil our hopes for them was an indication that Africans in general were not yet ready to fill positions of high responsibility in the public service. Nothing could, in my view, be further from the truth. I worked with many African civil servants who were hard-working, competent, honest, and got on well with colleagues and with all the people they were serving, rich or poor. When I retired from Tanganyika, my successor as the District Commissioner of Lindi District was a young Hehe who was still at school when I was a cadet in Iringa. He had only completed Standard X at school, but I had total confidence in him. He had joined the civil service as a clerk, and been promoted very quickly on real merit. He eventually became the Permanent Secretary of one of the Ministries in Dar.

The difficulty with Ozzy, in my view, was that he was completely self-centred, and was not sufficiently interested either in the progress of his country or in his relationships with people he regarded as his inferiors.

It is a tragedy that such an exceptionally able young Tanganyikan graduate should have applied for a job which he seemed not to enjoy and for which he was temperamentally unsuited. Nevertheless, when the selectors considered his application, they probably had little to go on except his academic achievements, and these do not always give much indication of a person's character. If Ozzy's application had been turned down, it would have caused bitter resentment among the country's other future leaders, and, unless there was a very obvious reason for rejecting him, the selection panel in particular, and probably the whole Government as well, would have been branded as racists.

One Treasurer and Three Cashiers

The arrival of Ozzy in Mahenge meant that certain routine tasks which I enjoyed less than most of my other responsibilities could now be shared between three administrative officers rather than two. My colleagues and I all knew that proper financial control both of Central Government and of Local Treasury funds was essential if corruption was to be prevented, but we did not find it wildly exciting to carry out checks on all receipts and payment vouchers, and to add up columns of figures in cash registers to confirm that the balance of cash in hand was correct.

I found it tedious to count crumpled banknotes worth 20 shillings, 10 shillings, or 5 shillings apiece, and silver coins worth 1 shilling or 50 cents. However, counting banknotes and silver was nothing like so disagreeable as counting thousands of copper coins, each with a hole in the centre. These copper coins were worth 10 cents, 5 cents or 1 cent. During the 1950s, £1 sterling was worth 20 East African shillings, and each shilling was worth 100 cents. The hole was useful for tying the copper coins together with little bits of string into specified amounts.

Peasant farmers usually received their money in a single lump sum when they sold their crops, and then tended to spend it very slowly over the rest of the year. When cash is hoarded for a long time, it often gets dirty, and the coins received in the Local Treasury and in the District Cash Office were usually very grubby indeed. I always needed to wash my hands thoroughly after carrying out a cash check.

The treasurer of the Ulanga Local Treasury, Mr Mbulume Mtoahanji, was born in Ulanga District. He was a member of an aristocratic family. His brother was the chief of Kiberege, in the northern part of the district, and both Mbulume and his brother were highly respected by colleagues and by the general public. Like Mr Nair in the cash office, Mr Mbulume was very good at his job. He was well organised, conscientious, and experienced. He had been employed by the Local Treasury for many years, and there was no likelihood of his ever being transferred anywhere else. He was married and had a family, and he already had a circle of friends of his own by the time I arrived in Mahenge. He always behaved impeccably in all his dealings with expatriate officials, but I do not think he particularly wanted to make personal friends of officials such as myself, who were unlikely to spend more than a year or two in Mahenge.

People who were employed by central government, unlike local authority employees, were subject to frequent transfer, and it came as no surprise to any of us when we heard that C N U Nair was being transferred on promotion to a bigger cash office in Korogwe in Tanga Province. All of us who had worked with him were delighted about his promotion, but we were very sorry to see him go.

Apart from being an outstanding cashier, Nair was an extremely cheerful and likeable colleague, with wide-ranging interests. He was not married, and was more highly educated than any of the other Indians in Mahenge. He never complained about being lonely, but he clearly appreciated the friendship he was shown by the European officials stationed in Mahenge. He read avidly, and talked very interestingly about the books he had enjoyed. Jennifer and I offered to lend him any of our books. He always took great care of them, and returned them promptly. The

Bullocks also enjoyed his company, and they and we often invited him for meals at our homes. Although he was a Hindu, Nair was also always made welcome by Father Gerard, an exceptionally intelligent and saintly old priest who was in charge of the Roman Catholic Seminary at Kasita, just south of Mahenge.

A few days before Nair left for Korogwe, Father Gerard celebrated the fiftieth anniversary of his ordination as a priest, and the Bullocks, the Butlers, Ozzy, Nair, Jennifer and I were all invited to a festival service at Kwiro Mission. It was the first Christian service that Nair had ever attended, and he was delighted by both the simplicity and the joy of the whole occasion. The service was typical of the Capuchins in Ulanga District. It had dignity, the sermon preached by the Archbishop of Dar es Salaam was simple but excellent, and the choir and congregation sang very well. The cathedral was large and imposing, but there was no pomp or ostentatious display of wealth there. All the priests were dressed in the style of Saint Francis of Assisi. Nair told me how impressed he had been by the service and by the friendliness of all the people attending the reception after the service ended.

Just before he left, Nair invited his closest friends, six Europeans and seven Asians, to a farewell party in his house, where his guests were provided with delicious Indian food. He thanked us for our kindness to him during his time in Mahenge, and said he would never forget us, and hoped we would meet again. Jennifer and I had no idea at the time that forty years would pass before we saw him again.

When Mr Nair left Mahenge, he was replaced by an African cashier called Mr J H Sabuni. I had not expected Mr Nair's successor to be either as competent or as likeable as Nair. That would have been difficult. I nevertheless found Mr Sabuni exceptionally uncongenial. He was not very competent. He seemed hostile to all Europeans and Asians. Worse than that, in my view, was the fact that, like Ozzy Mwambungu, he treated African peasants and junior employees with contempt.

One day not long after Mr Sabuni's arrival, a telegram came from the Accountant General in Dar about a consignment of cash remitted from Mahenge. It had contained some currency notes whose numbers corresponded with notes stolen in transit between the De La Rue Factory, where they had been made, and Heathrow Airport. They were the first such notes to be recovered after a major robbery, and we were asked to check on whether we had any more stolen notes in the cash office.

A few more stolen notes were found. Antony Sarota had been transferred on promotion to Chief Inspector of Police, and his place had been taken by Senior Inspector Abubakari, who asked Sabuni if he remembered who had paid them in to the cash office. Sabuni said he believed that he had received them from the trader Gulamali Somji. Geoff Bullock then signed a warrant to search Gulamali's premises, and asked me to accompany Inspector Abubakari, who was to carry out the search. Geoff wanted me to be able to corroborate any evidence the Inspector might be required to give in what could perhaps prove to be a major robbery trial at the High Court in London. I was rather excited at the prospect of a trip to the Old Bailey in the middle of my tour of service.

Gulamali Somji's wife was in the last stages of pregnancy, and she sobbed hysterically throughout the search, begging us to have mercy on her husband and forgive him for his crimes. In fact, her husband was not guilty of anything. He did not have any stolen notes, but I was amazed at the amount of perfectly legitimate currency notes which he had hidden away very insecurely on his premises.

His shop was built of mud and wattle, and had a metal roof made of old four-gallon paraffin cans known as *debes*. When the shop was closed and unoccupied, the door was fastened with a very flimsy-looking padlock. It would not have taken a master criminal to break and enter the premises. I did not count the amount he had hidden away, but I guess it was getting on for two thousand pounds. These notes were not kept under lock and key, but were all kept in the kind of tinfoil wrappers used by tobacco suppliers to contain ten packets of 20 cigarettes. The wrappers were scattered round the shop and living quarters in places which a bright child would have no trouble in spotting. I suggested to Somji that his money would be safer in a bank, but he told me he did not trust banks, and was willing to risk fire and theft, so long as the money was kept under his own roof.

After Inspector Abubakari had satisfied himself that there were no stolen currency notes in Gulamali Somji's shop, he left, and I remained for a few minutes to try to console Mrs Somji, and to explain to her and her husband that the search had not been motivated by malice on the part of anyone. They accepted my explanation, and we parted on good terms.

I heard later that Sabuni had made a mistake when he suggested that the notes had been paid into the cash office by Gulamali Somji. They had in fact been brought into Ulanga District by a very young and inexperienced Swiss Capuchin Father about to be posted to a

particularly remote mission station. I never met him, but I understand that he was sent back in disgrace to Switzerland after he
admitted that he had bought them cheaply in Zurich before setting
out to join the Mission. He claimed that he had not even suspected
that the notes might have been stolen. He was not prosecuted. As far
as I know, the robbers and the men who had offered the notes for
sale in Zurich were never caught.

At the end of 1958, the Head Boma Messenger, Kilosa Mhali,
retired and was succeeded by Abdullah Likomiti, who had previously worked for me. This meant that he would in future be
working personally for Geoff Bullock, and a younger man called
Vitalis Cyril became my messenger.

One morning, Vitalis brought me a payment voucher to sign
authorising payment to someone who was waiting to receive his
money. I looked at the typed document prepared by Sabuni, and
saw that the numeral '4' was included in the amount in figures,
whereas the written amount due to be paid was spelt out in
words as 'five'. It was obvious that the voucher was wrong, and
would give rise to a query if it were passed for payment, but there
was no way of knowing which of the amounts mentioned on the
voucher was correct. I therefore sent Vitalis back to the cash office
to show the mistake to Mr Sabuni and ask him to correct it. Two
minutes later, Vitalis returned, saying, 'Mr Sabuni says you are
just annoying him for nothing, and there is nothing wrong with
this voucher.' I told him to call Mr Sabuni to my office at once.

A few minutes later, Mr Sabuni slouched into my office, sneer-
ing at me. He folded his arms across his chest and stood with his
weight on his left leg, with his right leg stretched outwards, with
his heel on the ground and his toes pointing upwards. If he had
been a soldier, his demeanour would have been described as
'dumb insolence'. Africans are normally extremely courteous,
and I was not accustomed to this sort of behaviour. It was the first
occasion on which I had seen an African official behaving in such
a way, and I am sure it was symptomatic of the growing hostility
of some Africans to the colonial regime.

I told Sabuni the voucher was wrong, and I tried to show him
the mistake he had made, but he did not even bother to look at
the document, and contradicted me very rudely. I then lost my
temper. I crumpled the voucher into a ball and threw it at him,
and said to Vitalis, 'Chuck this *shenzi* out of my office.' Mr Sabuni
left the office rapidly, without Vitalis laying a finger on him.

The word *shenzi* is defined in the dictionary as 'barbarian,
savage, a person untouched by civilisation', and it is regarded as

deeply offensive by Africans. I was thoroughly wrong to use such an insult to anybody, regardless of the provocation, and as soon as I had got over my anger, I went to the cash office to offer my apology for using such an objectionable word. Sabuni absolutely refused to accept my apology, and said I had only insulted him because he was an African. I denied this categorically, and then probably made matters worse, as far as Sabuni was concerned, by telling him that I had never once called any other African a *shenzi*, and had only used the word to him because he had himself been inefficient and impolite.

I then went to Geoff Bullock's office to tell him what had happened and to apologise to him for my behaviour. I also wrote a letter of apology to the Provincial Commissioner in Morogoro. The newly-arrived Deputy Provincial Commissioner, Denis O'Callaghan, who had been the District Commissioner in Tabora, replied to my letter in a way which I regarded as entirely fair. He told me that my knowledge of Swahili was quite good enough for me to understand how all Africans felt about the word I had used, and that the consequences would be severe if I ever repeated the offence. I am glad to say I never did.

Denis O'Callaghan then added the welcome news that he was arranging for Mr Sabuni to be transferred immediately to Rufiji District, and for him to be replaced as cashier in Ulanga by Mr Lotti Yonah Zachariah.

Zachariah was not much more competent than Sabuni, and he also had the disadvantage that he was epileptic, and was prone to have fits in the cash office. However, he was a very cheerful and likeable man. I felt sorry for him, not because of his illness but because of a financial rule which required cashiers to replace from their own pockets any deficiencies found on checking, and to take into revenue on a General Revenue Receipt any cash found surplus.

The cash balance when Zachariah was cashier was often incorrect, but there was a surplus just as often as there was a deficiency, and I am sure that he was completely honest. However, he forfeited a significant part of his monthly salary in refunding small losses, but he was not allowed to set these losses off against the surpluses found on other days. As far as the govenment rules were concerned, Zachariah was caught in a 'heads you lose, tails you can't win' situation. I think the problem was that he did not seem to be very good at mental arithmetic, and made bona fide mistakes both when he was adding up figures in the cash book and in his dealings with members of the public.

On one occasion when he had just had to refund out of his own pocket a sum which I was sure he could not easily afford, I asked him if he would like to apply for other duties, for example as a correspondence clerk or magistrate's court clerk, which would not put his salary at risk. He replied with a broad smile that he enjoyed being a cashier, and hoped to become better at the job as he became more experienced.

Tanganyika's First General Elections

For most of the time that Britain was responsible for the administration of Tanganyika, there were two assemblies which helped the Governor to carry out his responsibilities. The tasks of advising the Governor on policy matters and supervising the work of the various Government Departments were performed by Executive Council. Most of the members of Executive Council were very senior expatriate officials, although there were also some appointed 'unofficial' members as well.

Executive Council had great influence but no real power. Decisions were taken by the Governor, who could act in opposition to the advice of Executive Council. As far as I know, that never happened while I was in Tanganyika, but if he went against the advice of his Executive Council, the Governor was bound to make a report to the Secretary of State in London.

The task of Legislative Council was to advise the Governor on the enactment of laws. Like Executive Council, it had no real power, and until 1958 it was not democratically elected. The first Legislative Council was set up in 1926 by the then Governor, Sir Donald Cameron. It consisted initially of the Governor and thirteen other senior officials and seven nominated 'unofficial' members, five European and two Asian, who were appointed by the Governor. At its inaugural meeting, Cameron had explained that the native community could not yet be represented because at that time no native could be found with a sufficient command of English to take part in debates and to understand what was being said. The first two African members of Legislative Council, both chiefs, were appointed in 1945. The first African commoner was appointed in 1947. Until 1953, when a Speaker, Brigadier Scupham, was appointed, Legislative Council was chaired by the Governor himself. The first women members of Legislative Council, one African, one Asian, and one European, were not appointed until 1955.

Late in 1949, the year in which Twining became Governor, a

Committee on Constitutional Development was appointed under the chairmanship of the Attorney General, Sir Charles Mathew. Their terms of reference required them to 'review the present constitutional structure in the territory, both local and territorial, and to make recommendations for future constitutional developments'. Their report was completed in 1951.

The Committee recommended, among other things, that the membership of Legislative Council should be enlarged, and that an expert enquiry should be set up to examine the practical application of their recommendations. A Special Commissioner, Professor Mackenzie of Manchester University, was appointed to do this. His report reached Tanganyika in April 1953.

By 1958, there were sixty-seven members in addition to the Speaker. Thirty-four were on the Government side. The remaining thirty-three were known as 'representative members'. The representative members, eleven African, eleven Asian, and eleven European, represented geographical areas and special interests, and were all appointed by the Governor.

Professor Mackenzie's recommendations included proposals about the elective principle. In June 1956, a Bill providing for Elections to Legislative Council was passed. This established a common electoral roll based on a 'qualitative franchise'. Voters had to satisfy three conditions. A voter had to be at least twenty-one years old, and to have lived in Tanganyika for three out of the preceding five years. The third condition could be any one of three types of qualification – an educational standard of at least the equivalent of Standard VIII; an income of not less than £150 a year; or tenure of a 'listed office'. Holders of such offices included chiefs, headmen, and members of various advisory bodies. After the first general election, the qualification relating to education was amended to include anyone who was literate, and the qualifying level of income was reduced from £150 to £75 per annum. This was in order to increase the number of people entitled to vote. The candidates for election had to satisfy rather more demanding conditions than the voters.

In the first election, all voters were required to vote for three candidates, one from each of the three main racial groups. There were ten constituencies, and for administrative reasons it was decided to hold the election in two stages. The original plan was that the first group of five constituencies, which included Eastern Province, would vote in September 1958 and the remainder in September 1959. Turnbull later decided to bring the second stage of the voting forward to February 1959.

During the early years of British rule, people had shown little interest in the way that policies were decided and laws enacted by their colonial rulers. However, this attitude changed rapidly after India, Pakistan, and a number of former British colonies in West Africa became independent. One of the main demands of TANU was that Africans should be given a far greater say in the way their country was governed, and that the country's legislators should be elected democratically, not simply appointed by an expatriate Governor, however benevolent and wise he might be.

I, and many of my colleagues, agreed in principle with that point of view, but I was sufficiently paternalistic to feel that British administrators were generally less likely to abuse their power than some of the aspiring political leaders who seemed to be motivated by greed and personal ambition rather than a desire to serve their people.

When the proposals for the forthcoming election were announced, they were generally recognised as a major step towards 'responsible government', a term which meant that elected representatives would control some but not all of the functions of government. This represented the last stage of the journey that would lead to full independence. However, there was criticism from those who wanted a parliament based more closely on the Westminster model. 'Qualitative franchise' meant that virtually all peasant farmers and low-paid workers had no vote.

Those who did qualify for a vote were also dissatisfied. They were obliged to vote for three candidates, two of whom were members of different racial groups from their own. Although the new arrangements would mean that the proportion of Africans on Legislative Council would increase, many African leaders protested at the proposal that there should be equal numbers of Asian, European and African members of Legislative Council, since the number of non-natives was only a tiny fraction of the number of native Africans.

In the closing years of the 1950s, there was a marked change in public attitudes towards the colonial government and in the courtesy traditionally shown to those in authority, whatever their race. All over the country, TANU convened rallies which were attended by large and noisy crowds. Many of TANU's wiser leaders urged their audiences to work harmoniously towards a peaceful transition to independence, and stressed that the country would continue to need technical support from experienced expatriate officials, even after independence. There were others, however, whose speeches were inflammatory and designed to promote racial hatred. They made completely unrealistic promises about what Tanganyika would be like for Africans after getting rid of the non-natives. Hundreds of new schools and dispensaries would be built. Wages for all Africans would be increased enormously, regardless of their skill. There would be full employment. Taxes would be reduced or even abolished altogether.

Members of the audiences at such gatherings seldom asked how it would be possible for massive improvements in social services to be financed without increasing the level of taxation, but the belief was encouraged that by expropriating the wealth of non-natives there would be enough to make all Africans rich.

The colonial government might have tried harder to explain its policies, but there were too few officials with either the time or the rhetorical skills to respond effectively in Swahili to the messages that were being preached by extremists. Moreover, British officials, whatever their personal views, had grown up in the tradition that a loyal civil servant should try to appear impartial in democratic elections.

Many Africans, in particular young urban unemployed men, were encouraged to undermine the lawfully established courts, to resist the forces of law and order, to demonstrate against the colonialist oppressors who were sucking the blood of the people, and to withhold payment of their taxes. When Europeans passed through towns and villages, young men raised their fists in the air and shouted '*Uhuru!*' (freedom). Those Africans who appeared to be collaborating with the government ran the risk of being ostracised, intimidated, or even tried and punished by kangaroo courts.

Geoffrey Hucks, under whom I had served in Iringa, had been appointed Supervisor of Elections. The detailed planning of a huge and sparsely populated country's first general election is not easy, but Geoffrey carried out all his tasks brilliantly. He worked out procedures for the registration of voters; the designation of enough polling stations to enable every voter to reach one by foot from his or her own home; the rules of voting; the procedures to be followed by presiding officers; the drafting and distribution of explanatory briefing material in all appropriate languages for all who needed it; the supply of enough stationery and equipment for the election to be administered in accordance with the law; the handling of completed ballot papers; and the announcement of results.

Geoffrey Hucks was an extremely good organiser who always worked very hard and paid great attention to detail. His long experience of the country contributed enormously to the success of the election. His achievement was recognised in the Honours List the following year, when he was awarded an OBE. I was not alone in thinking he deserved a higher award than that.

During the period leading up to the election, officials through-out the country explained orally at public meetings what the arrangements for the election would involve, how people could register as voters, where voting would take place, and the dates and times when each polling station would be open. Many local TANU leaders were also very helpful in giving publicity to the practical arrangements for the election, and in urging their members to vote and to behave responsibly.

Candidates and their party spokesmen canvassed round their constituencies. The campaigning was generally done in an orderly way. I was told, however, that in Morogoro District some members of the TANU Youth League had thrown stones at the car in which Chief Patrick Kunambe, the African candidate for the United Tanganyika Party in Eastern Province, was travelling. There was no such disorder in Ulanga District, where, as far as I know, no UTP candidate ever came to campaign.

One day I happened to meet Amir Habib Jamal, the Asian candidate for Eastern Province supported by TANU, when he was canvassing near the ferry across the Kilombero River at Ifakara. I listened to what he said to the crowd and I chatted to him after he had finished his address. I had never met him before, but I was greatly impressed by his pleasant personality, his ability to communicate with Africans, and by the practical good sense of what he set out as his political programme. I was not at all surprised when he was elected with a substantial majority. His subsequent political career was very successful, and a model of how non-Africans of high calibre could work harmoniously with Africans. Jamal became one of Nyerere's most able and trusted Ministers. His reputation grew steadily, and in 1979 he was elected Chairman of the International Monetary Fund/World Bank Governors' Annual Meeting in Washington.

The TANU African candidate for Eastern Province was Julius Nyerere himself. I never discovered exactly why he chose to stand in Eastern Province, as he was a Zanaki tribesman from Musoma District in Lake Province, where his father was a chief. One of his aims, however, was to weld the whole country into a single nation, rather than perpetuate the tribal rivalries which later led to so much violence in other newly independent countries such as Rwanda.

As in many other Districts, the voting in Ulanga took place over several days. The reason for this was that polling stations were often a long way apart, and there were not enough responsible officials to staff all of them on the same day. I was appointed to preside at a number of different polling stations on consecutive days. My main tasks were to ensure that the voting was carried out in an orderly way, to check on the identity of those who applied to vote, to issue each voter with a ballot paper, and to ensure than no one voted more than once.

Printed ballot papers listed the names of every candidate in that constituency, and each candidate was allowed to choose a symbol which was printed beside his or, in very rare cases, her name. There were no women candidates in Eastern Province. Candidate A, for example, might choose a pair of clasped hands, Candidate B a lion, Candidate C a bicycle, and so on.

When a voter was illiterate (and there were a number of holders of a qualifying office in Ulanga who could not read or write), the presiding officer had to explain the ballot paper, read out the names of all the candidates, and then fill in three crosses, one for a candidate from each race, where he was asked by the voter to place them. Julius Nyerere did not have a symbol printed beside his name, and I was surprised that each of the illiterate voters who asked me to record his votes chose symbols rather than specifying by name the candidate for whom he wanted to vote. Nyerere was elected with a very comfortable majority, but his majority might well have been even larger if he had selected a symbol for himself, as his opponent Chief Patrick Kunambe had done.

Most of the polling stations in Ulanga District had very few voters, some less than a dozen, and each morning they all arrived quite early to cast their votes. This meant that my work as presiding officer was usually over by noon, but I was nevertheless required by law to keep the polling station open until the official closing time, even if all the registered voters had voted, in case someone arrived and claimed that an impostor had been given a ballot paper to which he was not entitled. This did not happen in any of the polling stations where I presided. I had some very restful days, and made friends with the likeable young TANU political agent who had been asked to monitor the work of TANU in the same polling stations as I had been allocated to. We spent many pleasant hours playing noughts-and-crosses with each other, and chatting about every subject we could think of except politics, which was taboo.

It took some time for the results to be announced. This was partly due to the state of the roads, but also because the election was held in two stages, the second five months after the first.

Even before all the votes had been counted and detailed results were known, it was quite clear that TANU had won a sweeping victory. None of the candidates from UTP was successful. In Southern Highlands Province, Lady Chesham, who was supported by TANU, inflicted a crushing defeat on the Chairman of UTP, Ivor Bayldon. In every constituency, TANU candidates of whatever race won by large majorities.

After the 1958–59 election was completed in an orderly way, pressure for immediate 'responsible Government' mounted. Both Sir Richard Turnbull and Julius Nyerere understood the danger to the country's political future if Tanganyika descended into lawlessness and chaos. The Governor was told by his advisers that Nyerere feared that he might not be able to control his own party members unless some concessions were made to appease their frustration and to speed up progress.

In March 1959, the Governor announced plans to give Ministerial responsibility to four (later increased to five) elected representatives. In May 1959, a Council of Ministers was introduced, five of whose members were elected Members of Legislative Council.

A Post-Election (Constitution) Committee was set up under the Chairmanship of Sir Richard Ramage, who had previously served in Nigeria, the Gold Coast, and Sierra Leone. Its task was to plan the next steps forward. It recommended that Legislative Council should be enlarged to consist of seventy-one elected members and a smaller number of nominated members. Constituencies were redefined, and instead of ten Provinces each with three members, the general plan was to have one member for each District. In addition, eleven seats would be reserved for Asians and ten for Europeans, but the proportion of Africans would be higher than ever before.

A further general election would be required as soon as possible to implement these proposals. Before that could take place, however, voters who qualified under the new rules would have to be given the opportunity to register.

Later in 1959, the Governor announced that the country would achieve responsible government in 1960. This did not go as far as the more extreme members of TANU wanted, but it was sufficient to enable Nyerere to retain the confidence of his party while he was also building up a relationship of mutual trust and respect with Sir Richard Turnbull.

The country held its second General Election in September 1960. This reinforced TANU's overwhelming victory in 1958–59. They won seventy out of seventy-one seats. However it did not involve much work for officials in Ulanga, as the TANU candidate there was returned unopposed. The full results were announced just as my family and I were setting off from Mahenge to begin our home leave in Britain.

Pyrexia of Unknown Origin

In November 1958, two months after the voting in the first part of the general election, I became ill. I was working in my office when I suddenly became extremely thirsty, and sent my messenger to G M Gulamali's shop to buy me a bottle of fizzy orangeade. I did not want to drink the water from the taps in the Boma. I went home before the Boma closed, and Jennifer sent for the doctor. Gary Butler was on safari, and one of the Medical Assistants, Samson Mwaruanda, came to examine me. He gave me an injection and some analgesics, and promised to go on visiting me regularly in my house until Gary returned. Samson was very well meaning, but did not inspire confidence. The symptoms of my illness were appalling headaches and muscular pains with a very high fever, followed by prodigious sweating, which brought my temperature down but left my pyjamas and bed completely saturated.

There were no Grade 1 facilities in Mahenge Hospital, and as soon as Gary saw me he decided that I needed to be admitted immediately to Ifakara Mission Hospital. I think he drove me there in his own car, but my memories of the journey are not very clear. The fevers and sweating continued for several days, while I was treated by Dr Karl Schöpf, the extremely competent doctor in charge of the hospital, and nursed by nuns. The hospital carried out several laboratory tests, but were not able to make a diagnosis.

One evening, a few days after my admission, I suddenly felt infinitely worse than I had ever felt before, and I rang the bell by my bedside to call a nurse. She took a look at me and immediately sent for Karl Schöpf, who clearly thought that I was critically ill. I thought I was dying.

Intensive care in hospitals in developed countries now involves being attached to machines which monitor a patient's pulse, temperature, blood pressure, and a mass of other things as well. The machines print out the results, and sound warning noises or flash lights to alert the nurses if there is a crisis. Ifakara had no such sophisticated apparatus. Its intensive care had two hands, a beautiful face, a veil over her head, and was called Sister Alphonsina. She sat by my bed throughout the night, holding my hand and helping me to drink whenever I felt thirsty. I was aware that she was praying beside me, and I felt completely serene and confident in the love that surrounded me.

Next morning the worst of the crisis seemed to be over, but Karl Schöpf had to go to Morogoro for some urgent work that could not be postponed, and he did not think it safe to leave me in Ifakara hospital without a doctor there. He therefore decided to take me with him in his car and transfer me to the Government Hospital in Morogoro.

I already knew the Medical Officer in Morogoro, a highly competent Austrian called Valentin Schuppler, who had been with me in Iringa. Soon after my admission to Morogoro Hospital, he sent a telegram to Jennifer to tell her where I was, and to advise her not to come to collect me from hospital yet. This telegram was incorrectly transmitted, and Jennifer got a message asking her to come to Morogoro to collect me. She was not very used to driving on Ulanga's appalling and muddy roads, but set off with Ruth, Ina, and Mohamed. Mohamed was exceptionally good on safari and capable of changing a wheel or carrying out roadside repairs to the car if it proved necessary. By the time Jennifer reached Morogoro, I had been transferred once again, this time to the Ocean Road Hospital in Dar es Salaam.

The hospital in Dar was better equipped than the one in Morogoro, but the staff seemed no better in 1958 than they had been when I had been sent there from Iringa at the end of my first tour in 1954.

Jennifer followed me to Dar, and after a couple of days in a hotel she was offered self-catering accommodation in a flat belonging to the Women's Service League, even though she was not a member. She spent Christmas and the New Year there, while I was being pumped full of medication in the hope that something would make me feel better.

After trying a large number of other drugs, I was given one called Aureomycetin, and the effect was clearly beneficial. My fever dropped and my aches got better, and the hospital said that

I could be discharged, but would have to stay in Dar, take my own temperature each morning and evening, and report to the Outpatients' Department once a week for a further blood sample to be taken. It took nearly three months for my diagnosis of 'pyrexia of unknown origin' to be replaced by a firm diagnosis of brucellosis, a disease which takes various forms, and is sometimes known as undulant fever, Malta fever, Gibraltar fever, Bang's disease, goat fever, or contagious abortion. I lost nearly four stone in weight while I was in hospital, and was told that in order to avoid the risk of contaminating other people I should never be a blood donor.

While I was convalescing as an outpatient in Dar, a Crown Counsel called Alistair Troup (no relation to his namesake Donald Troup, the Provincial Commissioner in Mtwara) invited us to housewarm his house in Oyster Bay and look after his Siamese cats, Ming and Periwinkle, while he was in Moshi, prosecuting in what was generally referred to at the time as the 'Chagga Torture Trial'.

Some over-enthusiastic Local Authority messengers near Mount Kilimanjaro were charged with several offences of pouring boiling water through a tube into the private parts of suspects to make them confess. The messengers were brutal, but they were not particularly important people. The main question on everbody's mind concerned the possible involvement of the Paramount Chief of the Chagga.

The Chagga were regarded by many people as the most sophisticated tribe in Tanganyika, and their cultivation of coffee had made them one of the richest. The British policy of indirect rule had encouraged the creation of an African elite, and Thomas Marealle was thought of as one of the best examples of the success of this policy. He had graduated at a British university, and had later been appointed as a member of Executive Council. Many people thought of him as the prototype of the African leaders who would govern the country after independence.

While the accusations of torture were being investigated, the simple question, 'Did you know what was going on?' put the Chief on the horns of a dilemma. If he said he did not, he would be blamed for not being aware of what his subordinates were getting up to. If he said he did, he would be blamed for condoning the flagrant abuse of human rights in his chiefdom. He chose the lesser evil of pleading ignorance, but there was a lot of publicity, and the Chief's reputation as one of the success stories of the policy of indirect rule was badly damaged.

The trial took quite a long time to complete, and I continued to convalesce in Alastair Troup's house. Jennifer and I took Ruth to swim in the Indian Ocean nearly every day. One afternoon, when Ruth was splashing about in a calm sea, a freak wave came and knocked her over. She was under the water for what seemed a terrifyingly long time while Jennifer and I both rushed to pick her up. She came up laughing merrily at what the naughty wave had done, and eagerly waiting for the excitement of a few more big waves just like the first one. She was eighteen months old at the time!

I was starting to feel much better, although I still continued to have a high temperature every evening. However, my spell of leisurely convalescence was about to come to an unexpected end.

In February 1959, there was a nasty incident in a notorious village called Buguruni, on the outskirts of Dar. Three uniformed policemen on night patrol in a brand new Standard Vanguard van equipped with a radio transmitter–receiver set came across a house where what appeared to be voodoo-like rituals were taking place. The policemen entered the house, and were immediately attacked by the frenzied participants in the ceremony. Two of the policemen managed to get away and hide in a nearby shop owned by an Arab, who provided them with plain clothes to wear instead of their uniforms, which he concealed. He then helped them to make their escape by mingling in the angry crowd.

The third policeman, Mwitu Kitongu, ran for his life, but when he was trying to climb over a wire netting fence around the compound of the Metal Box Company, the crowd caught up with him and brutally stoned him to death.

The crowd also attacked the car, which had only been on the road for nine days. I later saw what remained of it. I found the piles of blood-stained stones and the shattered remains of the car very sinister. The windscreen and windows were smashed to smithereens. The steering wheel was bent double. The doors had all been ripped off their hinges. The bodywork was bent and crumpled. The new tyres were torn to shreds. Even the cylinder block had been dislodged from its mountings. About the only thing that the mob had omitted to do was to set fire to the petrol in the tank.

No tools were ever found that could have provided an explanation of how such damage could have been inflicted, and several people suggested that the crowd were in such a diabolical frenzy of rage that they had been able to do it all with just their bare hands. Mob violence can be very frightening, and I felt horrified that a young policeman on duty should have lost his life in such dreadful circumstances.

Not surprisingly, the police themselves were eager to charge those responsible. They found fingerprints all over the car, many of which were identified as those of people living in Buguruni who had criminal records. However, the villagers all refused to cooperate with the police investigation. They claimed that the fingerprints were all left by sightseers who came the morning after the killing to see the damaged car. Even those who lived close to the wreck of the car or to the spot where the policeman had been killed insisted that they had seen and heard nothing unusual during the night. No one was ever charged either with killing the policeman or with malicious damage to the car.

The police then mounted a campaign to arrest all the tax defaulters they could find in Buguruni. The campaign was perfectly legitimate, but no one attempted to conceal the fact that the main motive of the police was vengeance for the death of their colleague. About 900 people were arrested for non-payment of tax. Some of them paid their arrears straight away, and were discharged, but those who could not pay were remanded in custody in overcrowded cells in Ukonga Prison, a few miles out of the centre of Dar.

This sudden flood of people awaiting trial put a great strain on the police, the prison staff, and the magistrates normally stationed in Dar. I was therefore asked to join the team of magistrates that was to try the cases, and was given special extended powers to try cases arising within the District of Dar es Salaam, even though I was still nominally stationed in Ulanga District. However, the doctors insisted that I was not yet strong enough to work a full day, and should only work in the mornings.

The cases were heard at great speed. Trials were normally held in open court buildings, but it was feared that there could be further disturbances if the villagers of Buguruni awaiting trial were transported by lorry between a prison in Ukonga and a court in the centre of Dar. Legal advice was sought about whether the trials could lawfully take place within the walls of the prison, and we were told that it would be lawful, provided that the prison gates were kept open while the trials were taking place. Guards were therefore posted outside the open prison gates while the trials were going on, but there was no more trouble, and no one ever challenged the legality of the proceedings.

Each morning I went out to Ukonga by car. I worked side by side with all the other magistrates in a very large hall within the prison. Those who wished to plead guilty, the majority, formed a long queue. The small minority who decided to plead not guilty were told that they would have to wait until all the pleas of guilty were dealt with before their cases could be heard.

I normally felt that the dignity of the judicial process and of the accused person required me to take my time before depriving anyone of his liberty, but this was an exceptional situation, and I sacrificed dignity to speed. One day I counted the number of cases I had heard that morning. It was thirty-four. I stopped counting after that.

I had a problem one morning. A prison warder brought before me two men whom he said I had convicted the previous day. They both had exactly the same Islamic name, Saidi, name of father, Mohamed, tribe, Mluguru, and home village, Buguruni, but one had been convicted for one year's tax default and the other for three. The one convicted on three counts was to serve a longer sentence than the other, and the warder asked me to identify which was which. I was totally unable to do so, so I asked the two men themselves to tell me. There was no dispute between them about which had the longer sentence, so I simply added the names of their respective grandfathers to their commitment warrants, and then went on trying other cases.

While I was still undergoing treatment in the Ocean Road Hospital, I was told that there had been a radio announcement to the effect that a new multi-racial preparatory school at Rungemba would be opening on 1st January 1959, and that I was to be its first headmaster. Neither Jennifer nor I had been told about the proposed date of opening, and we thought the time for preparation was grossly inadequate, and in any event I was certainly not yet well enough to tackle a new and very challenging job.

Early in 1959, some of the members of the committee of trustees responsible for the management of Rungemba School held a meeting, and Jennifer and I were invited to attend it. We were kept waiting for an inordinately long time in a passageway outside the committee room before being summoned in. When we eventually met what would in Britain be described as a Board of Governors, I asked the same questions which I had already put privately to Spencer just after we had returned from leave the previous year.

Spencer reneged totally on the assurances that he had given me, in particular the undertaking that pupils leaving Rungemba would continue their education in a multi-racial secondary school. Jennifer and I got the impression that none of the committee had been told about the matters I had discussed with Spencer at the start of my tour of service.

The members of the committee had each been appointed to represent a particular community, and each seemed to think that his objective was to obtain preferential treatment for pupils of his own race or creed. The representative of the Ismaili community insisted that if the Aga Khan contributed a certain percentage of the costs of the school, that would automatically entitle his community to precisely that percentage of the places in the school. There was then an acrimonious argument involving the representatives of the less wealthy communities, who wanted their share of the subsidised places to be based on their need rather than on their cash contribution towards the cost of setting up and running the school. The committee had no plans about exactly how pupils should be selected, and whether places should be awarded on the basis of academic merit or membership of a particular community or race. They were nevertheless very reluctant to delegate to the headmaster designate any responsibility for the admission of pupils.

On the question of religious and moral education, one of the committee thought the problem of different religious backgrounds would be solved by having an assembly each morning where pupils would sit silently for five minutes having pious thoughts. Jennifer and I were not totally convinced that the thoughts of ten-year-olds forced to remain silent for five minutes would necessarily be pious ones. The committee ruled out one member's suggestion that religious leaders from outside the school should occasionally be invited to Rungemba to teach the pupils about their religion. Some objected to the idea of Christian boys being taught anything at all about Islam, or vice versa. Others thought such a scheme would cost too much. Our requests for the school to have a matron and a teacher of maths and science were not considered worthy of a reply at all.

Jennifer and I left the meeting convinced that the trustees would never work as a team, and that the school had no chance of success with such trustees. We told them that we were not very happy about the outcome of our meeting, but asked for time to discuss the matter between ourselves and with John Bradley, who had moved from Mwanza to take up a senior position in the Secretariat. John Bradley urged me not to accept the offer of a secondment, as I would be of more value to Tanganyika if I

remained in the Provincial Administration. Jennifer and I reluctantly agreed with him. We were sad to take a decision that
would disappoint Twining, but he was no longer the Governor,
and we were sure we would get no support from those now in
power. After agonising for a few days, we wrote to say that we no
longer wished to be personally involved with the school. We got
a very curt reply to our letter. The plans for the school were
discontinued, and it never opened.

Towards the end of January, we had bad news from Mahenge.
Ina got a telegram to let her know that her youngest son Joseph
was very ill. We arranged for her to return to Mahenge immediately. Two days later, after Ina had already left Dar, a second
telegram arrived to say the boy had died. Ina had herself decided
that while she was away Joseph should stay with his grandmother. She thought he would be happier in Mahenge with his
grandmother than living with strangers in the humid climate of
Dar es Salaam. None of us expected that there would be a serious
outbreak of measles in the area surrounding Kwiro Mission
while we were away, or that little Joseph would be one of its
victims.

My temperature continued to go up every evening, but, by the
end of February, Jennifer and I were getting worried that the
rains would start and the Kilombero Ferry be taken out of service
early in March, and that we might be unable to get back to
Mahenge until the end of the rainy season if we remained in Dar
much longer. Ruth and I were also covered with prickly heat,
which would get better in a cooler climate. I was therefore
allowed to return home, subject to the proviso that Jennifer
would share the driving with me if I got tired, and that I would
ask Gary Butler to go on monitoring my health in Ulanga District.

Just before we left Dar, we invited some of our friends to
supper. They included an exceptional District Officer called
Randal Sadleir, who had been an usher at our wedding, and a
newly-married African couple called Anthony and Martha
Bulengo. Martha and Jennifer had taught together, but because of
my illness we had not been able to accept an invitation to her
wedding in Tabora. Anthony was one of the first Tanganyikans to
qualify in Britain as a doctor. He later worked for the World
Health Organisation in Ghana, and during the 1980s asked us to
be guardians of two of his children while they were at school in
England.

We had no problems on our journey home. When we arrived,
Juma and Omari and their wives were all there to welcome us.

The Bullocks had paid them their wages on our behalf during our absence, and our house was immaculate. Both our dogs were in perfect condition. Juma had been provided by the Bullocks with the cash needed to buy food for our animals during our absence, and also for a delicious hot meal for us, which was ready almost as soon as we arrived.

Jennifer, Ruth, Mohamed and I were all delighted to be back home at last. Ruth was thrilled to see her old friends again. She was as devoted to Juma, Omari and Ina as they were to her. There was no doubt that Ina's grief about Joseph was genuine, but she showed great courage in seeming to be perfectly happy whenever she was with Ruth. Ruth was also very fond of Mgeni binti Jumanne, Juma's buxom and dignified wife, and she always treated Ruth like a well-loved granddaughter.

The only gloomy face when we arrived home was Juma's. He could not wait to tell us about the appalling thing which had happened during his stewardship. While we had been away, one of my muscovy ducks had fallen ill, and, as Ulanga had no vet, Juma had walked to the government hospital carrying the duck under his arm, to tell Gary Butler that it was my duck, and to ask him to give it the right medicine to make it well again. In spite of Gary's ministrations the duck had died, and Juma felt that he had let us down badly. He became cheerful again when we did not rebuke him for negligence but thanked him for taking so much trouble to seek the doctor's help on our behalf, and for the splendid way he and Omari had looked after our home and our property during our absence.

Swiss Capuchins and Danish Lutherans

The only secondary school in the district was run by the Capuchins at Kwiro, a mile or two west of Mahenge. About a week after we got back to Mahenge following my illness, Father Gustav, the Vicar General, arrived at our house one evening and invited Jennifer to join the staff of Kwiro School as a part-time teacher. Her subjects were to be English, history, and the British system of local government. Jennifer was flattered, but she reminded Father Gustav that we were Anglicans, not Roman Catholics. He replied, 'Of course we all know you are not Roman Catholics, but the Archbishop has already given his approval to our appointing you, and we really would like you to join us'.

Jennifer had come to Tanganyika in order to teach, and the

opportunity to return to teaching delighted her. She gladly accepted Father Gustav's invitation, and her close contacts with Kwiro School confirmed the impression we had already formed that it was well run and that the teaching staff were excellent. Most of them were men from Switzerland, but there was one Indian, Father Joseph Pais, and one nun, Sister Maria Pia.

The history of the whole continent of Africa provides many examples of appalling cruelty and exploitation by greedy adventurers. The man who was largely responsible for the establishment of the German East Africa Company in 1884, Karl Peters, was quite ruthless, and advocated a policy of terror (*Schrecklichkeit*) as the best way to rule a primitive country. Hitler later described him as a 'model, if stern, administrator', and in 1934 the Nazi regime issued a set of commemorative postage stamps in Karl Peters' honour.

There were, however, many other Europeans who travelled to East Africa in the nineteenth century whose motives were very different. In 1857, David Livingstone delivered a speech to the undergraduates of Cambridge University urging them to carry on the work which he had begun of opening up in Africa a path to 'Commerce and Christianity'. The idea of preaching the Christian message to people who had never heard it before was not a new one, but the opening up of Africa led to the establishment there of a large number of missions staffed and financed by various churches and missionary societies based in developed countries.

The first missionaries who came to Ulanga District were Benedictines who came from the monastery of Saint Ottilien in Germany in 1902. I never discussed the work of the Benedictines with any African who was old enough to remember them personally, but I understand that they collaborated rather too closely with the harsh German colonial rulers who suppressed the Maji-Maji rebellion between 1905 and 1907.

When Germany lost its colonies at the end of the First World War and Britain was given the mandate to administer Tanganyika, Capuchins from Switzerland assumed responsibility for the activities which had been carried out by German Benedictines until they were expelled from the country. The Swiss had no previous experience of missionary activity, and I was told that when they started to work in Ulanga District they had inherited a mission which was not in a particularly flourishing state. By 1958, however, when Jennifer and I arrived in Ulanga, the Capuchin mission was clearly thriving.

The Capuchins were indeed outstandingly successful in every-thing that a mission sets out to do. Most of the African population of Ulanga claimed to be Catholics. The seminary at Kasita, just south of Mahenge, provided, under the leadership of the saintly Father Gerard, a high standard of education for young men wanting to train for the priesthood. The mission hospital in Ifakara enjoyed the reputation of being the best hospital in Tanganyika. I certainly never came across a better hospital there. The cathedral at Kwiro was large, though not so large as one or two in other parts of the country, and the building managed to be beautiful without flaunting its wealth. There were also about twenty smaller Catholic mission stations in the outlying parts of the district. Like Kwiro, they all avoided the extremes of being either too shabbily poor, which did not draw in many converts, or too ostentatiously rich, like the missions run by certain societies, in particular those from the United States of America. I did not admire those missionaries, from whatever country, who lived a luxurious life-style.

I assume that the Capuchin Mission as a whole received gener-ous financial aid from its supporters in Switzerland, but the feature of the mission which impressed me most was not the material resources at its disposal but the quality of those people, whatever their race, who worked for it. Whether they were employed in teaching, health care, evangelisation, or manual work, the missionaries, both male and female, were skilled, compassionate, tolerant, and seemed to radiate spirituality and joy in their day-to-day lives. They all dressed very simply. The priests normally wore sandals and the rough brown habits seen in pictures of Saint Francis. When the weather was very hot, they changed their brown habits for white cotton ones. The nuns wore simple long white dresses and veils, and they also wore sandals.

Some of the priests in positions of high authority were men of outstanding intellect and great learning, but they combined this with a degree of humility not always found in church leaders. Father Gerard had a profound understanding of all world reli-gions, and I heard from others that he knew fourteen different languages, though he himself was far too modest ever to boast about it. He sometimes came to have a simple meal with us – he was a vegetarian and a teetotaller – and one evening after supper we played him a recording of Verdi's *Requiem*. He had never heard the work before, and was thrilled. He told us about the years he had spent in London before the war. He had often attended concerts there. He remembered one in particular, an unforgettable performance by a 'brilliant young boy violinist called Yehudi Something-or-Other'.

Those who were not particularly well-educated were given tasks that were appropriate. Each mission station had its own experienced Father Superior, but it also had Brothers who were not necessarily highly educated. The Brothers had the gift of teaching manual skills which were valuable to rural Africans. Brother Mathias, for example, had been born in an Alpine village and could barely read or write, but he provided care for a group of epileptics and mentally or physically handicapped people who, under his guidance, tended the gardens and the domestic animals at Kwiro Mission, and who, without the help of the mission, would almost certainly have lived alone and depended for their subsistence on begging. One day Brother Mathias brought us as a present a pair of rabbits. They later had quintuplets. We found it hard to determine the sex of the baby rabbits, so we gave each of them the name of a biblical musical instrument – Sackbut, Psaltery, Dulcimer, Trumpet and Cymbal. Ruth loved them. She always referred to Cymbal as Simba, and Dulcimer as Dull Simba, *simba* being the Swahili name for a lion.

Many of the priests visited us regularly and became close friends. They were always able to accept our invitations, and many from the outlying stations would simply drop in on us whenever they were visiting Kwiro. The rules were much stricter for the nuns. When Jennifer asked Sister Maria Pia and another nun called Sister Lamberta to come to tea with us, they said they could not accept until they confirmed that their rules allowed them to do so. Next day they said that their rules did not allow it, but invited Jennifer to tea with them instead. I, of course, was not included. Sister Maria Pia said she was glad that the ruling was clear and gave her guidance about what was allowed and what was not. She felt no disappointment at being denied a simple pleasure.

It was not surprising that the proportion of Africans in Ulanga who described themselves as Catholics was large. I believe that it was higher in Ulanga than in any of the other districts in which I served. Every Sunday, and on every church festival, services in the Catholic churches in all the different tribal areas were attended by large congregations. Many Africans in villages all round the District wore rosary beads, crucifixes, or images of the Virgin Mary.

There was also a Protestant mission in Ulanga District. In 1947, the Danish Evangelical Lutherans had established a small church in Mahenge itself. The church was solidly built and functional but not beautiful.

The congregation in the Lutheran Church in Mahenge consisted almost entirely of public sector employees and their families. They were members of various Protestant denominations, and had been posted to Mahenge in the course of their careers, but they did not expect to remain there permanently. These officials included clerks, policemen, health-care workers, agricultural instructors, prison warders, teachers, and a few expatriates like Jennifer and me.

It worried me that even though most of the Africans in the Lutheran congregation were, by local standards, in well-paid employment, the total amount they contributed to the offertory Sunday after Sunday was derisory, usually less than five shillings (25p) a week from a congregation of about forty or fifty people. At that time few, if any, African churchgoers, Catholic or Protestant, ever gave more than a copper coin worth a tenth of an old shilling to the church collection. Although many educated Africans were already aspiring to achieve political independence, this did not bring with it any concept of assuming a share of the responsibility for paying for the benefits that were at that time being funded from abroad.

The missionary in charge of the Lutheran Mission was a Dane from Copenhagen called Thygessen. He lived with his plump and unattractive wife in a small brick-built house near the church. Their house was always spotlessly clean, but it was not comfortable or welcoming.

Mr and Mrs Thygessen were approaching retirement, and were anxious about how they would manage financially in their old age. Mr Thygessen's sermons were among the most boring and lugubrious I have ever heard. He had been sent out to minister to Africans, and he explained to us that his own academic qualifications were considered good enough for pastoral work in Africa, but were not sufficient to secure him a comparable post in a Lutheran church in Denmark, and he had no other skills.

Jennifer and I were told later that after his retirement from the mission he had got a job as the caretaker of a block of flats in Copenhagen, and that he was not enjoying that any more than he had enjoyed working in Africa.

Very soon after we arrived in Mahenge, Thygessen asked Jennifer if she would play the harmonium at Sunday services, and asked me if I would be willing to take services in Swahili on his behalf when he was not in Mahenge. We agreed to both these requests.

When we had been in Mahenge for a few months, Thygessen asked me to give a job as a District Office messenger to the one Pogoro member of his congregation. He explained that the man he wanted me to help was the only convert whom he had attracted into the Lutheran Church during all the years he had been working in Mahenge. Unfortunately, the convert had none of the qualities which might have enabled me to find him a regular job in Government service.

The Thygessens abruptly ceased to be friendly towards us as soon as Jennifer accepted the invitation from Father Gustav to teach at Kwiro. They never asked us to their house again, and they always refused invitations to ours. They nevertheless continued to rely on our help at services on Sunday mornings.

Jennifer and I felt sorry for the Thygessens. Thygessen was not very well educated or clever, but he was not a bad man, and he was quite intelligent enough to recognise that his work as a missionary had been a failure. Mrs Thygessen seemed to be a very unhappy woman. She grumbled about everything, and had given up any pretence of actually liking Africans. They both seemed totally opposed to delegating any responsibility to African members of the congregation, even though in other places in Tanganyika there were already many outstanding examples of African churchmen in senior positions. The Roman Catholic Bishop of Kwiro, Elias Mchonde, was an African. I myself had been licensed as a lay reader by an Anglican African Bishop, Yohana Omari. In 1960, Laurian Rungambwa, a Haya tribesman from Bukoba District, became the first African Cardinal, but these facts were not likely to impress the Thygessens. Even if they had been more charismatic personalities, however, they would still have found it very difficult to attract new converts in an area where the Catholic mission was so successful.

In addition to the Thygessens in Mahenge itself, there were three other Danish Lutheran missionaries in Ulanga District. They worked at a small mission hospital in a village called Malinyi, in the western part of the District occupied by Bena tribesmen. I never got to know them very well, but I liked and respected Dr and Mrs Sorensen and Sister Christiansen. Unlike the Thygessens, they had a sense of humour. They even managed to be cheerful as they set about repairing the damage when the River Furua, a tributary of the Kilombero, changed its course during an overnight rainstorm and washed away many of the buildings of Malinyi Hospital, and also took with it most of the equipment and drugs, which the mission found very hard to replace.

Sister Christiansen and I were both involved in an incident which revealed clearly the contrast between her and Mrs Thygessen. The Government Hospital in Mahenge was staffed by Gary Butler, the Medical Officer, and by two Medical Assistants, Samson Mwaruanda and Walter Mulaga. One night, when both Gary Butler and Geoff Bullock were away on safari, Walter Mulaga knocked on my door at about 3 a.m. and asked for my help. A patient who had been suffering from a strangulated hernia for five days had just been carried into hospital on a bed made of woven grass, and Walter was certain that he would die unless he was operated on immediately.

Jennifer and I knew Walter well. For some months he had been coming to our house regularly to receive free private coaching in English from Jennifer. He had only completed Standard XI at school, and he wanted to improve his chances of promotion by passing his Overseas School Certificate, which was normally taken at the end of Standard XII. Jennifer and I had already formed a high opinion of his competence and integrity.

Walter was the only person available to operate, but he was not a qualified doctor, and wanted someone senior to himself to see the state of the patient and endorse his clinical judgement in case the operation he was willing to perform proved unsuccessful. I therefore went with him to the government hospital. When we got there, I was shocked to find that the only light available was an old-fashioned paraffin hurricane lamp with a smoky glass. The light it provided was so dim that I was sure that it would add to the risks of the operation, so I drove home again and fetched my own Tilley pressure lamp and some methylated spirits to light it with. My lamp was not perfect, but it did at least provide a bright enough light to let me see the patient, and for Walter to see what he was doing if he decided to operate.

As soon as I got a clear view of the patient, an elderly man called Pius Ferdinand, I felt quite certain that Walter's prognosis was correct. Unless he received treatment immediately, Pius was going to die. I asked Walter if he had assisted in operations for strangulated hernias, and whether he felt capable of doing one himself. Walter's replies to my questions were encouraging, and I concluded that, if he operated, the patient might perhaps survive, but that without an operation he was sure to die. I therefore told

Walter that I thought he ought to go ahead with the operation, and promised that, if the worst happened and Pius died, I would speak out in Walter's defence if he were accused of carrying out an operation he was not authorised to perform.

One of the orderlies at the hospital then mentioned that he had seen Sister Christiansen that afternoon in Mahenge, so I drove to the Lutheran Mission to see if she was still there, and to ask if she would be willing to help Walter during the operation. She gladly agreed to do this. The operation was successful, but when it was over Walter and Sister Christiansen both agreed that Pius still needed very skilled post-operative care which could only be provided at Ifakara Hospital.

As soon as the sun rose and the ferry across the Kilombero River opened, I drove Pius, with Sister Christiansen in my car to monitor his condition, to Ifakara Hospital. When we got there, we were received by an elderly Swiss nun called Sister Arnolda. The love and respect which the Protestant and the Catholic sister showed for each other, and for their patient, seemed to me to be an outstanding example of how Christians of different denominations ought to behave to one another.

My point of view about this was not shared by Mrs Thygessen. She was furious with Sister Christiansen for wasting time on helping a Catholic patient when she had been asked to come from Malinyi to Mahenge in order to bake some cakes for a tea-party that Mrs Thygessen had arranged. Sister Christiansen was not just a good nurse and a loving personality. She had also qualified as a cook.

The whole idea of Christian Unity was anathema to Mrs Thygessen. She was convinced that all her ideas about religion were directly inspired by God, and that, if anyone disagreed with her views, then the other person must, by definition, be in error.

I was told that on one occasion when she was visiting the hospital at Malinyi, Mrs Thygessen had ordered a dying Catholic patient to be ejected from the ward where he was lying and to be taken out to die in the shade of a mango tree close to the hospital. She was not willing to tolerate the presence of a Capuchin priest to administer the Catholic last rites inside a Lutheran hospital. Not surprisingly, that sort of behaviour did not endear her to people of whatever race or creed.

The Guilty and the Innocent

There were not quite so many criminal cases in the District Court of Ulanga as in some of the other districts in which I was stationed, but there were fewer magistrates to deal with them, so I spent a fair amount of my time in court. Sometimes the caseload became too heavy, and then the Resident Magistrate stationed in Kilosa, who also had jurisdiction to try cases in Ulanga District, came to Mahenge to help out. This was a pleasure for Jennifer and me, as the RM at Kilosa at the time was Charles Rees, who had served with us in Tabora, and was a very good friend. He was some years older than me, but he had been Twining's Private Secretary when Twining was Governor of North Borneo, and he had also graduated from the same college as me at Cambridge. We shared many common interests. Sadly, he was suffering from a serious heart condition, and died during the course of his tour in Kilosa, but whenever he came to Mahenge he always stayed with us. When I first had to attend High Court Sessions in Kilosa, Jennifer, Ruth and I stayed with Charles, his wife Celia, and their ten-year-old daughter, who was also called Jennifer. On our subsequent visits to Kilosa, after Charles became too ill to have friends to stay, we were always invited to stay with the Assistant Superintendent of Police, Tom Moore, and his wife Leslie. They also were very good friends of ours, and stayed with us regularly when they came to Mahenge.

The most common reason for my journeys to Kilosa was that I had been summoned as a witness to give evidence before the High Court about statements made to me by people in custody. The first occasion when I gave evidence in Kilosa about a confession made to me in Ulanga District concerned a particularly gruesome murder committed in Utengule, an area occupied by members of the Bena tribe.

Normally I recorded confessions in the Boma, but on this occasion I was on safari to Utengule Local Court, and Chief Towegale told me that he had three people in custody whom he had arrested on a charge of murder, and that they all wished to make statements. I agreed to Chief Towegale's request to record their statements on the spot.

The first accused was a man called Saidi Walema. I satisfied myself that he genuinely wanted to make a statement to me, and he then gave me his account in Swahili of what had happened. He said he was the lover of a married woman called Sinababa Malile. One day he had been to a beer-club where Sinababa and her husband Kisokoro were also drinking, together with Sinababa's cousin, a woman called Hawa. Saidi said that Sinababa had come up to him in the beer-club, and urged him to help her kill Kisokoro while he was too drunk to defend himself. Saidi and Hawa both thought this a good idea, and the three of them persuaded Kisokoro to come with them into the bamboo forest. There Saidi Walema had cut a bamboo stick and sharpened it to a point. Saidi and Sinababa had then supported Kisokoro in an upright position, while Hawa took the bamboo stick in her right hand and stabbed Kisokoro in his left eye, killing him instantly.

Saidi had then taken the blood-stained bamboo stick and burned it near to his own hut. He said he knew perfectly well what he was doing, but had collaborated in killing Kisokoro because he had been tempted by Sinababa, who desired her lover more than she desired her husband.

The dresser in charge of Utengule rural dispensary later confirmed Saidi's description of the cause of death, and said he had measured the wound and found that it was six and a half inches deep.

I then started to record a statement by Sinababa herself. This was more of a problem. Sinababa spoke only Kibena. She could understand a little Swahili but could not speak it. Kibena and Kihehe are very similar languages, and when I had studied Kihehe for an interpretership while I was in Iringa District I had occasionally referred to an indifferent grammar book in German called *Bena-Hehe Grammatik*. However, I had no formal qualification in Kibena, and I would have found it difficult to swear on oath in court that what I had recorded corresponded exactly with what Sinababa had said. This quandary did not arise, however. Sinababa's statement, which I repeated back to her in Swahili after she had made it to me in Kibena, was never used. She agreed that what I had written was what she had said, but her statement was a vehement denial of involvement in her husband's murder. I was not required to give evidence about it before the High Court. Hawa simply told me that she wanted to remain silent and not to make a statement at all.

A former District Commissioner of Ulanga, A T Culwick, had collaborated with Chief Towegale in producing a book published in 1935 called *Ubena of the Rivers*, which said that the best way to reach Ubena was by river. More than twenty years later the roads were still appalling, and the best way to reach the area was still by river, usually in a large dug-out canoe. I had myself arrived in

Utengule by canoe, accompanied as usual by a messenger, a cook, and some porters.

When we set off to return to Mahenge, the canoe's load had increased. We now had with us three people charged with a very nasty murder, together with male and female escorts to prevent them escaping. Saidi seemed quite friendly, and no one seemed in the least afraid of him. Sinababa and Hawa, on the other hand, seemed to me to be thoroughly evil. No one spoke to either of them.

All three were committed for trial by the High Court. The magistrate who committed them thought the circumstantial evidence against the two women might just be strong enough to warrant putting them on trial, but the High Court did not agree. The uncorroborated evidence of an accomplice is not sufficient to convict an accused person, and the High Court held the view that the only direct evidence against the two women was Saidi's, and he admitted to being an accomplice. This meant that Sinababa and Hawa were not made to stand trial. On the evening that we received orders from the Attorney-General's Office that the two women were to be released from custody immediately unless held on another charge, I happened to spot them sitting on the ground near the market place in Mahenge. They were both drunk, and stared triumphantly at me with malevolent expressions on their faces. Saidi was convicted of murder and sentenced to death. His sentence was not commuted, and he was executed.

Some months later, after Jennifer had been invited to teach at the Roman Catholic Secondary School at Kwiro, one of her pupils asked her in class which was worse, to sin and to confess one's guilt, or to sin and then deny it. Jennifer gave the obvious answer. The pupil then asked why the British had executed a murderer from Ubena who owned up to his crime, but had failed to punish the two women who had also taken an active part in plotting the crime, one of whom was the person who had actually stabbed the victim. The boy who asked this question was Emanuel Towegale, the Chief's grandson. He and his classmates were not convinced by Jennifer's explanation about the rules concerning uncorroborated evidence of an accomplice, or about the assumption of innocence until a person is proved guilty. They all thought such rules were not appropriate in Tanganyika. I myself have no doubt that Saidi had told me the truth, and that the women were just as guilty as he was.

It is frustrating for those concerned with maintaining law and order when a guilty person gets away with a serious crime, but I was also involved in a case which very nearly led to a man being hanged for a murder he did not commit. To convict an innocent person is, in my view, far worse than to acquit a guilty one.

The marriage of Crispin Max and Kalimarita Gabriel was not a happy one. Crispin was a violent man, and beat his wife up frequently. He had five previous convictions imposed by the Chief of Chilombola, Bernardin Mbinji, for violence on Kalimarita. One afternoon Kalimarita took her husband to Chilombola Court to accuse him for the sixth time. The Chief said it was too late to start hearing the case that evening, and told them to return next morning, when the case would be heard. Kalimarita and Crispin both set off together in the direction of their home, arguing furiously.

Forty-five minutes after they had left the Court, Kalimarita's body was found lying beside the path leading to their home. Her neck was broken. The place where she was found was about forty minutes' walk from the Court, so she must have been killed within about five minutes of her body being discovered by a passer-by.

Crispin was arrested and charged with murdering his wife, and was taken under escort to the Boma. The police carried out their investigation, and summoned all the prosecution witnesses to the Boma. I began to take the preliminary inquiry, and heard evidence from many people, all of whom seemed reliable.

No one had actually seen Crispin kill Kalimarita, but there are plenty of murders committed when the killer and the victim are alone. Crispin claimed that he and his wife had been quarrelling so bitterly on the way home that he had got fed up with her noise. He said he had left her walking on the direct path home, and had himself taken an alternative route back. He never saw his wife alive again.

The Chief did not believe his story, The Inspector of Police did not believe his story. I did not believe his story. I had no doubt at all that Crispin would be convicted of murder, and that, because of his previous record of violence, he would be executed. There was no great hurry to commit Crispin for trial, however, as the High Court had only just finished its Sessions in Kilosa, and would not be returning for some months. I therefore remanded him in custody until the Medical Officer returned from safari, when I would take evidence about the post-mortem examination that the doctor had carried out on Kalimarita, who had been five months pregnant.

While Crispin was still on remand awaiting the completion of the preliminary inquiry, Inspector Abubakari brought another man before me to have a statement recorded. He looked about twenty years old, and his name was Martin Manji. I put him in the custody of my messenger. As was usual in such cases, the police had given me no indication of his alleged offence before Martin began his statement. He told me he was a peasant farmer living in Chilombola Chiefdom. Two days previously he had been walking in the forest and had seen a woman he desired, and had attempted to have sexual intercourse with her. She had screamed, and he had let her go and she had run away. He had then spotted another woman whom he found attractive, and had tried the same thing with her. He then heard other people approaching and he let the second woman go as well. The two women both reported the incidents to Chief Bernardin, who sent his court messenger to arrest Martin, who was put in the Chief's lock-up for the night.

I was slightly puzzled that Inspector Abubakari should think the cases were serious enough to justify holding a preliminary inquiry, when the powers of magistrates in subordinate courts were normally regarded as adequate to deal with cases of indecent assault. However, I thought that having started to record Martin's statement I might as well complete the task.

Martin then went on to explain to me that Chief Bernardin had asked him to answer the accusations of the two women, and he had agreed that he had sexually assaulted them just as they said. While Chief Bernardin was still considering what sentence to impose, he had asked Martin, 'Where did you get that *kaniki* cloth you are wearing?' (a *kaniki* is a piece of cotton or calico worn by winding it round one's body) and he had replied to the Chief, 'This is the kaniki cloth I took from the body of the woman I killed last month.'

It was only then that I realised, to my amazement, that I was dealing with a case of murder, not just of indecent assault. Within minutes of Kalimarita having been left alone in the forest by her husband, Martin had arrived and used such violence in attempting to rape her that he had broken her neck.

As soon as Martin admitted that it was he who had killed Kalimarita, the police withdrew the charge against Crispin, and he was released from custody. Martin was later committed for trial on a charge of murder. He was convicted but not reprieved. In due course he was executed.

When I next visited Chilombola I asked Chief Bernardin why he had asked Martin the question about the *kaniki* cloth, and whether anyone had previously noticed that it was missing from Kalimarita's body. The Chief replied very simply, 'God put it into my mind that I wanted to know.' He told me that he had had no idea at all what the answer would be when he asked the question, and that no one had noticed that Kalimarita's *kaniki* cloth was missing.

That case worried me enormously. Martin was a violent sex offender, but he had no criminal record. If he had moved from his home in Chilombola to a different district, or even to a different part of Ulanga District, after he had killed Kalimarita, I am absolutely certain that Crispin, who was no saint but was not a murderer, would have been executed for a crime he did not commit. If a person is wrongly sentenced to imprisonment, at least there is a possibility that the conviction may be quashed if additional evidence comes to light, but once a person has been convicted of murder in a country where the death sentence exists, there is no way he can be restored to life after he has been executed.

I had always hated being involved with cases of murder, which carried the death penalty. It gave me no satisfaction whatsoever to commit anyone for trial on a murder charge. I also hated the task of preparing detailed reports about the life and background of murderers who had been convicted by the High Court, and the circumstances of their crimes. Such reports were required in order to help Executive Council to make a recommendation to the Governor on whether or not to exercise the prerogative of mercy. After the murder of Kalimarita, I hated these tasks even more.

Not all the cases in which guilty people escaped punishment were cases involving murder. I tried many cases involving theft of government or local treasury revenue. The temptation for very poorly-paid clerks and messengers to steal money which they were delivering to the Boma was very strong. During the harvest season, when most peasant farmers paid their tax, a messenger earning perhaps £2–£3 per month might have responsibility for the custody of a cash box containing several thousand pounds. As mentioned previously, a prison record carried very little stigma, and the surprise was not how many junior employees stole, but how many remained honest.

I tried one case which was not typical. This case did not involve one accused person who pleaded guilty, but two who did not. The system for delivering money to the Boma was quite straightforward. A local court messenger had to carry a locked metal cash box full of money and documents, while the court clerk held the key and accompanied the messenger who was carrying the cash box. In theory, neither could have access to the money without the collaboration of the other.

The clerk and messenger of Mbingu Local Court in the north of the District set off on foot together to deliver tax and other revenue to the Boma, and had to stay overnight in Ifakara before continuing their journey to Mahenge. There was a dance being held in Ifakara the night they arrived there, and the messenger asked the clerk if he could go to it, and if he could borrow the clerk's trousers to wear at the beer-club, as they were smarter than his own. The clerk agreed, and lent the messenger his trousers.

The stories told by both the clerk and the messenger had been identical up to that point, but then their versions began to differ. The clerk said that he inadvertently left the cash box key in the trousers the messenger had borrowed, and that while he was asleep the messenger had unlocked the box and stolen the money, and hidden it away during the night. The messenger said that the trousers he had borrowed had not contained the cash box key, and that when he had left the cash box in the care of the clerk he had forgotten to ask the clerk to hand him the key. The clerk had therefore had charge of both the cash box and the key, and he had opened the cash box and stolen the money while the messenger was attending the dance at the beer-club.

The police were satisfied that the theft had not been carried out by an outsider, and decided to charge both the clerk and the messenger. It is quite possible that they carried out the theft together, and were both equally guilty. What was quite impossible was that both men were telling the truth. Their versions of what happened were not compatible. If the messenger was telling the truth, the clerk was guilty, and if the clerk was telling the truth, then the messenger was guilty.

I was unable to decide which of the two was lying, and could not be certain beyond a shadow of doubt who was the guilty one. I therefore had no option but to acquit them both. I did so very reluctantly. They were both sacked from their jobs for failing to comply with the rules concerning the custody of cash in transit, but I doubt whether that worried the thief who had managed successfully to hide the loot where the authorities never found it.

Family Affairs

Just after Jennifer and I got back from Dar, the family who lived in the house nearest to ours in Mahenge, Mavis and Ken Pouncett and their baby son, went on leave. Ken wanted to train as a teacher, and resigned his appointment as Sleeping Sickness Settlement Officer.

A very high proportion of the land area of Ulanga District was uninhabitable, due to infestation by blood-sucking tsetse fly, which carry sleeping sickness. This disease, if untreated, can kill both human beings and animals. Tsetse fly need shade in order to breed, however, and the policy adopted by the Government in order to protect the human population was to create 'settlements'. Clearings just wider than the distance tsetses can fly were made by cutting down all the shade-giving trees and bushes around designated villages and cultivated areas. Humans were all required to live inside the protective barrier, while the tsetse continued to live outside it. This policy was very unpopular, as it prevented peasant farmers from choosing for themselves where they wanted to build their houses and cultivate their crops, usually close to the graves of their ancestors, and the job of the Settlement Officers who were responsible for implementing it could be stressful, particularly if they were sensitive and found it hard to communicate in Swahili. We were not very surprised when Ken resigned.

A Game Ranger, Alan Rees (no relation to Charles) moved with his family into the house the Pouncetts had vacated. Alan and his wife Margaret had two sons: Neil, who was already at boarding school, and Michael, who was a little older than Ruth. Michael was plump, slow-moving, and immensely good-natured. He and Ruth became great friends, and the whole family were delightful neighbours. Michael Rees was probably Ruth's best friend among all the young children in Mahenge, but she had plenty of friends of about her own age to play with.

As far as European adults were concerned, however, there were very few planned amenities in Mahenge. It had no Grade 1 Hospital, no club, no electricity, no swimming pool, no golf course, no cinema, no bank, no Anglican church, no maintained airstrip, and no garage. Radio reception was so bad that news bulletins from Dar were often inaudible. There were no European-owned shops, and the three Indian-owned shops were very poorly stocked. There was also mounting political tension in the country as a whole, and Mahenge was so isolated that

Europeans living there would have been very vulnerable if there had been any violence.

In spite of all the apparent disadvantages, Ulanga was a 'happy station'. Jennifer and I both loved Mahenge from the moment we arrived there, and, though we experienced many crises, we continued to love it throughout our tour of service. I think that part of the credit for that must go to Geoff and Anne Bullock, who were both extremely kind, but my time as the Governor's Private Secretary had given me the opportunity to visit many up-country stations, and Mahenge had seemed very congenial under Geoff's predecessor, Charles Beauclerk, and the high morale continued after Geoff went on leave and was replaced by Mike Dorey.

Paradoxically, I think its lack of amenities and its vulnerability were factors which helped to make Mahenge such a happy place. We all relied on each other for companionship and simple hospitality in each other's houses. We knew each other much better than was possible in larger stations, where people tended to form cliques, and snobbery was rife. All the expatriate officials worked very closely together, and we often went on safari with our colleagues. The shops had no expensive imported luxury goods, but locally-grown fresh fruit, vegetables, eggs and chickens could always be bought in the market. Firewood was cheap, and we enjoyed sitting by cosy log fires in the evenings. We had big enough gardens to rear our own sheep, ducks, chickens and rabbits. Whenever a sheep was killed, the carcass could not be deep frozen, so it was shared with colleagues. Whenever any of us drove down to the Kilombero River, we always brought back fresh fish not only for our own needs but to distribute to friends. The cost of living in Mahenge was far lower than in any of the other stations where I served, and we had no money worries there.

There were only two European settler families in Ulanga District. Watty and Isabel Paul, and George and Jean Pletts lived on farms near Kiberege in the northern part of the district. In contrast to the settlers living in some other districts, who seemed to be hostile to government officials, Watty and George and their wives were invariably hospitable and friendly, and made it a pleasure to call in at their houses either on safari, or on journeys to or from Kilosa or Morogoro.

The wives of all the expatriate officials and of the two settlers also all shared a major interest. They all had very young families. The only European wife in the District who did not give birth while we were in Ulanga District was Mrs Thygessen, who was past child-bearing age. She seemed to think that the young mothers and ayahs all spoilt their children when what was really needed was a bit of firm discipline.

The Capuchin Missionaries also had no children of their own. They had taken a vow of celibacy, but all those whom we got to know well seemed very fond of children in general, and left us in no doubt about their love for Ruth in particular.

Jennifer and I had arrived in Mahenge at the start of the heavy rains in 1958. During our second rainy season there, we had pleasures which we had not been able to enjoy the previous year. Jennifer's piano had arrived, and she was able to play it in the knowledge that our servants enjoyed music and that the noise would not reach the houses of our nearest neighbours, which were at least a hundred yards from ours.

During my period of convalescence in Dar, we had also bought a portable battery-powered record player. This enabled us to listen again to the long-playing records that we had enjoyed in Dar and Tabora, where there was electricity. The new machine consumed torch batteries at a terrifying rate, and when they were starting to lose power the music went horribly flat. It nevertheless gave us a lot of pleasure so long as we took care to have a good supply of spare batteries.

The old clockwork gramophone that I had brought out with me from England and which could only play 78 r.p.m. records continued to be in regular use for Ruth. We thought she showed signs of musical precocity when her very favourite of our old records was of Elisabeth Schumann, a great soprano of the inter-war years, singing Mozart's *Hallelujah*. Ruth called it 'Hallo Loola', and she never tired of listening to it. We were also encouraged in our hopes that she would grow up to be a musical genius by her reaction whenever she listened to one particular record which my mother had bought at Woolworth's for my brother and me when I was about three. In it a plummy contralto called Jane Bartlett sang a nursery rhyme called 'Go to sleep my little piccaninny', and went terribly flat half way through the second verse. As soon as Ruth heard her going out of tune, her mouth turned down and she started to cry. She always cheered up again as soon as the record was changed. In my wish to prove that this was not just a coincidence, I confess that I played Jane Bartlett two or three times in quick succession, in order to make quite sure that it really was the ghastly noise that was upsetting Ruth. It was. Jennifer accused me of cruelty to our own daughter, and I never repeated the offence. Ruth has grown up with a good ear and a pleasant singing voice.

As Ruth grew from being a baby to a toddler, I began to be conscious of an important ingredient that was usually lacking in the privileged lives of European children of pre-school age in Tanganyika. They grew up with their parents, but normally only saw their grandparents, uncles, aunts and cousins while on home leave for five or six months at the end of a tour of service lasting nearly three years.

My mother had come out to Tanganyika for our wedding, but she never visited Africa again. Frances, Jennifer's mother, had employed a nanny to look after Jennifer as a child, and Frances had therefore spent much less time with her daughter than the average mother. As a grandmother, however, she wanted to see as much of her first granddaughter as possible. She was unwilling to wait until we returned on leave to England, when Ruth would be more than three years old. She therefore arranged to travel out to Tanganyika at the end of June 1959, and to spend about six weeks with us in Mahenge before returning home in the middle of August.

When she landed in Dar, Frances was welcomed by Pip Fraser-Smith, an outstanding secretariat official, and by Father Joseph Pais, the Indian teacher at Kwiro school, who brought her the latest news from Mahenge. She stayed for a couple of nights at the New Africa Hotel, and visited Dr Marion Phillips at the Anglican Mission Hospital at Minaki, a few miles outside Dar, for whom she had been raising funds in her home village in Surrey. She then travelled by train to Morogoro, where I met her with my car.

Morogoro presented a difficult choice. It had two hotels. Jennifer and I were told that the Acropol had a reasonably good chef, but its bedrooms and bathrooms were filthy. The Savoy, on the other hand, had clean bedrooms and a pleasant view, but the food was disgusting. We solved the problem by advising Frances to have dinner on the train before it reached Morogoro, and then to sleep at the Savoy. Even the appalling cook at the Savoy could not do much damage to cornflakes and a banana at breakfast-time.

Jennifer had tried to teach Ruth to pronounce the word 'Granny', but Ruth pronounced it 'Bangy' (with a hard 'g'), and Frances was always known to all our children as Bangy. My own mother had the more orthodox title, as Ruth was able to say 'Granny' correctly by the time we got back to England in October 1960.

Frances and I made the journey from Morogoro to Mahenge at the best time of the year, when the road was dry but not too dusty, but I think she was a bit startled by it. The 200-mile journey took about eight hours, including the time it took to cross the Kilombero Ferry, and Frances, who was seventy years old at the time, was extremely tired when we at last arrived.

I was again struck by her ability to charm everyone, and by her self-confidence. We always spoke in Swahili to our servants, but it never occurred to Frances that they might not understand her if she spoke to them in English. In fact, both Juma and Mohamed understood her well, but Omari and Ina did not.

I think Jennifer found it irritating that her mother tried to re-organise our domestic routine in her own way, and had not the slightest idea about keeping little children out of danger. Jennifer and I had not even heard that Frances suffered from angina until we found Ruth playing with a bottle of Bangy's heart pills. We were even more exasperated when she let Ruth run around playing with her embroidery scissors. When I remonstrated, she replied, 'But Ruth's a good little girl!' as if being good or naughty had anything to do with a toddler of two getting accidentally hurt.

Perhaps the thing about Frances which astonished me most was her snoring. It was unbelievable. She slept in our guest room, across a passage from the bedroom where Jennifer and I slept. The noise of snores penetrated two walls and a corridor, and totally drowned any conversation which Jennifer and I might want to have between ourselves. Fortunately, Ruth did not appear to be troubled by the racket.

After Frances had been with us for nearly a week, Doug Webb, the Revenue Officer from Morogoro, paid a duty visit to Mahenge, and as usual he and his wife Eleanor stayed with Jennifer and me. The Webbs were good friends of ours. I had travelled out by ship with them when we came out to Tanganyika on first appointment, and Jennifer had stayed with them in Morogoro on her way down to Dar when I was in the Ocean Road Hospital.

When we made plans for their visit, Jennifer and I arranged that Doug and Eleanor should sleep in our room, I should sleep on a camp bed in Ruth's nursery, and Jennifer (poor thing!) would endure the snoring and sleep in the same bedroom as her mother.

Doug mentioned casually soon after he arrived that a tsetse fly had bitten him during the journey from Morogoro. While we

Tsetse fly

were all having dinner that evening, he suddenly looked extremely ill, and I noticed that his arm had swollen up like a balloon. He asked to leave the table, and on his way to the lavatory, he collapsed. Juma and I lifted him and laid him on my bed, and Jennifer rushed out of the house and jumped into our car to fetch the doctor as quickly as possible. We had no telephone.

When Jennifer reached the Medical Officer's house, she found that Dr Patel, an Indian Sub-Assistant Surgeon who was standing in for Gary Butler while Gary was on leave, was not at home, but was on a visit to Dar. He had been given permission to go there, but he had not told any of us that he would not be available.

Jennifer then called at the house of the Medical Assistant. The able and dedicated Walter Mulaga had recently left Mahenge to go to Britain to train as a pharmacist, and the only Medical Assistant left in Mahenge was the elderly Samson Mwaruanda. He had already gone to bed when Jennifer arrived, and he had to get dressed again. He then had to rouse the orderly who kept the operating theatre key and get him to light a paraffin stove in order to boil the water to sterilise the hypodermic syringe that would be needed to give Doug an injection.

By the time Jennifer got back with Samson in the car, she had spent an hour and forty minutes in her attempt to get medical help. Fortunately, Doug had come round and was talking to us again. I think Frances and Eleanor were both more shocked by the whole episode than Doug himself.

Samson beamed amiably, and announced with satisfaction that the patient was now all right again, and that if he had been going to die he would already have done so.

Frances was quite restrained about expressing anxiety concerning the example she had just witnessed of the inadequacy of Mahenge's medical services. However, Jennifer did not want her mother to fuss, so we waited as long as possible before breaking the news that Jennifer was expecting a second baby. We thought that the pleasure for Frances of knowing that she was to have another grandchild and that Ruth was to have a brother or sister might be outweighed by worry for Jennifer's health, with non-existent ante-natal care, and the birth of the baby needing to take place in Ifakara Hospital, nearly fifty miles away.

After the Webbs left, the remaining weeks of Frances's visit were more tranquil. All our friends invited her to meals in their houses and welcomed her very warmly. Robin Blackall, the Field Officer (Agriculture) arranged a delightful picnic for us all beside a pretty little waterfall on a green and shady part of the Mahenge Massif.

Even the Thygessens invited her to their house. I did not go, but Frances said they had both seemed quite cheerful, and had taken a lot of trouble to give her a nice tea.

Father Gerard invited her to Kasita, and showed her all round the seminary. Like everyone else, she found Father Gerard an exceptionally interesting man, and was impressed by his spirituality. She was also captivated by the charm and good manners of all the theology students she met at Kasita.

I think the visits that she enjoyed most were on two consecutive days to Kwiro Mission. On the first day we were all shown a film covering every aspect of the Mission's work in Ulanga. The film had been made primarily for audiences in Switzerland for publicity and fund-raising purposes, and the sound-track was in German. The photography and the commentary were both excellent, and we all assumed that it had been made by a professional film director until we were told that one of the brothers working in Ulanga had been entirely responsible for making it.

The next day we were again invited to Kwiro. This time we attended a service and reception to celebrate the silver jubilee of the ordination of three Capuchin priests. It was just as joyful an occasion as Father Gerard's golden jubilee had been the previous year.

The three priests included one who was thin and had a wispy beard. He reminded me of paintings of early Christian martyrs. The second looked more robust, His beard was thicker, and he seemed serene and placid. They both came from outstations which I seldom visited, and I did not know either of them well.

The third was Father Berthold, the Father Superior of Malinyi

Mission, near the upper reaches of the Kilombero. I visited Malinyi often, and knew Father Berthold very well. He had the physique of a circus strong-man, a beard which came down nearly to his waist, startlingly blue eyes, and an ebullient sense of humour. He used a motor cycle to visit the villages in his parish, and his parishioners gave him the nickname of Father Two-Beards, as one half of his enormous beard trailed behind him over his left shoulder and the other half over his right shoulder as he was riding along on his motor cycle, known in Swahili as a *piki-piki*.

Father Berthold was in his own way just as lovable a man as Father Gerard. He was never boring, and when he was being serious he could discuss his beliefs cogently and in a stimulating way. He was very knowledgeable about his flock, and the political and economic situation in his parish and in other parts of the world.

At other times, Father Berthold was like a mischievous school-boy. I was not sure whether he was joking or not when he told Ruth that he had grown such a long beard so that he could roll it up in a ball and tuck it under his ear when he wanted to go to sleep and hadn't got a pillow.

He was one of the Fathers who always dropped in on us whenever they came to Mahenge. One evening he told us, in a conspiratorial whisper and with a wicked twinkle in his eye, that he tried to time his trips from Malinyi so as to reach Mahenge just as the sun was setting. Mahenge was the last rest stop on the journey from Malinyi to Kwiro. Priests were normally expected to stay in mission houses if they arrived before dark, but if they had not reached their destination by nightfall, then they could ask for overnight shelter somewhere on the way. He said that he preferred to stay with us rather than at Kwiro if he could possibly justify it.

His visits to our home always gave us great joy, and I was always invited to stay overnight at the Capuchin mission rather than at a rather dreary unfurnished rest-house whenever I visited Malinyi. Without any suggestion of being envious, Father Berthold managed indirectly to make Jennifer and me more aware of how a vow of celibacy involved, both for men and women, sacrificing the possibility of a happy family life with children of one's own. When Catherine, our second daughter, was born, Father Berthold showed just as much love for her as he did for Ruth, and said that her eyes reminded him of the beauty of lakes in Switzerland. He never met our son, Philip, who was born in Lindi after we had left Ulanga.

Our friendship with Father Berthold lasted many years. Every

Christmas, even after he had retired to a monastery in Switzerland, we continued to get a card with all his news and greetings, and including loving messages to each of our children. We felt that he really meant it when he wrote that he remembered us all daily in his prayers. He continued to write year after year until, after we had come back to England, we got a letter from another priest to tell us that Father Berthold had died.

After the silver jubilee celebration at Kwiro, Frances enjoyed several short outings by car, walks with Jennifer and Ruth, and sitting in the shade in our lovely garden, but I think that the jubilee was probably the high point of her visit to Ulanga. In the middle of August she returned to England. I drove her as far as Morogoro, and she took a train to Dar before flying back to Heathrow.

Between mid-August and mid-September Jennifer suffered from unpleasant bouts of morning sickness. Dr Patel had only stayed in Mahenge for a few weeks, and another Indian doctor, Dr Dhebar, came to see her and gave her some tablets. He said they were not as effective as a new drug which was now available in Britain, but had not yet reached Mahenge. When we later discovered that the drug Dr Dhebar would have prescribed if he had been able to do so was thalidomide, and heard about the damage it had done to unborn children in other places, Jennifer and I thought that morning sickness had been the lesser evil.

It was a very inconvenient time for Jennifer to be suffering from morning sickness, as we had even more house guests than usual that month. A newly appointed cadet, Roger Searle, arrived with his pretty young wife Brenda, and stayed with us for a few days until they could move into the quarter vacated by Ozzy Mwambungu.

Geoff Bullock was reaching the end of his tour, and just after the Searles had moved into their own quarter, Geoff's successor, Mike Dorey, arrived in Mahenge with his wife Sheila and their little daughter Helen. Anne Bullock was not well at the time, and in spite of Jennifer's morning sickness we agreed to invite the Doreys to stay with us until the Bullocks left, and the Doreys could move into their house.

We were very sorry to see Geoff and his family go. They were very good friends, and we did not yet know the Doreys. However, they too were pleasant colleagues, and Mike was just as conscientious and hard-working as Geoff had been. Sheila was quiet and seemed rather shy, but she was very kind, and Ruth and Helen got on splendidly.

The government did not expect its officials to provide hospitality entirely at their own expense to anyone who happened to visit
their station on official business. Officers were entitled to claim
hospitality allowance if they put up a colleague who was travelling on duty. Those who were travelling on duty but stayed in a
rest-house or a tent could claim safari allowance for the nights
they were away from their homes. The rules were complicated,
but I thought they were reasonable. The amount of the
allowances was not large – a District Officer could claim 8s (40p)
per night for putting up an official guest or when he himself was
on safari. This was intended to compensate either for the cost of
feeding one's guest, or of running two households simultaneously. No one could be paid safari allowance for the same night
that someone else had claimed hospitality allowance for putting
him up. When one's guest was not working for the government,
for example when a missionary or a settler came to stay, there
was no set pattern, but the normal arrangement was that the
guest left a tip for the host to give to his domestic servants, and
hospitality was usually reciprocated later. We never felt exploited
by people who came to stay with us, although some of our visitors were much more congenial than others.

One day in September Father Cyprian, the Father Superior of
Kisawasawa Mission near Kiberege, who was one of the Fathers I
liked best, brought me a present of a python skin nearly twenty feet
long. The snake had been spotted in the mission garden, and an
African had killed it with his spear. There was just one hole made by
the spear immediately behind the snake's head. The skin was cured
for us by one of the Brothers at Kwiro. More than ten years later,
when Jennifer was teaching at a secondary school in Surrey, she
often showed it to her pupils. They all found it scary but exciting.
Few English schoolchildren have much idea of just how long a
python can be, or of the courage a man needs to succeed in killing
such a large and dangerous reptile with only a spear.

Three days after Father Cyprian had brought me the python
skin, a local court messenger from the chief's court at Ifakara
came into my office in the Boma carrying a letter and a very large
sack, which looked as if it contained something heavy.

I read the letter, which was written in Swahili and addressed to
me personally by the Chief himself, Nkosi Ahamadi Mahawanga.
In it he sent his greetings and told me he was sending me a
present of a *kakakuona* as a token of his respect. I had never come
across the word before, and had no idea what the chief was
giving me, though I guessed it was alive. I asked the messenger to

open the sack. He carefully took out a large animal which was rolled up in a ball and seemed to be fast asleep. It looked like a reptile, but was, in fact, a mammal.

I looked up the word *kakakuona* in the *Standard Swahili–English Dictionary*, and discovered that what the Chief had given me was defined in it as 'an animal like an armadillo – some natives believe that if its scales are burned wild animals will not come near'. I learnt later from a book on African wildlife that the correct name for this animal was 'pangolin' or 'scaly ant-eater'. This book went on to say that its flesh was considered a delicacy by natives, and that its scales were often used to ward off evil.

None of the natives then present in the Boma mentioned anything about burning the kakakuona's scales or warding off evil spirits, let alone eating the Nkosi's present to me, but they all found it very exciting, and several of them insisted that the animal had magic powers and could answer questions about the future like an oracle if asked in the right way. No one was able to advise me about the right way to ask a pangolin a question. However, it was clearly a very great compliment that the Nkosi was paying me, and I wrote a warm letter of thanks for the messenger to take back to him.

I tried to find out a little more about how to look after pangolins. When the one I had been given was relaxed enough to unroll itself, I saw that it (I never discovered whether it was male or female) was nearly four feet long. It had a very small head, a long nose but apparently no ears, a long broad tail, and strong claws on its front paws. These claws were used for digging up the termite mounds and anthills from which it got its food. I did not see its tongue, but learned later that a pangolin's tongue is extremely long and sticky. The animal lives in open country, bush or light woodland, sleeps during the day, is strictly nocturnal, and is very rarely seen.

I wondered how a pangolin whose previous habitat had been in the low-lying chiefdom of Ifakara would take to living on the

Mahenge Massif, but I did not want to offend the Nkosi by returning his present, so I decided to take the pangolin home with me. I lifted it very gently, and was surprised at its weight. It rolled itself into a ball again as soon as I touched it. When we reached my house, I asked Atanasi, our gardener, to put some dry grass in the corner of the inspection pit in our garage, and we laid the animal there. I hoped it would not be attacked, and would be warm enough during the night. I left a bowl of milk in the inspection pit, though I doubted whether the pangolin would drink it.

Next morning the milk was still untouched, and there was no trace of the pangolin in the garage or anywhere around the house. It had climbed out of the pit, and escaped. I have no idea whether it survived in its unfamiliar surroundings. Nkosi Ahamadi Mahawanga never asked me how the pangolin was getting on, and I never told him that it had disappeared.

By the time I brought the pangolin home from the Boma, Ruth was already asleep, and she would have been very intrigued by it. Jennifer and I would have enjoyed showing it to her, so its disappearance was rather a disappointment. However, it also proved to be something of a relief. I had not been aware of the fact, but pangolins were included in the schedule of 'Royal Game', which could only be hunted with a Governor's Special Licence. It might have caused embarrassment both to the Nkosi and me if we had been questioned about being in possession of a pangolin without the proper authority. Ignorance of the law is no excuse, especially if the two people concerned are both involved in the enforcement of laws which include the Fauna Conservation Ordinance.

A Birthday Treat

Jennifer's morning sickness ended as abruptly as it had started, and by the middle of September she was feeling quite well again, but we both agreed that it would be sensible for her to give up classroom teaching until after the baby was born. Jennifer had thoroughly enjoyed her spell of teaching at Kwiro, and getting to know the staff and pupils at the school. She was sorry that she had only been working there for such a short time, but all the staff at the school regarded pregnancy as a cause for rejoicing, and the best possible reason for a young married woman to leave her job. The Headmaster was very grateful for what Jennifer had achieved in a short time, and said he intended to ask her to undertake special tasks for the school whenever he needed her help.

A few days after Jennifer stopped teaching at Kwiro, Alan Rees proposed that we should all come with him and spend the first weekend of October visiting the Selous Game Reserve. We could travel down on the Saturday, spend one night in a small camp a few miles from Ifakara, and return to Mahenge the next day. We thought this was a splendid idea. Any weekend would have been enjoyable, but the date Alan suggested, 4th October, happened to be Jennifer's thirtieth birthday and we thought this would give us the chance to celebrate it in a really exciting way. Alan had some work to do in the Game Reserve, and he offered to follow in his Landrover to come to our rescue if we had any trouble in our Peugeot.

The first part of the journey was quite easy. On the road down to Ifakara we met George and Jean Pletts, who were driving up to Mahenge, hoping to pay us an unexpected visit. I wrote a note in Swahili for George to take to Juma asking him to welcome George and Jean at our house until we ourselves returned. We told Juma that we had invited them to join us for a meal on Sunday evening, and that they would be returning to their home on Monday. We then drove on, and turned off the Mahenge–Ifakara road on to the track which led to the camp. Alan had assured us it would be quite passable for our car, but it barely was. There were so many gulleys and potholes that we began to have doubts about whether we should have attempted the journey at all. Our car had to descend into the gulleys and we then had to try somehow to get out on the other side. Sometimes, when the front of the car was pointing upwards, the rear end tipped back and the petrol tank hit the dried-up bed of the stream with an almighty bang. Luckily, there were no sharp stones to penetrate it. Short wheel-base Landrovers are much more suitable for that type of terrain, but my legs are much too long for me to be comfortable when I am driving a Landrover.

We arrived at the camp just as the sun was starting to set, and we were glad we had not turned back. The camp was a blissful place. It was built on a bank that overlooked a particularly beautiful stretch of the Kilombero. It consisted of one large thatched rondavel and a number of smaller huts. The huts were primarily for Game Scouts and their families, but could also be used for domestic servants.

We were all hungry when we arrived, and Jennifer produced

a birthday cake which she had herself baked before we left Mahenge. We gave Ruth some cake with her supper, and she then went to bed without a murmur while Mohamed cooked a celebration dinner for Jennifer, Alan and me. I had secretly hidden a bottle of Chianti in the car, and after Ruth was safely asleep we ate our dinner sitting in front of the rondavel, sipping the wine, listening to the hippo in the river immediately below us, and enjoying the fragrance of a tree that was a mass of delicate yellow blossom. We hung my safari lamp on a branch of another tree a few yards away, where it attracted hundreds of moths and other insects which might otherwise have irritated us.

Jennifer, Ruth, and I slept in the rondavel. Alan assured us that he often slept in the open air on safari, and he put up his camp bed and mosquito net a few yards from the rondavel.

The next morning we all got up at about six o'clock, when the sun was rising, and set off, first by car and then on foot, to look for animals. We saw a few impala and some waterbuck, and when we came to a different stretch of the river we saw a large number of crocodiles, some quite small, others enormous. We would probably have seen more animals if Ruth had not been quite so vocal in her enthusiasm. It was delightful walking in the cool of the day, and at about half past eight we stopped to look at the graves of four German soldiers who had died in 1894 and 1895. The youngest had been twenty-three and the oldest twenty-nine.

It was beginning to get really hot by the time we got back to the camp, and we all tucked into an enormous breakfast that Mohamed had cooked while we were away. We then spent the rest of the morning sitting very lazily in front of the rondavel looking out on to the river and watching elephant and hippo which were almost as lazy as we were, and an immense variety of brightly coloured butterflies and chattering river birds. Ruth was particularly fascinated at the way elephants used their trunks to put food in their mouths, and how the mother elephants suckled their newborn babies. When Mohamed brought us lunch, Ruth called out to the baby

elephants to invite them to share her lunch with her, but they did not accept her offer.

We set off soon after lunch to return to Mahenge. Alan did not come with us on the homeward journey, as he had not yet finished his work. We passed six enchanting zebra on the way. When they heard our car they started to run, but then they all stopped and turned and stared at us, standing with their heads parallel and equal distances apart. They looked like performing animals in a circus, or, as Mohamed put it, like askaris on parade.

The journey back was at least as uncomfortable as the outward journey had been, and my car actually got stuck in one of the gullies. We had to unload all our luggage and passengers, and I drove and Mohamed pushed as hard as he could before we finally got it out. Meanwhile Jennifer, Ruth and Ina were all standing by the track wildly flapping towels to keep the tsetse fly from biting us. Ruth thought her crusade against the bad *dudus* ('dudu' is the Swahili word for insect) was the high spot of the whole expedition.

As soon as the car was safely out of the gulley, we reloaded it and I drove along a reasonably flat stretch of the track. However, our adventures were not yet over. It was the dry season, and many parts of the Game Reserve were already parched. On each side of the track, and on stretches of the track itself, there was dry grass several feet high. I was not pleased to see the number of small fires that had started, and Mohamed and I had to extinguish one right in the middle of the track before we drove over the ashes. If there had been a strong wind, the fires might have spread rapidly, and I drove as fast as I could to get out of the danger as quickly as possible. The car hit a large pot-hole, and Ruth made us all laugh by exclaiming 'Gosh!' very loudly. She had never used the word before. When we reached the Mahenge–Ifakara road we were thankful that Peugeot cars were so reliable. It could have been disastrous if our car had broken down.

Looking back on it, I now think we were crazy to undertake a trip of this kind with a little child in our car and while Jennifer was pregnant. However, watching African wildlife is like an addictive drug.

I had a fortnight's local leave due to me, and shortly after we had spent the weekend in the camp by the Kilombero River, Alan asked us if we would like to visit another Game Department camp, this time overlooking the Ruaha River. This camp was some miles further from Mahenge, but Alan assured us that it was more accessible than the camp where we had spent Jennifer's birthday. We accepted eagerly.

It was a great privilege for us to be allowed to use the Game Department's camps, but the benefit for the Game Department was that the presence of a District Officer inside the Reserve might discourage poachers.

Alan also knew that I would not harm the animals. Unlike a certain elderly American missionary in Central Province, who boasted that he had once shot ninety zebra in a single day on the Wembere Steppe during the good old days when zebra had been regarded as vermin, I much preferred living animals to dead ones. During the whole time I was in Tanganyika, I never used a gun. Alan knew my views on the subject, and in particular about people who killed in order to make money from selling ivory and rhino-horn on the black market.

A Fortnight's Local Leave

Between her birthday and our local leave, Jennifer came down with me to Ifakara Hospital for a check-up while I was paying a quick visit to Ifakara on other business. Rolf Diethelm, the doctor who was temporarily in charge during the absence of Karl Schöpf, told her that everything was going well. It was the only ante-natal medical examination she had until we all moved down to Ifakara four months later so as to be near the hospital in time for her confinement.

Before she stopped classroom teaching, Jennifer had agreed to give a short course on the pronunciation of English to a group of teachers from Capuchin Mission primary schools. Swahili is a very easy language to pronounce. Words are pronounced exactly as they are spelt, and spelt exactly as they are pronounced. There are few, if any, exceptions to the rules about the stress on particular syllables. The pronunciation of English is much more complicated than Swahili. One has only to look at pairs of words like 'ear' and 'bear' and 'cough' 'plough' to see that the same letter or combination of letters can be pronounced in different ways in English. The stress in words like 'photograph' and 'photographer' causes real problems to speakers of other languages.

Many pupils in Tanganyika were taught English by teachers whose pronunciation was not good. The mission authorities therefore decided that it would be valuable if primary school teachers in their schools received instruction from someone whose mother tongue was English. Even though most of the Fathers who came from Switzerland spoke English fluently, they could not teach pronunciation as well as Jennifer.

Jennifer enjoyed getting to know a number of eager and like-able primary school teachers from around the district, and giving them lessons which interested them, but it was quite strenuous work for her. When the course ended, she and I both agreed that we would spend our local leave as restfully as possible.

On the last day before we planned to set off for the camp on the Ruaha River, we had a visit from two Anglican priests from the Church Missionary Society in Morogoro, one a very gentle and caring Australian called Arblaster, the other a delightful African pastor called Lusinde, whose daughter, like ours, was called Ruth. She had been one of Jennifer's very brightest pupils at Tabora. They both stayed with us for two nights, and we deferred our departure to Ruaha by one day.

They took an evening service in the Lutheran Church when they arrived. After the service there was a buffet supper for the whole congregation in our house, which was attended by twenty-three people. The following morning they held a well-attended communion service. I was very struck by the way that both priests talked personally to everyone, and gave the impression that they really cared about each of them. Both priests spent the whole of their second day on pastoral visits to people in Mahenge, many of whom had not been visited by a priest for a long time.

One of my criticisms of Christian missionaries in Tanganyika concerns the rivalries which existed between some of the representatives of different denominations. I also regretted the way that some hard-working missionaries, including a number of Anglicans, seemed to think that the pastoral care of expatriates was a matter of very low priority, particularly if the expatriates happened to be working in a remote station. Neither of those criticisms could fairly be levelled at Ted Arblaster.

Not long after Jennifer and I arrived in Mahenge, I had written to the bishop of the diocese in which we believed that Mahenge was situated, to ask for occasional visits from an Anglican priest. He replied saying that he could not help us as Mahenge was not in his diocese, and suggested that we write to the bishop of the adjacent diocese instead. That bishop replied in exactly the same way, and advised us to apply to a third bishop, who advised us to make our request to the bishop we had written to in the first place. None of them seemed either to know or care in whose diocese Mahenge was situated, and each made the excuse that the cost in money and time of visiting Mahenge was disproportionately high. They showed no interest in the pastoral care of a few expatriates who were out of sight and out of mind.

After the bishops had declined our request, Mr Thygessen very kindly volunteered to give communion from time to time to Anglicans who wanted to receive it, provided that the Anglican Bishop of the diocese concerned, whichever it happened to be, gave his consent to this arrangement. We did not know who to approach, so we approached all three. They all refused.

As soon as the two Anglican priests had left on their homeward journey to Morogoro, Jennifer and I set off for the camp by the Ruaha River. Our Peugeot, which had a roof-rack, was very heavily loaded. It carried Jennifer, Ruth, Ina, Mohamed and me, and all the paraphernalia that we expected to need for the next two weeks: camp beds, bedding, mosquito nets, safari chairs and tables, a canvas safari bath, lamps, paraffin, clothes, toys for Ruth, food and drink, and miscellaneous household articles. We also brought luxury items like our radio, our record player with spare batteries, playing cards, Monopoly, Scrabble, and a large number of books and long-playing records. We were determined to enjoy our leisure, whatever the weather might do. Fortunately, the track leading to the Ruaha camp was not quite so bad as the one to the Kilombero camp, and we had no trouble on the journey in either direction.

As soon as we got to the Ruaha camp, we realised how lucky we were, and how idyllic the place was. It seemed incredible, but I believe that the camp on the Ruaha was, if anything, even more beautiful than the one on the Kilombero. It stood on a bend in the river. It had been built by Watty Paul, who had lived there while he was building his permanent house at Sanje Estate, a few miles away. When Watty had moved out, the Game Department had acquired the camp buildings, and they had been carefully maintained.

The camp consisted of one rectangular mud and wattle hut, with a number of smaller huts behind it. The smaller huts were used as a kitchen and as accommodation for domestic servants and game scouts. The latrines were holes in the ground, but the holes had been dug recently, and were not as insalubrious as some of the pit latrines that I came across in other places.

The mud and wattle hut we slept in was quite large. It had two big rooms and a shady verandah looking out over the river. We used one room as a bedroom, with Ruth's bed placed between

Jennifer's and mine. The other was theoretically our sitting room, but we spent far more time sitting on the verandah looking out on to the Ruaha river immediately below us. On the other side of the river a few miles away there were beautiful hills which reminded Jennifer of the hills that rise up behind Scottish lochs. I had never visited Scotland, so I could do no more than agree that they were amazingly beautiful by day, with a narrow waterfall dropping over a thousand feet down one of the hills, and even more beautiful at night, with the moon shining and a few small fires glowing on the hillside. There was a full moon during our second week at the camp, and almost every evening we sat on the verandah listening to the animals and to our long-playing records. Some hippo responded noisily when we played them a recording of Verdi's *Il Trovatore*, with Jüssi Björling in the leading role.

Every day we went for short walks with Ruth, who learnt quite quickly that she would see the animals more closely if she kept as quiet as possible. The animals did not seem to be in the least afraid of us and never threatened us at all. We saw various types of mammals, including large numbers of antelope, monkeys, zebra, hippo and elephant. I was not disappointed that we saw few if any predatory animals or scavengers such as lions, leopards or hyenas.

The bird life was even more varied than the mammals. The field guide said that the bird life in the Selous Reserve was similar to that in the Game Park at Mikumi, and went on to list 320 different species of bird to be found in the Mikumi Game Park. We did not see anything like that number, and we were not able to identify accurately most of the birds that we did see, though we could classify many of the broad groups such as eagles, hawks, storks, doves, owls, hornbills, kingfishers, bee-eaters, bulbuls, weaverbirds, and sun-birds. Mammals are seldom very brightly coloured. Predatory ones want to get as close to their prey as they can without being seen, and their victims have an even stronger reason for being inconspicuous. Birds are different. Male birds in particular want to impress their mates by looking as dazzlingly beautiful as possible, and the colours of many African birds are quite stunning.

Ruth was particularly keen on a family of warthogs. There were six enchanting young ones, and they frisked along behind their parents with their tails sticking up in the air. They all got quite used to us, and we saw them almost every day. There are other animals which are prettier than warthogs, and the tusks on the side of adult warthogs' faces look as if they could be danger-

ous, but we all became rather fond of our warthog family. Every day they came close enough for us to be able to watch them, but never close enough to cause us any alarm.

The only animals whose company we did not much enjoy were the rats. They had made nests in the thatched roof of our hut, and every night we heard them scratching about above us. One night a rat dropped on to the top of Jennifer's mosquito net, but it got no closer than that. Another night a rat took a fancy to one of Ruth's dolls made of something which felt like rubber but was probably plastic, and smelt of very cheap and nasty scent. Ruth failed to put it away when she was going to bed, and a rat had started to chew it. The rat gave up when it decided that it did not care all that much for the flavour. However, for the rest of its days Ruth's doll had a rat's toothmarks on its elbow. Ruth herself did not seem to mind very much. She spent a large part of each day in the canvas safari bath washing all her dolls and their clothes, and we managed to get through an immense amount of soap on our holiday.

Jennifer and I had decided as soon as we reached the camp that we did not want Ruth to go into the river, even with us standing near her. The water was shallow during the dry season, but it still flowed quite fast and there were also a number of pools where a little girl of two would have been out of her depth. Ruth was perfectly happy to obey us about not going into the 'bad water', but after she was safely asleep Jennifer and I thoroughly enjoyed having a cool dip in the river, taking care that Ruth did not wake up and see us swimming in the water which we had told her was bad. I doubt whether she was quite old enough to understand that what was quite safe for grown-ups might be unsafe for her.

We had expected that we would not see many of our friends while we were on holiday, but our social life was just as active in the camp as in Mahenge. We saw George and Jean Pletts the day before they left Kisanambega Estate for a holiday of their own on the island of Mafia, south of Zanzibar. They visited us again on the day after they got back at the end of a disappointing and expensive week in an appalling hotel which did not even provide clean drinking water for them. Watty and Isabel Paul visited us several times, and invited us back to meals with them at Sanje Estate. Father Cyprian, the congenial Father Superior of Kisawasawa Mission, called on us and had pot luck lunch with us, and invited us all to visit the mission a couple of days later, when we swam in a very cold stream which flowed down from the hills above the mission. Ruth enjoyed her bathe very much, and made great friends with Father Cyprian, who seemed just as fond of children as Father Berthold.

As well as the friends who lived in the north of Ulanga District, between the Kilombero and the Ruaha Rivers, we also received unexpected visits from anyone who happened to be travelling between Mahenge and either Kilosa or Morogoro. Robin Blackall, when he was visiting Morogoro on duty, brought us our post with him from Mahenge, and stayed overnight before leaving for Morogoro, taking with him all the letters we had written and posting them on our behalf in Morogoro.

Mohamed was always at his best when we had guests or when we were on safari, and every day he used simple ingredients to produce delicious meals for us and anyone who happened to be visiting us. Ina was as devoted as ever in the care she gave to Ruth, though Ruth spent the greater part of her time with us.

At the end of two weeks we returned to Mahenge, feeling refreshed and that we had had a perfect holiday, even though we looked forward to getting back to a house with a flush loo. The journey home took considerably longer than the journey down to the camp, as we made courtesy calls on the way home on the Pauls, the Plettses, Father Cyprian, and Nkosi Hamisi Mtoahanji, the Chief of Kiberege, in whose area we had been staying, and a purely social visit to Rolf Diethelm and his wife Charlotte.

Father Cyprian asked Ruth to deliver a puppy from him to one of the Brothers at Kwiro. Ruth tripped up over a saucepan and fell on to the puppy, but was much more concerned about the puppy than about herself.

When we got to Kwiro, we thought she might be unhappy about handing over the puppy which she had been fondling in the car for hours, but she gave it one big kiss and passed it over to the Brother without complaining.

Nkosi Hamisi provided tea for Jennifer and me at Kiberege.

Ruth was not yet very keen on tea, so he offered her some fruit instead. The Diethelms at Ifakara were no less hospitable, and dusk was falling by the time we eventually reached Mahenge.

That holiday lives on in our memory, but we were never able to repeat it. During the next rainy season, the Ruaha flooded and the river washed away the bank on which the camp had been situated, and all the buildings where we had stayed.

Jennifer spent the day after we returned invigilating pupils taking the Standard X examination at Kwiro School. This caused an unexpected problem. In the morning, when she opened a properly sealed envelope which was marked as containing sixty-five copies of the mathematics question paper, she found that there were only forty copies in the envelope. There were fifty-nine candidates, and each candidate needed his own copy of the paper, in addition to one for the invigilator.

After a hasty consultation, Jennifer and the Headmaster decided on a solution. The paper that was scheduled to take place in the afternoon was brought forward to the morning, and twenty additional copies of the maths paper were quickly prepared in secret so that each pupil and the invigilator could have their own copies in the afternoon. Such a procedure might have provided a chance for dishonesty if there had been any way in which pupils at Kwiro could have contacted pupils or staff at other secondary schools, but because of the lack of communications between Ulanga and other districts, the risk was negligible. A telegram was nevertheless sent to the Education Department in Dar to inform them of the position, and to recommend them to check on what had happened to the missing copies. If they had been misappropriated and might have been shown to candidates at other schools, then the original maths paper would have had to be abandoned, and a new one set for all the secondary schools in the whole country. Luckily, this was not the case.

Mad Dogs, Witches, an Elephant, and a Hungry Lion

District Officers in up-country districts normally spent a week or more every month on safari. In Swahili, the word *safari* simply means 'a journey', and is used to refer to many kinds of journey which would not be described by an English speaker as safaris. On the other hand, some English dictionaries give the word a definition which seems too narrow, for example – 'a hunting or scientific expedition, especially in East Africa; a sightseeing trip to see African animals in their own habitat'. Those are examples of particular types of safari, but not all safaris could be defined in those terms. I am not a hunter or a scientist, and, while it was something I enjoyed, looking at wildlife was never the main objective of the time that I spent on safari.

District Officers travelled round their districts in order to promote good government, just as hospital consultants go round the wards to see how the patients are getting on. No two safaris were the same. There were wide variations in the duration, the distance, the method of travel, the number of people travelling together, the places where they halted overnight, and in the aims of the safari.

The distance one travelled and the time it took depended on the size of the district and the state of the roads. Ulanga was a big district and such roads as existed were atrocious. I preferred to go on safari during the dry season, but that was not always possible.

In Ulanga there were up to six different methods of transportation, and on most safaris two or more would be used for different parts of the journey. Every District Office had its own Government Transport car, colloquially referred to as a 'GT'. When I was a cadet in Rungwe District, the GT there was an old box-body Ford V8, but in most districts, including Ulanga, the Boma GT was a short wheel-base Landrover. I found its leg-room horribly cramped, and preferred to use my own Peugeot car on safari whenever possible.

The District also had its own motor boat, imaginatively named *Ulanga*. For about the first year of my tour, the *Ulanga* was out of service, awaiting delivery of a spare part from Britain, so we had to visit riverside villages by dug-out canoe paddled by local fishermen. Even after the motor boat had been repaired, we still needed to use canoes where the river was too shallow or too narrow to allow passage to the motor boat. On one particular safari, when I was visiting villages on a tributary of the Kilombero, the motor boat got stranded in thick clumps of water hyacinth, and my companions and I all had to get out and push. Luckily, the water was only waist high and there was no danger of drowning, and there were no crocodiles or leeches, but it was not a very pleasant experience.

There were other places, for example forests or very isolated villages, which were not accessible to cars or by river. We normally parked our cars as close to such places as we could, then walked the last few miles. Foot safari had the great advantage that one could chat informally to the people one met; the disad-

vantage was that it was very slow, and involved long absences from the Boma. It was also costly. Loads had to be carried by porters who needed to be paid, not only for the days they were carrying loads, but also for days of idleness when the District Officer remained for more than one night at a particular stopping-place.

My messenger and I sometimes rode bicycles along paths which were too narrow for a car, or on stretches of road between rivers whose damaged bridges still had to be rebuilt after the rainy season. We carried our bicycles across the river beds, and arrived at our destination in time to start work long before the porters arrived.

The night-stops themselves also varied greatly. Every Boma was equipped with its own large tent, and I generally enjoyed sleeping under canvas, even though tents sometimes let in the rain. Tents were also heavy, required several porters to carry them, and took time to put up and take down.

In larger villages, there was usually an unfurnished government rest-house with a bedroom, a kitchen, and a latrine. The kitchen was sometimes under cover, but often it was in the open air, and consisted of a stove made of of three large stones supporting a sheet of metal. A wood fire was lit under the sheet of metal, and pots and pans were put on top of it. Rest-houses did not have running water, and the chief usually arranged for someone to bring a container of water to the rest-house before the visitors arrived. The water was often dirty and tasted nasty, and my cook always boiled it before I drank it. My usual drinks on safari were tea or bottled beer.

Some of the rest-houses were clean and situated in pleasant surroundings, but others were unattractive, stank of bat-droppings, and were full of creepy-crawlies. The nastiest of these were small but very fierce red ants, known in Swahili as *siafu*. Hordes of siafu could get up one's trouser-leg and inside one's shirt unobserved, and then all attack simultaneously. Bashfulness and modesty were abandoned as one stripped off clothing to brush them off one's skin as quickly as possible. Being bitten by mosquitoes carried a risk of malaria, but mosquitoes did not actually hurt in the way that siafu did at the time one was being bitten.

Different types of safari had different objectives. Many were routine visits to one or more Local Courts. The basic aim of such visits was to check up on whether the chief and the local authority personnel, such as teachers, clerks, and health care staff, were doing their jobs properly, and to give guidance about how they could improve their performance. Court records and cash were examined. Local Authority buildings were inspected and urgent repairs put in hand. Shops in the trading centre were visited. Crops under cultivation and supplies of food were examined. Petitions and complaints from villagers were heard, and applications for exemption from poll tax were approved or rejected.

District Officers also took the opportunity to give news on matters such as the country's political progress, or to deliver homilies about whatever seemed appropriate – the value of education and the need to enrol children in the local primary school; the adoption of measures to promote health; ways to improve crop yields; the obligation to pay tax promptly; or the need for orderly behaviour as Tanganyika approached independence.

The aim of certain safaris was to carry out a specific task, for example the payment of a gang of road labourers; or work connected with elections; or arbitration in boundary disputes; or assessing the compensation payable to farmers evicted from forest reserves; or consultations about applications for the alienation of land to non-natives. In spite of TANU's general opposition to the alienation of land to non-natives, some applications got support from villagers who hoped that investment from outside would provide job opportunities and stimulate the local economy.

Every safari needed to be planned in advance, and an experienced messenger was invaluable in recommending the best route to take and estimating the time needed for each stretch of the journey. Chiefs had to be notified in good time for porters to be recruited, canoes hired, and people who wanted to see the District Officer told when and where he would be available. The only exception to this rule was when misconduct was suspected. A safari might be unannounced if there was any risk that evidence could be destroyed or witnesses suborned.

I never went on safari completely alone. I was always accompanied by my Boma messenger and my cook. Chiefs and their retinue usually walked with me when I was on foot in their areas. I often travelled with colleagues from other government departments. District Officers were jacks-of-all-trades, but they were not experts in matters such as agriculture, forestry, fauna conservation, animal husbandry, or health care. It was useful and pleasant for expatriate officials to work as a team and we learnt a lot from one another.

We did not always achieve our objectives. One safari I did in the area to the west of Ifakara with a jovial Irishman called Dennis Kelly, the Provincial Veterinary Officer from Morogoro, was a total failure. I blamed this on bureaucracy in Dar. There was a serious rabies epidemic in one corner of Ulanga District, near the boundary with Iringa District. At least eleven people died agonising deaths after being bitten by mad dogs, and the Veterinary Department asked Dennis to inoculate all the dogs in the infected area. The vaccine was too expensive for poor peasant farmers, so, as a special concession, officials in Dar decided to charge only half price for each dose. The local African villagers had never seen or heard of rabies vaccination before. They misunderstood the purpose of the safari, and, despite all my attempts to reassure them, they insisted on calling the campaign a new 'dog tax', which they refused to pay. Not a single dog was inoculated. If the control of rabies was the overriding objective, as the Veterinary Department claimed, then the vaccine should have been made available completely free of charge.

Safari often brought serious abuses to the notice of a visiting District Officer. While I was serving in Tabora, the corruption of Chief Nassoro Saidi Fundikira had come to light as a result of information which my colleague Peter Hopkins and I received while on safari.

Most of the Chiefs in Ulanga District meant well and were honest, though some were lazy. However, there was one who was a villain. The Chief of Mtimbira was called Rafael Njahite. He was as corrupt as Fundikira, but he had none of Fundikira's better qualities.

Mtimbira was situated between the foothills of the Mahenge massif and the Kilombero River. It was a nasty village. Crops were neglected. The local authority buildings and the huts of the peasant farmers were shabby and dilapidated. Attendance at the primary school was bad. Tax defaulters were not pursued. Month after month, the number of pending cases awaiting trial in the Chief's court grew larger and larger. The feature which struck me most about Mtimbira, however, was its sinister atmosphere. The people all seemed to be living in a state of fear. There was no laughter or friendly banter between villagers. They all seemed deeply suspicious of one another. As I got to know the place better, I reached the conclusion that its menace was due to the prevalence of witchcraft in the area, and the personal involvement of Chief Njahite in exploiting it.

People in developed countries tend to laugh at the idea of witchcraft. They think of it as a superstitious belief in ugly and malevolent old women with pointed hats riding around on broomsticks after midnight, and reject the idea of certain individuals having occult powers. Sophisticated people rely on actuaries to assess the risks of calamities such as bereavement, sickness, fire, injury, theft, crop failure, or loss of one's job. However, the traditional view among many Africans is that such events are not fortuitous, but are caused by an enemy with occult powers. The more successful a person appears to be, the more likely he is to arouse the hatred and jealousy of his neighbours and become the victim of witchcraft. This attitude has an adverse effect on the country's economy, as people with the skill to become successful entrepreneurs are often afraid to do so.

Another feature of the beliefs common in Ulanga District is that the most effective defence against traditional sorcery is traditional medicine, and the identification of the sorcerer or witch who is responsible for the mishap, whatever it may be. If a person is wasting away after being threatened with death, treatment with European drugs in a Government Hospital is not considered likely to cure him. If a person is accused of being a witch, a process of cleansing, sometimes known as 'going to be shaved', needs to be undertaken.

I am no expert on the motives of witches and sorcerers who practise evil, but I believe they include envy, hatred, and malice towards the person being bewitched. They probably also include lust for power and a desire to be paid well for exercising their professional skills. I presume that Ali Athmani, the corrupt Head Tax Clerk, paid the women he engaged to bewitch me, and that they had no personal animosity against me, as they had never met me before. I have no idea how much they were paid, but I suspect it was quite a lot. Medicine-men who use occult treatments to heal the sick or to protect people from sorcery probably also receive generous payment in cash or in kind for their services.

Njahite was a very inefficient and lazy chief, but the actions which eventually led to his being deposed included conspiring to force everyone in the chiefdom to undergo witchcraft tests, for which they were compelled to pay, and then sharing with the medicine-man the very large amount paid as fees by the innocent and the allegedly guilty.

Fear of witchcraft was seldom far from the surface in Ulanga, but it came to a head in Mtimbira when nine apparently healthy people all died suddenly in a very short period. The cause of their deaths might possibly have been meningitis, but that was never proved or disproved. The opinion of most of the villagers was that the victims had been bewitched. Njahite then invited a Ngindo witch-doctor from outside his own chiefdom to come and discover who was responsible for the deaths. Every man and woman who lived in Mtimbira Chiefdom was ordered to drink a cup of bright red fluid. Some people estimated that between one and two thousand people were forced to drink the potion. I later put a tiny drop of it on my finger and tasted it for myself. It was extremely bitter but did me no harm. Those who were made to drink a full dose were all ordered to pay a shilling for it. That was the equivalent of a day's pay for a labourer.

Those who had taken the medicine without any adverse reaction were pronounced innocent, but anyone who was unwell after drinking it was declared to be guilty of being a witch and ordered to undergo a cleansing ritual before setting off on the journey home. This involved drinking a different fluid, which I believe had a soporific effect, though I never tasted it. The charge for the cleansing medicine was ten shillings. All those people were told that if they tried to leave before the cleansing had been completed, they would surely die on their way home. Several of the people alleged to be witches objected to being charged so much, and one woman declared loudly that she was a devout Christian and refused to pay or to sleep it off. She set off towards her home, and collapsed and died before she got there. Her death crushed any public resistance to the rituals that Njahite had ordered.

I have no adequate explanation for these tragedies. Medicine-men know a lot about herbal medicines, including poisons. Some of the villagers might have been allergic to the red fluid. The medicine-man or his henchmen might have knowingly tampered with the medicine or administered an overdose to a small proportion of the villagers. The woman who died was probably poisoned, but she might also have died of natural causes. The cause of her death was never established.

I do not vouch for the truthfulness of my informants, who

seemed reluctant to answer questions, but I formed the impression that between 10% and 20% of the people who drank the red fluid became unwell, and that for several days in succession large numbers of people were made to undergo cleansing. Everyone seemed to agree about the prices charged for the two types of medicine, and that Njahite and the witch-doctor had each received enough money to make them, by the standards of Ulanga at the time, very rich men.

A Witchcraft Ordinance had been enacted in 1928 and revised in 1958. It outlawed the practice of witchcraft, and accusing others of being witches except before a court or a local authority. However, there were few successful prosecutions under it. The evidence of witnesses in such cases was often unreliable. Many people were too frightened to make sworn statements, and others might well commit perjury. No one was charged in connection with the affair at Mtimbira.

While I was still at Mtimbira, I asked Njahite to come to see me in the rest-house. He was tipsy when he arrived, but I nevertheless told him what a bad chief I thought he was. He then astonished me by offering meekly to resign his appointment. I asked him to confirm his offer in writing, and he was sober enough to draft in his own words a paper which he handed to me. I told him I would read it aloud in his court the following day. I accepted his request to be allowed a reasonable period of notice before his resignation took effect. Next morning, the people in the court heard the announcement in stunned silence. There was neither jubilation nor fury.

Geoff Bullock himself went to Mtimbira a few weeks later to preside over the selection of Njahite's successor. When he returned to Mahenge, he told me that the people had refused absolutely to allow Njahite's resignation to be accepted, and that after some discussion he had agreed that Njahite's son, Rafael Rafael Njahite, should be appointed his father's deputy to help his father with a work-load which was beyond his capacity. I expressed my disappointment, but Geoff assured me that, in his judgement, the solution he had agreed to was the least bad option.

Rafael Rafael Njahite proved to be even more corrupt than his father, and about a year later I convicted him on a charge of burglary from Mtimbira Mission. He appealed, but the High Court upheld the conviction. His imprisonment meant that he ceased to be the chief's deputy.

Rafael Njahite himself was eventually the subject of investigations carried out under the supervision of Charles Sutcliffe, the Senior Superintendent of Police who had also investigated the Fundikira affair. An experienced District Officer called John Adams was sent from the Secretariat to prepare a special report into the activities of Rafael Njahite. This led to Njahite's being deposed by order of the Governor.

In Tanganyika, witchcraft was, and still is, a serious matter. President Julius Nyerere, himself a devout Christian, regarded it as the biggest influence on the lives of Africans, not just in rural areas but even among educated town-dwellers. All denominations of the Christian church are in agreement that the practice of witchcraft is incompatible with the teachings of the New Testament and the Christian way of life, but some of the people who get baptised do not abandon their traditional practices, and many people who do not themselves practice witchcraft nevertheless acknowledge its power.

On a later safari, Father Vincent, the Father Superior, invited me to supper at Mtimbira Mission, and we chatted about the Njahite affair, and the problem of witchcraft. He explained that those who dedicated themselves completely to serving a God of love were often able to work miracles. At the other end of the spectrum, however, there were people who were wholly dedicated to evil, and their power to do harm was comparable to the power of saints to do good.

Fear of the forces of evil permeates the lives of many Africans. Sadly, in the 1950s there were certain Christian missions who made that fear worse by threatening their flocks with hell-fire if they did not conform exactly to a set of punctilious rules. I spoke recently to an educated African who was on a postgraduate course in Britain. For him the most important feature of Christianity was the day of the week on which he went to worship God, and going on the wrong day was an abomination. Becoming a Christian does not always liberate converts from fear. However, those who accept that God is omnipotent and that He loves them as individuals are probably able to deal better with their fears than those who adhere solely to traditional beliefs.

* * *

There were about twenty Local Courts in Ulanga District. A few were accessible by car from Mahenge, and were visited regularly. Safaris to courts that were harder to reach normally had to be made during the dry season, after all the bridges on the approach roads had been repaired, or else by foot, bicycle, or boat. There was one Local Court which was so remote that it was hardly ever visited at all. The court at Matumbi in Ulanga District (there are villages called Matumbi in other districts as well) was five days' walk beyond the village where the road along the foothills south of the Kilombero River came to an end. When that road was impassable, as it was for much of the year, the journey between Matumbi and Mahenge took sixteen days each way.

Towards the end of 1959, I went on safari to Matumbi. I was the first official to do so for about ten years. I drove through Mtimbira and Malinyi as far as Kilosa-kwa-Mpepo, where I left my car in the care of the chief, Nkosi Ludwig Kapungu. Chief Ludwig was the head of a small group of Ngoni descended from tribesmen who had fled from South Africa at the beginning of the nineteenth century in order to escape from the warriors of Chaka, the powerful Zulu ruler. The invasion of Southern Tanganyika by the Ngoni led to the defeat of some of the existing tribal communities there, but the Ngoni also succeeded in bringing together certain groups of Mbunga, Ngindo, Pogoro and other tribes which had previously lived in isolation. The Ngoni introduced negotiating skills which were practised in dealing with coastal traders, and military tactics which were used later in the century in their resistance against the German colonial forces. By the late 1950s, there were about 60,000 Ngoni living in Songea District and about 5,500 in Ulanga. Their influence was far greater than their numbers might suggest.

I held a public meeting, generally referred to as a *baraza,* at Kilosa-kwa-Mpepo. I was pleased with what I found there. Nkosi Ludwig Kapungu was energetic, intelligent, and, as far as I could judge, completely honest. I discovered later that he was also brave. I praised him for the way he ruled his chiefdom, the cleanliness of his village, the excellent state of the school, the dispensary, the local authority buildings, tax collection, and the administration of justice in his Court. I told him I was looking forward to seeing him again on my way home from Matumbi a couple of weeks later.

When I had written to the Nkosi from the Boma about my plans to call at his village and then continue my safari as far as Matumbi, I had asked him to engage porters to carry my loads. I told him that I had arranged to send two bicycles down from Mahenge to await my arrival. I intended to travel by bicycle with my messenger, Vitalis Cyril, while the porters and Mohamed, my cook, went by foot. During the time I saved by riding a bicycle, I hoped to meet as many local villagers as possible and to listen to their problems. I wanted to learn as much as I could about each of the places I was passing through.

After spending a day and a night at Kilosa-kwa-Mpepo, everything was ready for us to set off early the following morning. As expected, it took us five days to reach Matumbi. I slept in a tent each night, and the journey was uneventful.

Matumbi was exceptional in three ways: it had a special dispensation from the rule that Local Courts were required to submit their cash and records to the Boma at least once a month; its Chief was a woman; and it had no visible sign of economic activity.

The Chief of Matumbi was a woman called Ottilia Filiang'afu. I guessed that her father's name was Ng'afu and that she had learnt from Italian missionaries at Ifinga, a few miles away, to refer to herself as 'filia' – the Latin word for daughter. She was middle aged and seemed pleasant and intelligent. She had completed Standard VI at school. This was an achievement, since she must have gone to school at a time when education for African girls, even those of high birth, was not yet thought of as being particularly important. I assumed she was married, but I did not meet her husband. In contrast to most of her subjects, the clothes she wore were clean and tidy. There were not many civil or criminal cases in her Court, but she appeared to deal with them justly and without undue delay. Her people appeared to respect her, and I saw no reason to blame her personally for the backwardness of her chiefdom.

Chief Ottilia was accompanied by a man who seemed to fulfil the role of court jester. He was an extraordinary figure. He jumped up and down, squatted close to the ground and twirled his legs round at great speed like a Cossack dancer. He then leapt high up into the air and put his face within inches of mine, grinning at me in a way which I found extremely disconcerting. All the teeth on the left side of his upper jaw and all the teeth on the right side of his lower jaw had been removed. I have no idea how he managed to chew his food. His energy and agility were astonishing, but he looked hideous. As Chief Ottilia showed me round her village, he followed a few feet behind us, making grunting noises. I did not hear him speak coherently and wondered what accounted for his strange behaviour, but thought it would be impolite to ask.

The feature of Matumbi which particularly struck me was the

lack of a money economy. The farmers saw no sense in attempting to grow cash crops when there was no trader to buy them, and the nearest market was five days' walk away. This meant that the people grew only food crops. The land was very sparsely populated, and the method of cultivation they adopted was to burn and slash down forests, plant their crops on hilly soil until the topsoil was eroded, then move on to repeat the process somewhere else. None of the farmers knew or cared about soil conservation. They did not have enough money to buy tools, paraffin, or clothes. None of the men had dressed up in special clothes for my visit. Indeed, some of the clothes they wore were in such tatters that they bordered on indecency. After sunset, all the huts were dark.

I was told that men usually had to go to other parts of the country to seek temporary or permanent employment in order to earn money to pay poll tax for themselves and their relatives. In other parts of the country there might be famine when there was too much or too little rain, but when I visited Matumbi the people did not seem to be starving. They were just desperately poor. Until links could be created with the rest of the country, I could see no way for them to escape from their grinding poverty.

The people of Matumbi saw so few Europeans that I was welcomed more warmly there than in other villages where political discontent was becoming rife. Nobody shouted '*Uhuru!*' at me.

While I was at Matumbi, I received an invitation to have supper with the Father Superior of Ifinga Mission. Ifinga was just inside the administrative district of Ulanga, but it was not in the same diocese as the Capuchin Missions in Ulanga District. I believe it was part of the vicariate of the Benedictines of Saint Ottilien at Peramiho, in Songea District. This might have been the reason why the Chief of Matumbi was called Ottilia.

The Father Superior, accompanied by a servant with a lamp, arrived at my camp as the sun was going down, and we started to walk to Ifinga. It was quite dark by the time we got there, so I was not taken round the Mission, but got the impression that the buildings were unnecessarily large for such a small congregation. The meal which the two of us ate together was not very appetising. It was served on a big refectory table whose size was not conducive to informal conversation between two strangers. The Father Superior seemed kind and sincere, but I think he was extremely lonely, as indeed I would have been working on my own in such a place. He told me how pleased he was to welcome me, and when I left to return to the camp, he insisted on coming with me and carrying the lamp himself. It was late in the night when I got back to my tent, and he then had to walk back to the mission.

I had very mixed feelings about Matumbi. I felt that the Government as a whole, and the British officials stationed in Ulanga, had been guilty of neglect, and that the area could have made more progress if we had provided active help and encouragement. At the same time, when I compared the incredibly primitive standard of living in Matumbi with the progress being made in other parts of the country, I appreciated more fully what had been achieved the during the period of British rule in those areas which were visited regularly on safari.

The journey back to Mahenge was more eventful than the outward journey had been. I set off by bicycle from Matumbi with Vitalis, and we had not been riding very long when, quite unexpectedly, it started to rain. I was wearing a shirt and shorts, and was soon soaked to the skin. I was also rather worried that the rain might make the road back from Kilosa-kwa-Mpepo impassable for my car. The rain stopped as suddenly as it had started, but the path along which we were riding had some quite deep puddles. I glimpsed to my left, and saw a small herd of elephants about a hundred yards away. While I was looking in their direction, my bicycle suddenly came to an abrupt halt, with the front wheel stuck in a deep pot-hole. As the bicycle came to a halt, I was thrown forward, and one brake handle penetrated the skin of my right thigh. We looked to see what had made the pot-hole, and discovered that it was the footprint of a very large elephant.

The bicycle was not damaged, and the wound bled a little, but did not seem serious, so we carried on. When the porters arrived in camp with the loads that evening, I unpacked my first-aid kit, applied some antiseptic cream to my thigh, and thought no more about it. However, by the time we got to Kilosa-kwa-Mpepo four days later, my leg was swollen and inflamed.

We reached Kilosa-kwa-Mpepo at about noon. In normal circumstances I would have been pleased to see his enthusiasm and initiative, but I was concerned to learn that Nkosi Ludwig had convened another *baraza* on his own initiative, even though it was only two weeks since I had held the previous one. I wanted to get back to Mahenge with as little delay as possible, but I agreed to hold the *baraza* on the understanding that it would be a short one.

While we were all exchanging the usual greetings, a young Ngoni rushed into the court building and spoke to Chief Ludwig in Kingoni. Ludwig then turned to me, and asked, in Swahili, 'Have I your permission to go and shoot a lion?' I agreed, and five minutes later I heard wild jubilations and ululations in the village. The lion was dead. Its carcass was then dragged to the space in front of the court building, while the rejoicings became louder and louder, and the crowd got bigger.

The lion had died of two bullet wounds, but it had already been in very poor condition. It had no flesh on its body, and its ribs stuck out in a way which reminded me of photographs of concentration camp victims. I congratulated Nkosi Ludwig on his marksmanship, and he explained what had happened.

While he and his wife and children were all in bed the preceding night, they had heard a big animal inside their room. Ludwig Kapungu thought it was a hyena, and picked up his rifle and told his family to stand behind him while he shot at the animal, although he could not see it as the house was completely dark at the time. The animal escaped, and Ludwig then lit a lamp and discovered bloodstains and what he identified as a lion's footprints. At dawn he sent out all the young men he could get hold of, and told them to go and trace the wounded lion. The man who had spoken to him in the court had just spotted it sheltering under an evergreen shrub less than five yards from the path along which Vitalis and I had just been cycling.

The lion was near to starvation, and I presumed it was looking for a human child to eat, but I felt sorry for it that it had chosen to enter the house of one of the very few Africans in Ulanga District who owned a rifle. Permits to own rifles were very strictly controlled.

Driving my car back to Mahenge was agonisingly painful. My leg was swollen, red, and throbbing, and it hurt to press the accelerator. Applying the footbrake was even worse. When I eventually got home, Jennifer sent for Gary Butler, who had recently returned to Ulanga after home leave. He took my temperature, which was over 103°, gave me an anaesthetic, and lanced my suppurating wound. It was some days before he allowed me to get out of bed.

I still have a small scar on my thigh, though it is now barely visible. However, after my family and I finally returned to England, it amused me in a harmelss way to tell people that it had been caused by an elephant.

An Unforeseen Tragedy

It was nearly Christmas by the time I got back from Matumbi. We had invited Peggy Fowler to spend Christmas with us, and she arrived before I had completely recovered. Jennifer's pregnancy was progressing well, but she was not very mobile, so when Father Gerard sent us a present of a large Christmas tree, carried up from Kasita by two young seminarians, Peggy volunteered to decorate the tree herself while Jennifer and I sat and watched.

The tree was looking very festive when Juma, Mohamed, and Omari (all Muslims) came to admire it. Omari suddenly exclaimed that he had seen a snake emerging from the tree, and Juma agreed with him. Jennifer, Peggy, Mohamed, and I had not spotted it, and we could not see it anywhere in the living room. Omari and Juma were convinced they were right, however, and insisted on lifting all our rugs, taking the cushions off the chairs, and looking behind every stick of furniture in the room. They then tackled the bookshelves, while we were becoming more and more sceptical. Omari was just taking the last books out of the bottom shelf when he announced triumphantly that the snake was there, hiding behind the books, and killed it with a piece of wood.

The snake was greenish, less than three feet long, and quite slender. It would have been very hard to spot in the branches of a Christmas tree. I am not an expert on snakes, and had no idea whether or not it was poisonous, but the Africans round us all assured us that its bite was so lethal that its victim would be dead before he reached hospital. We were very thankful that it had not bitten anyone. We did not want to seem ungrateful to Father Gerard, but decided that it was essential to warn him that some of Kasita's other Christmas trees might be harbouring uninvited guests as well. He was horrified, and promised that they would all be examined very closely before being brought into a house or a church to be decorated in time for Christmas.

Jennifer and I were more concerned about Ruth's safety than our own. Snakes cannot move very fast on polished surfaces, and Ruth had occasionally seen me stamp on the heads of small snakes that had managed to get into the house. One day I saw her pretending to stamp on something, and using the Swahili word *nyoka* (snake) as she did so. A small snake would not have been able to bite through my shoes, and I knew where to stamp on it and weighed about sixteen stone, but Ruth often wore rubber flip-flops on her feet, and a snake could easily have nipped her little ankle, or her finger if she had tried to pick it up. Jennifer and I spent a long time explaining that Daddy was allowed to stamp on snakes, but that children were not allowed to do so in any circumstances. I think she understood the message without getting too terrified, or her spirit crushed.

Jennifer and I were not very active over the festive season. The day after Boxing Day, John Crabbe, the Headmaster of Tabora Boys' School, arrived with his wife Dorothy to spend a few days with us. The Crabbes and Peggy all left Mahenge just after New Year. We enjoyed their visit very much, but spent most of the time chatting rather than doing anything energetic.

As the expected date of the baby's birth drew closer, we arranged to move down to Ifakara. The ferry did not operate at night, so expectant mothers who wanted to give birth at the Mission Hospital always spent the last days of their pregnancy on the north bank of the river in case the baby chose to arrive after the sun went down.

Mike Dorey was very considerate. A second general election was to be held later in the year, and he made me responsible for supervising the arrangements for the registration of voters in the northern part of the district. This gave me a valid reason for remaining on duty in Ifakara while Jennifer was waiting to go into labour and be admitted to the Mission Hospital there.

Jennifer, Ruth, and I travelled down to Ifakara towards the end of February. Ina, Mohamed, and Vitalis came too. While we were in Ifakara, a tragic accident occurred for which I felt myself indirectly responsible.

On their most recent visit to Ulanga, auditors from Dar had spotted that a messenger working at the Pogoro Chief's court at Vigoi, a mile or two from Mahenge, had only been appointed on a temporary basis, and that the court therefore had one messenger in excess of its approved complement. The auditors therefore wanted his appointment to be terminated at once.

I was not at all happy about this. The messenger had been working for more than twenty years, and Chief John Mlolera spoke very highly of him. The muddle had occurred through no fault of the messenger's, and I thought it unfair to dismiss him without notice after such long and satisfactory service.

I called him to my office to explain the situation to him, and asked whether he would be willing to accept a transfer to another Local Court as soon as a genuine vacancy arose, subject, of course, to the approval of the chief for whom he might be working. The messenger immediately agreed to this proposal.

A few weeks later, a messenger from Mngeta, one of the Ndamba courts, left his job, and I asked Chief Daftari Mtwanga whether, in the exceptional circumstances, he would agree to interview a highly recommended messenger from Vigoi as a possible replacement, even though he was not a Ndamba tribesman. Chief Daftari accepted him, and the messenger and his family moved down to Mngeta, close to the Kilombero River. Daftari was not one of the most diligent chiefs in Ulanga, but my opinion of him went up when he accepted a member of a different tribe to work in his court.

Soon after he arrived in Mngeta, the messenger was asked to deliver a box of voters' registration papers to the Boma. This task involved making part of the journey in a dug-out canoe.

Ndamba tribesmen are very competent fishermen and learn to handle canoes from an early age, but the Pogoro messenger came from the Mahenge Massif, and was an inexperienced canoeist and a non-swimmer. He capsized the canoe and was drowned. The registration papers were all lost.

The radio news bulletins from Dar contained reports on how the registration of voters had been completed smoothly in all constituencies but one, and after a few days they began to include critical comments naming Ulanga District as the culprit. If the bulletins ever included an explanation of the tragic reason for our delay, I never heard it. It still saddens me that a well-intentioned action of mine should have resulted in the tragic death of the person I had been trying to help.

Ulanga had very few voters, but it would clearly have been wrong to deprive any of them of the opportunity to vote because their registration papers had been lost in the Kilombero, so the process of registering had to be repeated in the area affected. In the event, this proved a waste of time. The TANU candidate was returned unopposed, and none of Ulanga's registered voters needed to go to the polls later in the year.

A Sister for Ruth

Most Government officials staying overnight in Ifakara chose to sleep in a new rest-house a couple of miles north of the village. It was in a quieter situation, and was better equipped than the old one in the centre of the village. It even had a concrete bath, though the water to fill it had to be carried in four-gallon *debes*.

Jennifer and I preferred, on this occasion, to stay as close to the Mission Hospital as possible, even though the rest-house sanitary arrangements were very primitive, and the softboard ceilings were sagging under the weight of bat droppings and urine. At first we found the smell most unpleasant, but we got used to it. As far as bathing was concerned, the doctor and his wife were kind enough to offer us the use of the bathroom and shower in their house attached to the hospital whenever we wanted it.

Rolf Diethelm examined Jennifer soon after we arrived in Ifakara, and said it was not possible to forecast accurately, but he thought the baby might be born within the next day or two. We hoped the waiting would not take too long. Ifakara was much hotter than Mahenge, and we wanted to get home before the rains made the car ferry unserviceable. We were very glad we were already in Ifakara, as there were two occasions when Jennifer thought she was going into labour. These proved to be false alarms, but if they had occurred when we were still in Mahenge we would have had to set off immediately on a journey that would have been very stressful.

For the last week or two before the baby was born, I took Jennifer and Ruth for several evening outings in the car after I had completed the day's work. I did not attempt to avoid pot-holes in the road, as I thought this might hurry things up a bit. I was quite wrong. The baby stayed put, but I managed to break one of the car's rear springs.

We had already been in Ifakara for nearly three weeks before Jennifer was admitted to hospital. She spent much of each day sitting playing with Ruth on the rest-house verandah, but our social life was, if anything, even more active than in Mahenge. Anyone who was travelling to or from Mahenge had to pass through Ifakara, and there were others whose journey ended at Ifakara. We had over thirty visitors of all races in the days leading up to Jennifer's confinement, and we were often invited by Rolf and Charlotte Diethelm to their house. Ruth particularly enjoyed going there, not just to have a bath in their bathroom but also to play with a pet monkey which really belonged to Karl Schöpf, but which the Diethelms were looking after while Karl was on leave.

One evening the Diethelms had supper in the rest-house with us, and after supper we listened to records of Mozart's *Don Giovanni*. They invited us back to listen to Richard Strauss's *Ariadne auf Naxos* the following evening, but Archbishop Edgar Maranta arrived unexpectedly from Dar, so we all spent the evening chatting instead. We listened to *Ariadne auf Naxos* on a later evening, and enjoyed it very much.

The Archbishop was a delightful and unassuming man whom we had already met at Father Gerard's golden jubilee celebration at Kwiro. He was always sweet to our children. When he was paying us a visit in Mahenge he took off his gold ring and let Ruth play with it. After Catherine was born, he brought us up a bundle of new nappies which Peggy had bought on our behalf in Dar. I doubt whether many Anglican babies have had their nappies delivered in person to their homes by a Roman Catholic Archbishop.

Jennifer started to go into labour one evening when we had two young bachelors from the Water Development Department having a meal with us. She was embarrassed about mentioning to them what was happening, and concentrated on appearing unperturbed. Being preoccupied, she was less careful than usual about mosquitoes in the house that night.

The labour was a long one, and Jennifer did not need to be admitted to hospital until early the next morning. Ruth and I spent most of the day with her, but in the late afternoon I took Ruth to the Diethelms' house to play with the monkey and chat to Charlotte, whom Ruth referred to as 'Mrs Doctor', while I returned to be near to Jennifer.

Catherine Jane was born soon after five o'clock on 17th March – Saint Patrick's Day. My first glimpse of her was when she was one minute old, being carried upside down by Sister Alphonsina, who held her feet between the fingers of one hand. After Catherine had been washed and dressed properly, and put in a Moses basket ready to meet her big sister for the first time, I went to the Diethelms' house. I did not tell Ruth that Mummy had had her baby, but invited her to come with me and find out for herself. She scampered along, holding my hand. As soon as we got to the room where Jennifer was in bed, Ruth rushed to the

Moses basket in the corner and exclaimed triumphantly, 'There she is!' The idea that the baby might be a boy did not appear to cross her mind.

I sent telegrams to Jennifer's mother and mine to tell them the news. My mother seemed quite pleased, but Frances replied to the effect that she hoped we were not too disappointed that it was only another girl. Catherine was just as perfect as Ruth. I was very angry at Frances's reaction to the birth of a second grand-daughter. Right up to her death, Frances adored her first grand-child, Ruth, and her first grandson, Philip, who was born nearly two years after Catherine. She bought Ruth and Philip generous presents, but showed little interest in Catherine, who was just as sweet, pretty, and intelligent as her brother and sister. Catherine was not to blame at all. Frances was prejudiced against her before they had ever met, simply because of her gender. My own mother, on the other hand, was especially fond of Catherine. I find it very odd that grandmothers can discriminate between their own grandchildren in such a way.

Ruth was thrilled to have a sister, and sat on Jennifer's bed holding the baby on her lap. When Catherine was three days old, Ruth suddenly did what she had often seen African women do, and took her dress off her shoulder, and tried to breast-feed Catherine.

The rains were starting to fall heavily, and when Catherine was six days old we were told that the ferry would close before Jennifer could leave hospital. I decided to take the car across the river and drive up to Mahenge with Ruth, Ina and Mohamed and as much luggage as I could get into the car. Ruth thought it a great adventure to get the house ready for Mummy and her new baby. We spent one night in Mahenge before we drove down again. I then left my car on a small mound beside the road on the south bank of the river, about a hundred yards from the ferry.

When Catherine was nine days old, Jennifer suddenly became unwell. She had a very high fever, and Rolf Diethelm feared she might be getting some sort of post-natal complication. He took some tests, and came back smiling, 'Thank God for that,' he said, 'it's only malaria!'

Jennifer had taken her prophylactic pills regularly, but they were not 100% reliable, and the mosquitoes in the rest-house the night before Catherine's birth had caused Jennifer's very first attack of malaria.

Rolf advised us to go back to Mahenge as soon as possible. Jennifer was not well, but she was not in any serious danger.

Malaria was a killer for young children, however, and, if a mosquito were to bite first Jennifer and then Catherine, it could be fatal. There were no mosquitoes in Mahenge, so we decided to return home the following morning.

After we told him of our plans to return to Mahenge, Rolf thought it might be our last opportunity to hear a magnificent new recording he had just bought. He brought his record player into Jennifer's room and played us the whole of Richard Strauss's *Salome*, fortissimo.

The oldest and most experienced nun at the hospital, Sister Arnolda, sat outside the door. Sister Arnolda was in reality sweet and gentle, but she did not care for *Salome*, and was not going to pretend to anyone that she did. She remained silent and stony-faced throughout the opera.

Catherine did not much like *Salome* either, and made her views on the matter known by crying continuously from the first bar to the last, not quite drowning the lascivious screeches of the soprano singing the role of Salome and the pulsatingly erotic rhythms of *The Dance of the Seven Veils*. Rolf himself was the only member of the audience who seemed to be enjoying it.

Jennifer told me next day, when we were on our journey back to Mahenge, that the music had made her headache much worse. There are many operas by Richard Strauss which we both enjoy, but *Salome* is not one of them.

My car was waiting for us on the far side of the river, so we started our journey in an open diesel lorry owned and driven by Rajabali Ladha, one of the Indian shopkeepers in Ifakara. The first stage was from the rest-house to the hospital. Mohamed, Vitalis and I supervised the loading of our luggage on to the back of the lorry, and Rajabali then drove to the hospital to pick up Jennifer and the other passengers.

Jennifer sat in the front seat with a Norwegian doctor called Louise Aal, who was doing research at the hospital. I stood in the back of the lorry with Ruth. Sister Alphonsina in her white robes sat on a crate holding Catherine in a carry-cot. Also in the back of the lorry were Ina, Mohamed, Vitalis, the care-taker of the rest-house, and about half-a-dozen other Africans who had come to make themselves useful. Two of them were holding a stretcher, in case Jennifer needed to be carried. There were four-teen people in the back of the lorry and three in the front. As we left the hospital, Sister Arnolda, the African nurses and medical staff, the Fathers and Brothers working in the Mission, and every patient who was able to get out of bed came to see us off. Rolf and Charlotte Diethelm followed behind the lorry in their Landrover.

Rajabali had arranged for one of his African employees to walk through the floods in front of the lorry, pointing out the line of the submerged road. The lorry bubbled along very slowly indeed. Rolf and Charlotte had to abandon their Landrover and follow us on foot. Ruth – and everyone else including Rolf himself – burst into fits of laughter as Rolf tripped and fell face first into the floods, creating a splendid splash.

Rajabali drove extremely carefully, while the water got deeper and deeper, rising first to the guide's knees, then to his thighs, then his hips. When the floods were as high as the guide's waist, Rajabali leaned out of the driver's window and called up to me to say that he did not think he could drive his lorry any further. No one disagreed with him. He had done a splendid job.

We waited for some minutes for a large canoe to arrive. When it did, Jennifer got into it, followed by Ruth and me, Sister Alphonsina and Catherine, Ina, Mohamed, Vitalis, and our luggage. We said goodbye to the others who had accompanied us on the first part of our journey, and thanked everyone, especially Rolf, Charlotte, and Rajabali very warmly indeed for all their help and kindness.

There were dozens of children on each side of the submerged road trying to catch small fish that were swimming around in large numbers. While we were in the canoe crossing the river slowly from north to south, a load of passengers who had come down from Mahenge in N G Gokhale's bus crossed us, wading through the water for the last few miles into Ifakara.

One of the passengers was a Capuchin Father. He had lifted his white cassock to stop it getting wet, and I was surprised to see that he was wearing a pair of bright purple underpants. Many of the African passengers were carrying assorted baskets and bundles of luggage on their heads. One had even got a bicycle balanced on the top of his head. They all greeted us with enormous enthusiasm, and were thrilled to see Jennifer's new baby.

Jennifer found it much more restful to travel by canoe than by road, but in the middle of the river there was a stretch of the road which was not yet flooded. There was no alternative but to cross that by foot. We all got out of the first canoe, and Jennifer held my arm as we walked very slowly for about a mile to where a second canoe was waiting for us at the other end of the sandbank.

The journey in the second canoe was more adventurous than the first. There was a slight breeze, and the weather was overcast.

It looked as if it might start to rain any minute. We were surrounded by a large group of hippos who opened their mouths very wide, snorted, and wiggled their ears at us. They seemed perfectly friendly, but hippos are large and can occasionally be aggressive.

Ruth was very happy. Crossing the river thrilled her. Jennifer's memory of it consists of psychedelic colours and a total lack of worry, presumably caused by the drugs Rolf had given her to deal with malaria and having had a baby. My own feeling on reaching the south bank of the Kilombero was one of profound thankfulness and relief. My love for Jennifer and our two little daughters had made me feel desperately vulnerable as we were all crossing the river. I also managed to spare a thought for Sister Alphonsina and the others who had come with us so far, and would be crossing the river a second time to get back to Ifakara. I silently prayed that we would all reach our destinations safely.

We had a drink of fruit juice and ate a few sandwiches before continuing our journey by car. The first four miles had taken over three hours, but we had an unexpected piece of good fortune before we drove away. One of the two bachelors who had had a meal with us the evening before Catherine was born met us. He was also on his way to Mahenge, and offered to follow us in the Water Development Department's Landrover and to help in any emergency. I found this offer very reassuring.

The road up to Mahenge was as muddy as I had ever seen it. The bus which had carried passengers down to the Kilombero earlier in the day had churned up the mud and left enormous ruts, but luckily for us the worst damage had been caused on the stretches of road where the bus had been going uphill, and we were going downhill at those places. From time to time we skidded alarmingly, and the hairpin bends on the escarpment leading up into Mahenge itself were nightmarish, but we reached home at last. It had taken well over five hours to travel less than fifty miles. Juma, Omari, and our dogs were all delighted to see us again, and to meet Catherine for the first time.

We had another problem to deal with on our return. Ina was a widow, but when she had been hanging out some clothes of Ruth's to dry I had spotted that she was pregnant. She wanted to go on working for us for as long as possible, but she did not think that she would be able to continue after her baby was born. This meant looking for a replacement for her.

Ruth was extremely fond of Ina, and we wanted her to have the chance to get to know her new ayah before Ina left. We took on a young woman called Louisa (she spelt it Lwiza) whom Ina wanted to train for the job. At first Louisa seemed keen and pleasant, but she was a disappointment. After a couple of weeks she failed to arrive at work, and Ina told us that she was now interested only in her new boyfriend, and would not be coming back to us. We then took on a more mature woman called Evona. Evona was casually employed as a wardress at Mahenge Prison whenever there was a female prisoner there, but that happened very rarely, and we thought it was worth engaging a woman who was used to responsibility. When we interviewed Evona she seemed kind and reliable, but she too was a disappointment, and Ruth, who usually got on well with everybody, did not appear to like her at all.

We were glad when Ina had a little daughter Maria, and asked if she could have her old job back. Other members of Ina's family had offered to help her care for her new baby. Ruth was absolutely delighted. Sadly, after the death of her little son Joseph while Ina was with us in Dar during my illness, she did not want ever to leave Mahenge again, so we were only able to employ her until the end of my tour in Ulanga, unlike Juma, Omari, and Mohamed, who all came back to us after the end of our home leave.

The End of a Tour

Catherine was born two years after we had arrived in Ulanga, and tours for expatriates normally lasted two and a half years. When we got back from Ifakara with our new daughter at the end of March, Jennifer and I started planning for our next leave.

We were determined that we would not repeat the mistake we had made on our previous leave of attempting to divide our time equally in the houses of two over-possessive mothers. Both our mothers had counted every minute we spent in Surrey and in the Isle of Wight respectively, and each one claimed that her rival was getting more than her fair share. My mother had asserted that she was still employed as a hospital doctor, and could only be with us after normal working hours, so we ought to spend twice as many days at her house near Ventnor as we spent at Frances's house in Churt. That method of calculation would enable her to spend the same number of hours in our company as Frances.

Frances, on the other hand, had insisted that, as my mother

could only be with us in the evenings after she finished work, this meant that any day we spent on the Isle of Wight was a day wasted. It was obvious (to Frances) that we ought to spend the whole of our leave at her house in Surrey. She even tried to persuade her doctor to order Jennifer to remain in her centrally-heated house rather than risking her own health and Ruth's by being exposed to the cold conditions in my mother's house, which did not have central heating.

I suppose it would have been even worse if neither of our mothers had wanted to see us at all, but we had not enjoyed being wrangled over. We did not want to go through the same arguments a second time, so I wrote from Mahenge to seek the help of my godfather, Hugh Raymond, a retired naval commander who lived in Hayling Island. We decided to spend our forthcoming leave on Hayling Island, partly because it was my birthplace and had a pleasant beach, but mainly because it was was halfway between Churt and Ventnor.

Hugh negotiated with the owner of the house next door to his own, a prep-school headmaster, and rented very cheaply on our behalf for the winter months a delightful detached house near the sea. The owner continued to pay the gardener, and we ourselves engaged the gardener's wife as a daily cleaner. In fact, Mrs Evans was so besotted with Catherine that it was Jennifer and I who did most of the domestic chores while she spent many happy hours holding Catherine on her lap.

Our leave in Hayling Island proved far more enjoyable than our previous leave had been. We took full advantage of the chance to invite our own friends to visit us, and not to have to fit in with routines which took little account of the needs of small children.

Our lives continued to be eventful during our last six months in Ulanga. Some incidents were sad, others cheerful, but things were never dull there. On Good Friday, Laurie Butler, the doctor's wife, gave birth to a baby boy, William, in Ifakara Hospital. Sadly, he was very severely handicapped, and only survived until Whit Sunday. He was buried in a shady corner of the Butlers' garden.

On Ruth's third birthday at the end of April, we gave a party in our garden for Ruth and all her friends with their parents. Ruth found an extremely large and hairy caterpillar, and picked it up. Her arm immediately turned bright red and became very swollen. She was scared and in considerable pain. Fortunately Gary Butler had brought his little black medicine-case with him, and immediately gave her an injection of what I believe was adrenalin. This quickly cured the effects of the hairy caterpillar, but it made Ruth overactive. She did not stop scampering round the garden and the house at full speed until the not-so-early hours of the following morning. All the other children had gone to bed, and their parents had done the same, but Ruth's energy was inexhaustible, and Jennifer and I thought we ought to stay up with her.

The flooding of the Kilombero continued for longer than in previous years, and in the middle of May there were places where the river was still about seven miles wide. Before the floods subsided, I went on safari by motor boat upstream from Ifakara towards the villages of Chita and Merera.

Before I set off, one of the Fathers from Ifakara Mission came to look for me at Nkosi Ahamadi Mahawanga's Court to ask for my help. He told me that Father Balthasar of Mchombe Mission was desperately ill with what was believed to be a combination of pneumonia, malaria, and dysentery. There was no doctor at Mchombe, and Father Balthasar was being nursed by a lay sister called Sister Olive Schmidt. He could not possibly make the journey along the flooded road back to Ifakara Hospital, even if porters carried him on a stretcher. His only hope of getting the skilled medical attention he needed urgently was if he could be brought to the point on the Kilombero River that was nearest to Mchombe, and then travel the rest of the way in the Boma motor boat.

I agreed to help, but I said that I was not planning to visit Mchombe, and that the Fathers at Ifakara would themselves have to get the message to Mchombe Mission that I would be waiting for Father Balthasar the following Thursday evening at the confluence of the Kihanji and the Kilombero Rivers.

Just after I had agreed this plan with the Father from Ifakara, I happened to recognise one of the Africans who came to me with a complaint against his village elder. He was a Ndamba tribesman, and told me he was afraid to take it to his local chief as the village elder was one of the chief's cronies, so he had come to Ifakara to try to get help there. He was the cook at Mchombe Mission. I told him I refused to help him until he helped me first. I promised to deal with his complaint, but only after he had done me a favour by delivering an extremely urgent letter from me to the Mission at Mchombe. He was as good as his word, and delivered the message, and I later sorted out his problem for him.

I arrived as planned on Thursday afternoon at a mound close to the confluence of the rivers, and Vitalis and Mohamed put up my tent, camp bed, and safari chair. We then all began to wait for

Ulanga – river safari

Father Balthasar. The sun went down, and Mohamed lit my pressure lamp. I had almost lost hope that they would reach us, and was just preparing to have supper and go to bed when I heard a group of people wading through the floods towards my tent. The reeds were so tall that I could not see them until they were only a few yards away. Father Balthasar was sitting in a deck-chair which was tied to two long bamboo poles. A gang of porters had been taking turns to carry him for nearly ten hours. He was barely conscious when he arrived, and I told Sister Olive that Father Balthasar was welcome to spend the night in my camp bed while I slept in the motor boat. I suggested that she should use my safari chair.

Sister Olive nursed Father Balthasar until he fell asleep, and I wondered whether he would survive the night. Olive then changed her shoes. She did not make any complaint, but I could not help noticing that her feet looked like pieces of raw beefsteak. She had walked for many miles through the floods in unsuitable shoes which had rubbed great patches of the skin from her feet. She must have been in pain herself, but she ignored her own needs in order to care first for her patient.

Olive and I then ate a meal that Mohamed had prepared some hours previously, and we all tried to get some rest. The motor boat was not at all comfortable, but I must have slept quite soundly on it. During the night, a rat chewed a corner of my pyjamas without my noticing it.

Next morning, the porters set off by foot through the floods to get back to Mchombe, and those of us who were travelling in the motor boat all embarked on our return to Ifakara. As soon as we got there, Father Balthasar was admitted to hospital and began, very slowly, to recover.

Shortly before Jennifer and I went on leave, Father Gustav, the Vicar General, visited our house and told us that the Mission wanted Sister Olive to spend a few months in England in order to improve her English. He asked us if we would be willing to have her to stay with us in England. Olive had trained as a nurse in a children's hospital in Switzerland, and loved children. She would like to help us with Ruth and Catherine in exchange for her board and lodging and an opportunity to converse with us in English. We agreed immediately, and while we were on leave we found Olive a great help and a delightful companion.

Communications in Ulanga were always erratic, especially during the rainy season. In 1959, towards the end of the government financial year, the Provincial Commissioner had sent a message to Ulanga to ask if we would agree to the transfer of a small unspent balance in one of our votes to another district which was in danger of overspending its allocation. He then sent a reminder. He then sent a telegram. This was followed by a furious additional reminder by telegram, asking why we had not replied to his earlier communications. All four documents reached Mahenge in the same mailbag on the head of the same porter.

In 1960, the problem was even worse than in other years. It was not just the floods which caused delays. The African Postal Workers' Union convened a series of strikes, and Mahenge's postmaster was a union member and went on strike. The strikes had no chance of success. In the larger Post Offices there were Asian and European employees who carried on working normally, and the country was much too poor to meet the strikers' demands for huge pay increases.

While the postmaster in Mahenge was out on strike, however, those of us who wanted letters posted relied on colleagues who were visiting Morogoro or Kilosa to take our letters with them and post them at a Post Office that was still functioning. The strike leaders were obstinate and vain, and refused to enter into negotiations involving compromise about their demands. The strikers eventually came to the conclusion that low earnings were better than no earnings at all, and returned to work. Union leaders then claimed it as a great triumph that the employers had agreed not to victimise any of the strikers after the strike ended.

Robin Blackall, the Field Officer in the Agricultural Department, went on leave at the end of May, and resigned from Government Service in Tanganyika in order to train to become an agricultural missionary with the Church Missionary Society in Nigeria. Robin was a hard-working and popular colleague, and, the night before he left Mahenge, Jennifer and I hosted a farewell party for him in our house which was attended by twenty-three people.

We heard early in June that Ozzy Mwambungu had married Blandinah Robert, but none of his colleagues at Mahenge got to the wedding. Also in the first half of June, I went down with a particularly nasty tummy bug which led to my admission once more to Ifakara Hospital. I remained there for about a week.

I recovered more quickly from that than I had from brucellosis, and in the middle of July I was selected to represent Ulanga in the Provincial Athletics Championships. I was then selected to represent Eastern Province in the Territorial Athletics Championships. That year both functions took place in Morogoro, and Jennifer, Ruth and Catherine came with me. We were invited to stay with the Provincial Agricultural Officer, Jim Tuckett, and his family.

My partner in the Eastern Province team in both the discus and shot events was John Hucks, Geoffrey and Aline's son, who was nearly seven feet tall, and towered over me. Neither of us was able to defeat a white Protestant missionary from the United States, who was representing Northern Province, and had the physique and appearance of an amiable gorilla. There was no racial discrimination about who was selected to compete in which event, but it was noticeable that Africans were far more successful than Europeans in the track and jumping events, where speed and stamina were needed, but that heavily built Europeans usually did well in the events that depended largely on strength and technique. The atmosphere at inter-racial athletics championships was always very friendly, although local rivalries sometimes made for rowdy behaviour at football matches.

While we were still in Morogoro, I was given a task which kept us there longer than I had expected. I was asked to meet a number of trains on their way down to the coast from Kigoma, on Lake Tanganyika. The trains were carrying hundreds of Belgian refugees fleeing from the violence that was engulfing the Congo after the army had mutinied there. I had a degree in French, and was given the job of acting temporarily as interpreter and welfare officer for those passengers who were not able to communicate in either English or Swahili.

It was a harrowing experience. When Jennifer and I had spent part of our honeymoon in the Congo four years previously, we had both been appalled at the way the Belgian regime exploited Africans while the Belgians themselves lived in affluence. We had also been uneasy, even then, about the way that the Belgian authorities tolerated the divisions which existed between the Tutsi aristocracy and the Hutu majority. The Hutu seemed to have no share in the country's administration. It was no surprise that independence in a country that had been badly administered as a colony should be followed by disorder.

However much one might feel, as Jennifer and I did, that the Belgians were largely to blame for their own predicament, I felt very sorry for the individual refugees I was trying to help. They had left their homes in haste, often without time to collect even the barest essentials for the journey. My aim was to ask passengers what they needed urgently, and to arrange for it to be distributed in as humane a way as possible, and to let them know that more help would be provided after their train reached the coast.

I did not have the time to ask many questions, but I gathered that some of the women had been raped or violently attacked. There were far more women than men on the trains, and many did not know whether their husbands were alive or dead. Nearly all the children and some of their mothers were sobbing. They seemed hungry, shocked and bewildered at what was going on. A few of the very young ones were sleeping uneasily in their mothers' arms.

The Belgians had transferred power without giving adequate preparation either to the Europeans who would have to start a new life in Belgium, or to African political leaders. Many of the country's new rulers turned out to be even more ruthless and corrupt than their former colonial bosses, and managed to outdo them in impoverishing a mineral-rich country for their own personal gain.

People sing the praises of a democratic form of government, but its success depends on the ability of voters to distinguish between honest candidates and rogues. Adolf Hitler was democratically elected, and the voters in the Congo were less sophisticated than voters who gave power to the Nazis.

Before we left for Morogoro, Gary Butler had vaccinated Catherine against smallpox, but it had not taken. Immediately we got back home it had to be done again.

A few days after our return, I felt slightly unwell and had some mild aches and pains. A day or so later, Ruth had the same symptoms. After a few more days, Juma's young granddaughter, who was visiting her grandparents, became ill. Gary Butler diagnosed polio, and she suffered very slight paralysis in one leg. Gary's daughter Helen had had polio severely, and Gary suggested to us that we might want Catherine to be inoculated against the disease. He than warned us that there was a risk, albeit a small one, that inoculating a child for polio while a smallpox vaccination had not yet healed might result in permanent brain damage.

We were very worried, but decided that polio for a child who was not yet mobile would be a lesser evil than brain damage, and we declined Gary's offer. Fortunately, Juma's granddaughter made a full recovery, and Catherine did not become ill at all. I still have no idea whether or not Ruth and I had both had an extremely mild attack of polio, or whether Juma's granddaughter had caught the illness from someone else.

During our last few weeks in Ulanga, there were a number of changes. Roger Searle had started his career very well, but cadets were still required to serve in two or more districts during their first tour, and he had been transferred elsewhere. He was replaced by John Illingworth, a District Officer starting his second tour of service. John spent only a short time in Mahenge itself, and was then moved to a new sub-station in Ifakara. I did not work with him for long, but I liked him very much, and thought him exceptionally competent.

At about that time we got an unexpected letter from Teddy Kingdon, my first District Commissioner. He said he would like to pay a visit to Mahenge, and asked if it would be convenient for us if he spent a couple of days with us. We were delighted to extend an invitation to stay for as long as he could manage. Jennifer did not yet know him well, but we both found it a very great pleasure to welcome him as our guest, and to show off our two daughters, whom he had not met before.

Another arrival in Mahenge was a new cadet who arrived on first appointment after completing the Overseas Service Course at Oxford. He seemed pleasant enough on first acquaintance. Teddy Kingdon's recent visit had reminded me of all the kindnesses he had shown to me when I was still a cadet, in particular when he offered me the use of his car while he was on home leave. I thought it would be a friendly act to make a similar offer to the new cadet when Jennifer and I went on leave.

This proved to be a great mistake. When I got my car back at the end of my leave, I saw that it had a big dent caused by 'an unavoidable tree' (his words, not mine). The cadet wrote me a letter which I regarded as both ungrateful and discourteous. The gossip I heard from former colleagues still in Mahenge contained nothing complimentary about either his work or his conduct there, and he did not stay in Tanganyika very long.

We also had fairly long visits from the Provincial Superintendent of Police, Charles Sutcliffe, and John Adams, the experienced District Officer appointed to carry out the inquiry into the misdeeds of Chief Rafael Njahite of Mtimbira. The thorough investigation led to Njahite's deposition by order of the Governor. I never met the man appointed to be the new Chief of Mtimbira, but he could not have failed to be an improvement on Njahite.

Another visit was by a senior official from the Secretariat, Paul Haile, a plump red-faced man who told me that after my leave I would be posted as District Officer in Songea, in Southern Province. I told him this was a posting I did not want. He replied in a way I found extremely pompous that he was 'a Founder Member of the Friends of Southern Province League'. I replied that I had already visited Songea on a Governor's safari and had served as Provincial Commissioner's Staff Officer in Southern Province, and that if there were any of my colleagues who actually liked the place, then they were welcome to go there rather than me. I do not think Paul Haile was very pleased with my reaction.

Jennifer and I decided that, as a farewell gift to the schoolchildren of the district, we would present an athletics trophy to be awarded to the Middle School which won the largest number of points at an annual sports day. I asked one of the best local carpenters to make a carved wooden shield, and was delighted at the quality of the work he did for us.

The first time the sports were held, they attracted a large crowd of spectators. The only Local Authority Middle School beat all the Capuchin Middle Schools very easily, despite the fact that Father Gallus, the Capuchin Education Secretary, had represented Switzerland as a middle-distance runner when he was young. At the end of last race, Sheila Dorey presented the shield to the captain of the team from Nawenge Local Authority Middle School.

The Indian shopkeepers in Ifakara, Mahenge and other trading centres also entered into the spirit of the occasion. They all contributed towards the cost of dozens of small presents, one to be given to each of the children who took part, not just the winners. As a gesture of good-will, it was very welcome.

Asian traders were not always popular with their African customers. One of the bones of contention arose through the Government's policy on price control. This aimed to protect peasant farmers from exploitation in times of either shortage or surplus. District Officers issued price control notices for each of the markets in their districts. These were routinely calculated on the basis of the price the crop would fetch at the coast minus the cost of transport to get it there. The same principle was applied in reverse to imports. The up-country controlled price was made up of the price at the port of entry plus the cost of transport to the market. This seemed quite reasonable, but the system failed to reflect what very often happened. Many farmers did not have proper facilities to store their own produce and prevent it from being eaten by rats or other pests. The farmers of Ulanga had not set up the kind of Growers' Cooperative Unions which existed in some other districts. They therefore sold part of their crop at harvest-time to a local trader, who then kept it until the farmers' own food stocks were running low. Hungry villagers would then return to the trader to buy back the grain they had themselves sold him a few months earlier. When the trader insisted on a price which had been agreed by the Boma but reflected the cost of two journeys which the grain had never actually made, the farmers became angry. TANU made vigorous protests about the way Asian traders were blood-sucking parasites, and I suspect that the traders' generosity on such occasions as a schoolchildren's sports day may have had an ulterior motive.

My successor, Denis Gardner, arrived a few days before we left. I had met him when I was a member of the Higher Standard Swahili Oral examining board which had passed him while I was stationed in Mtwara and he, I believe, was at Kilwa. He seemed very capable, but I never got to know him well.

Parting from friends is always sad, even when one is going on home leave, and we had made very many good friends of all races in Ulanga – as well as one or two enemies. I felt that the District had made real progress in the thirty months we had spent there. The Secretariat had at last decided that the complement of District Officers had not been adequate for the district's needs. When I arrived, I was the only District Officer under the District Commissioner. When I left, there were three.

Early in October, just after Jennifer's birthday, Catherine was christened in Morogoro Church while we were on our way down to Dar to board the ship to England. Peggy Fowler was the only godparent able to get to the service. The former Governor, Lord Twining, now a life peer, had agreed to be Catherine's godfather, but there was no chance of his being able to attend a service together with the other godparents, so the Tucketts, who had invited us all to stay overnight with them in Morogoro, acted alongside Peggy as proxy godparents.

The christening was carried out by a friendly Australian priest called Kevin Engels. It was a simple service, punctuated by a certain lack of solemnity when Ruth announced in a stage whisper audible right through the church, 'He's washing her hair!'

Chapter 8

Songea District

(March–April 1961)

A Tiresome Journey

My family and I left England by sea on board the S.S. *Uganda*, a liner of the British India Steam Navigation Company, on 10th February 1961. We had travelled home on the same ship four months earlier. The comfort and the quality of the service on the homeward journey had, with one exception, been excellent. The crew included many Asian cabin and table stewards who all did their jobs well and courteously. Nearly all of the ship's officers were very friendly, and we felt total confidence in their skill. The only exception was the 'children's hostess', a woman with the status of an officer who appeared to have no interest whatsoever in children, and who sat all day long reading books in those parts of the ship where children were not allowed to go, leaving her subordinate, the 'children's stewardess', on her own to look after the children in the nursery for excessively long hours.

On our journey home to Britain, I had been elected chairman of the passengers' entertainments committee, and just before we arrived the committee asked me to write to the B I Head Office on their behalf in order to complain about the children's hostess. When we got on board the ship for our journey back to Dar, I felt apprehensive that she might have heard that it was I who had complained about her, and seek revenge by being vindictive to Ruth or Catherine.

I need not have worried. As soon as Jennifer and I checked in at the purser's office, the purser himself greeted us with enormous enthusiasm, thanking us for having told the company about the idle and unfriendly children's hostess, whom he himself described as 'ballast'. No passenger had ever bothered to make a complaint about her before, but my letter had triggered off an inquiry into how she was doing her job, and the company had dispensed with her services. A new children's hostess was just about to start her first journey on board the *Uganda*.

The new hostess proved to be extremely hard-working, cheerful, fond of children, and imaginative. She had a huge repertoire of ways to keep children safe and amused when they were playing in the nursery. Jennifer and I were very glad she was so well suited to her job, as we later needed to rely on her far more than we had expected.

It is not easy to go ashore with a baby who cannot yet walk, so when the ship reached Gibraltar, Jennifer stayed on board with Catherine while I took Ruth with me to see the sights. We watched the Barbary apes for a while, then hired a horse-drawn carriage to look round the island. I suspected that there might be fleas in the upholstery when I noticed spots coming up on Ruth's arms and legs, but I was quite wrong. When we got back to the ship, Ruth was completely covered with spots, and the ship's doctor diagnosed chicken-pox. He very reasonably ordered Ruth into the ship's isolation ward to prevent the spread of an epidemic.

The isolation ward was up on the poop deck, right at the stern of the ship, above the propellors. It was much less stable than the cabins in the middle of the ship. It was also subject to extremes of temperature. At night, when the ship was heading eastwards through the Mediterranean, it was so bitterly cold that Jennifer and Ruth needed hot-water bottles to keep themselves warm. As the ship approached the Equator, however, the isolation ward turned into an inferno whenever the tropical sun was beating down in the middle of the day, and the painted metalwork became far too hot to touch with bare hands.

The interior walls were painted a depressing shade of olive green, and the floor was covered with dark green linoleum. There was a huge lock on the door, and heavy iron bars had been placed over the darkened windows. We were told that the lock on the door was to prevent mentally ill passengers from escaping, and the purpose of the bars across the windows was to prevent suicidal passengers from climbing out of a window and throwing themselves overboard. Any urge which passengers might feel to take their own lives would not have been calmed by the exorbitant extra charges for each day spent in the isolation ward, or by the high cost per visit of the ship's doctor.

Ruth was far too young to be left in such a gloomy place on her own, but Jennifer and I were the only people who were available to keep her company night and day. Catherine, fortunately, was quite content to spend several hours each day in the nursery with the hostess or the stewardess, though Jennifer and I took it in turns to give her her meals. Ruth's meals were brought to her by the ship's nurse, and Ruth ate them with Jennifer or me at her side. Other crew members were not allowed to bring meals for Jennifer or me to the isolation ward, and it was not the nurse's job to serve meals to passengers who were perfectly fit. This meant that Jennifer and I both had to eat in the dining saloon, but we were not able to have our meals together. One of us had to look after Ruth while the other was eating a meal. The dining saloon was situated down in the bowels of the ship, about as far away from the isolation ward as it was possible to be. We worked out a routine that I usually ate before Jennifer. As soon as the doors opened, I rushed down to the dining saloon and bolted my meal. I then rushed up to the isolation ward to relieve Jennifer, who then hurried to reach the dining saloon before it closed. Most of the other passengers were nearly finishing their meals by the time Jennifer arrived. At night, we arranged that Jennifer would sleep with Ruth in the isolation ward while I slept in our cabin and looked after Catherine. It was grim.

Most of the other passengers were very sympathetic, but a few were not. One scrawny woman of uncertain age with a very shrill voice advanced towards me and screamed, 'You'll be popular. You'll be the most popular family on the ship!' as if we had given our daughter chicken-pox intentionally, just to endanger the health and safety of our fellow-passengers.

The situation got worse when the ship docked at Port Said. The Egyptian authorities, who were not very friendly to the British so soon after the Suez Crisis, refused to accept the doctor's diagnosis that Ruth had chicken-pox, and tried to insist that she was suffering from smallpox. They threatened, as a precautionary measure, to refuse permission for the ship to pass through the Suez Canal, and only relented when we were able to produce Ruth's internationally valid smallpox vaccination certificate.

When we reached Port Sudan, my morale plummeted still further. A letter was waiting for me from Pip Fraser-Smith, the senior secretariat official who had welcomed Jennifer's mother when she passed through Dar on her way to Mahenge. It was a very friendly letter, and Pip apologised for sending me unwelcome news, but he said he had only just been told of my request to Paul Haile not to be posted to Songea, and by the time he had heard about it, it was too late to post me anywhere else. He sent us all sorts of good wishes and words of encouragement, and hoped I would not find Songea as uncongenial as I feared. I muttered to Jennifer a few uncomplimentary things about Paul Haile, and resolved to make the best of it.

We had a pleasant surprise at Aden. Griff and Betty Farr, whom I had first got to know on my visit to Zanzibar and who had become good friends when I had been stationed in Mtwara, paid us a visit in the isolation ward. Griff had been the Provincial Medical Officer in Southern Province, and had recently been promoted to the post of Director of Medical Services in Aden. Neither he nor Betty was in the least scared of chicken-pox, and they cheered us up enormously by their kindness to us and also to Ruth, whom they had never met before.

When Jennifer and I had got married, Griff and Betty had sent us a cheque for a wedding present, and Griff had sent a covering letter apologising for giving us something as dull as a cheque. He explained that he did not want to send us 'the seventh travelling clock'. If he had in fact sent a travelling clock, it would have been the seventh.

To our surprise, neither Catherine nor any of the other children on board caught chicken-pox. When the ship reached Mombasa, Ruth was discharged from the isolation ward, and we all resumed normal family life.

The ship's doctor sent us his bill, and it was much smaller than we had expected. We asked if he had miscalculated. He replied that he had charged us less than the standard rate as we had been the only passengers to use the isolation ward who had not complained bitterly about it. We certainly would have done if we had thought it might have done any good. We had complained successfully about the former children's hostess, but nothing could be done to improve the isolation ward while we were using it, so we decided on this occasion to suffer in silence. We were glad we had done so.

While we had been on leave in Hayling Island, we had got to know two charming Indian girls of about fifteen. They were pupils together at an independent school in Wiltshire, and we met them while they were spending their school holidays with a couple called Frank and Margaret St George. Frank and Margaret were both teachers who had become good friends of ours.

The girls were not sisters, but they both came from Mombasa, and had written to let their parents know that we would be passing through Mombasa on board the *Uganda*. Their parents invited Jennifer and me to visit them for tea with our children on two consecutive afternoons. It was very kind of both couples to offer hospitality to Europeans whom they had never met, but Jennifer and I found the first afternoon rather disappointing. The mother hardly said a word, while the father spent the whole afternoon telling us how rich he was, how much his house and every article of furniture had cost, and about his plans to enlarge his business and get richer still. Neither of them took any notice of our children, and they did not seem at all interested when we attempted to tell them the latest news about their own daughter in England. It sounds very ungrateful to say so, but we felt that the probable reason for inviting us had been to provide the head of the family with a captive audience while he pontificated about the joys of making money.

After listening to him, Jennifer and I did not look forward much to spending another afternoon in a similar way. However. the second couple we visited were completely different. Neither mother spoke English fluently, but the second one clearly loved children, and got on magnificently with ours. The father asked us for news about the girls in England, about Frank and Margaret, about our journey, and about Tanganyika. He expressed interesting opinions about the political situation in Kenya. The conversation never flagged for a moment, and from time to time the husband interpreted in Gujarati to his wife something he thought she might like explained to her. He was obviously well off, but he did not talk about money and never mentioned the price of anything. We both found them really congenial hosts.

As soon as my posting to Songea was confirmed, we started to plan how to get there. In theory there were three options. Plan A was to collect my car in Dar, and drive south along the coast road as far as Lindi, then change direction and travel westwards through Southern Province as far as Songea, with a lorry following on behind with our baggage. That would probably have been the best choice during the dry season, but the Dar–Lindi road was not passable in March.

Plan B involved making the journey to Southern Province by sea in a coaster called the *Seyyid Khalifa*, which plied to and fro along the coast, calling at Zanzibar and the ports of Kenya and Tanganyika. If the *Uganda* reached Dar in time to connect with the *Seyyid Khalifa* on its southbound journey, this would have been better than attempting the whole journey by road through Eastern Province and Southern Highlands Province, and arriving in Songea from the north-west. Unfortunately, just as the *Uganda* was arriving in Dar harbour, the *Seyyid Khalifa* was leaving, and we would have had to wait a month until its next journey to Southern Province.

This left us with Plan C, which was to make the whole journey by road through Morogoro, Iringa, and Njombe. The drive would take four days, and we would stay overnight in those three places. The final stage of the journey would involve crossing some steep hills to get to Songea. The whole journey would be arduous, and I agreed to travel by that route on the understanding that the District Commissioner of Songea would send his Boma Landrover to meet us in Njombe and accompany us on the last stretch of the journey. I also needed to be sure that my car was in good condition before embarking on such a long and difficult journey with two very young children.

I had written two letters to the cadet who was using our car. I sent one from England and the second from the Mediterranean, but got no reply. I then sent him a telegram from Mombasa, reminding him yet again of his promise that my car would be waiting for me as soon as I got off the ship. However, when we disembarked in Dar there was still no word from the cadet, and no sign of the car. I explained to Pip Fraser-Smith that I could not travel to Songea until my car was returned to me, and he sent a furious telegram to the cadet. Even then he did not bother to deliver the car to me in person. When it at last reached Dar, it was being driven by the Provincial Commissioner's driver from Morogoro, who handed me a letter from the cadet which I found offensive. The car was filthy, badly dented, and in very poor condition. Even if it managed to get as far as Songea without breaking down, it would certainly not last for another tour taking me regularly on safari. I therefore left it with the Peugeot agent in Dar, asking him to sell it on my behalf, and I bought a nearly new Peugeot 403 Station Wagon instead.

When Jennifer and I left Ulanga, Juma and Omari had returned to Tabora for a few months' holiday, and Mohamed stayed in Mahenge. We paid each of them a retainer while we were away, and sent them the money for their fares to Songea. We were convinced that loyal and efficient servants deserved to be treated generously. We arranged for Juma to travel by train from Tabora and meet us in Dar, while Omari made his way independently to Songea, and Mohamed kept an eye on our baggage on its journey by road from Mahenge to Songea.

While I was still waiting for my Peugeot 203 to turn up, I was asked to work for a few days in the Chief Minister's Office. It sounded very grand, but nobody knew how long it would be before I could set off for Songea, so I was given only dull routine tasks to perform. This convinced me that working in an up-country district, however uncongenial that district might be, was preferable to pushing paper in the Secretariat.

The drive from Dar was tiring. We had no problems as far as Iringa, but in Iringa, on her first birthday, Catherine became unwell and had a high temperature. However, the doctor advised us that she was fit enough to continue the journey, and the sooner we reached our destination the better, so the next day we drove on towards Njombe, with dire warnings that the rains were imminent.

Njombe was one of the few districts which I had not visited before, and I liked what I saw of it. It was the only Boma in the country with an altitude of over 6,000 feet above sea level, and the hotel was simple but clean and comfortable. The food was good. All the guests seemed friendly, and there was a huge log fire glowing cosily in the hearth.

One of the guests was Archdeacon Woolley, an Anglican missionary, who apologised to us for having failed to arrive on a pastoral visit to Mahenge while we were there. There was another very elderly guest who told us he had lived in Tanganyika ever since the time of the Germans. The District Commissioner, Bill Tulloch, who was an amusing raconteur, came to see us with his smart wife Georgina.

During the night there was a tropical downpour comparable to the one which had greeted our arrival in Mahenge three years earlier. Next morning we woke up to find Njombe drenched. We had been promised that the District Commissioner at Songea would send his Boma Landrover to Njombe and escort us for the last stage of the journey, through very hilly country. The Landrover had not arrived, and Bill Tulloch showed me a telegram he had received from Len Manson, the District Commissioner at Songea, saying that his Landrover was not available, and asking for the Njombe Landrover to escort us instead. The District Office at Songea would reimburse the cost of using the Njombe Landrover. Bill said this could not be done, as his Landrover was off the road and in need of major repairs. He therefore hired on our behalf the Landrover of a local Indian shopkeeper, asking the trader to submit his invoice directly to the DC at Songea, which he agreed to do.

Our departure was delayed by these negotiations, and we set off later than planned. The road was even worse than we had feared. We had off-loaded everything we would not actually need on the journey into the Landrover, and our Peugeot 403 coped excellently with the steep gradients and the mud on the road, but the journey of a little over 160 miles took nearly ten hours, and it was already dark by the time we reached Songea. The Landrover which was supposed to be escorting us got completely stuck in the mud, and did not reach Songea until the following afternoon.

When at last we reached Songea, we reported our arrival to Len Manson, the DC, who told us he could not put us up himself but had arranged for us to stay for a few days with a young married cadet and his wife, John and Patricia Woodley.

The Woodleys had an enchanting baby daughter who was a few months younger than Catherine. They were perfectly civil to us, but did not hide their displeasure at having been told to put us up, whether or not they wanted to. They explained that they had not been expecting us to arrive until the following day, and that no evening meal had been prepared as they were planning to go to a party at the Songea Club. They suggested that we should go with them, and that their ayah should look after our children as well as theirs.

Jennifer and I were not very happy at the idea of leaving Ruth and Catherine in the care of a stranger in a house they had never seen before, while we went off gallivanting in the Club, but we trusted Juma, who stayed with them. We told him how to reach us if any problem arose. A meal was prepared for the children, and they were both so tired after the journey and their supper that they fell into a deep sleep the moment we put them to bed. They did not wake for hours. The Woodleys gave us time to wash and put on a change of clothing. They then took us with them to the Songea Club, where the party was already in progress. Jennifer and I would have preferred to go straight to bed.

That's Songea – that was!

As we walked with the Woodleys into the Songea Club, we saw two rows of faces glowering at each other from opposite sides of the dance floor. There were a few small groups of people whispering to each other, but others sat in silence. There was dance music playing on the gramophone, but few, if any, members were dancing. The Woodleys were not very gregarious people. The four of us each had a drink and a buffet supper, and sat together chatting, but they did not take us round introducing us to the other members. They saw that we were very tired and anxious in case our children should wake up and be worried by our absence, so we all left as soon as we decently could and went to bed.

There had not been a club in Mahenge, but in every other station where I had served, a member of the club committee would as a matter of course introduce himself to any newly-arrived European, and encourage him and his family to apply for membership. This did not happen to us in Songea. I did not take it as hostility directed at us personally. The whole atmosphere in the club was lugubrious, and nobody seemed to be enjoying the party at all. Jennifer and I accepted that we would in due course be expected to join and take part in the social activities for Europeans, but we felt that membership would be a duty rather than a pleasure. We decided to wait until we had settled in before we visited the club again. In fact, we left Songea without ever applying to join.

Songea was generally regarded as quite an attractive station. The district was described in 1958 in the *Handbook of Tanganyika* as 'fertile and productive, with a valuable tobacco industry and coalfields still to be developed'. To the west of Songea township, the road descended to Lake Nyasa, which I had seen when I was in Rungwe District, and knew to be very beautiful. The Boma was situated in 'pleasant hilly country', 3,800 feet above sea level (slightly higher than Mahenge). Nights were always cool. In 1952, the population of Songea Township consisted of 739 Africans, 196 Asians, and 48 Europeans. The African population of Songea Township was about 50% larger than Mahenge, but the size of the non-native population in Songea was very different. There were nearly three times as many Europeans in Songea as Mahenge, and more than ten times as many Asians. There were also many European missionaries of various denominations working in other parts of the district.

At the time we were there, a regular weekly air service made a circular trip anti-clockwise from Dar via the airports of Southern Highlands Province and Southern Province and back to Dar again. Songea had a bank, a garage, a Roman Catholic and an Anglican church, more and better shops than Mahenge, and, in addition to the usual public football field, there were facilities for golf and tennis available exclusively to members of the European Club.

On paper, Songea might have looked a better place to live than Mahenge, but we did not find it so. When I had visited it in 1955 on safari as Robert Stapledon's Private Secretary, I had formed an unfavourable impression of the place. Five years later, when Paul

Haile told me of his plan to post me there after I returned from home leave, I had asked him to send me somewhere else instead.

The town was in an airless hollow surrounded by lowering hills, and did not enjoy such splendid views as Mahenge. The air service meant that it was possible to obtain luxury items like bacon, sausages, fresh butter, cheese, and better wines than any of the traders in Mahenge could offer. However, the prices of imported foods were exorbitant, and the cost of living was far higher than in Mahenge.

The District Officer's house that Jennifer and I moved into after my predecessor went on leave was about the same size as our house in Mahenge, but it was gloomy and charmless. My predecessor had not bothered much about the garden, and the grass was about two feet high when we moved in. Jennifer and I engaged the ayah, Kathrin Hamisi, who had looked after my predecessor's son, but we found her surly with adults and harsh with children, and we did not ask her to come with us to Lindi when we left Songea after only six weeks.

We wanted our children to be able to play in the garden as Ruth and her friends had all done in Mahenge, but we were concerned that snakes could be hard to spot in such long grass. I therefore borrowed a big motor mower normally used for rural road maintenance, and spent my first free Saturday afternoon using it. After we had cleared the lawn, we found a number of ornamental plants which had probably been planted some years earlier, but had been almost smothered by the long grass.

Jennifer masterminded the transformation, with the help of Juma, Omari, and Mohamed, of a dismal lodging into a reasonably welcoming home. We genuinely made an effort to become enthusiastic about Songea and to make friends with our colleagues of all races.

It is not easy to analyse exactly why one station is generally regarded as a 'happy station', as Mahenge certainly was, while another outwardly similar one is not.

In Mahenge, there was nowhere else to offer hospitality, so people entertained in their own houses. Everyone got to know everyone else, and even those who would probably not have become friends on a bigger station enjoyed each other's company.

The trouble with Songea was that I saw few signs of community spirit there. The missionaries did not seem to fraternise with the officials, and some of the officials themselves were at loggerheads with one another. The wife of one of the expatriate officials in Songea was a graduate, and was said to look down on the rest of the European wives who were not so highly educated as she was. When Jennifer arrived, however, that woman seemed to regard another wife who was also a graduate as a rival.

The District Commissioner was able and hard-working and had a charming wife, but he was also irascible, and it worried me to think that I, as his second-in-command, might be involved in dealing with the consequences if he lost his temper with one of the local political firebrands, as had happened in a previous station.

We were glad to have an Anglican church in the town, and Jennifer was asked to play the harmonium there. She agreed, but asked to attend one service before playing, so that she could see what she was expected to do. However, at the first service she attended, the African priest rebuked the congregation furiously for failing to welcome her properly, or provide her with a hymn-book with music. A crowd of willing worshippers then rushed her to the harmonium and gave her a hymn-book with the tunes printed in tonic sol-fa, which she could not play from. She had to explain that she had never intended to play for them on this first visit. In fact, the singing was in excellent harmony, and there was no need for a harmonium accompaniment at all.

Towards the end of the service, two young women were called forward to sit on the penitents' stool and be vilified by the priest and threatened with eternal hell-fire for having had sex out of marriage. There was no attempt to name and shame the boyfriends who had caused the girls' humiliation.

* * *

The European children in Mahenge, many of whom were girls, had all got on well with one another. In Songea most of the children were boys, and seemed to squabble all the time. There were two young brothers, who were aged about six and three, and hated each other so much that it looked as if the elder might cause serious harm to his sibling. He was always kicking and punching his little brother, and I was told that on one occasion, soon after the younger boy was born, the older boy had tried to smother him in his pram with a pillow. I thought their parents were largely to blame for this situation. The mother had arranged to be admitted to the hospital in Provincial Headquarters for her second confinement, leaving her older son at home in a smaller station being cared for during the day by his ayah, and by his father in the evenings and overnight. When his mother was discharged from hospital after not having seen her son for several weeks, the boy was suffering from a cold and was not allowed to go near the new baby in case he passed on the infection. He saw his mother breast-feeding the new arrival, but was told to stay away. At the time, he was only about three years old, and could not possibly have understood why his mother appeared to be rejecting him. The mother, who herself told us the story, acknowledged that she and her husband ought to have shown more sympathy.

Another small boy had a mother who was paralysed and confined to a wheelchair. The boy took no notice of what she said to him, as he knew she could not catch him if he ran away. He was not an attractive child, but his father boasted to me one day that his son was very brave, and bore pain without ever crying. He then called his son, and tried to prove his point by gratuitously giving him a hard smack on the bottom. The boy promptly burst into tears, to the chagrin of his father.

However, it was not the children who were to blame for the acrimony we had spotted the night we arrived in Songea. That was caused by mutual distrust and resentment. One official was known to have had an affair with a colleague's wife while her husband was on safari. People's sympathies were sharply divided on the matter. Moreover, some husbands were worried when they went on safari that unwelcome attentions might be paid to their wives during their own absence from Songea. Whatever the circumstances, adultery was always bad for the morale of a station. This particular case affected Songea worse than any other station where I had served.

* * *

The work-load in Songea District was divided geographically, as it had been in Iringa, rather than functionally, as in Rungwe. After a week or two, I went on a short safari to visit my part of the district and meet the people I would be working with. I do not remember much about the personalities I met. The whole country was then in a state of high excitement about the rapid political developments that were taking place, and my experience had taught me that African peasants take a little while to know and trust newcomers, and that my first task should be to listen carefully to what the people told me about their problems and aspirations before I started to suggest possible solutions.

At the beginning of April, Raymond Tubbs, the Provincial

Commissioner, visited Songea with his wife Vivian. I had met them both when I was in Government House, but did not know them well. Len Manson decided to give a sundowner party in their honour, and asked me if Juma would be willing to help in serving drinks and snacks to the guests. I said I was sure he would be delighted, and then I remembered that, before he had started to work for me, Juma had worked for Vivian and her first husband, Roly Wheeler, before that marriage had ended in divorce. I wondered if it would cause embarrassment to Tubbs and his wife to meet Juma again, but Len insisted that if Juma were willing to meet Mr and Mrs Tubbs again there was nothing to stop him doing so.

At the party, Vivian Tubbs saw Juma, and greeted him with great enthusiasm, then called to Raymond and said, 'Darling, you remember Juma, don't you?' Raymond Tubbs looked disconcerted and said, 'Yes. Jambo!', and promptly turned away.

The following afternoon I was sitting in my office in the Boma when Raymond Tubbs came in and started asking me all sorts of questions about my plans for the part of the district for which I was to be responsible. He listened to me very carefully, and sometimes asked for my opinion about suggestions he put forward himself. He spent nearly the whole afternoon with me, and when I got home I told Jennifer how impressed I had been to have a new Provincial Commissioner who really paid attention to the views of a subordinate.

By the next incoming airmail, I received through Len Manson a letter from Raymond Tubbs. It started with an apology for uprooting Jennifer and me and the children so soon after we had arrived in Songea and seemed to be settling in so well there (his comment, not mine!). However, I was to pack up my bags and proceed immediately to Lindi. What he himself described in the next paragraph as 'the sugar on the pill' was that Brian Weeks, the current District Commissioner in Lindi, would be going on leave at the beginning of July, and that I would take over as the new DC of Lindi when he went.

I was taken completely by surprise by this news, and went straight home to tell Jennifer about it as we had no telephone in Songea. I had excluded Lindi mentally from my prejudice against all the other districts of Southern Province, and would gladly have accepted a transfer there as an ordinary District Officer, but the prospect of taking charge as District Commissioner far exceeded my wildest hopes.

We left Songea on 26th April, less than six weeks after we had arrived there. Before leaving, we gave a children's party to celebrate prematurely Ruth's fourth birthday. We did not think we would be able to give one for her in Lindi on her real birthday, 30th April, only three days after our arrival. Ruth enjoyed her farewell party enormously, and was particularly delighted with an iced cake Jennifer had made. It was exceedingly pink, as Jennifer had been heavy-handed with the cochineal, but the children all approved.

We spent one night on the journey with our friends Anthony and Geraldine Mayle in Tunduru, and reached Lindi the next evening. The journey through mile after mile of *miombo* woodland was dull, but as we got nearer to the coast the countryside became greener and more attractive, though it also became much hotter and more humid. I was not complaining. We had not enjoyed Songea much, and we were thankful that we were unlikely ever to see the place again.

Chapter 9

Lindi District

(April 1961–June 1962)

A Pleasant Old Town by the Sea

Lindi is one of the ports which line the coast of East Africa. Its contacts with the outside world date from long before the time when Livingstone and other explorers reached the interior of the country during the nineteenth century. Every year from about November to March the north-east monsoon blows steadily from Arabia and the Indian sub-continent towards Africa, and from April to September the south-west monsoon blows in the opposite direction. For centuries, perhaps even for millennia, this has enabled dhows to sail to East Africa with one monsoon and return with the next.

Some merchant adventurers spent nearly all their lives at sea, but others left their ships to set up trading posts on the coast of East Africa, for example in Dar es Salaam, Bagamoyo, Kilwa, Mikindani and Lindi. The methods the rich traders employed were often cruel, but the buildings which they used as forts, prisons, markets, mosques, and homes for themselves were solidly built, and many were very beautiful. They reflected several different styles and traditions – Shirazi, Omani Arab, Portuguese and German. The bungalows and single-storey office blocks put up during the period of British administration were functional and probably cheaper to build than two-storey buildings, but they were nothing like as attractive to look at.

Tourists who visit East Africa nowadays are usually interested either in the wildlife of the country's interior, or in spending their holidays in luxury hotels beside warm sandy beaches. They tend to overlook the character and charm of the old towns on the coast. I had visited Lindi three times before I was posted there. In 1955, when I was Provincial Commissioner's Staff Officer in Mtwara, I had been a member of two Higher Standard Swahili Oral boards convened in Lindi to examine District Officers from various other

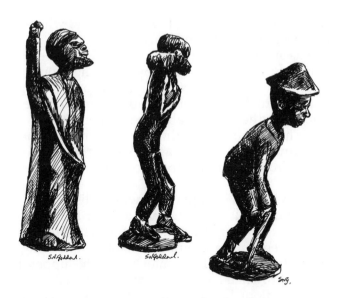

Ebony figures carved by Makonde tribesmen

districts. Later that year I had accompanied Robert Stapledon, the Acting Governor, when he visited Southern Province on safari. I already knew that I liked Lindi better than anywhere else in the province.

Lindi District is about the same size as Jamaica, but, judged by the standards of Tanganyika, it is not a particularly big district – only 4,144 square miles, a sixth the size of Tabora District. However, the population of Lindi District during the 1950s was about 230,000, the largest in Southern Province. It consisted largely of Mwera or Makonde tribesmen, who were also to be found in the adjoining districts. The Makonde had, and still have, the reputation of being about the best sculptors in East Africa, and were also known for their tradition of stilt-dancing, which I often heard about but seldom saw.

A census carried out in 1952 listed Lindi as the seventh largest township in Tanganyika, with 11,330 inhabitants, 159 of whom were European, 1,542 Asian, and 9,629 African. The township's importance and economic survival seemed quite secure until the disastrous Groundnut Scheme was set up in 1947, and work began soon after that on the development of a harbour with a deep water berth at a fishing village called Mtwara, about seventy miles south of Lindi and ten miles south of Mikindani. A railway link was also constructed between 1947 and 1954 from

384

The Flags Changed at Midnight

Mtwara to Nachingwea, about 130 miles away, where optimists hoped that groundnuts would flourish.

When I was stationed in Mtwara in 1955, I had seen for myself how little benefit had been gained by investing money there. Six years later, when I was posted to Lindi, I saw that money had been pumped into Mtwara in total disregard for the probable consequences for the long-established settlements of Lindi and Mikindani. The economic decline became irreversible in 1953, when the Provincial Office was moved from Lindi and the District Office from Mikindani to the ugly sprawling new town of Mtwara.

Moving Provincial Headquarters was a disaster for most of Lindi's inhabitants, but the cloud had a silver lining for whoever happened to be the District Commissioner. The Provincial Office in Lindi had been on the ground floor of an imposing mansion built during the period of German rule. The upper floor had provided the Provincial Commissioner's official residence. In 1953, the upper floor became the District Commissioner's residence, and the lower floor a flat to accommodate his guests. For the next few years, District Commissioners of Lindi were thus provided with a home that was far more splendid than their status really justified. I was one of the officials who benefited from this situation, and I cannot deny that it gave me pleasure.

The house had in all twenty-two rooms. Some were just small closets, but there were three bathrooms, the dining room was large, and the living room was enormous, fifteen metres long and ten metres wide, with a polished stone floor. The upstairs bedrooms were larger than in any other house I have ever occupied. At both the front and the back of the house there were imposing flights of steps leading up to heavy double doors. Both sets of portals had decorated arches above them.

Lindi had electricity, and the main rooms were kept reasonably cool by very thick walls and by large electric ceiling fans. There was a verandah circling the whole of the upper floor. One part of the verandah was open to the sea breezes, while another was protected by wire gauze to keep mosquitoes out. The house was even provided with a double ration of government furniture at no extra cost to its tenants. The authorities in Dar had agreed that just one sofa and two armchairs in the living room, and six dining chairs and one standard size table in the dining room would look ridiculous in such enormous rooms.

The house stood in the middle of a spacious though not particularly fertile garden overlooking the estuary of the Lukuledi

River. A road along the Sea Front ran between the low garden wall and a sandy beach. The Lindi Club, which was still racially segregated, was situated about fifty yards away, between the road and the beach. There was a narrow peninsula jutting out into the Indian Ocean on the far bank of the estuary. The view from the upstairs verandah of the house was superb, both in sunny and in stormy weather, but was at its best by the light of the tropical full moon on a calm night.

The main colour in the garden came from massive bougainvillea shrubs which climbed up both the back and the front walls of the house. The flowers of bougainvillea are small and insignificant, and the bright colours associated with the shrub come not from the flowers themselves but from a special type of magenta, white, or salmon pink leaves known as bracts.

When Jennifer and I arrived from Songea with our children, my predecessor, Brian Weeks, invited us all to stay for a few days in his guest flat before we moved temporarily into a pleasant but much more modest quarter on Wireless Hill.

We had brought our trusted servants Juma, Omari, and Mohamed from Songea with us, but one of the first things Jennifer and I did in Lindi was to engage a new ayah to replace Kathrin Hamisi, the surly girl we had left in Songea. The girl we recruited was also the daughter of a man called Hamisi, an Islamic name commonly given to boys born on a Thursday. Our new ayah was called Margaret Hamisi, and she proved to be as devoted to our daughter Catherine as Ina had been to Ruth in Mahenge. The majority of Africans in coastal districts were Muslim, but one sign of the spread of Christianity was that it was more common to find an African whose own name was Christian with a father whose name was Muslim, than it was to find the reverse.

On Wireless Hill

Comparatively few expatriates lived in houses on the sea front. Most of them lived on a hill on the outskirts of Lindi called Mtanda Hill, a mile or so from the town centre. There was also a little group of older government quarters on Wireless Hill, which was closer to the town and overlooked the bay. The house which we were allocated there was about the same size as our houses in Mahenge and Songea. We did not like it as much as the house in Mahenge, but better than the house in Songea.

Unlike our houses in Mahenge and Songea, it had electricity and a telephone.

We had no European neighbours living close to us. The house next to ours was occupied by the family of a teacher at the Indian Secondary School. Mr and Mrs Pillai were pleasant neighbours, and had a son of six who made friends with Ruth and played well with her in spite of language problems. Ruth was quite happy to chatter in Swahili to Africans or in English to Europeans, but she found it hard to understand either language when it was spoken with an Indian accent, and she had not learnt any Gujarati. We would have liked a neighbour with a child close to Catherine's age, but Catherine was not as gregarious as Ruth, and was quite happy playing with her own family and her new ayah, Margaret.

About a fortnight after we moved into our house, we noticed a little Siamese cat miaowing outside our door. We discovered that she had belonged to the family of an official of the Public Works Department who had been transferred from Lindi just before we arrived. We assumed that the cat had run away to hide when she saw the upheaval when her owners were about to leave. They had apparently made no attempt to find out what had happened to her, or to get her returned to them. The cat was obviously very hungry, and we gave her something to eat, but she was also very timid, and ran away as soon as we approached her. She did not dare to come into our house for several days, but she then suddenly decided to adopt us. Ruth, Catherine, and our two dogs were all very happy about this arrangement. She was a sweet little cat, and after she got used to us she purred loudly whenever she was picked up and stroked. She never scratched anyone, even when one of the children lifted her clumsily. We learned later that her previous owners had called her *Nyuki*, the Swahili for bee, and we continued to use the same name.

* * *

Early in June 1961, all expatriate administrative officers received a personal letter from Julius Nyerere requesting them to stay on after independence to help the new government. He told us that we would continue to be needed for a long time. He praised the sense of mission which had brought us out to Africa in the first place, and reminded us of all the challenges which still faced the country. I found the tone of his letter extremely encouraging, but I had some misgivings about whether it represented the views of all the elected political leaders of the country.

It was becoming increasingly obvious that most of the expatriates who had once expected their careers to last until they
retired on a pension at the age of 55 would leave Tanganyika
before they reached that age. They would be paid compensation
for loss of career. This would be calculated on a complicated
formula based on age, years of service, and final salary, and
would be paid in instalments, the first of 50%, the remainder
spread annually over a period of six years. We would also be paid
whatever pension we had already earned, but for those who
retired prematurely after only a few years' service and when they
were still low down on the salary scale, this pension was likely to
be very small.

Expatriate officials were offered three options, either to resign
at the beginning of 1962, to enter into a contract to continue to
serve for two more years, or to continue on their present terms of
service subject to six months' notice on either side.

I heard in July that about 20% of European officials, mainly the
old-stagers who could not accept the idea of serving under an
African, had already opted to resign on January 1st. Another 10%
had signed contracts for two more years' service. The remaining
70%, which included me, were still undecided. Many of us
wanted to go on doing a job which we thought useful and which
we enjoyed immensely, but we did not want to endanger
ourselves and especially our families by committing ourselves to
stay on even if the country degenerated into violence and chaos
after it became independent.

* * *

A few weeks after we moved into our house on Wireless Hill, our
dog Wol, Susan's daughter, became ill. Wol was solid and
clumsy, and far less intelligent than her mother. I was fonder of
Susan than I have ever been of any other dog, but we were also
quite attached to Wol except when she had rolled in something
particularly evil-smelling. Piles of discarded fish-entrails were
her favourite perfume, but, when fish were in short supply,
cowpats were a good substitute. We were less gentle when we
gave Wol a bath than when we washed Susan, and I think Wol
eventually cottoned on to the idea that her choice of scent was not
ours. However, we never could fully rely on her not to roll in
something horrid as soon as our backs were turned.

When Wol fell ill, she had a high fever, her back legs became
paralysed, and she was in some distress, but there was no quali-

fied Veterinary Officer in Lindi. The Field Officer (Veterinary) was knowledgeable about cattle, but told us that he was far less skilled at treating dogs than a former Assistant Veterinary Officer who was, I believe, a graduate of Makerere College, and was currently serving a sentence in Lindi Prison for theft.

With the prior approval of the Provincial Veterinary Officer and the Chief Warder, for the next few days the delinquent vet spent his working hours at our house, with a warder to escort him, giving Wol constant care, and administering the drugs which he asked us to buy for her. Sadly, his efforts were not successful, and Wol died. She was eight years old. Catherine was not old enough to understand, but Ruth was very unhappy, and Jennifer and I were thankful that her first encounter with death involved only a pet rather than a human friend or relative.

I was so busy that we did not have the time to entertain as many friends as we had done in Mahenge, but we did nevertheless have a small dinner party on our wedding anniversary at the end of June. There were six guests, including a charming young Swiss couple called Niederhäusern. He was a manager on one of the sisal estates in the district, and they had been married for some years and were still desperately longing for a child of their own. They doted so much on Ruth and Catherine that we thought it might upset them if we told them that Jennifer was now expecting our third baby.

The following evening we were invited to dinner at Brian Weeks's house. Jennifer was getting ready to go out when she called me from the bathroom and asked me to phone the doctor urgently, as she was having a haemorrhage. I was thankful that Lindi had a telephone system, and that it was in good working order at the time.

The Medical Officer, a Maltese doctor called Paul Grech, arrived within minutes. Paul was one of the outstandingly good doctors who worked in Tanganyika. He told us what we already feared, that Jennifer was starting a miscarriage. He advised us that if she were driven along bumpy roads to be admitted to Lindi Hospital there was hardly any chance that the baby would survive, but that if she remained completely still in bed at home for some days it might just be possible to save the baby.

He insisted that Jennifer would not be able to get out of bed for any reason whatsoever, and would need round-the-clock attention. It would not be possible for a nurse from the hospital to be made available, but he knew of an Asian girl who would be suitable. She was the eighteen-year-old daughter of the Assistant

Postmaster, and had completed her schooling at the Indian Secondary School. She had been accepted to start training as a nurse in England at Newmarket Hospital in October. Paul promised to ask her if she would be willing to care for Jennifer by day, while I was working in the Boma. She agreed, and arrived at our house early the following morning.

Miss Sirisena was kind and intelligent. She had been born in Tanganyika, but her parents came from Ceylon, now known as Sri Lanka. In a candid moment she told Jennifer that her father had said to her that, in order to be successsful, girls must either be beautiful or be educated, so she would need to be educated. I think I would have tried to express it more tactfully than her father, but Miss Sirisena (it was rare for Asians to be addressed by their first names) was not very pretty. She was heavily built, and had hairy legs. Within her own home she always used English, as her parents' native language was not generally understood in Tanganyika, even by other Asians. Like families of mixed race, Miss Sirisena and her family were not accepted on equal terms either by Europeans, Indians, or Africans. However, we will always be extremely grateful to her for helping our unborn son to survive, and to Paul Grech for his skilled care and for arranging for Miss Sirisena to come and help.

While Jennifer was still not allowed to get up, Nyuki took us all completely by surprise by having two premature kittens on her bed. One was stillborn, and the other died after only two days. Ruth was not so upset about the death of two kittens she had not yet got to know, but she commented that they would get to heaven much quicker than Wol, as they were so much lighter.

About thirty years later, I travelled to Malta on business, and went by ferry from Malta to its sister island of Gozo to visit Paul and his wife Mary, who was also a doctor. They had retired from work in the British National Health Service. All Paul's previous publications had been medical reference books, but, using a *nom de plume*, he had just had a detective novel published in which the detective was called Inspector Grech, and the main themes were Malta, scuba diving, and AIDS. He gave me a copy which Jennifer and I both enjoyed very much.

They were then living in an enchanting villa on the side of a hill overlooking the Mediterranean. Paul and Mary had never met our son, as Paul had been transferred to Dar to become the specialist radiologist there shortly before Philip was born in January 1962. However, he remembered the threatened miscarriage well, and they were both delighted to hear that Philip and

his two sisters were now all married, and had children of their
own.

Bishop Trevor Huddleston

During the dry season just after I arrived in Lindi, I took the
opportunity to visit as much of the district as possible while the
roads were still in reasonably good condition. After Jennifer's
threatened miscarriage I stayed in Lindi until she recovered, but
as soon as she was well again I resumed a programme of safaris
round the district. These did not involve such long journeys as in
bigger districts like Iringa, Tabora, or Ulanga, and I was usually
back home after a night or two.

On routine safaris in my previous tours of service, I had
usually addressed villagers on topics of permanent interest such
as hygiene, education, ways to improve the productivity of the
land, and the need to pay taxes. In Lindi District in 1961, the
emphasis was different. My main objective now was to make sure
that independence would be achieved that year in an orderly
way. I stressed the need for everyone to play a part in working for
the development of a country which would earn the respect of the
world after it became independent. I frequently quoted from
speeches by Julius Nyerere himself, preaching the message that
hard work and self-reliance were essential to the success of an
independent Tanganyika. I also emphasised that Nyerere himself
totally repudiated the claims of some extremists who purported
to speak for TANU when they promised to provide new schools
and dispensaries and at the same time to reduce or even abolish
taxation. My praise for the way Nyerere was conducting the
negotiations leading up to independence was sincere, and I never
encountered any anger or hostility on my safaris in Lindi District.

Just before I took over as DC from Brian Weeks, I went on a
short safari to the Rondo Plateau, about 2,000 feet above sea level.
The plateau had a temperate climate, was pleasantly wooded,
and I thought it a very attractive place.

This safari was for a special purpose. I wanted to take part in
discussions concerning the future use of some land and buildings
there. A timber firm, Steel Brothers, had been granted a concession over land in the Rondo Plateau some years previously, and
had been producing up to 6,000 tons of sawn timber a year. This
had provided jobs for many Africans. However, the firm had
decided to cut back their business in the area, and the

Universities' Mission to Central Africa (UMCA) were interested in buying their buildings and installations and adapting them for use as a theological college for African ordinands. The Chief and his people all had the right to express their views about a change which could have a profound effect on their daily lives.

I was one of the two expatriate government officials present at the meeting. The other was the District Forest Officer, Len Yull, who lived in a house on the Rondo Plateau with his wife Liz. They both became very good friends of ours.

The spokesman for Steel Brothers was their Manager, Verney Lovett-Campbell, an eccentric but likeable man with many years of experience in the forests of Burma. His brother was the Consultant Physician to the Colonial Office who in 1950 had passed me as physically fit for service in Tanganyika.

The spokesman for the UMCA was the Bishop of Masasi, Trevor Huddleston, who had been consecrated in 1958. His book *Naught for your Comfort*, published in 1956, had called the attention of readers all over the world to the plight of non-white people in the apartheid regime in South Africa. I had already read it, but until that day on the Rondo Plateau I had never met Huddleston himself.

I had agreed entirely with the views expressed in *Naught for your Comfort* about the evils of apartheid, but I had initially felt some misgivings about the style in which Trevor Huddleston wrote. I feared that fulminating against the supporters of apartheid with all the indignation of one of the angrier Old Testament prophets might be counter-productive, and I was concerned about the controversy the book caused, even among senior churchmen. I later became convinced that he had been absolutely right to denounce apartheid so forcefully, and that condemning a sin does not necessarily involve hating the sinner.

One of the main purposes of the meeting was to get agreement about the future use of the limited water resources on the Plateau. The supply of adequate clean water was one of Tanganyika's biggest problems, and while the villagers had regarded it as fair and reasonable that the employees of Steel Brothers should use some of the available water in return for the job opportunities the firm would provide, a college full of students and teachers would probably use more water and provide fewer jobs for locally-recruited manual workers. Before the UMCA committed itself to taking over the buildings, the participants at the meeting wanted to be sure that all the arguments for and against the Mission setting up a theological college had been considered fully. A clear and unambiguous document was needed to confirm various matters on which agreement had been reached orally. These concerned the respective rights of the college and the local villagers, particularly the right to use water, and the proportions which would be reserved for the villagers and for the college.

The meeting went very smoothly. Steel Brothers wanted the buildings to go on being used rather than being abandoned and falling into disrepair. The UMCA thought they would be ideal for their purposes. The premises were available immediately, and would cost the mission less than putting up brand new buildings. There were a few farmers, mainly Muslims, who were rather uneasy about having an Anglican theological college close by, but, in contrast to the coastal plain, Muslims seemed to be in a minority on the Rondo Plateau. The chief and most of the villagers were eager to welcome a college which would be of social and economic benefit to the area. If I remember rightly, I wrote a draft note in both English and Swahili, setting out all the conclusions which had been reached, and this draft was later approved and signed by those who had taken a major part in the discussion.

One feature of the meeting which particularly impressed me was the courtesy of all the participants, and in particular Trevor Huddleston. His Swahili was still not very fluent, but he listened with total attention to every word which was said, and gave lucid and honest answers to all the questions that were put to him. During the three years or so that he had been Bishop of Masasi, he had earned the absolute confidence of all the Africans who knew him, regardless of whether or not they were Anglicans.

I met Trevor Huddleston several times over the next few months. He came to Lindi from time to time to take services there, both in English and Swahili. When I arrived in Lindi, there was an English priest there, Frank Begley, who was later transferred to Lushoto. He was replaced by an African archdeacon, whose pastoral care for all the members of his congregation, black or white, was exemplary. On most Sundays, there was a priest in Lindi to take Anglican services, but the Bishop authorised me to take services there, just as I had done in other districts.

Like many of the Capuchin priests we had got to know in Ulanga, Huddleston had a deep love for children of all races, and even very young children always responded to the love which he showed for them. A biography of Huddleston published in 1999 has on its cover a photograph taken in Sophiatown of Huddleston touching the head of a little black girl of about two, while a little black boy of about three holds the bishop's cassock and gazes up adoringly at him. The village children of Masasi Diocese reacted to him in exactly the same way.

On the first occasion when Trevor Huddleston stayed overnight with us in Lindi, his secretary telephoned us after he had set off from Masasi. She asked us to make sure that we were not late in giving him a meal when he arrived. He suffered from diabetes, and took insulin regularly, but he became unwell if he went too long without food. Her concern for his health was apparent from the way she spoke.

Jennifer had a special reason to want to meet Trevor Huddleston. In 1952, a year or two before she was selected to become an Education Officer in Tanganyika, she had worked as a volunteer in the newly established Africa Bureau, set up in London by the Reverend Michael Scott. He had worked as a priest in the diocese of Johannesburg in the 1940s, and, like Trevor Huddleston, he had become very unpopular with white racists for supporting the rights of black people. In 1947, he appealed to the United Nations on behalf of two of the oppressed tribes in South-West Africa. He later wrote several books about South Africa.

Many of the papers which Jennifer dealt with in the Africa Bureau had referred to the work of Father Trevor Huddleston. Jennifer did not want to boast as soon as she met him about her earlier involvement in the work of the Bureau, but she had no need to mention it to him at all. He already knew.

Conversation with Trevor Huddleston was fascinating. Though his love of Africans was profound, he was not blind to their faults. He was depressed by the reluctance, even of comparatively rich Africans, to make a realistic contribution towards the cost of the services provided by the UMCA and other missions. He thought it would be difficult for former African colonies to become truly independent as long as they continued to rely so heavily on financial support from donors in other countries.

His reputation and his charisma made him very successful as a fund-raiser, and he obeyed the calls which were sometimes made on him to visit developed countries, in particular the United States, but he did not enjoy holding out the begging bowl to rich patrons. Jennifer's mother had collected a sum of money to support UMCA from her friends in Churt, and had posted a cheque for Jennifer to hand to the Bishop. We were glad that it did not damage our friendly relationship with him.

He admired Julius Nyerere, whom he regarded as a great human being who preached the need for self-reliance and gave an example, rare in political leaders anywhere, of humility, honesty, and approachability. However, he was also aware of the dangers posed by certain other African leaders, some democratically elected, who used their power to enrich themselves and to exploit their people. He acknowledged that many potential donors in rich countries would like to give more to charities working in Africa, but were put off by the thought that money given to feed the poor might not reach the hungry people for whom it was intended.

Trevor Huddleston's love of children that was noted during his time in Sophiatown and in Masasi was not confined to those who were black or deprived. He showed it just as clearly when he met Catherine and Ruth, who were both devoted to him. One evening, when Ruth was going to bed, the Bishop asked if he could go and say goodnight to her. Jennifer and I gladly agreed, and some minutes later he came back with a broad smile on his face. Ruth and he had had a serious discussion about which were better, angels or fairies. Ruth had at first been a supporter of fairies, but she had changed her mind and decided that the Bishop was quite right – angels really were the best! The following morning Trevor Huddleston returned to Masasi, and Ruth commented to us after he had gone, 'I like my Bishop. Please ask him to come here again.'

When Brian Weeks went on leave, the new District Officer posted to Lindi to work with me was Anastasios Christodoulou, known to us all as Chris. He and his wife Joan had two daughters, Stephanie and Andrea, who were roughly the same ages as Ruth and Catherine. Joan was expecting a third baby a few months before Jennifer. In March 1962, Trevor Huddleston christened two little boys at the same service in Lindi Church, Nicholas, the son of Chris and Joan Christodoulou, and our son Philip. Joan was proxy godmother to Philip, and I was proxy godfather to Nicholas.

In 1968, six years after we had ourselves returned to Britain, Trevor Huddleston left Tanganyika, by now linked with Zanzibar and called Tanzania, and became Bishop of Stepney, in the East End of London. He visited us from time to time at our home in Surrey, and I was present when he gave a memorable lecture in Guildford Cathedral. In 1978, he was appointed Archbishop of Mauritius, and we did not see each other for some years.

In 1993, Jennifer and I were privileged to attend Trevor Huddleston's eightieth birthday celebrations in Central Hall, Westminster, and to hear the eloquent tributes which great leaders of many races then paid to him.

We were also deeply moved at the memorial service held in Westminster Abbey on 29th July 1998, before a congregation which completely filled the Abbey, to give thanks for his life. To quote the words of Archbishop Desmond Tutu, 'The world is a better place for having had Trevor Huddleston.'

District Commissioner

A few days after the meeting about the theological college on the Rondo Plateau, Brian Weeks went on leave, and I took over as the new District Commissioner. The rules about handing over and taking over a District involved checking and signing for all cash, documents, and equipment. The formalities took some days to complete, and I was glad when the task was over.

I felt proud to be put in charge of an important district at such a crucial stage in the life of Tanganyika. I was told that I was the youngest British District Commissioner that Lindi had ever had, and I looked forward to the challenge.

There were other reasons to be pleased. My family and I would be living in a really lovely house, though we did not move into it at once. It needed a few repairs, in particular to the mosquito-gauze over the windows of the rooms where Ruth and Catherine would be sleeping.

Our financial position would also be improved because, as a District Commissioner, I would now qualify for a 'responsibility allowance'. Lindi was designated as an 'A' district, which carried the highest rate of allowance.

Becoming a District Commissioner did not mean abandoning the old tasks one had done as a District Officer, but there were certain new tasks which were the District Commissioner's personal responsibility

I became a first-class magistrate, but in Lindi this was not very onerous, as we had a Resident Magistrate who dealt with most of the judicial work.

I became, *ex officio*, a member of the Town Council and of its Finance Committee, and also of the District Council, which was quite separate from the Town Council. I became the Chairman of the 'District Team', an informal gathering of all the officials in charge of the various Government Departments in the District. The Town Clerk and the Secretary of the District Council were usually invited to attend meetings of the District Team.

The District Comissioner himself (there were at the time no

women District Commissioners in Tanganyika) monitored the political situation in the district, and informed the Provincial Commissioner of any developments or problems. He also compiled an annual report made up of contributions from members of the District Team. He represented the District at the annual DCs' Conference, held under the chairmanship of the Provincial Commissioner. It was expected that the District Commissioner would usually offer hospitality to the judge presiding over High Court sessions, and to other important visitors.

Except in districts which were also headquarters of a province, the District Commissioner was also the Queen's representative in the district. This was normally a titular function, but in 1961 it meant that I would represent Her Majesty the Queen at the parade in Lindi to celebrate the independence of Tanganyika.

I delegated as much responsibility as I could to the District Officer, Chris Christodoulou, and to the two Assistant District Officers, but even so I was always busy.

Within a few days of my taking over, I had to organise an important meeting in Lindi, attended by the elected Ministers of Transport and of Agriculture from Dar es Salaam, the Provincial Commissioner from Mtwara, the General Manager of East African Railways and Harbours from Nairobi, Gordon Mackay, and their aides.

Its purpose was to agree the logistics of closing the port of Lindi. The ports of Lindi and Mtwara were both currently running at a loss, but if all the lighters and other equipment now in Lindi were moved to Mtwara, and all the business went there too, it was just possible that the port of Mtwara might break even financially. Lindi could be sacrificed in order to rescue Mtwara.

I realised immediately that I was the lone voice speaking up for the interests of Lindi, and that it would be a waste of breath to try to get the rest of the meeting to reverse a decision that had already been taken at a high level. However, there were a number of long-established import–export dealers in Lindi, and the sisal estate owners, traders, and peasant farmers in Lindi District would all be badly hit by the closure of the port there. Their losses might be mitigated, however, if there were a reliable all-weather road between Lindi and Mtwara. The existing Lindi–Mtwara road was atrocious, and regularly became impassable during the rainy season.

I therefore pleaded as eloquently as I could for a stay of execution, and eventually managed to secure a promise that the plan would not be implemented until after the road between Mtwara and Lindi had been upgraded.

At midday, those who had attended the meeting were driven up to our house on Wireless Hill to have lunch. There were too many people to seat at our dining table, so we had arranged a buffet lunch for the guests, who sat on a miscellany of chairs in the dining room, the living room, and on the verandah.

The visitors were served by Juma and Omari, each dressed as smartly as possible in a long white calico gown, a maroon waist-coat and a fez. Our cook, Mohamed, always cooked excellently when we had visitors.

The guests all seemed to enjoy their meal. Minister Paul Bomani, a portly man with a limp hand-shake, enjoyed it so much that he helped himself to two plates of the main course, and then retired into a corner to eat voraciously by himself. He did not bother to converse with anyone else. I was glad to chat once more with Minister Amir Habib Jamal, whom I had first met by the river near Ifakara three years previously. I had formed a favourable impression of him then, and the good sense he showed that day at the meeting and the courtesy he showed as a guest enhanced the respect I already had for him.

The District Council builds its first Middle School

Lindi's two separate Councils, one for the town, the other for the rural areas of the district, were very different, but the District Commissioner was *ex officio* a member of both. I never heard any rumours of dishonesty in the District Council.

When I first arrived in Tanganyika, Indirect Rule was still the official policy, and there were several hundred Native Authorities in the country. Their powers covered most aspects of the life of Africans in tribal areas. They were responsible for maintaining law and order, for collecting taxes and local rates, and for a wide range of executive functions comparable to those carried out by units of local government in Britain. When councils were set up, they at first consisted largely of chiefs, headmen and people with special experience. In certain more progressive districts, a few commoners were co-opted. The democratic election of councillors began towards the end of the period of British rule, when virtually every elected member was supported by TANU, whose policy was to reduce the power of hereditary chiefs.

The size of Tanganyika created problems, both at district and at village level. Town Councillors usually lived within walking distance of Town Council Offices, but District Councillors often had to make very long journeys to attend meetings. The progress of rural District Councils was hampered by the cost of bringing councillors from outlying areas, and while they were absent from their home areas councillors were not able to perform their normal duties.

An additional problem at village level was that many peasant farmers lived several hours' walk from the nearest dispensary or primary school. As a result, many children did not go to school and remained illiterate, and many sick people were not strong enough to reach the nearest dispensary, and went without treatment or else relied on the traditional medicine-man. The other side of the same coin was that many teachers were paid a salary to teach in classrooms that were half empty, and health-care workers had often seen all their patients by mid-morning, and were paid for doing virtually nothing for the rest of the day.

African villagers everywhere wanted improved social services, but Tanganyika was too poor to afford the buildings and the staff that would be needed if every village were to have its own primary school and dispensary. There were also too few people with the necessary skills, and it would take years to train all the staff that would be needed.

After independence, Julius Nyerere tried to solve this problem by a strategy for rural development that involved the compulsory resettlement of farmers in so-called *Ujamaa* villages. 'Ujamaa' is the word used by Nyerere to describe his concept of socialism. This policy proved very unpopular with small-holding farmers, who wanted to go on living near the graves of their ancestors, and Nyerere was honest enough to acknowledge in due course that it had been a failure.

Woman of Lindi District

The people of Lindi District seldom went hungry. Farmers grew cash crops which included cashew nuts, sesame, and copra, and food crops of rice, maize, sorghum, millet, coconuts, and cassava. Those who lived near the coast also included fish in their diets. However, the standard of literacy among the mainly Muslim population was not so high as in predominantly Christian areas further inland, and I thought that if the social and economic standards of living were to improve in the district, then education was a matter of high priority.

The system of education for Africans provided for three stages of schooling: primary – up to Standard IV; middle – up to Standard VIII; and secondary – up to Standard XII, though many secondary schools did not go beyond Standard X. Education was not compulsory, and admission to middle or secondary schools was based on the results which pupils obtained in their Standard IV and VIII examinations. The fee for primary education was usually very low, about 5s (25p) a year. Middle schools were usually boarding schools, and fees were higher, usually about 200s (£10) a year. Schemes existed in certain parts of the country for the remission of part or all of the fees, but even so many bright pupils dropped out of middle school because their parents could not afford the fees. Secondary schools were free, but the proportion of pupils from all over the country who qualified for admission was very small.

In the coastal areas of Tanganyika, the majority of the population were Muslims. Much of the pioneering work in African education had been done by Christian missions, however, and some Muslim parents were reluctant to send their children to mission schools in case they abandoned Islam and were converted to Christianity. Many Muslims also had an old-fashioned attitude to women, and did not appreciate the value of educating girls, even though the children of literate mothers had a much lower infant mortality rate than the children of illiterate ones.

At the time I arrived in Lindi, the district still had no local authority middle school. I thought that setting one up should be a matter of great importance for the District Council, but I doubted whether a direct appeal to councillors to fund the creation of such a school would be welcomed by the more conservative members.

At the first meeting of the Council which I attended, I took a gamble. A high proportion of the Council's skilled employees like teachers, clerks, and dressers, were Christians who came from inland districts, mainly Masasi and Newala, and had been educated at mission schools there. I might just have stirred up jealousy and xenophobia, but when I heard the name of an employee who came from outside the district, I sometimes drew attention to his origins, and expressed mild regret that our own district was not able to provide enough suitably qualified candidates to fill all the Council's vacancies for trained staff.

There were two outstandingly able men at the meeting. Both of them carried out the functions of chiefs, but were designated as *Liwalis*. Liwali Paul Norbert and Liwali Petro Nyale were both in their late thirties. Paul was jovial and rotund. Petro was tall, muscular, and looked very distinguished. Both had been educated at mission schools up to Standard X, and I trusted them.

After the meeting, I took them both into my confidence. I told them that I hoped that councillors would agree to the setting up of a new middle school, but I did not want the idea to seem to come from me. My remarks about the origins of certain members of the council's staff who came from other districts had not been made to stir up animosity. I just wanted to make our councillors aware that the educational standards of pupils who had been born in Lindi District had to be improved if we were to become self-reliant in meeting our own need for trained staff. The local treasury had enough money to pay for a new middle school, and what was now required was to harness the political will.

They both warmly supported the idea, and Petro suggested that his village of Mtama would be an ideal spot for the new school. It was the junction of the North–South and the East–West main roads through the district, and was easily accessible from all parts of the district. It was fertile, healthy, had a good water supply and a level space for a football field. His people would all welcome a new middle school there. Paul Norbert and I agreed that Mtama seemed a very suitable place, and we discussed the tactics we would adopt at the next council meeting.

Paul Norbert was one of the office holders of the council, and it was he who announced, after the routine items on the agenda had been dealt with, that he would like to give the floor to Liwali Petro Nyale. Petro then invited all the councillors to be his guests at Mtama to see a site which he would like to offer to the council for the construction of a new middle school. Transport had been arranged and was available to take them to Mtama. He gave the invitation so diplomatically that the whole council responded eagerly, and enjoyed the outing. No one put forward a rival bid to have the school in his part of the district, and the capital expenditure was voted and approved. In a surprisingly short time the school had its headteacher and premises, and was ready to admit pupils to Standard V. I still feel proud to have sown a seed which came to fruition so quickly and successfully.

One of my other tasks was to be the Chairman of the District Education Committee. It had responsibility for approving the marks given by the African Schools Supervisor and his team in the Standard IV examinations, and thus deciding who would be offered admission to Standard V.

I was worried by the wide disparity between the results of the best and the worst schools. Thirteen out of the top sixteen candidates in the whole district came from the same school, Lindi Town Primary School. The reason for this was not hard to find. Many pupils were the children of parents who were themselves well educated. They were all well fed, and had prompt access to the hospital if they became ill. They either lived in houses with electric light or had access to the town library or welfare centres where they had the opportunity to read after the sun went down, The teachers at the Town Primary School all wanted to work there, and were enthusiastic and good at their jobs. The school was often visited by senior officials, and was regarded as a show-place. Perhaps the most important advantage of all was that the pupils lived within easy walking distance of the school.

The school with the worst results in the district also had compelling reasons for being so bad. It was not that the children were all of lower than average ability, though none of its pupils gained admission to Standard V. The school was situated in a remote village, and the buildings were in a dreadful condition. The enrolment was too low to fill four separate classes, and the headteacher, who had no assistant, had to teach two or more classes in the same classroom at the same time. The teacher himself was lazy and discouraged. Whenever I visited the school, even quite early in the morning, his breath smelt strongly of beer. The school's catchment area was large, and some children walked many miles to get to school, and were already tired by the time they arrived there.

A few never arrived at all. An old lion which had become too slow and feeble to catch wild animals took to eating children instead, and killed three little boys before it was shot by a Game Scout. Attendance at that school was never good, but it plummeted when the boys died. It did not pick up again, even after the danger from the lion had passed.

Hospitality, Human Rights, and a Visit by Julius Nyerere

One of the contrasts between the life of a British official working in a District Office in Tanganyika and the life of a commuter travelling to work in a big city in Britain lay in the matter of hospitality. Expatriates in Tanganyika entertained guests in their homes far more often than is usual in Britain. Some up-country stations did not have a hotel or a restaurant at all. Where hotels did exist, they were usually either shabby or expensive, and it was easier and pleasanter to invite friends into one's home for a meal or to stay overnight. There were servants to do the cooking, wait at table, launder, and clean the guest's bedroom, and most guests left a tip to reward the servants for their extra work.

After I left Tanganyika, I worked in London for over twenty years, and I rarely met the wives or families of my work colleagues. I occasionally invited a particular friend to visit us with his family on a Saturday or Sunday, but they never stayed overnight, and most of my contacts at a personal level took place over lunch in the staff canteen or at a pub near my office.

The contrast in the types of hospitality in Tanganyika and Britain had a profound effect on the depth and durability of the friendships one formed with one's colleagues. I still have some friends whom I got to know during the years I worked in London, but they are far outnumbered by the friends Jennifer and I made in less than half that time in Tanganyika, many of whom will remain very close friends for the rest of our lives.

There were some expatriates who were willing to invite other Europeans into their homes, but who did not invite Asians or Africans, however well-educated or cultured they might be. The most bigoted of the white racists were mainly the less well-educated Europeans. Perhaps they feared that the emergence of Africans and Asians with better qualifications than their own might put their own jobs at risk. However, as the country developed politically and socially, racial prejudice slowly abated, though it did not go away altogether. It was not a matter for which whites were exclusively to blame. There were also some Africans, including a number of politicians, who opposed peace and reconciliation, and preached a message of racial hatred. Tanganyika has not been cursed with the kind of violence and xenophobia which has caused so much suffering and bloodshed in other newly independent African countries, but it is not blameless.

The number of politicians who visited Lindi during my first few months as DC was very high. We had already received visits from Amir Habib Jamal and Paul Bomani at the beginning of August. Later in August, Oscar Kambona, who was at the time Minister for Education, arrived with a large retinue of officials. He had been a close associate of Julius Nyerere in the formative years of TANU, and had been the party's Organising Secretary. He was extreme in his views, and wrote abusive attacks on Sir Richard Turnbull, who was building up a sound working relationship with Julius Nyerere. I also had some personal and disquieting advice. The District Commissioner of Lindi was *ex officio* a member of the Town Council and of the Finance Committee. Soon after I became the District Commissioner, the Deputy Minister for Local Government, Austin Shaba, visited Lindi and told me that the reason for his visit was to investigate a complaint to the Minister by an African employee of the Town Council, alleging that I was a racist and should be removed from Lindi at once. I had made a suggestion at a Finance Committee meeting that we should introduce a new method of verifying that the council had in fact received the goods which it had been asked to pay for.

Austin, who later became the Minister for Health, completely exonerated me and said I would not be moved from Lindi on this occasion, but he advised me privately not to quarrel openly with any African officials because in the current political situation, in an overt disagreement between a white DC and an African official, the African would win, regardless of the merits of the case!

A few months later, the council had a meeting to re-elect its own office-bearers. The Council Chairman, Councillor S Amin, a likeable and hard-working Asian shopkeeper, was re-elected unanimously. The Finance Committee Chairman, Councillor Lucas Joseph, who was the Provincial Vice-Chairman of TANU, declined to be proposed for re-election for a second term and himself proposed me to be his successor as Chairman of the Town Council Finance Committee. In spite of my attempts to persuade Councillor Lucas to agree to stand for re-election, his nomination of me was immediately seconded by Councillor Shaibu Mohamed, the District Chairman of TANU, and I was elected unanimously. My new position was radically different from what it had been when I was an unelected member of a colonial regime. The official who had complained about me applied to be seconded on a training course to another council, and the costs about which I had been uneasy were significantly reduced.

When Julius Nyerere arrived at Lindi Airport, there was a large crowd there to welcome him, but he did not stay there long. He was driven to my house, where Raymond Tubbs, the Provincial Commissioner, and I were waiting for him.

All three of us then went together to a meeting of the District Team. Nyerere repeated, with every appearance of sincerity, what he had written in his letter to expatriate officials, urging them to stay on after Independence because the country needed them and they were friends not enemies. He answered many questions in a sympathetic way, and created a very good impression. He then surprised me by his reply to a question by Raymond Tubbs. This concerned a recent reference he had made to Jomo Kenyatta as 'the spiritual leader of East Africa'. Nyerere replied that as a matter of conscience his remark had been indefensible, but as a matter of politics it had been justifiable and necessary. The candour of his reply was refreshing, but the implicit admission that he did not always mean what he said made me feel uneasy.

A few years later, he showed a similar frankness when he explained his reasons for supporting the introduction of the Preventive Detention Act of 1962. That Act gave the President power to detain people without trial. Nyerere argued that, in the circumstances of a new nation, other factors than individual human rights needed to be taken into account, and that it was preferable for innocent people to suffer preventive detention than for a possible traitor to wreck the nation. Such an argument might perhaps be credible when the President is an honourable man who only makes use of his power in a genuine emergency, but the power to detain without trial can very easily be used by a tyrant to justify the crushing of all political opposition.

After the end of the District Team meeting, Julius Nyerere came back to my house for tea, and he got into conversation with our daughter Ruth. He had great personal charm and humour, and got on splendidly with young children. His nickname was known as *Mwalimu* – teacher. He asked Ruth, who was four, if she was going to school yet, and Ruth explained that her Mummy was teaching her together with two other children whose names were Margaret and Michael. Nyerere then asked if she could read yet, and Ruth replied that she could, and read him a few sentences to prove it.

Nyerere then said, 'You're a very clever girl, aren't you, Ruth?' Ruth paused for a moment before replying, 'Yes.' Then, thinking that one friendly compliment deserved another, she added, 'And you speak very good English, don't you?'

I was appalled. I thought that the remark would be taken as an example of a bright little white girl being patronising to the country's African leader, but Nyerere took no offence whatsoever, and laughed uproariously.

People often criticise Nyerere's misguided economic policies and the fact that he ordered the preventive detention of some of his political opponents, but he nevertheless stands out as one of the greatest African leaders of the twentieth century. At a time when many African leaders in other countries seemed only to be interested in getting rich and hanging on to power, Nyerere lived very modestly. He retired voluntarily from the Presidency in 1985, after serving his country for more than twenty years. His conversation with Ruth illustrated in a way which Jennifer and I will always remember his humility, his approachability and his humour. Those personal qualities will be remembered long after his mistakes have been forgotten.

The week following Julius Nyerere's visit, we had another visit from an old African friend. Stephen Mzinga had been the Head Clerk at Government House when I was the Governor's Private Secretary, and his daughter had been a pupil of Jennifer's at Tabora Girls' School. He visited Lindi as part of a training programme to improve the skills of Africans in running Local Government. He stayed with us, and we gave a small dinner party in his honour. I found myself thinking how likeable, competent, and honest Stephen was, and what a pity it was that the country's elected politicians included so many ambitious and unscrupulous men, some of whom had only gone into politics after being dismissed from the civil service following a conviction for dishonesty.

After Stephen Mzinga's visit, three senior officials from the Education Department came to visit Lindi, and stayed with us for a night. One of them was our very dear friend Peggy Fowler. She was delighted to see her god-daughter Catherine again. Another of the visitors was Ralph Elwell-Sutton, who later married Peggy.

Towards the end of September, Joan Christodoulou, the wife of the excellent District Officer who had been posted to Lindi at the same time as I became the DC, gave birth to a son in Lindi Hospital. Chris and his two daughters came to stay with us while Joan was in hospital. Although we had only known them for a few months, Jennifer and I were already extremely fond of Chris and Joan, and Ruth and Catherine also got on very well indeed with Stephanie and Andrea.

We had a less congenial visit at the beginning of October from members of the Minimum Wages Board. Their aim was to promote better living standards for unskilled labourers. I was in sympathy with their objectives, but I was doubtful about the effectiveness of attempts to enforce a minimum wage. Most of the population of Tanganyika were very poor peasant farmers, and when an employer invited people to work for him there were always far more applicants than there were jobs to fill. Not all employers exploited their work force, though some certainly did, but trade union leaders had not had much success in improving conditions of work for their members, and I saw no reason to believe that staff working for the minimum wages board would be any more successful.

In mid-October the annual DCs' Conference was held in Mtwara under the chairmanship of Raymond Tubbs. All eight District Commissioners in Southern Province assembled in Mtwara for the occasion, and those who came from other parts of the province all stayed with friends stationed in Mtwara.

A few weeks before the conference began, I received a pressing invitation from the Deputy Provincial Commissioner, John Cawthra, to stay with him, bringing Jennifer and the children with me. John and I had worked together in Iringa. In 1953, he had stayed for three weeks in my house before his predecessor, Geoff Bullock, went on leave with his family, and John moved into the house that Geoff had vacated.

John and I were good friends. He was still a bachelor, and he asked me to bring our cook and the children's ayah, so that his servants could work under the guidance of mine in providing the routine our daughters were used to and the meals they enjoyed. John was quiet and rather shy, but he was extremely competent and an exceptionally thoughtful and considerate host. Jennifer later told me how much she had enjoyed hearing me tell her nice things about John's work in Iringa, and that, when she was alone with John, she had enjoyed hearing him say equally nice things to her about me.

The conference agenda was rather vague, partly because nobody had a very clear idea of who would remain in the same job after Independence. Several expected to have left the country by Christmas, and long-term planning seemed inappropriate. Much of the time was devoted to an important discussion on the plans for the celebration of Independence. We also discussed the arrangements for the proposed goodwill visit of a naval ship, H.M.S. *Striker*, during the weeks just prior to Independence, but that only involved the District Commissioners of the three coastal districts of Kilwa, Lindi, and Mtwara.

There was only one African DC in the Province at the time, and I had not met him before. He was a Kenyan called Harold Chipeta, and I thought him outstanding. His contributions to the discussion were wise and well-informed, and he was a delightful person. It was heartening to know that there were Africans of such calibre ready to fill positions of responsibility after expatriate DCs had left the country.

During the Conference, Raymond reminded us all that he and his wife Vivian would shortly be leaving Tanganyika on retirement. The rest of the participants at the conference arranged to host a dinner party in their honour at the least bad hotel in Mtwara, which, to give it its due, produced a very good meal and decorated the hotel dining room very attractively for the occasion. I was sad that Raymond Tubbs would soon be leaving. Some people said that he was harsh to his subordinates who made mistakes, but he was always extremely kind to Jennifer and me.

I was not at all pleased to hear that Raymond's place would be taken temporarily by an Acting Provincial Commissioner – Denis O'Callaghan, who had been my District Commissioner at Tabora and then my Deputy Provincial Commissioner in Eastern Province, when I was stationed in Ulanga. I had little respect for him. Unfortunately, I think he was already aware of my opinion of him.

A few days after Jennifer and I got back from the DCs' Conference, Denis and Sybella arrived in Lindi by ship on their way from Dar to Mtwara. While their ship was anchored in the bay, they came to have dinner with us. Denis mentioned during dinner that he had been the DC in Lindi from 1948 to 1950, when Lindi had still been the Headquarters of Southern Province, and that Sybella had been ill while they were in Lindi. They both seemed amiable, but told us they were very jealous of our having a much grander house than they had had.

Towards the end of October, two officers of the King's African Rifles came to Lindi on a recruiting safari. One was a British major, the other Lieutenant Alexander Nyirenda. Alexander had been at Tabora Boys' School when Jennifer and I had been in Tabora, and he had been one of the first two boys from Tanganyika to be accepted for training at Sandhurst. I knew him well, and liked him very much indeed. We invited both officers to stay with us while they were visiting Lindi.

The major was amiable enough, but no one could have described him as lively. Alexander was fun! He told Ruth stories which had them both convulsed with laughter. He played games

The Flags Changed at Midnight

with our dog Susan, who was ten years old, but responded to Alexander like a young puppy. He was extremely smart in his appearance, had impeccable manners, and his conversation was sensible and amusing. We enjoyed his tales about Sandhurst and listened with respect to his opinions about the political developments taking place in Tanganyika. We were happy to hear that he had been chosen to perform the task of climbing to the top of Mount Kilimanjaro on Independence Night to hoist the new Tanganyikan flag at the summit. After Alexander and the major left us, we got a charming thank-you letter from Alexander, but not a word from the major.

The word 'paternalistic' is now often used as a term of abuse, although Julius Nyerere was often called *Baba wa Taifu* – Father of the Nation. I freely admit that in much of my work for Africans I was paternalistic, and much of my job satisfaction came from the pride I felt in the achievements of Africans like Alexander.

The Last Weeks before Independence

The whole of Tanganyika bustled with activity in the closing months of 1961. Newly-appointed Ministers travelled all over the country to see for themselves the problems they would inherit from the previous administration, and to make themselves known to the people. Officials were transferred from place to place like pawns on a chess board, often to take over essential jobs from colleagues who had retired prematurely.

Paul Grech, the District Medical Officer who had saved Jennifer's unborn baby, was transferred to Dar es Salaam as Specialist Radiologist. C J Patel, a Fellow of the Royal College of Surgeons, who had worked under Paul Grech, became Lindi's new District Medical Officer. Within a few months of Mr Patel's successfully taking charge of Lindi Hospital, he was himself transferred to Mwanza on promotion. He was replaced in Lindi by an Irish doctor who, I later discovered, was not as experienced as his two predecessors.

The transfer of men to other districts meant that their wives went with them, and other women had to be recruited to take on the tasks that were commonly done by expatriate wives. Jennifer, in spite of her pregnancy, was invited to become the new Lindi correspondent of the *Tanganyika Standard*, the country's main English-language newspaper. She was required to use her own initiative in submitting to the editor reports about local events.

She was to be paid a small fee for anything the editor decided to publish. The rate would be fifty per cent higher if the report appeared on the front page.

She also heard from a firm of publishers in London, Routledge and Kegan Paul, that they were about to publish *Wellington Road*, a book which Jennifer had written under a *nom de plume*. Jennifer spent several evenings checking the proofs. It was first published in January 1962, and was reprinted in April. It later came out in paperback as a Penguin book.

Wellington Road concerned a multi-problem family with whom Jennifer had lived as a lodger for six months between completing her teacher training course and sailing out to Tanganyika. The father was work-shy, the mother a part-time prostitute, the children ragged and unwashed, the dog untrained, and the house filthy. The father later went to prison for living off his wife's immoral earnings, and the family broke up. I never met them.

When the book appeared, several reviewers acclaimed it for its penetrating analysis of people who, in spite of being provided with good housing, excellent schools, doctors and social workers, are still not able to cope with the demands of modern life. Jennifer told me that she much preferred the members of the problem family, whose impulsive generosity was part of the cause of their insoluble money problems, to the petty bureaucrats who treated them with contempt, or the door-to-door salesmen and debt-collectors who exploited their inadequacies.

Jennifer was also elected as the new chairperson of the Lindi Branch of the Tanganyika Council of Women. Mrs Patel, the doctor's formidable wife, was the Secretary. The TCW was similar in many ways to the Women's Institute in Britain, but it placed special emphasis on being multi-racial. The refreshments offered at TCW receptions were an assortment of African, Indian, and European dishes, many of which I had not tried before, but found delicious.

Mrs Patel had a bee in her bonnet about family planning, and wanted to promote the use of contraceptives. This was not a cause which appealed greatly to Africans, and Jennifer, whose figure was a clear indication that she was shortly to have another baby, was not a very good advertisement for Mrs Patel's message.

The arrival of AIDS in Africa in the 1980s introduced a powerful new argument in favour of the use of condoms to prevent the spread of sexually transmitted diseases, but during the 1960s most Africans wanted large families. The fact that many cities in India were overpopulated did not then seem relevant in a

sparsely populated country like Tanganyika. The long-term
threat of a world with too many inhabitants is not of pressing
concern to unsophisticated people living in a country with no
system of social security. Most peasant farmers and their wives
loved children. They were also well aware that, if they themselves became too old and frail to cultivate their land, they would
get no sickness benefit or old-age pension. They would therefore
need the support of others, usually their own families, in order to
stay alive. The more children they had, the more people there
would be to share the burden of caring for aged relatives.

Parents who had succeeded in bringing up many children were
respected both for their fertility and for their skill at parenting.
Highly educated parents often had very large families who
became an asset to the country. Moreover, the cash cost of rearing
children in Tanganyika was much lower than in developed countries. Parents in Tanganyika seldom had to buy warm clothing or
shoes for their children. Mothers carried their babies on their
backs, not in prams. Babies were breast-fed. Older children ate
food grown by their parents. Toyshops for the children of peasant
farmers did not exist. School was not compulsory, and from an
early age children helped in rural tasks like scaring grain-eating
birds away from crops, or keeping an eye on the family's cattle
and calling for help if they were in any danger.

* * *

In Lindi District the main cash crop grown by peasant farmers
was cashew nuts, and the market usually opened in mid-
October, with growers selling directly to traders, as there was
as yet no cooperative growers' union in the district to market
the crop.

Cashew nuts grow in a very unusual way, at the bottom end of
a fleshy pear-shaped fruit called a cashew-apple. The nuts are
delicate, and Indian girls with nimble fingers were regarded as
more skilled than Africans in detaching the nuts without breaking them. Much of the value of the crop was wasted by having to
transport it to India for processing. One of my plans for improving the prosperity of the cashew growers of Lindi District was to
recruit a few workers with dexterity who could train the growers'
wives and daughters in ways to detach the nuts without breaking
so many. Sadly, this scheme had made no progress by the time I
retired.

A completely unexpected crisis occurred just as the cashew

markets were due to to open. I received a directive from Dar that the markets should remain closed until 1st November, and that they should then be run as cooperatives. There was not enough time to travel round the district explaining this to the farmers, and it was a very inopportune time to try to force peasants to accept a new system. There was no suitable infrastructure. Even if experienced staff could be brought in from other parts of the country by the beginning of November, they would not be known or trusted by the producers. To make matters worse, the world prices of cashew were much lower in 1961 than in 1960, and producers would blame the new system for their reduced income.

I tried to warn the authorities in Dar that disturbances might be caused by the rigid application in local markets of a dogma dictated from Dar without any thought for the consequences on the ground.

As I feared, there were conflicting instructions from different ministries in Dar. I did not hear of any actual violence at markets in Lindi District, although there were noisy protests. The only violence I heard about occurred in Dar itself, where two of the Ministers involved in the controversy allegedly came to blows in public, with the loss of a few teeth.

Lindi had its own quarrel too, but this did not lead to fisticuffs. It involved two Europeans, both of whom were Field Officers working in the Agriculture Department. Pat Lewis had a very loud voice, chewed his food noisily, had a hairy paunch which bulged through his shirt-front, and always looked dishevelled. He was fond of his beer, and after a glass or two was liable to make ill-advised remarks. He had also won a medal for bravery in the war, worked immensely hard, was liked and trusted by African farmers, and was a generous friend. Pat's wife Doreen was the District Commissioner's very competent and discreet personal secretary.

The trouble arose when Pat's colleague threatened to sue him for defamation of character after Pat had opened his mouth too wide in the bar of a hotel in Mtwara. The last thing I needed was to have two expatriate members of the Distrct Team involved in a lawsuit. I called them both to my office together. Pat did not deny making the remarks, and I told him I thought his behaviour had been outrageous and disloyal to his department. If he had evidence of corruption, then he should have reported it in private either to the Provincial Agricultural Officer, the Superintendent of Police, or to me. A hotel bar was not an appropriate place to make derogatory comments about one's fellow-worker.

I then turned to Pat's colleague, and said he was perfectly within his rights to sue Pat if he wanted to, but I warned him that, if he did so, Pat was likely to defend himself by claiming that what he had said was true. If the court accepted that Pat's allegations about him were well-founded, the consequences for him could be disastrous.

Tears were streaming down Pat's cheeks as he apologised for his behaviour, and shook hands, first with his colleague and then with me. Both men took notice of the warnings I had given them. I was very conscious, as I read them the riot act, that they were both considerably older than me. I was fond of both Pat and Doreen, and hated making Pat so miserable.

* * *

The climate in Lindi did not suit our dhobi, Omari. At the end of October he was admitted to hospital with pneumonia. When he was discharged from hospital, he asked to go back to Tabora, and we paid him off with a gratuity and our warm thanks. We were very sad to see him go. He had worked faithfully for us, starting as a garden boy before we promoted him to be our dhobi in Tabora. He then continued to work for us in Mahenge, Songea, and Lindi. He was diligent, honest, had been excellently trained by Juma, our Head Boy, and he never touched alcohol. We were glad to give him a glowing reference. Omari's successor, an elderly man called Hassani, was much more experienced than Omari. He had good references dating back as far as 1930, but we found that his work was nothing like as good as Omari's.

* * *

The idea of sending a warship to a Trust Territory just two weeks before it gets its independence, and describing it as a 'goodwill' visit seemed odd. Gun-boat diplomacy normally implies the reverse of goodwill. However, when I was told that H.M.S. *Striker* would be paying visits to various ports along the Tanganyika coast and would be in Lindi from 27th November to 2nd December, I called a meeting of the District Team, with a few co-opted non-officials, in order to discuss plans and arrange a draft programme. The explicit aim of the visit was to foster goodwill, and we all agreed to do our best to make it a success. We thought it would also be useful as a dress rehearsal for some aspects of the celebrations for Independence a week later.

The ship would arrive in Lindi from Mtwara, having previously called at Bombay, ports in the Persian Gulf, and Mombasa. It would remain in Lindi for five days, then sail northwards towards Kilwa and Dar es Salaam.

The Chairman of the Lindi Club, Edgar Spencer-Payne, was a long-term resident of Lindi. He was employed by one of the shipping companies which had offices in Lindi, and, because of the reduction of traffic in the port of Lindi, he was not excessively busy. He was also a very good organiser, and on friendly terms with members of all the racial groups in Lindi. Edgar volunteered to co-ordinate the arrangements for the naval visit. He promised to ask the Club Committee to agree to make its facilities and premises available to all members of the crew.

A few days before H.M.S. *Striker* arrived, Edgar outlined a draft programme which he had worked out. He had already got several people to promise to provide hospitality to members of the ship's crew, and had arranged motor transport for the visitors.

A few hours before the ship was due to arrive, Denis O'Callaghan telephoned me from Mtwara to warn me that the crew were a bunch of drunken hooligans who had been rowdy and behaved appallingly while in Mtwara. One seaman had even exposed himself indecently in front of the wife of one of the senior officials stationed there. I felt profoundly uneasy, but decided to go ahead with the programme as planned, and hope for the best.

On the first night of the visit, the *Striker* held a sundowner party on board the ship for residents of Lindi. One of the guests fell on the steep and slippery gangway, but she was not badly hurt. Jennifer and I were both especially careful on Thursday evening, when we visited the ship for a small dinner party given by the Captain.

The part of the programme hosted by Lindi included accompanied visits to the beach, a variety of sporting events against opponents from all races, visits by small groups of crew members to private houses, to sisal estates, and to villages a few miles inland. There was a barbecue party on the Wednesday evening in the Lindi Club, and a dance at the Club on the Friday evening. Before Jennifer and I went on to the dance, we gave a small dinner party for the Captain and a few others.

The only flaw in Edgar's planning was that there were not

enough women to provide partners at the dance for all the men, so the dance turned into a sing-song, with individuals doing their party-pieces. Jennifer, tired by her pregnancy, went home around midnight, but many of those who stayed on were very talented, and the party did not end till three o'clock on Saturday morning. The ship sailed soon after sunrise.

I had been pleased at the good behaviour of the whole crew, but puzzled that they should have created such an unfavourable impression in Mtwara. Towards the end of the sing-song the reason became clear. When they were taking their leave and thanking us for the welcome they had had in Lindi, many of the crew contrasted Lindi with Mtwara. They described Mtwara as 'a dump', 'a hell-hole', 'rotten', 'horrible' and various other graphic terms of abuse. Lindi, on the other hand, was 'bloody brilliant'. One slightly tipsy seaman put his arm round my shoulder as he was leaving, and told me in a confidential whisper that he had never been treated like a toff before, and would never forget it.

I do not doubt that some sailors behaved badly in Mtwara, but I put most of the blame on those who planned a programme in which snobbery prevailed. Officers were acceptable in Mtwara, but naval ratings were treated as second-class citizens. Very little had been arranged for the ratings, so they got bored and spent their leisure time drinking in grotty bars. The sailor who had allegedly exposed himself had probably drunk too much beer and could not find a public convenience.

I loved Lindi, and disliked Mtwara, and it reassured me that so many of the crew of the *Striker* with no axe to grind shared my opinion.

Uhuru

On the same day that H.M.S. *Striker* sailed from Lindi, I was the invited guest of TANU at a large public meeting in Lindi Stadium, where the TANU District Chairman, Shaibu Mohamed, made a simple but wise speech, stressing the need for people of all races to work together for the progress of the country, and for everyone to behave with dignity and good manners at the Independence ceremony. He ended with a very gracious tribute to the British and some kind remarks about me. I was then invited to address the crowd. I reiterated Shaibu's message, and I think I left them in no doubt about my pride and happiness at being part of their great day, and about my affection for the people among whom I had been working. I made equally complimentary remarks about Shaibu Mohamed.

Tanganyika got its Independence – *Uhuru* – on Saturday 9th December 1961, exactly a week after H.M.S. *Striker* left Lindi. The eyes of the world were fixed on the ceremony in the capital, Dar es Salaam, where leaders form many countries gathered to celebrate a freedom won without violence. In the rest of Tanganyika every district celebrated the occasion in a similar way, but with variations of detail.

In Lindi, we started planning for Uhuru Day as soon as the date was announced. Each district was allocated a certain amount of money, and was given authority to raise additional funds from local businesses and individual citizens. Traders responded very generously.

Fund-raising could only be done by properly authorised collectors and receipts were issued for cash contributed. Each collector was given a defined area to collect from so that potential donors would only be approached once. We asked for the money to be subscribed before a definite target date so that we could know as soon as possible exactly how much we would be able to spend.

Members of the District Team were made responsible for specific tasks and were asked to say how much money and manpower they would need. Representatives of TANU collaborated eagerly with officials of central and local government. Preparations for Uhuru Day were to have priority over other day-to-day commitments. Routine tasks could be postponed if necessary until after 9th December; tasks connected with the Independence ceremony and celebrations could not. However tempting it might be to say, 'It'll be all right on the night!' we were all determined not let the people down on Tanganyika's greatest day. Nothing could be allowed to go wrong, and we rehearsed everything.

I remembered the effort my colleagues and I had devoted in Iringa in 1953 to making the celebration of the Coronation of Queen Elizabeth II a success there, but this was something else. The Coronation had taken place in Westminster Abbey, thousands of miles away. Uhuru was about to happen in Tanganyika. It would be the culmination of what the citizens of Tanganyika had been struggling to achieve for seven years, ever since TANU was founded on 7th July 1954.

People who have lived in Britain all their lives and have never been ruled by anyone else may find it hard to understand the depth of the feelings of the Tanganyikans who were about to become a free nation for the first time.

The planning committee held several plenary meetings and I also kept in close touch with those individuals who were responsible for particular tasks. I needed to make sure that everything was going well, and, if necessary, to allocate more money or more manpower to tasks which were giving rise to problems.

We were sure that many of the people living in rural parts of the district would want to come into Lindi to take part in the festivities but we had no idea how many. We needed an estimate of the number of people who would need overnight shelter; how much food and drinking water to supply; how many temporary latrines to build and where to put them; and how many people would want transportation into Lindi and back home again after the celebrations. TANU leaders volunteered to get this information from their local branches in all the villages, and their estimates proved very accurate.

Certain tasks needed people with particular skills. Electricians were in great demand for the lighting and public address systems. Engineers and artisans from the Public Works Department took charge of purchasing the materials and putting up the dais on which the ceremony of lowering the old flag and unfurling the new one would take place.

The District Foreman took charge of the arrangements for a firework display. The Health Inspector and his staff supervised the arrangements for sanitation and rubbish disposal. Cooks were recruited to prepare the curry and rice which would be available free over the holiday period. The smartest police askaris were selected to form a small Guard of Honour to take part in the ceremony. The rest of Lindi's police contingent were instructed to maintain law and order and supervise crowd control.

The green-shirted members of TANU Youth League volunteered to help the police in controlling the crowds and before the ceremony started they searched people entering the stadium to make sure they were not carrying weapons. No one was found to be armed, and I was told later that the frisking was done in a very good-natured way and that everyone accepted that the process was a wise precaution.

The leaders of TANU were just as determined as government officials that the day would not be spoilt by drunkenness and a law was enacted prohibiting the sale of alcohol anywhere in Tanganyika for the whole period of four days while the celebrations lasted.

Everything seemed to be progressing smoothly until three or four days before Uhuru Day. The rains came much earlier than usual in 1961 and by early December the road between Dar and Lindi was impassable. The telephone line between Mtwara, Lindi, and Dar was also out of order for much of the time.

The *Tanganyika Standard* had announced that it would print in advance of Uhuru Day full details of the programme of events for every district but when copies of the paper reached us we discovered that the details about Lindi which we had sent off in good time for publication had been left out, so we had to distribute as many hastily run-off copies as possible to remind everybody of what was happening where.

The fireworks for Lindi had missed the last lorry to leave Dar before the coast road closed. They had to be brought to Lindi by an inland route, as, for safety reasons, aeroplanes were not allowed to carry fireworks.

A speech recorded by Julius Nyerere, the new Prime Minister, would be included in the ceremony, and the climax was to take place at exactly midnight, when the Union Flag would be lowered slowly to the sound of *God Save the Queen*, and the lights would all be put out and there would be a moment of total silence. The music would then change to the new Tanganyika National Anthem – *Mungu Abariki Tanganyika* – *God Bless Tanganyika*. The tune was the same as the African National Congress hymn *Nkosi Sekelele Afrika*. The lights would be switched on again to reveal the new green, black and gold flag of Tanganyika.

The Province's supply of new national flags was delayed in transit. We were anxious when ours did not reach Mtwara until long after they should already have arrived in Lindi. Worse still, though the recording of Julius Nyerere's speech was intact, the recordings of both the National Anthems had been badly packed and they arrived in pieces and could not possibly be used. We all agonised about what to do until someone suggested that the proprietor of the local cinema might be able to help. He gladly did so. *God Save the Queen* had been played at the end of each cinema performance for years, and he had recently invested in a record of the new National Anthem to be played at future performances. The worn record of *God Save the Queen* sounded a bit scratchy, but no one minded about that. At least it was recognisable, and what people really wanted to hear was *God Bless Tanganyika*.

Supplies of bunting and banners for decorating the town had

arrived in good time and had been adorning the streets for some days, but the rain had soaked them and made them look rather bedraggled.

The football stadium provided seating for some spectators of all races, and there was standing room for several thousand more. Jennifer and I wanted our servants all to have the chance to attend the ceremony, but someone had to watch over Ruth and Catherine, who were much too young to be left alone, so Jennifer stayed at home with them. She listened to the live ceremony in Lindi and to a radio broadcast of what was going on simultaneously in the capital. In Dar, the crowds were unable to contain their glee for long enough for Julius Nyerere to complete his speech, and over the radio it was inaudible. In Lindi, the crowds listened in total silence to the recording of Nyerere and of the new Anthem and paused for an instant in complete and reverent silence before bursting into jubilant cheers which went on for the whole night.

Her Majesty the Queen was represented in Dar es Salaam by the Duke of Edinburgh. Julius Nyerere himself represented Tanganyika. In Lindi and in other districts, the newly independent country was represented by the District Chairman of TANU. The Queen was represented by the District Commissioner, so I myself had the great privilege of representing Her Majesty on the occasion that had been the target towards which I had been working for just over ten years.

I was very glad that the representative of TANU was Shaibu Mohamed. During the short time I had been in Lindi, he had made a habit of dropping in unexpectedly to my house after sundown to discuss the district's problems with me and to have a cup of tea. If I was busy or had other guests, he just asked my houseboy to give me his greetings and left. I found our conversations pleasant and useful. There were some members of TANU who did not approve of collaboration with British officials, but Shaibu was not intimidated by them. He was not a racist or an extremist. He showed no sign of personal ambition or greed for his own advancement. I was extremely lucky to have a man like Shaibu as the TANU Chairman in my District. We became good friends, and I only wish that all the political leaders who came to power at Independence had been like him. Unfortunately many were not.

I had another reason to be pleased after the Independence ceremony was over and had been acclaimed as a success. The formal white uniforms worn by District Commissioners were extremely

uncomfortable. The trouser-legs were like drainpipes, and were held in place by pieces of black garter elastic strapped under the insteps of long black leather boots concealed under the trouser legs. Outside our left trouser-legs we carried swords. The collars of our tunics were tight and held together by hooks and eyes that were hard to close and even harder to open. On our heads we wore large, hard, and very uncomfortable white helmets with brass badges. I had worn my uniform from time to time as the Governor's Private Secretary, and also when Princess Margaret visited Tabora. Although it was described as 'tropical kit', I nearly always got prickly heat after wearing it during the hours of daylight. Even at midnight, I was dripping with sweat as I wore it in Lindi, and I was thankful that I would never have to wear it again.

* * *

The festivities carried on over Saturday, Sunday, and Monday. Events had been arranged to suit people of all ages. The very young took part in children's sports. Footballers played football. The elderly sat outside their houses watching the young people enjoying themselves. People of all ages danced and sang for three whole days without a break. They were all completely sober and blissfully happy.

Huge bowls of curry and rice were available at several places in the town for people to help themselves when they got hungry. As soon as the amount of food seemed to be getting low, the cooks went to get more from the kitchens and refill the bowls. There were no knives or forks. People used the fingers of their right hands to eat with – the Swahili for the right hand is *mkono wa kulia* which means literally 'the hand for eating with'.

I walked around the town greeting as many people as possible, and I was often invited to join a group of people who were eating. The curry was delicious, and I enjoyed it. If the others were seated on chairs, they would always insist on bringing an additional chair for me. If they were sitting on the ground, I sat on the ground as well. Many of the residents of the town already knew me, and many people who had come in from the rural villages had seen me at the midnight ceremony. I was happy to be treated as a friend, and the welcome that was extended to me was extended to other expatriate officials as well. There had been a time a couple of years earlier when politically minded Africans had often shouted abuse at Europeans, but now that Julius Nyerere was Prime Minister and Tanganyika was independent all the rancour seemed to be a thing of the past.

The dancers seemed to have limitless energy, but I was tired, and decided to go home to spend a few hours relaxing with Jennifer and playing with Ruth and Catherine. We had told all our servants that we could manage without them until Tuesday and they could go and join in the celebrations, but they chose Juma as their spokesman, and he told us that they had all agreed among themselves that one servant would stay on the premises in case of an emergency. I assume he was thinking that Jennifer might have to be rushed to hospital to have her baby, but he was much too polite to say so.

On the Monday after Independence we were very surprised when Denis and Sybella O'Callaghan arrived at our house at midday. They were passengers on the coaster between Dar and Mtwara, and the ship had just arrived in Lindi, so they had decided to pay us a call. Our recently recruited dhobi Hassani was in the house at the time, and he was not a cook. We therefore apologised for not being able to offer lunch for guests as we ourselves were only going to have bread and cheese. The O'Callaghans said that sounded delicious so we asked them to join us, and I laid the table while Jennifer got out a tin-opener to open a tin of Camembert cheese which her mother had sent us as a present from England.

Unfortunately, the cheese had gone bad, and as soon as Jennifer pierced the lid of the tin a jet of liquid under high pressure shot up into the air and descended on the top of her head. The smell was like a barrack room where a platoon of infantrymen have just taken their boots off after a route march. Jennifer excused herself and went to have a shower and wash her hair. The O'Callaghans were highly amused by the incident. Our picnic meal was delayed. After lunch it started to pour with rain, and Denis and Sybella stayed on in our house until a few minutes before their ship was due to sail. The conversation was lively, and I began to hope that working under Denis in Southern Province might not be quite as unpleasant as I had feared.

Bearing False Witness

The total euphoria in Lindi lasted only for a few days after Independence. When the public holiday was over and I had spent a couple of days trying to catch up with the arrears of paperwork in my office, a group of six or seven TANU members came to the Boma and asked to see me. My office messenger told me they had a serious complaint about a Swiss engineer called Romann, who was employed on one of the District's sisal estates that was a long way from Lindi itself. I had only met him once but had heard that for various reasons he was not popular with those who worked for him.

I called the men into my office and asked their spokesman to tell me what had happened. He said that, on Independence Day, metal badges with a picture of the face of Julius Nyerere had been given away for people to attach to their clothes. He told me that Romann had taken a number of these badges, and had then fixed them on to the collar of his dog, with a remark to the effect that his dog was just as good as any African.

Among Muslims such a remark was certain to give particular offence. I listened with growing astonishment that anyone could want to insult and humiliate Africans on Uhuru Day. It seemed not just nasty but also stupid to make a remark that was likely to provoke violence against oneself. I assured the group that Romann's comments did not reflect the views of Europeans generally, and that they should now go to the Police Station to make a formal complaint, so that the matter could be investigated and dealt with in a court of law.

As soon as they left my office to go to the Police Station, I telephoned the Superintendent, Michel Le Bars, to let him know that they were on their way. I asked Michel to investigate the allegations very thoroughly, and he promised to send out his best inspector and a good detective-constable, both of them Africans, to take statements from all the witnesses at the sisal estate where Romann worked. I then telephoned the Provincial Office to let Denis O'Callaghan know the situation.

The police Landrover got badly stuck in the mud, and took several days to make the journey to the sisal estate and back again. Meanwhile, without waiting for confirmation of the allegations, the authorities in Dar es Salaam issued an expulsion order requiring Romann to leave the country. The time he was allowed to pack up seemed short, and I believe he had to abandon many of his belongings. I had initially taken the complaint at its face value, and thought that Tanganyika would be better off without him.

When the Landrover at last got back to Lindi, however, the inspector reported that the complaint had been a tissue of lies. Even though Romann was unpopular, he had committed no offence involving badges or racist remarks. The inspector himself said that he thought the expulsion order ought to be cancelled, and those who had complained to me should themselves be charged with maliciously making a false statement to a person in authority. Regrettably, this was quite a common offence.

I discussed the problem with Michel Le Bars and with Chris Christodoulou, whose judgement I respected greatly. We all thought the inspector's views seemed reasonable, but we did not have the power to rescind an expulsion order, and we were all worried that arresting a group of TANU members on such a charge could cause serious disturbances. I therefore decided to consult Denis O'Callaghan, my senior officer, before doing anything else. Michel went back to the police station, and I promised to get in touch with him again as soon as possible.

When Denis answered the phone, he said that the problem was much too hot for him to handle, and that if I said later that I had consulted him personally about it he would deny it. He warned me that as he was senior to me, his word would automatically be accepted rather than mine.

I remembered how spineless Denis had been in dealing with the affair of the corrupt Chief Fundikira in Tabora District, but I never expected him to be quite such an abject coward. I beckoned to Chris to stand very close to me with the phone midway between our ears while I asked Denis to confirm that I had understood him correctly. After I put the phone down I explained to Chris that if it should ever come to a point where Denis and I gave accounts which were incompatible, I would be glad of a completely trustworthy witness to corroborate my word.

Romann's lawyer protested that the expulsion order had been issued without verifying the facts, but the authorities in Dar did not admit that they had made any mistake, and Romann had to leave the country.

There were two very able and honest Asian lawyers practising in partnership in Lindi at the time, G M Pardhan and Y N Lilani. Pardhan was Romann's lawyer. He asked to come to our house to discuss Romann's case with Jennifer and me, and to request Jennifer to submit to the editor of the *Tanganyika Standard* a report quoting him verbatim in his protest about the unjust way his client had been treated.

As Pardhan spoke, my admiration for him grew. I warned him that making a statement on the lines he proposed would make him very unpopular with the authorities, and that he might himself be victimised. He replied quite calmly that he had been born in Tanganyika and had recently taken out Tanganyika citizenship. He felt it was his duty to protest about any injustice done by the leaders of his country. Jennifer endorsed my warnings, but our efforts were unavailing, and a few days later Pardhan's words appeared on the front page of the *Tanganyika Standard* under the banner headline THIS IS NOT JUSTICE – SAYS LINDI ADVOCATE.

* * *

A short while later I was told of another case in the adjacent District to Lindi involving a British official whom I never met. A cow on the research farm where he worked died of a disease which he suspected might be anthrax. In that case the animal would not be fit for human consumption, so he ordered the carcass to be buried. A group of disgruntled labourers who had hoped to eat the meat then went to the police and complained that the official concerned was guilty of the new offence of 'showing disrespect to the national flag' by saying the new flag was only fit to be used to wipe one's arse. He was charged with this offence, which he denied absolutely, insisting that he had complete respect for the flag, and that in any case his knowledge of the language was not good enough for him to express in Swahili the indelicate views that he was said to have uttered.

He was suspended from duty and he and his family were advised for their own safety to stay indoors at home until the case came before the court. He had been a member of TECSA, the Tanganyika European Civil Servants' Association, which had ceased to exist when Independence came, and the balance of TECSA's funds was used to pay for a good lawyer to defend the case.

The lawyer had no difficulty in discrediting the prosecution witnesses. They all agreed about the main element of the charge, but in cross-examination the lawyer asked questions on matters of detail about the allegation against his client. When he asked when the offence took place, some said in the morning, others in the afternoon. Some said it had happened inside the office of the accused, others that it had happened on the verandah, others in the open air. Some said the accused had been sitting down, others that he had been standing up. Some said the accused spoke Swahili well, others that he spoke it badly. The discrepancies were so blatant that no court could possibly convict on the evidence of such unreliable witnesses.

The official was acquitted, but no action was taken on this occasion against those who had given false evidence in court. I was worried that others motivated by envy or malice might also plot to make false allegations, especially against non-natives. If they did so, they could well have learnt the lesson that, when giving perjured evidence in court, a group of conspirators should always prepare in advance consistent answers to the questions which they might be asked in cross-examination.

My concern was not just for Europeans and Asians in general. I was also worried on my own behalf. I had already been the subject of one malicious letter written by the Town Clerk to the Minister for Local Government, and, though I had won a significant battle on that occasion, I had no wish to be falsely accused a second time. However, in the course of doing my duty I had made another powerful enemy. The Member of Parliament for Lindi had seemed very friendly when I arrived in Lindi and when I took over as DC. However, he became hostile when I refused to let him take out of the Boma an official file classified as 'secret'. I do not know why he wanted the file, but I would have been guilty of an infringement of the security rules if I had agreed to his request. His anger at my refusal made me uneasy, and I was sure I could not rely on Denis O'Callaghan to support me in any emergency.

Some months after my family and I had returned to Britain, I got a letter from Lilani telling me the latest news about Pardhan. He could not be expelled from the country of which he was a citizen, and he had committed no crime. The new Government nevertheless bore a bitter grudge against him for speaking out on behalf of Romann, and it had served a restriction order compelling him to reside in Tunduru Minor Settlement and not to engage in any business outside Tunduru District. There was no possible way for a lawyer to make a living in an economic backwater like Tunduru. The new Government of a supposedly free and independent Tanganyika had effectively deprived an honest citizen of his right of freedom of association, to move where he wanted, and to earn his living as a lawyer.

Uhuru Day had been a very joyful occasion. A democratically elected Government had taken over from a colonial power. The Prime Minister was widely admired. Racial harmony seemed to prevail. Within a few weeks of Tanganyika becoming independent, however, there had been examples of the abuse of human rights, particularly the rights of racial minorities, and Julius Nyerere had resigned and been replaced as Prime Minister by Rashidi Kawawa.

Lilani's letter made me sad, and very sorry for Pardhan. I nevertheless felt relieved that my family and I were safely back in England, and that I was no longer working for a Government which had such a huge majority that it did not always feel it necessary to respect the basic human rights of minority groups. Tanganyika never produced a brutal tyrant like Idi Amin in neighbouring Uganda, but some of its elected leaders abused their power, and even Julius Nyerere's record in the field of human rights was not unblemished.

In Peril on the Sea

On Christmas Day it was our custom each year to invite all our unmarried colleagues who would otherwise spend the day by themselves to join us for lunch. In Lindi, we also gave a party just before Christmas for thirty-one children and another one for about forty members of the Tanganyika Council of Women. Our house was big enough for a large number of guests, but the Christmas festivities a few weeks after Independence were spoilt by oppressive heat and very heavy rain. The jellies that Mohamed had prepared for the children's party were left in the coldest part of the fridge the previous day, and still had not set by the time the children arrived.

The roads out of Lindi were all impassable, and the level of the River Lukuledi, which entered the Indian Ocean at Lindi, rose higher and higher. The problem of soil erosion was serious in the rainy season, and every year the Indian Ocean, which was normally bright blue, became discoloured near to the mouths of all the big rivers as thousands of tons of fertile top-soil from inland were washed into the sea, making the water look like thick brown soup.

Fisherman with outrigger canoe

On Saturday 30th December, exactly three weeks after Independence Day, the weather changed. It stopped raining for a few days, and the sun shone brightly for the first time for weeks. Children came out to play on the sandy beach, which shelved so gently that at low tide an aeroplane could take off and land without any difficulty.

Officials worked a five-and-a-half day week in Tanganyika, and Chris Christodoulou and I were just preparing to leave the Boma and have lunch. Expatriates normally enjoyed a large curry lunch every Saturday. Suddenly Police Inspector Saidi ran to my office and told me that three boys had been spotted far out to sea and were in danger of drowning in the bay.

Chris drove me to the point on the sea front closest to the boys, who had got separated. Two were not far from a fishing canoe which appeared to have seen them, but the third was by himself, with no boat anywhere near him to pick him up. A crowd of Africans was standing by the water's edge. Some were muttering that it was '*Shauri ya Mungu*' – 'the will of God'.

Chris and I and an African Police Constable who came from the shores of Lake Nyasa took off our shirts, shoes, socks and watches and ran into the water to try to swim out and rescue the boy. The policeman was not a strong swimmer, and turned back quite soon. I was amazed at how fast Chris and I were swimming, and we reached the boy far quicker than I had expected. I got to him first, and lifted him on to my back and turned round to swim back to the shore. Chris followed a yard or so behind me in order to take a turn at carrying the boy if I got tired.

It was only after we turned towards the shore that I understood why we had made such good speed out to the boy. We, like him, had been carried out to sea by the ebb tide and the spate of water flowing down the Lukuledi into the sea. Reaching the boy had been easy, but getting back again against the current was quite a different matter. We just managed to make slow headway when we were swimming as hard as we possibly could, but as soon as we paused to get our breath back the tide immediately began to carry us out to sea again. If we were to survive, we would need to go on swimming without taking a rest at all.

We were still a few hundred yards from the shore when I noticed that Chris himself seemed to be in some difficulty, and I had the horrifying thought that a really outstanding District Officer with a lovely wife and three delightful children might lose his life in an attempt to rescue an unknown small boy.

My moment of panic did not last very long. I am nearly two metres tall, and, when we were still a long way off the shore, my toe touched the bottom of the sea. Chris is not so tall as me, and he was still out of his depth. He would have had to swim much further than I did, but I was able to walk with the boy still on my back and holding Chris's hand till we all reached safety.

The spectators on the shore told me that the other two boys had been picked up by the fishing boat, and the boy I had saved told me that his name was Mohamed Ibrahim Himboti, and that there had been only three boys playing together by the water's edge. I was thankful that they all now appeared to be safe. I do not think I could have made the journey a second time.

Chris and I retrieved our clothing and returned home for a very late lunch with our families. When Jennifer saw me she said my face was ashen, and she felt what seemed like her first contractions. The contractions stopped, however, and the baby was not born until more than three weeks later.

That afternoon, I was told that the boy whom Chris and I had saved had misled us. There had in fact been six boys playing on the shore, and three were still missing, presumed drowned. One of the missing boys was the son of the Chief Warder of Lindi Prison, whom I knew and respected.

Jennifer and I had invited Len Yull, the Forest Officer from Rondo, and his wife Liz to stay with us to celebrate the New Year. The sun was setting on New Year's Eve when Len looked out over the bay from our verandah, and saw the body of a small boy lying on the sand just below the wall in front of our house. I followed Len to the water's edge, where a small crowd of spectators had gathered. One of them identified the boy as the Chief Warder's son, and we went to phone for the boy's father and to call the Hospital Landrover to take the body to the mortuary.

The body of a dead child is always a poignant sight, even when the child has died from natural causes and is laid out peacefully on a bed. The twisted little body of a child with rigor mortis whose death is due to drowning is unbearably distressing. I watched the tears trickling gently down his father's cheeks, and was not able to find words to express adequately the sympathy I felt for him. As far as I know, the bodies of the other two boys were never recovered from the sea.

New Year's Eve was a Sunday, and as soon as the Landrover had returned to the Hospital with the Chief Warder and his dead son, Liz and Len went with Jennifer and me to evensong in the Anglican Church. When the service was over, we felt an obligation to go to the Lindi Club to see the New Year in with our friends, while Margaret, our ayah, looked after Ruth and Catherine, but we did not enjoy ourselves, and returned home immediately after midnight.

When the Boma opened again after the New Year holiday, Denis O'Callaghan telephoned me from Mtwara. He congratulated Chris and me on saving an African *toto* (child), and said he thought that such an action was 'politically very expedient so soon after Independence'. I made no reply.

A week or two later I got a letter from my mother. Her views were very different from Denis's, but they displeased me just as much. She was absolutely furious that I had risked my own life, and the future security of my wife and two daughters I loved, and an unborn baby, in order to save a black boy I did not even know. I got the impression that she might not have minded quite so much if the boy had been white.

I am not a brave person. I swam out to rescue the boy before I had any idea of the strength of the current, and it was over-confidence rather than courage that prompted me to do so. If I had known the danger, I might have been too scared to attempt the rescue, but I hope not.

The Master has Arrived

In a few up-country stations there was a 'judge's rest-house' where the judge stayed when he came to preside over High Court sessions. In Lindi it was assumed that the judge would stay with the District Commissioner. There were two problems about having a judge to stay. Some judges were said to be extremely demanding and pompous guests. It was also hard to predict how long the judge and his retinue would remain. If all the accused pleaded guilty, the sessions could be over in a couple of days, but if they all pleaded not guilty, and all the evidence from prosecution and defence witnesses in each case had to be heard and taken down in writing, then the judge might remain for much longer.

Jennifer and I were not very pleased to learn that High Court sessions would take place in Lindi during the week that Jennifer was expecting to be admitted to hospital to have her baby. We were also unenthusiastic when we heard that we would have not one but two guests to stay. The presiding judge was to be accompanied by his wife. Jennifer was tired, and did not relish the prospect of keeping the judge's wife amused while the judge himself was in Court and I was in the Boma. We had already met them both in Tabora, and did not think of them as being personal friends. The next few days totally changed our opinion about them both.

When Philip Biron had been a Senior Resident Magistrate, he had visited Tabora in order to preside over the very long trial of a British lawyer charged with subornation of perjury (see Chapter 6). While he was working temporarily in Tabora, his interest in Rita Colville, the Matron of Tabora Hospital, had given rise to a few uncharitable comments about middle-aged people behaving like lovesick teenagers. Jennifer and I were rather surprised to hear some time later that they had got married.

As soon as they arrived in Lindi, it became obvious that the Birons were devoted to each other and extremely happy. They were appreciative and thoughtful guests. Rita was a very experienced midwife, and took a great interest in our daughters, in the unborn baby, and in Jennifer's health. I was glad that Jennifer had someone so friendly and competent to keep her company during the hours I had to spend in my office.

Philip Biron had a keen sense of humour, and conversation with him was never dull. I was also very glad that, on the only occasion when I had ever thought of consulting a lawyer about a personal matter, there was an exceptionally able judge staying with us as a guest, and he gave me his legal advice without making a charge for it!

The problem was quite a simple one. The Government was demanding money from me which I did not think I owed. At the beginning of my tour, when I was travelling with my family to Songea, I had been promised in Dar that a Landrover would escort us from Njombe to Songea, the last and most difficult part of our journey. Unfortunately, the Boma Landrovers in Songea and Njombe were both being repaired at the time, so the District Commissioner of Njombe had hired the Landrover of a local Asian trader to accompany me, and asked the trader to submit his bill to the District Commissioner of Songea.

I thought no more about the matter until nearly a year later, when I got a demand from the Accountant General's Office ordering me to meet the hire charge from my own pocket, even though I had been promised, first in Dar, then in Njombe, and finally in Songea, that the cost would be borne by the District Office in Songea.

I told Philip Biron the whole story, and he immediately drafted a brilliantly worded letter for me to send to the Accountant General. All I had to do was to start my reply with the words 'I have consulted my legal adviser, who has expressed the following opinion –'. A few weeks later I got another letter from the Accountant General withdrawing the claim he had made against me.

The due date of Jennifer's confinement had passed, and Mr C J Patel, the Medical Officer, said he would induce the birth on 22nd January. When he heard that the Birons were still staying with us, however, he deferred the date of Jennifer's admission to Hospital until the following day, when our guests left Lindi.

* * *

On the same day that the Birons left, astonishing news reached Lindi. We heard that Julius Nyerere had resigned from the position of Prime Minister, only seven weeks after Uhuru, in favour of Rashidi Kawawa. The news caused tension across the whole country, and in Lindi I feared possible unrest. Many people concluded, quite wrongly, that Nyerere must have got involved in some financial scandal. He himself gave as his reason for resigning that he wanted to concentrate on reorganising TANU. I was sceptical about this. Most people brought up in Britain think that the position of Prime Minister is much more important than that of the leader of a political party. In fact, Nyerere's explanation may well have been quite genuine. He strengthened his leadership of TANU, and on 9th December 1962, exactly one year after Uhuru, he was elected as Tanganyika's first President, with an enormous majority. He polled over a million votes. His opponent, Zuberi Mtemvu of the extremist African National Congress polled just over 20,000. Nyerere remained President until 1985, when he retired voluntarily.

Kawawa was less extreme than Mtemvu, but much more outspoken in his anti-European views than Nyerere. I did not trust him, and reluctantly decided that the time had come for my family and me to leave Tanganyika. I did not want to give notice without discussing the matter fully with Jennifer, however, so I waited until until after the baby was born before I gave six months' notice of my wish to retire.

On the evening of 24th January, I received a phone call from Mr Patel announcing proudly, 'The Master has arrived!' He told me that our son's umbilical cord had been wrapped round his neck, and that his life had been saved by Mr Patel's professional skill. I still regret that the political tensions caused by the change of Prime Minister meant that I was not with Jennifer at the hospital as I had been when Ruth and Catherine were born. During the first five days of our son's life, I was with him for less than an hour.

There was a retired Anglican Bishop, Frank Thorne, in the adjacent room to Jennifer's in the hospital, and as soon as he heard the baby crying he wrote to Jennifer telling her we should call him Timothy, as 24th January was Saint Timothy's Day. Jennifer's refusal was a masterpiece of diplomacy. We had thought about calling a boy Philip long before Philip and Rita Biron came to stay with us, but while they were our guests we got used to the sound of the name and liked it, so we decided to call him Philip Michael. I signed his birth certificate in two places, one as the parent notifying the birth, and the other as the Official Registrar of Births in the District where he was born.

Jennifer and the baby both got bad prickly heat in hospital. There was a fan beside Jennifer's bed, but she was advised not to use it in case the baby got a chill. When they both came home, however, we laid Philip out naked on a clean towel where he could cool down in the gentle breeze provided by the ceiling fans in our living room.

Hassani, the new dhobi who had replaced Omari, was lazy, and had not ironed the towels on which Philip lay. The purpose of pressing towels with a hot iron was not to make them look elegant but to kill the eggs of an unpleasant insect called a mango-fly, which laid them on clothes left drying in the sun. These eggs then turned into maggots which burrowed under the skin of the person wearing the unironed clothes – or lying on the unironed towel. When Philip was only a few weeks old, his back was covered with sore spots caused by larvae which had to be removed by smothering the wounds with vaseline. Philip's back remained scarred for several months.

* * *

On 18th February I drove up from Lindi to the Rondo Plateau to attend the opening ceremony of the new theological college there. I loaded the car with many of the things we would need on local leave, and the following day I drove up again with the whole family, including our dog Susan, to begin a couple of weeks of local leave.

Just as we had done in Ulanga District, we took our cook and ayah with us. We stayed in a house which was empty following the departure from Rondo of Steel Brothers, the forestry firm. The house was only fifty yards from the house where Len and Liz Yull were living, and they made us very welcome. Before we arrived, Liz had put bowls of lovely flowers in every room. They invited us to dinner on our first night. The next night they came to us.

Prickly heat was quickly cured at an altitude of two thousand feet above sea level, and we enjoyed the beautiful view, the peace and quiet of the plateau, and the company of two good friends. Ruth and Catherine loved it, and Jennifer and I relaxed, enjoying gentle walks with the children, reading light books, and listening to our long-playing records – there was electricity on the Rondo Plateau. We did nothing energetic. We both felt too exhausted.

Philip was still too young to join in, but the rest of the family's favourite game on the Rondo was snail-racing. The snails on the plateau were enormous – some were larger than my fist. A monster snail was chosen by each of us, given a name, and then lined up alongside its rivals to start the Great Snail Race. The first snail to cross the line at the winning post was declared the winner, but the results were quite unpredictable. One snail would start at a splendid pace (for a snail), but would stop half way down the course while the others all overtook it. The result was never a foregone conclusion, as each snail stopped and started just as the mood took it, and their steering was erratic. Sometimes one snail would win one race and come last in the next. The girls thought it a magnificent game, and Jennifer and I enjoyed it too. The only disappointment was that there were no similar snails on the coast to play with after we all got back to Lindi.

On our last day on the Rondo Plateau there was a heavy rain-storm, and the road down to Lindi was very muddy. The Christodoulous had planned to follow our example, and take a short spell of local leave on the plateau a few days after we returned, but they had to turn round and go back to Lindi, as there were floods three feet deep on the road.

A Time of Change

The change of Prime Minister led to some rapid changes of policy by the Government. I had taken at its face value the letter which Julius Nyerere had written before Uhuru, assuring expatriate civil servants that they would be needed after independence. As soon as Rashidi Kawawa came to power, however, it became apparent that he had other ideas. He seemed willing to tolerate expatriates with technical qualifications such as doctors or engineers because it was clear to everybody that there were not enough Africans with the relevant professional qualifications to meet the country's needs. However, TANU had promised the electorate that it would 'Africanise' posts in government service as quickly as possible, and Kawawa's two main targets for rapid Africanisation were the Police and the Provincial Administration.

Within days of assuming power, Kawawa had got rid of the expatriate Commissioner of Police. He had also removed from office Charles (Kim) Meek, the Head of the Civil Service who had served as Secretary to the Cabinet and as Permanent Secretary in the Prime Minister's Office while Julius Nyerere had been Prime Minister. I did not know the Commissioner of Police personally, but I had enormous respect for Kim Meek's ability and for his sincere dedication to the social and economic development of Tanganyika. I thought it wrong to dismiss, just because he had a white skin, the man generally regarded as the most able and experienced administrator in the country's civil service.

In February 1962, Kawawa went further in pursuing his radical policies. He appointed a number of politicians to become the 'Regional Commissioners' of what had been known as Provinces and were now called Regions. The senior British civil servants who had been Provincial Commissioners were given a new designation as 'Administrative Secretaries', and were lower in the hierarchy than Regional Commissioners. In due course, he would also appoint 'Area Commissioners' to political posts in what had previously been known as Districts.

I was told a depressing little story about one newly-appointed young Regional Commissioner who had called a public meeting at which he humiliated the former Provincial Commissioner by ordering him repeatedly, in front of a large audience, 'Stand up – sit down – stand up – sit down,' and then gloated to the delighted crowd 'You can all see who is in command now!' That sort of behaviour was not at all typical of the courtesy which Africans traditionally showed to people of any race, but in particular to those who were older or wiser than themselves. The impression which reached Lindi was that Kawawa, in contrast to Nyerere, seemed to encourage rudeness to anyone who represented the old regime, including expatriate officials and the hereditary chiefs who had been the key to the system of Indirect Rule.

It was not difficult for a mob orator to discredit the old regime. He had only to quote passages from the vitriolic abuse of colonialism in publications that arrived in large quantities, mainly from the United States and the Soviet Union. There were admittedly some expatriate officials who were lazy, incompetent, tyrannical or corrupt, but they were a very small minority. However, TANU wanted to Africanise the whole civil service, and under Kawawa they stepped up their campaign to vilify the large number of expatriates who were honest, efficient, and genuinely doing all that they could to improve the lives of the local people.

TANU's success in the elections had shown that consent to be ruled by Britain no longer existed, and no country can be democratically governed without the consent of its people. Britain therefore had no option but to grant Independence when it did. Further delay would almost certainly have led to violence and bloodshed.

My own relationship with the African political leaders in Lindi was peculiar. Lawi Sijaona, the Constituency MP for Lindi, had visited me in my office for a chat before Kawawa took over from Nyerere, and he had then told me not to worry about public pressure to remove all Europeans from positions of responsibility. He said that he had heard nothing but praise for my work, and wanted me to remain in Lindi for the foreseeble future. His attitude changed completely after our disagreement, mentioned above, about his request to take a secret file from the Boma. After that he supported the Kawawa line about Africanisation.

The District Chairman of TANU, Shaibu Mohamed, never

wavered in the support he gave me. After Kawawa took over, Shaibu was challenged by some of his party members about being too friendly with a white DC, and he answered that I was indeed his friend, and that he would not allow anyone else to interfere with our friendship.

Like Shaibu, the Regional Commissioner also tried to keep me on as District Commissioner in Lindi. I was told that he had a serious row with Sijaona about it, and, even though he was not successful, I was grateful to him for his efforts on my behalf.

* * *

There are many newly independent countries in Africa which are now governed by incompetent, corrupt and brutal politicians who have plundered their countries' economies for their own gain, denied the human rights of minorities, carried out policies of genocide against their traditional enemies, stifled any criticism of their misrule, and stopped at nothing in order to keep themselves in power.

Tanganyika was ruled brutally by the Germans for nearly forty years up to the end of the First World War. British rule lasted slightly longer, but the policies of British rulers were based on a mandate to promote the well-being and development of the indigenous people. There were some mistakes and some abuses of human rights by the Government of Tanganyika, both before and after Independence, but these were trivial when compared with the atrocities which took place in many other African countries. I sincerely believe that the rapid progress which Tanganyika made between 1919 and 1961 in the field of education, health care, agriculture, and political development was due to the combined efforts of indigenous people who were learning to live in the modern world, and of those expatriates who taught them.

It is easy to criticise Britain for handing over independence without providing enough time to train the country's future leaders thoroughly. There were many officials who felt that prolonging British administration for a few more years would have prepared Tanganyika better to assume responsibility when it eventually reached maturity. During the early years of TANU, some senior British officials regarded Africans who wanted independence immediately as troublemakers, and as enemies to be kept under control, rather than as future leaders of their country.

My own opinion is that the risk of disaffection and violence was too great to make the postponement of independence a viable option. Julius Nyerere and his ministers made a number of serious mistakes, particularly in their economic policies, but I doubt whether the country's recent history would have been any happier if it had spent a few more years under British rule.

The Last Few Months

Early in March, the Regional Commissioner told me that I would continue to be needed in Lindi for the foreseeable future. Less than a week later I received a letter telling me that I was to be transferred in April to the Ministry of Local Government in Dar es Salaam. My task there would be to draft in Swahili a new manual about the procedures for running local government.

Lawi Sijaona had recently been appointed as a junior minister in the Ministry of Local Government, and I did not relish the prospect of working alongside him after our earlier disagreement.

I was much more worried, however, about the stress my instructions put on 'procedures'. The problem in both central and local government was not that cashiers, treasurers, committee secretaries and clerks were ignorant of the correct procedures. It was the broader issues of principle that needed to be addressed; to raise revenue in a vigorous way; to determine priorities fairly when planning expenditure; to eliminate overspending of budgets; and to keep corruption under control. During the colonial regime, African politicians had encouraged people to regard the Government as an organisation run by foreigners for the benefit of foreigners. As I have already mentioned, there had been very little stigma attached to embezzling public funds. In a newly independent country there was a need for a change of attitude, but, with several top jobs now being filled by self-interested people with criminal records, I doubted whether a booklet written by any expatriate would have much influence. I suspected that my proposed assignment to the Secretariat was simply a ploy by politicians to get rid of me from Lindi District.

Nyerere himself set an example of frugal living and hard work, and, unlike some other African leaders, his honesty was never in doubt. His objective was to achieve 'socialism in action'. However, his approach to the problem of poverty involved paying very low salaries even to those with high qualifications and in positions of responsibility. He argued that if the country as a whole had paid for the privileged education of a tiny minority, then the beneficiaries of the system ought, as a matter of principle, to repay their debt to the people after completing their education. This policy was often counterproductive, since it tempted many highly skilled public sector workers either to seek well-paid employment abroad in international organisations or to find clandestine ways locally to supplement their incomes. There had been corruption in Tanganyika before Independence, but it got worse afterwards.

* * *

Catherine celebrated her second birthday on 17th March, and we had a very small birthday party for her. Unlike her more gregarious sister, Catherine preferred to play with a few close friends and did not like crowds. The following day, Bishop Trevor Huddleston came to Lindi from Masasi. He took the Sunday service in the Anglican Church, and baptised both Nicholas Christodoulou and Philip.

After the service, the congregation came back to our house to have a glass of champagne and a piece of cake. Trevor Huddleston chatted about Jennifer's book *Wellington Road*, and compared it to his own best-seller about apartheid in South Africa, *Naught for your Comfort*. He felt that both books had been inspired by compassion for underprivileged people and indignation against those who exploited them.

A respected Asian politician called Nazerali happened to be in Lindi on business that month. He somehow learnt that Jennifer was the author of *Wellington Road*, which had been published under a *nom de plume*. He telephoned us to say that he had read a review of her book in the *New Statesman*, and asked if he might pay us a visit in order to discuss it with her. When he came, Jennifer and I were struck by the similarity of the views expressed by an Asian politician who was not a Christian and the views of an Anglican bishop. In spite of kind comments by readers and many very good reviews, the book did not make us rich.

* * *

At the beginning of April, I became ill with a high fever. Mr Patel had been replaced as Medical Officer by Dr Halahan, an Irishman, who initially diagnosed pleurisy and ordered me to stay in bed. After ten days in bed at home, I was admitted to

Lindi Hospital. I told Dr Halahan that my symptoms were the same as those I had had three years previously, when I had eventually been diagnosed as having brucellosis. Fortunately I also remembered the name of the drug which had proved effective in 1959, and he prescribed it for me. I made a quicker recovery from my second than from my first attack, but even so I lost nearly twenty kilos in weight in a month.

Dr Halahan was probably a less experienced clinician than either Dr Grech or Mr Patel, but I was very grateful to him for fighting on my behalf against the Ministry of Local Government. He insisted that I would not be fit to travel on transfer to Dar on 21st April, as I had been ordered to do, and that I was still very seriously ill. He said I would need to undergo further treatment for about a fortnight in the Hospital for Tropical Diseases in London, probably followed by a period of up to three months' convalescence in a temperate climate.

While I was in hospital, Chris Christodoulou had had to do all my work as well as his own. When he had been posted to Lindi he was already well over half way through his tour of service, and he was due to fly from Lindi on home leave at the end of April. Joan and he had decided to retire prematurely at the end of their tour and start a new career in Britain. This was a wise decision. Chris went on to have a very distinguished career as a university administrator, first at Leeds University, then as Secretary of the Open University, and finally as the Director of the Federation of Commonwealth Universities.

Many of the colleagues with whom I served in Tanganyika were able and congenial, but I can think of none whom I would have preferred to have as my second-in-command than Chris. We only served together in Lindi for about nine months, but they were very important and busy months. Jennifer and I knew that we would miss the whole Christodoulou family enormously when they went on leave.

On their last night in Tanganyika, Denis O'Callaghan paid an overnight visit to Lindi to say goodbye to them, and called at their house to have a farewell drink. Chris had no whisky in his house, but Denis insisted that that was what he wanted, so Chris borrowed a full bottle from his neighbour. Denis was not normally a heavy drinker, but he was without his wife on this occasion, and had drunk more than half a bottle by the time he left Chris's house to come back to have supper at ours. Chris phoned to warn us that Denis was a bit tipsy.

Over supper, Denis told Jennifer and me how much he sympathised with Africans who were caught with their fingers in the till and convicted for it. He insisted that everyone cheated Government if they thought they could get away with it. Jennifer and I made no comment.

Next day the Christodoulous left, with the affection and good wishes of all their friends, and the plane which took them as far as Dar es Salaam was the same plane which brought Stephen Galinoma, my successor designate, to Lindi.

Before being posted to Lindi, Stephen had been the District Commissioner of Mafia District. This consists of a small group of islands south of Zanzibar and east of the mouth of the Rufiji River. The largest island, Mafia, itself, is only 152 square miles in area, and the population of the whole District was then just over 12,000. Lindi District was more than twenty times as big as Mafia, and had nearly twenty times the population, so Stephen Galinoma's transfer to take charge of Lindi District was a big step forward in his career.

I was immediately struck by Stephen's friendliness and good manners. I soon came to appreciate his competence and integrity. He was a Hehe from Iringa District, and he remembered me from a visit I had paid in 1953 to Malangali Secondary School, when he was still a pupil there. He had left school after completing Standard X – two years before School Certificate – and had entered Government Service as a clerk. His reporting officers spotted very quickly that he was exceptionally promising, and he was soon promoted to the rank of Assistant District Officer. He continued to do well. After serving as DC in Lindi District, he worked successfully in the Secretariat, and the latest information I had about him was that he had retired from the civil service with the rank of Permanent Secretary in one of the most important Ministries – I believe it was Finance.

The job security of a pensionable civil servant is greater than that of a politician, who may lose his seat at the next election. If Stephen Galinoma had chosen to stand as a parliamentary candidate, I am sure he would have been elected. The choice to remain a civil servant was his. Nevertheless, it seemed a pity that a country should elect as its rulers people whose records in many cases proved that they were far less fitted for positions of leadership than the civil servants to whom they gave instructions.

Stephen could have required me to move out of our house to make way for him and his large family – he already had six children. However, he did not want to ask me to make an additional move when I was still so weak after my illness.

He had not had a car of his own in Mafia, but he would need one in Lindi, and agreed to apply for an advance of salary from the Accountant General's Department in order to buy my Peugeot 403 when I left the country. The Accountant General took several months to approve the payment, and I was kept waiting for the money I was owed, but it was not Stephen Galinoma's fault.

Within a few weeks of his arrival, he was told that the 'DC's house' would be allocated to the new Area Commissioner as soon as one was appointed, so Stephen was glad of the generous way he had treated me. He said that it spared him the humiliation of settling in to a splendid house only to be evicted from it a short while later in order to make way for the Area Commissioner.

* * *

Early in May, I received a surprising telegram from the office of East African Airways informing me that passages had been booked for me and my family on the next plane to London. Dr Halahan said that I was not yet fit to travel, and the tickets were cancelled. The office of the Minister for Local Government insisted that they had no knowledge whatsoever of who had made the bookings or why, but we suspected some kind of skulduggery in the Secretariat, although we never discovered who was responsible.

As the flow of expatriates leaving Tanganyika grew faster and faster, Jennifer and I kept our servants informed of our plans. Hassani and Margaret lived in Lindi, and we would pay them off when we left. We decided to give Margaret a bigger gratuity than Hassani as she had worked for us for longer and done her job more conscientiously than he had. Government rules allowed domestic servants who accompanied their employers to be given travel warrants back to the place where they had been taken on, and we arranged for Mohamed Nganga to have a warrant back to Mahenge and for Juma Farjallah and his wife Mgeni Jumanne to have warrants back to Tabora.

Mohamed was still in his thirties, and he was quite cheerful about looking for another job. Juma and his wife told us that our pending retirement had solved a problem which they had been worrying about for some time. They felt that Juma was now too old to go on working, but they did not want to leave us. Our departure meant that now they could both go back to their home in Tabora with a clear conscience, and live the rest of their lives close to their children and grandchildren. The gratuities we gave to Juma and Mohamed were an attempt to show them how much we appreciated all they had done for us for many years.

Both Juma and Mohamed continued to write to us after we got back to England, and, though they were both Muslims, we sent them presents every year at Christmas-time. After a few years, we received a letter from Bilali Ali Mshoro, the Deputy Liwali of Tabora, which he had written at Mgeni's request to tell us that Juma had died. Mgeni herself could not write to us, as she was illiterate. Bilali's letter made it very clear that he too regarded Juma as a true gentleman and a loyal friend. Mohamed got an office job working for Saudi Arabian Airlines in Dar es Salaam, but some time later we stopped getting letters from him, and do not know what happened to him.

Another of our problems was solved for us in an unexpected way. Susan, my dog, was more than ten years old, a great age for a dog in Tanganyika, and she had not been in good health for part of our time in Lindi. Her daughter Wol had died there. There was no possibility of bringing Susan back to England, where she would have to spend months in quarantine, and we were reconciled to the thought that she would have to be put down when we left. I spoke to the Field Officer in charge of the Veterinary Department in Lindi to ask him to give Susan a lethal injection as soon as we left. He flatly refused to do so. He said that Susan was such an adorable little dog that he would like to take her himself, and go on looking after her as his own dog until she died of natural causes.

* * *

At the end of May, Dr Halahan pronounced me fit to travel, though he again forbade me to take any part in the packing, and insisted that I would need a long spell of convalescence in Britain before I started to work there.

I had not yet completed the period of six months' notice which expatriates were normally required to give, but the Minister for Local Government agreed that in the exceptional circumstances I could fly to London at the beginning of June, and would not be required to return to Tanganyika to serve out the remainder of my period of notice.

The terms of the independence agreement with Britain provided for compensation to be paid to those expatriate officers who had been confirmed in their permanent pensionable appointments and then retired prematurely. The amount varied according to one's age and years of service, but in my case I would receive one lump sum payment of about eighteen months' salary, and then the same amount spread in equal instalments over the next six years. I would therefore be able to put down the deposit for a mortgage on a house, and would have some financial help for a few years. The amount would not be enough to support the whole family, so I knew that I would need to find another job in Britain as quickly as possible. I feared that it would probably not be as satisfying as working in Africa had been.

Our last days in Lindi were very exhausting. There were farewell parties after farewell parties. The Town Council, the District Council, the Tanganyika Council of Women, the Local Branch of TANU, the Anglican Church, the Ismaili Community, the Hindu Community, the Lindi Club and our many personal friends invited us to parties that were all concentrated into a period of just a few days.

The speeches were predictable. Many referred to the love which Jennifer and I had shown for the people, and which had been proved by my willingness to risk my life by saving an African boy from drowning.

There were times when I felt close to tears when I replied to their tributes. I explained that I had met and married Jennifer in Tanganyika, and that she had herself come out to serve as a teacher at Tabora African Girls' Secondary School. All our children had been born in Tanganyika. My job had at times been difficult, but it had never been dull, and I had come to love the country and its people very deeply. I would never forget them, and I asked for God's blessing on the newly independent country.

I did not, of course, mention that I was worried that the future for the common people might become even harder under an independent but inexperienced government, or that the politicians now in power included some autocratic people I did not like or trust.

We left Lindi on 4th June. The airport was about ten miles out of the town, and we set off from our home much later than we had planned. I drove faster than usual so as to catch the plane. About five miles short of the airport, the car's silencer fell off on the roadside, and I drove on without stopping to pick it up. The noise of the car became deafening, and seemed much louder than the Dakota aircraft that we saw with its undercarriage lowered, already making its descent to land. The plane was scheduled to remain in Lindi Airport for only a few minutes, and I was afraid we were going to miss it.

When we got to the airport, the plane was still on the runway, and there was a crowd of several hundred people of all races waiting to say goodbye to us. The pilot, bless him, told me not to worry, and that he would wait until I had shaken hands with everybody. I apologised to Stephen Galinoma about the car's silencer, and promised to refund to him whatever it cost to fit a replacement.

At last Jennifer and I and the children were ready to embark on the plane. Ruth understood what was going on, and she was excited about the prospect of seeing her grandmothers again. Philip was only four months old, and he was sleeping peacefully. Catherine, who was just over two, had not really understood what we meant when we had told her we would soon be going back to England, but when her ayah Margaret hugged her for the last time she suddenly knew that this parting was not like anything she had ever experienced before. She wept long and bitterly.

As the plane took off and climbed slowly on its way to Dar, where we would change on to an international flight, I looked down over the town of Lindi, the rivers flowing into the brilliant blue sea, and the beautiful sandy beaches lined with thousands of coconut palms. I thought apprehensively about how our lives in Britain would compare with the years we had enjoyed in Tanganyika.

Boy climbing a Coconut-palm

Glossary

Swahili words commonly used by expatriates in
Tanganyika

asante – thank you
askari – soldier; policeman
ayah – African nurse
baba – father
babu – grandfather
bado – not yet
bado kidogo – just a moment!
baraza – public meeting or assembly; court-house; verandah
bibi – woman; wife; grandmother
bin – son of
binti – daughter of
boma – stockade or fortification; District Office
boi – houseboy (usually an adult)
bwana – mister; title used to address a man. (Often followed by
    words describing a person's job, e.g. Bwana DC – District
    Commissioner; Bwana Shamba – Agricultural Officer; Bwana
    Shauri – District Officer)
dawa – medicine (traditional or modern)
debe – four-gallon paraffin tin, often re-used to carry water or
    grain, or for roofing
dhobi – laundry-boy
dhow/jahazi – traditional Arab sailing vessel
duka – shop
fundi – artisan; skilled worker
gari – vehicle
gari la moshi – locomotive
habari – news
hakimu – magistrate
hakuna – there isn't any
hodi – a call made on approaching a door – 'May I come in?'
jambo – form of greeting: 'Hello'; matter
jumbe – headman of small village

kali – fierce

karibu – near; (used as reply to 'hodi') 'Come in!'

kanga – rectangular piece of brightly-coloured cloth worn by women

kaniki – a piece of dark calico or cotton worn like a kanga

kanzu – long white gown worn by men, often provided by employers for domestic servants

kikapu – basket

kipande – small piece; a card used to record work done by a labourer

kodi – tax

kuni – firewood

liwali – senior judicial or executive official in a town

maji – water

mtemi, mtua, mtwa, mwami, nduna, nkosi – titles given to tribal rulers

mtoto – child

mtumbwi – dug-out canoe

mwalimu – teacher

mzee – old person

ngalawa – outrigger canoe

ngoma – drum; dance

pipa – tub; forty-four gallon oil-drum

pole – slow, gentle (also used to express sympathy)

pombe – native beer

posho – daily rations as provided for porters on journey

safari – any kind of journey

sana – very

serikali – government

serikali ya madaraka – responsible government (last stage before independence)

shamba – piece of cultivated land

shauri – advice; plan; discussion; court-case; (Bwana Shauri – usual name for a District Officer in Tanganyika)

shenzi – uncivilized

shikamuu – respectful greeting to a superior (literally, 'I grasp your feet')

soko – market

uchawi – witchcraft

uhuru – freedom

ujamaa – socialism

upesi – fast

Note on Swahili prefixes

Every language has its own rules for indicating whether a noun is singular or plural, or the tense of a verb. In English, the appropriate changes usually occur at the end of a word – e.g. dog (singular) dogs (plural), walk (present tense) walked (past tense).

In many Bantu languages, including Swahili, the changes of meaning which, in English, are normally shown at the *end* of a word are indicated at the *beginning* of a word. Prefixes are used before nouns, verbs, adjectives and adverbs. Dictionaries normally omit the variable prefix, translating only the root of a Swahili word.

The main Swahili prefixes used with words relating to a nation or tribe are as follows:–

m–   a person (singular)
        e.g. *m*hehe = a Hehe person
             *m*swahili = a Swahili person

wa–   people (plural)
        e.g. *wa*hehe = Hehe people
             *wa*swahili = Swahili people

ki–   a language
        e.g. *ki*hehe = the Hehe language
             *ki*swahili = the Swahili language
                ('Kiswahili' is usually referred to in English as 'Swahili')

u–   (or sometimes *bu–*) a country
        e.g. *U*hehe = the land of the Hehe people
             *Bu*ndali = the land of the Ndali people

(Note – the country formerly known as Urundi is now called Burundi)

The prefix *u–* is also used to change an adjective into an abstract noun:

e.g.   –huru = free
            –gonjwa = sick
            *u*huru = freedom
            *u*gonjwa = disease

Select Bibliography

Allen, Charles (ed.), *Tales of the Dark Continent*, André Deutsch, 1979.
Amin, Mohamed, Willetts, Duncan and Marshall, Peter, *Journey through Tanzania*, Camerapix Publishers International, Nairobi, 1984.
Atieno Odhiambo, E. S., Ouso, T. I., and Williams, J. F. M., *A History of East Africa*, Longman, 1977.
Bates, Darrell, *A Gust of Plumes – a Biography of Lord Twining of Godalming and Tanganyika*, Hodder and Stoughton, 1972.
Cooke, John, *One White Man in Black Africa*, Tynron Press, Scotland, 1991.
Cross, Colin, *The Fall of the British Empire*, Paladin, 1970.
Denniston, Robin, *Trevor Huddleston – a life*, Macmillan, 1999.
Harris, Tim, *Donkey's Gratitude*, Pentland Press, 1992.
Huddleston, Trevor, Bishop of Masasi, *God's World*, Fontana Books, 1966.
Huxley, Elspeth, *Livingstone and his African Journeys*, Saturday Review Press, New York, 1974.
Huxley, Elspeth, *The Sorcerer's Apprentice – A Journey through East Africa*, Chatto and Windus, 1949.
Iliffe, John, *A Modern History of Tanganyika*, Cambridge University Press, 1979.
Joynson Hicks, Paul (photographs) and Sikujua Ng'maryo, Eric (introductions), *Tanzania – Portrait of a Nation*, Quiller Press Ltd., London, 1998.
Kinloch, Bruce, *The Shamba Raiders – Memories of a Game Warden*, Ashford Press Publishers, 1988.
Kirk-Greene, Anthony, *On Crown Service – a History of H M Colonial and Overseas Civil Services, 1837–1997*, I. B. Tauris, 1999.
Legum, Colin and Mmari, Geoffrey (eds.), *Mwalimu – The Influence of Nyerere*, the Britain–Tanzania Society in association with James Currey, Mkuki wa Nyota, and Africa World Press, 1995.

Lloyd George, David, *The Truth about the Peace Treaties*, Gollancz, 1938.

Longford, Ruth, *Frances, Countess Lloyd George, More than a Mistress*, Gracewing, 1996.

Moffett, J. P. (ed.), *Handbook of Tanganyika*, the Government Printer, Dar es Salaam, 1958.

Nyerere, Julius K., *Freedom and Development*, Oxford University Press, 1975.

Nyerere, Julius K., *Freedom and Socialism*, Oxford University Press, 1968.

Nyerere, Julius K., *Freedom and Unity*, Oxford University Press, 1966.

Pakenham, Thomas, *The Scramble for Africa*, Weidenfeld & Nicolson Ltd., 1991.

Perham, Margery, *The Colonial Reckoning*, Collins, 1963.

Pinker, Steven, *The Language Instinct*, Penguin Books, 1994.

Reader, John, *Africa – a Biography of the Continent*, Penguin Books, 1998.

Sadleir, Randal, *Tanzania – Journey to Republic*, the Radcliffe Press, 1999.

Smith, John (ed.), *Administering Empire – the British Colonial Service in Retrospect – proceedings of a Conference held in May 1999*, University of London Press, 1999.

Williams, John G., *A Field Guide to the National Parks of East Africa*, Collins, 1972.

Index